CONSTITUTIONAL CONFLICTS BETWEEN
CONGRESS AND THE PRESIDENT

By the Same Author

American Constitutional Law (with David Gray Adler,
7th ed. 2007)

In the Name of National Security (2006)

Political Dynamics of Constitutional Law (with Neal Devins,
4th ed. 2006)

*Military Tribunals and Presidential Power: American Revolution to
the War on Terrorism* (2005)

Nazi Saboteurs on Trial: A Military Tribunal & American Law
(2d ed. revised 2005)

Presidential War Power (2d ed. 2004)

The Politics of Executive Privilege (2004)

The Democratic Constitution (with Neal Devins, 2004)

Religious Liberty in America: Political Safeguards (2002)

Congressional Abdication on War and Spending (2000)

The Politics of Shared Power: Congress and the Executive
(4th ed. 1998)

Encyclopedia of the American Presidency
(with Leonard W. Levy, 1994)

Constitutional Dialogues: Interpretation as Political Process (1988)

*The Constitution Between Friends: Congress, the President, and
the Law* (1978)

Presidential Spending Power (1975)

President and Congress (1972)

CONSTITUTIONAL CONFLICTS BETWEEN CONGRESS AND THE PRESIDENT

Fifth Edition, Revised

Louis Fisher

UNIVERSITY PRESS OF KANSAS

First edition published in 1978 by St. Martin's Press under the title *The Constitution Between Friends: Congress, the President, and the Law.* Second edition published in 1985 by Princeton University Press under the present title.

Published by the University Press of Kansas (Lawrence, Kansas 66045), which was organized by the Kansas Board of Regents and is operated and funded by Emporia State University, Fort Hays State University, Kansas State University, Pittsburg State University, the University of Kansas, and Wichita State University

Library of Congress Cataloging-in-Publication Data

Fisher, Louis.
   Constitutional conflicts between Congress and the President / Louis Fisher. — 5th ed., rev.
   p.   cm.
   Includes bibliographical references and index.
   ISBN 978-0-7006-1533-9 (cloth : alk. paper) — ISBN 978-0-7006-1534-6
(pbk. : alk. paper) 1. Separation of powers—United States. 2. Executive power—United States.
3. Legislative power—United States. 4. Constitutional history—United States. I. Title.
   KF4565.F57 2007
   342.73'044—dc22

                                                                          2007016840

British Library Cataloguing-in-Publication Data is available.

Printed in the United States of America

10 9 8 7 6 5 4 3 2 1

The paper used in this publication meets the minimum requirements of the American National Standard for Permanence of Paper for Printed Library Materials Z39.48-1992.

To Ellen and Joanna with love and affection

CONTENTS

PREFACE

The first edition of this book, published in 1978 under the title *The Constitution Between Friends: Congress, the President, and the Law,* bucked a strong tide of disinterest in public law among political scientists. The response to the book, justifying another edition in 1985 under the title *Constitutional Conflicts Between Congress and the President,* was both gratifying and reassuring. Publication of a third, a fourth, and now a fifth edition provides welcome evidence that social scientists are less willing to accept the artificial separation that divides law from politics. This edition makes substantial cuts in many sections and augments others.

The neglect of public law coincided with, and helped encourage, the belief that presidential power was our best hope for promoting the public good and should be unfettered by constitutional and statutory restrictions. That assumption was shattered, at least for a time, by the records in office of Lyndon Johnson and Richard Nixon. The abuses uncovered during the Iran-Contra affair in 1987 supplied fresh evidence of the capacity of presidential assistants to defy statutory and constitutional restrictions. The U.S. "war on terrorism" after 9/11 brought with it new violations of legal rights.

A tension runs throughout the American system of government. Statutory and constitutional restrictions are erected to keep the actions of the executive and legislative branches within legal boundaries. The drive for political power continually tests those boundaries, often stretching them to do what the law forbids. Because the demarcations between the branches are imprecise and subject to varying interpretations, periodic protests about "encroachments" and "usurpations" are to be expected. At any given time one branch may appear to be dominant, the other subordinate.

A certain amount of friction is invited by the Constitution. Conflict between the branches serves the useful purpose of preventing an accumulation of power and the abuses that flow from unchecked power. Equally important, conflict develops public policies that have a broad base of support and understanding. However, as Attorney General Edward H. Levi has noted, the framers "hoped the system of checks and balances would achieve a harmony of purposes differently fulfilled. The branches of government were not designed to be at war with one another."[1]

1. Edward H. Levi, "Some Aspects of Separation of Powers," 76 Colum. L. Rev. 371, 391 (1976).

Although the nature of government and our constitutional system call for some overlapping of functions, and to good effect, it should be possible to clarify the authorities and responsibilities of each branch. In a search for clarification, this book examines the central legal and constitutional conflicts between the President and Congress today. For the most part, these conflicts are settled by the executive and legislative branches. Even when a dispute enters the courts, judges are likely to sidestep the issue entirely or provide only general principles to guide the two political branches toward a resolution. It is a simplification to say that courts have the final word on the meaning of the Constitution. Many constitutional issues never enter the courts. Those that do undergo a dialogue that involves all three branches and the general public.

Too often law and politics are viewed as isolated sectors of public policy. Regrettably, many citizens are reluctant to participate in informed debate on constitutional issues. Mere mention of a "legal" dimension seems to stifle further discussion. Why this is so I have never fully understood. Part of the resistance may come from the habit of associating political events with the real world while consigning legal matters to the realm of the remote and ethereal.

This is a puzzling attitude, for constitutional and legal questions have their roots in tangible and concrete injuries. Someone suffers and seeks relief. Strong beliefs and deeply held feelings cause plaintiffs to take their grievances to the courts, sometimes after being rebuffed by Congress and the executive branch. On other occasions, plaintiffs are rebuffed by the courts and seek relief from the elected branches and the fifty states.

The American Constitution is designed to protect individual liberties. That objective requires the consent and the understanding of the governed. When we shy away from constitutional issues, treating them as technical and abstract matters to be decided by legislators, executive officials, the courts, and a few academic specialists, democratic society suffers. A dependence on the people, Madison counseled in Federalist 51, is the primary control on the government. This book is written to encourage a broader public understanding of some of the central constitutional issues we face today. Each chapter represents a study of legal disputes within a political and historical context. The purpose is to leave the reader with a deeper understanding of the dynamics of government and the principles on which it operates.

At various points in its history, this book has benefited greatly from suggestions by the following scholars and colleagues: Phillip J. Cooper, Rogelio Garcia, Harold G. Maier, Arthur S. Miller, Ronald C. Moe, Walter F. Murphy, C. Herman Pritchett, Harold C. Relyea, and Morton Rosenberg. I also want to express my appreciation to the University Press of Kansas for giving early and enthusiastic encouragement to the publication of this edition. I am very pleased to add my title to the distinguished list of works on the presidency and constitutional law published by the Press.

NOTE ON CITATIONS

All court citations refer to published volumes whenever available: *United States Reports* (U.S.) for Supreme Court decisions, *Federal Reporter* (F.2d or F.3d) for appellate decisions, and *Federal Supplement* (F.Supp. or F.Supp.2d) for district court decisions. For cases not yet published in *U.S. Reports,* citations are to the *Supreme Court Reporter* (S.Ct.). There are also citations to *Opinions of the Attorney General* (Op. Att'y Gen.), *Decisions of the Comptroller General* (Comp. Gen.), and *Opinions of the Office of Legal Counsel* (O.L.C.) in the Justice Department. Decisions that focus primarily on federal rules of civil and criminal procedure appear in *Federal Rules Decisions* (F.R.D.).

Several standard reference works are abbreviated in the footnotes by using the following system:

Elliot
Jonathan Elliot, ed., The Debates in the Several State Conventions, on the Adoption of the Federal Constitution (5 vols., Washington, D.C., 1836–1845).

Farrand
Max Farrand, ed., The Records of the Federal Convention of 1787 (4 vols., New Haven, Conn.: Yale University Press, 1937).

Richardson
James D. Richardson, ed., A Compilation of the Messages and Papers of the Presidents (20 vols., New York: Bureau of National Literature, 1897–1925).

Wkly Comp.
Pres. Doc.
Weekly Compilation of Presidential Documents, published each week by the Government Printing Office since 1965.

CONSTITUTIONAL CONFLICTS BETWEEN
CONGRESS AND THE PRESIDENT

1

CONSTITUTIONAL STRUGGLES

Constitutionalism is more than a shorthand expression for a constitution and the case law that accompanies it. To be worthy of the name, a constitution embodies a philosophy of government with sovereignty resting with the people, not with elected officials or judges. It should promote the commonweal while protecting individual rights, including those of the minority. Especially crucial is the right of the people to meet together, to express their opinions individually and through associations, and to participate in free elections and self-government, including the shaping of constitutional values. Constitutions that merely sanction the use of governmental power without limiting it—those of autocratic and totalitarian states—are hostile to the concept of constitutionalism.

The Elements of Constitutionalism

The main elements of constitutionalism were identified by Bolingbroke in 1733: "By constitution we mean, whenever we speak with propriety and exactness, that assemblage of laws, institutions and customs, derived from certain fixed principles of reason, directed to certain fixed objects of public good, that compose the general system, according to which the community hath agreed to be governed."[1] As Bolingbroke notes, governmental behavior is guided not merely by laws but also by institutions and customs. Legal principles must be set forth in a written document. Even the "unwritten" constitution of England—an amalgam of major enactments, minor statutes, judicial decisions, custom and convention, and parliamentary debates—is secured by publishing the fundamental principles for all to see: the Magna Carta, the Habeas Corpus Act, the Petition of Right, and the Act of Settlement.[2]

Fixed principles of reason, Bolingbroke's second criterion, cannot be defined with any exact meaning and application. At the very least the concept excludes political regimes that act in an arbitrary, irrational, and capricious

---

1. Charles Howard McIlwain, Constitutionalism: Ancient and Modern 3 (1947).
2. H. R. G. Greaves, The British Constitution 15, 20–22 (1955); W. Ivor Jennings, The Law and the Constitution 32–40 (1943).

manner. Constitutionalism cannot survive, even in the presence of a constitution, if the principles and standards of behavior are matters of whim for
those in authority. Reason is more than an exercise in abstract logic or rational
analysis. It must be tempered and tested by experience. As John Dickinson
warned at the Philadelphia convention: "Experience must be our only guide.
Reason may mislead us."[3]

As a constitutional standard, fixed principles of reason evoke the idea of
natural law, "higher law," or *jus gentium,* which the Roman jurist Gaius called
"that law which natural reason established among all mankind."[4] Natural law
is given concrete meaning in a scene from Sophocles' *Antigone.* One of Antigone's brothers, Polyneices, participated in a military attack on the city of
Thebes. Among the defenders was his brother. Both men, meeting face-to-
face, died in battle. Although the regent of Thebes, Creon, ordered Polyneices' body left to rot on the battlefield, Antigone defied the proclamation by
burying her brother. When asked if she chose flagrantly to disobey the law,
Antigone responds:

> Naturally! Since Zeus never promulgated
> Such a law. Nor will you find
> That Justice publishes such laws to man below.
> I never thought your edicts had such force
> They nullified the laws of heaven, which,
> Unwritten, not proclaimed, can boast
> A currency that everlastingly is valid;
> An origin beyond the birth of man.

Even Haemon, son of Creon, tells his father that he is "at loggerheads with
open justice!" The chorus uses just eight words to define the issue of constitutionalism: "Where might is right there is no right."[5]

In one of the first examples of judicial review, Dr. Bonham's Case of 1610,
Justice Coke announced that when an act of Parliament was "against common
right and reason, or repugnant, or impossible to be performed, the common
law will controul it, and adjudge such Act to be void."[6] Common right and
reason, Edward S. Corwin concluded, meant something fundamental and
permanent: "It is higher law."[7]

---

3. 2 Farrand 278.
4. Edward S. Corwin, The "Higher Law" Background of American Constitutional Law 17
(1955).
5. Paul Roche, trans., The Oedipus Plays of Sophocles 179, 189, 194 (1958).
6. 77 Eng. Rep. 646, 652.
7. Corwin, The "Higher Law" Background, at 47.

The natural law doctrine enters American constitutionalism by way of John Locke's *Second Treatise on Civil Government* (1690). Locke believed that people living in the state of nature were governed by a law of nature, which obliged everyone to behave in a certain manner. Reason, "which is that law, teaches all mankind who will but consult it, that being all equal and independent, no one ought to harm another in his life, health, liberty or possessions." But humanity, biased and ignorant, failed to study the law of nature. When called upon to judge in their own cases, people punished others too harshly and excused their own transgressions. As a result, "inconveniences" (Locke's mild term) emerged in the state of nature and created the need for a common, unbiased judge to referee disputes.[8]

Although Locke regarded the legislative power as supreme, it could not be arbitrary. The purpose of the legislature was to preserve life, liberty, and fortune. If it became destructive of those ends, people would find themselves in a condition worse than the state of nature. Under such circumstances the people were at liberty to dissolve the government and establish a new legislature.[9]

Locke's philosophy animates the Declaration of Independence. The opening sentence explains that the rupture with England was necessary so that Americans might "assume among the Powers of the earth, the separate and equal station to which the Laws of Nature and of Nature's God entitle them." The idea of constitutionalism, emphasizing individual liberties and Locke's philosophy of government, appears in the very next paragraph:

> We hold these truths to be self-evident, that all men are created equal, that they are endowed by their Creator with certain unalienable Rights, that among these are Life, Liberty, and the pursuit of Happiness. That to secure these rights, Governments are instituted among Men, deriving their just powers from the consent of the governed; That whenever any Form of Government becomes destructive of these ends, it is the Right of the People to alter or to abolish it, and to institute new Government.

These sentiments lead to Bolingbroke's last two elements of constitutionalism: (1) government is directed to certain fixed objects of public good, and (2) the community gives its consent to be governed. Both points are consistent with Locke, who held that the legislature's power, "in the utmost bounds of it," was limited to the public good of the society. The executive's emergency power (the prerogative) was "nothing but the power of doing public good without a rule."[10]

8. John Locke, Second Treatise on Civil Government, §§ 4–6, 13, 124–25.
9. Id. at §§ 135–37, 220–22.
10. Id. at §§ 135, 166.

The principle of public consent and popular control is implicit in Locke's belief that human rights existed prior to government. If government fails to protect those rights the people can change the government. In this sense the *public's* interpretation of natural law and constitutionalism—as developed over a period of time—becomes the ultimate test of the legitimacy of civil law. The community can never agree to be governed by tyrannical or arbitrary regimes. It never loses control over the government it creates. Although regimes of that nature may exist, even supported by a written constitution, they are not constitutional forms of government.

The conviction that individuals retain certain rights, never to be surrendered to government, was basic to Spinoza. He believed that "no man's mind can possibly lie wholly at the disposition of another, for no one can willingly transfer his natural right of free reason and judgment, or be compelled so to do." Any government attempting to control minds was, by definition, tyrannical. It was an abuse of sovereignty to seek to prescribe what was true or false, or what opinions should be held by men in their worship of God. "All these questions," said Spinoza, "fall within a man's natural right, which he cannot abdicate even with his own consent."[11]

Sutherland and Friedrich: Modern Views on Constitutionalism

These elements of constitutionalism, debated centuries ago, are present in more contemporary studies. Arthur E. Sutherland, writing in 1965, emphasized the "freedom of men, acting through an organized majority, to control their own political and economic fate."[12] This principle rejects hereditary rule, divine right of kings, and rule by elites. Sutherland also said that government, to remain righteous and just, must create institutions to correct its own injustices. As Madison cautioned in Federalist 51: "In framing a government which is to be administered by men over men, the great difficulty lies in this: you must first enable the government to control the governed; and in the next place oblige it to control itself."

Sutherland recognized that his second principle could jar with the first. Government action may be unjust even if willed by a majority of the people. Judicial officers, less vulnerable to majoritarian pressures, may declare invalid any government action that is inconsistent with standards of constitutional justice.[13] This proposition is not the same as "government by judiciary." Charles Evans Hughes reached too far with his injunction: "We are

---

11. Benedict de Spinoza, A Theologico-Political Treatise 257 (2004).
12. Arthur E. Sutherland, Constitutionalism in America 2 (1965).
13. Id. at 2–3.

under a Constitution, but the Constitution is what the judges say it is."[14] The Supreme Court is a coequal, not superior, branch. In his inaugural address in 1861, President Lincoln denied that constitutional questions could be settled solely by Supreme Court rulings. If government policy on "vital questions affecting the whole people is to be irrevocably fixed by decisions of the Supreme Court . . . the people will have ceased to be their own rulers."[15] Constitutionalism is not entirely what the judges say it is.[16]

In many instances the judiciary concludes that Congress is a more appropriate forum for reconciling conflicts between individual rights and government action. Supreme Court Justices recognize that members of Congress take the same oath as they do to uphold the Constitution and that deference to legislative judgment on constitutional questions is often an appropriate course.[17] In performing their assigned constitutional duties, "each branch of the Government must initially interpret the Constitution, and the interpretation of its powers by any branch is due great respect from the others."[18]

Moreover, Congress frequently passes legislation that has the effect of modifying a previous decision of a court. Because of the "political question" doctrine, many important constitutional issues are left to Congress and the President. Even when the courts intervene they often regard as authoritative a set of practices already established by legislators and executive officials.[19] Still other constitutional questions never reach the courts because of problems of jurisdiction, mootness, standing, ripeness, and prudential considerations.

Sutherland points to three other criteria of constitutionalism. First, there must be fundamental equality among individuals. Although human beings are not identical, the standard of equality attempts to eliminate artificial and arbitrary inequalities, such as discriminatory treatment on the basis of race, sex, religion, or national origin. Second, the fundamentals of the constitutional system must be reduced to a written statement, either a concise constitution as in America or the fragmented, cumulative record of England. As a final element,

14. Charles Evans Hughes, Addresses and Papers 139 (1908).
15. 7 Richardson 3210.
16. Neal Devins and Louis Fisher, The Democratic Constitution (2004); Louis Fisher, Constitutional Dialogues (1988); Louis Fisher, American Constitutional Law (6th ed., 2005).
17. Rostker v. Goldberg, 453 U.S. 57 (1981), concerning male-only registration for military service.
18. United States v. Nixon, 418 U.S. 683, 703 (1974).
19. For legislative responsibility in shaping constitutional principles, see Neal Devins and Keith E. Whittington, eds., Congress and the Constitution (2005); J. Mitchell Pickerill, Constitutional Deliberation in Congress (2004); Louis Fisher, "Constitutional Interpretation by Members of Congress," 63 N. C. L. Rev. 707 (1985); Donald G. Morgan, Congress and the Constitution (1966); and William G. Andrews, ed., Coordinate Magistrates: Constitutional Law by Congress and President (1969).

Sutherland depends on structure to restrain government: dividing power first between the nation and the states and also within the central government (creating separate executive, legislative, and judicial bodies).[20] It is fashionable today to entrust individual freedoms and liberties to the courts, but the framers depended on structural checks to provide the basic safeguards.

To Carl Friedrich this division of power cuts across two planes: functionally (separation of powers) and spatially (federalism). The doctrine of separated powers has been heavily attacked in the twentieth century, first for impeding the flow of power to public administrators (who supposedly possess expertise not found among legislators), and second for interfering with the demand for centralized authority during World War II. Similarly, the push toward presidential power after the terrorist attacks of September 11, 2001, led to many executive abuses of basic freedoms. Friedrich warned that "many who today belittle the separation of powers seem unaware of the fact that their clamor for efficiency and expediency easily leads to dictatorship."[21] Nations that experimented with centralized, executive-oriented governments have come to learn the virtues of checks and balances.

The Doctrine of Separated Powers

The abuse of power by Presidents after World War II generated some conventional arguments about the separation doctrine. Opponents of presidential power claimed that the framers distrusted government (especially the executive) and attempted to fashion an instrument of checks and balances to prevent tyranny. Although the framers did indeed construct a system designed to restrain power, that was only part of their intention. It would be inaccurate and a disservice to their labors at the Philadelphia convention to believe that they created a document primarily for the purpose of obstructing and hampering the operation of government.

It is important to understand the practical forces that led to the creation of separated branches. The American structure of government owes its existence to the experiences of the framers, not the theory of Montesquieu or

20. Sutherland, Constitutionalism in America, at 4–7.
21. Carl Friedrich, Constitutional Government and Democracy 175 (1946). See his "Constitutions and Constitutionalism," Int'l Encyc. Soc. Sci. (1968), and "Separation of Powers," 13 Encyc. Soc. Sci. 664 (1935), as well as Charles H. Wilson, "The Separation of Powers Under Democracy and Fascism," 52 Pol. Sci. Q. 481 (1937). Arthur T. Vanderbilt, in the introduction to his Doctrine of the Separation of Powers and Its Present-Day Significance (1953), wrote that individual freedom and the progress of civilization were attainable only by adhering to the principles of the separation of powers.

precedents borrowed from England. The framers used Montesquieu selectively, adopting what they knew from their own experience to be useful and rejecting what they knew to be inapplicable. The product was more theirs than his. Having served in public life for many years, both in the colonies and in the fledgling republic, they knew firsthand the practical duties and problems of running a government. They were continuously and intimately involved in the mundane, down-to-earth matters of conducting a war and laying the foundation for a more perfect union. Their close familiarity with the classics in history and government, combined with the daily experience of public office, marked their special genius. They had vision without becoming visionaries.

British history, although valuable for the study of private and individual rights, is of marginal interest for the study of executive-legislative relationships in America. Questions of executive privilege, impoundment, and the war power cannot be resolved by harkening back to British practices. The Supreme Court made this valid observation in 1850: "In the distribution of political power between the great departments of government, there is such a wide difference between the power conferred on the President of the United States, and the authority and sovereignty which belongs to the English crown, that it would be altogether unsafe to reason from any supposed resemblance between them, either as regards conquest in war, or any other subject where the right and powers of the executive arm of the government are brought into question."[22]

It is said that powers are separated to preserve liberties. But separation can also destroy liberties. The French constitutions of 1791 and 1848 represented ambitious efforts to erect a rigid and dogmatic separation of powers. The first document produced the reign of Napoleon Bonaparte; the next effort led to the Second Empire.[23]

Instead of indiscriminately championing the virtues of the separation doctrine, we should remember that it can satisfy a number of objectives, not all of them worth seeking. The framers of the American Constitution did not want a political system so fragmented in structure, so divided in authority, that government could not function. Justice Story pointed out in his *Commentaries* that the framers adopted a separation of power but "endeavored to prove that a rigid adherence to it in all cases would be subversive of the efficiency of the government, and result in the destruction of the public liberties."[24]

Story's observation has been underscored by others. Justice Jackson correctly identified the multiple goals that motivated the framers: "While the

22. Fleming v. Page, 50 U.S. (9 How.) 602, 618 (1850).
23. M. J. C. Vile, Constitutionalism and the Separation of Powers 176–211 (1967).
24. Joseph Story, Commentaries on the Constitution of the United States 396 (5th ed., 1905).

Constitution diffuses power the better to secure liberty, it also contemplates that the practice will integrate the dispersed powers into a workable government. It enjoins upon its branches separateness but interdependence, autonomy but reciprocity."[25] In 1976 the Supreme Court noted that the framers recognized that a "hermetic sealing off of the three branches of Government from one another would preclude the establishment of a Nation capable of governing itself effectively."[26] And in 1988 the Court reiterated that "we have never held that the Constitution requires that the three Branches of Government 'operate with absolute independence.'"[27]

This conclusion is driven home by studying the political climate in which the framers produced their document. If they wanted a weak government, if they wanted it shackled and ineffective, they could have retained the Articles of Confederation. They rejected that option for very good reason. Having labored under a weak government from 1774 to 1787, the framers deliberately jettisoned that model in favor of stronger central powers. Consciously, at the national level, they vested greater powers in an executive.

The distrust of executive power in 1776 (against the king of England and the royal governors) was tempered by two developments over the following decade. Americans discovered that state legislative bodies could be as oppressive and capricious toward individual rights as executive bodies. Also, many delegates to the Continental Congress watched with growing apprehension as the Congress found itself incapable of discharging its duties and responsibilities. Support began to grow for an independent executive, in large part for the purpose of ensuring efficiency.

This interpretation challenges a famous dissent by Justice Brandeis, who claimed that the separation of powers doctrine was adopted *not* for efficiency but to preclude the exercise of arbitrary power.[28] His dictum, invoked regularly by those who urged legislative reassertion in the 1960s, is a half-truth. The historical record is clear and persuasive that the inefficiency of the Continental Congress convinced the framers of the need for a separate and independent executive.[29]

This practical source of the separation doctrine is generally overlooked or ignored. Much more satisfying, emotionally if not intellectually, is the belief that the Constitution was pounded into shape from abstract principles, with the name of Montesquieu leading the list of theorists. Gladstone reinforced

25. Youngstown Co. v. Sawyer, 343 U.S. 579, 635 (1952).
26. Buckley v. Valeo, 424 U.S. 1, 121 (1976).
27. Morrison v. Olson, 487 U.S. 654, 693–94 (1988), citing United States v. Nixon, 418 U.S. at 707.
28. Myers v. United States, 272 U.S. 52, 293 (1926).
29. See Louis Fisher, President and Congress 1–27, 241–70 (1972).

this impression by describing the American Constitution as the most wonderful document ever "struck off at a given time" by the mind of man.[30] But the framers did not create out of whole cloth the document that guides us today. They were alert to the excesses and injustices committed by state legislators. They were sensitive—very sensitive—to the demonstrated ineptitude of the Continental Congress, which had to administer and adjudicate while trying to legislate. One branch of government performed all the tasks.

Because of the repeated failings of the Continental Congress, it soon began to delegate power—first to committees, then to boards staffed by people from outside the legislature, and finally, in 1781, to single executive officers.[31] These events occurred prior to the Philadelphia convention of 1787. The Constitution marked a fortunate continuity with political developments already under way. John Jay, after serving as Secretary of Foreign Affairs under the Continental Congress, remained in office in the Washington administration until Thomas Jefferson could take his place. Henry Knox was Secretary of War under the Continental Congress and under President Washington. Because of this orderly transition, it has been said that the Constitution did not create a system of separated powers; rather, a system of separated powers created the Constitution.[32]

Several delegates at the ratifying conventions objected to the fact that the branches of government—legislative, executive, and judicial—had been intermingled instead of being kept separate. "How is the executive," demanded one irate delegate at Virginia's ratifying convention, "contrary to the opinion of all the best writers, blended with the legislature? We have asked for bread, and they have given us a stone."[33] This outcry attracted some support, but not much. By the time of the Philadelphia convention, the rigid doctrine of separated powers had been replaced by a system of checks and balances. One contemporary pamphleteer called the separation doctrine, in its pure form, a "hackneyed principle" and a "trite maxim."[34] Madison devoted several of his Federalist essays to the need for overlapping powers, claiming that the concept was superior to the impracticable partitioning of powers demanded by some of the Antifederalists.[35]

30. "Kin beyond the Sea," North Am. Rev. 127, no. 264 (September–October 1878), at 185.
31. Fisher, President and Congress, at 6–14.
32. 1 Francis Wharton, The Revolutionary Diplomatic Correspondence of the United States 663 (1889).
33. Quoted in 3 Elliot 280.
34. Quoted in Vile, Constitutionalism and the Separation of Powers, at 153.
35. Federalist 37 and 47 attempted to rebut some of the Antifederalist objections regarding blended powers. For the latter, see Morton Borden, ed., The Antifederalist Papers (1965), papers 47, 48, 64, 67, 73, and 75.

The system of checks and balances does not contradict the separation doctrine. Indeed, the two are complementary. Without the power to resist encroachments by another branch, a department might find its powers drained to the point of extinction. The Constitution allocated separate functions to separate branches, but "parchment barriers" were not dependable. It was necessary, Madison concluded in Federalist 51, that "ambition must be made to counteract ambition," while in Federalist 48 he warned: "Unless these departments be so far connected and blended as to give to each a constitutional control over the others, the degree of separation which the maxim requires, as essential to a free government, can never in practice be duly maintained."

The case for a strict separation of powers was tested in the form of an amendment to the Constitution. Three states—Virginia, North Carolina, and Pennsylvania—wanted to add a separation clause to the national bill of rights.[36] The proposed language read as follows: "The powers delegated by this constitution are appropriated to the departments to which they are respectively distributed: so that the legislative department shall never exercise the powers vested in the executive or judicial[,] nor the executive exercise the powers vested in the legislative or judicial, nor the judicial exercise the powers vested in the legislative or executive departments."[37] Congress rejected this proposal, as well as a substitute amendment to make the three departments "separate and distinct."[38]

Although powers are not separated in a pure sense, it does not help to characterize the federal government as a "blend of powers." The branches have distinctly different responsibilities, practices, and traditions. A certain distance between the branches is preserved by Article I, Section 6, of the Constitution, which prohibits members of either house of Congress from holding any other civil office (the Incompatibility Clause).[39] Article I, Section 6, also prohibits members of Congress from being appointed to any federal position whose salary had been increased during their term of office (the Ineligibility Clause). The framers wanted to prevent the executive from using the appointment power to corrupt legislators.[40]

36. 3 Elliot 280, and 4 Elliot 116, 121; John Bach McMaster and Frederick D. Stone, eds., Pennsylvania and the Federal Constitution 475–77 (1888).

37. Edward Dumbauld, The Bill of Rights and What It Means Today 174–75, 183, 199 (1957).

38. For the congressional debates, see 1 Annals of Congress 453–54 (June 8, 1789) and 789–90 (August 18, 1789). For action by the Senate, see U.S. Senate, Journals, 1789–1794, I, 64, 73–74 (1820).

39. But see Schlesinger v. Reservists to Stop the War, 418 U.S. 208 (1974), in which the Supreme Court denied standing to plaintiffs who challenged the right of members of Congress to hold a commission in the armed forces reserves.

40. 1 Farrand 379–82, 386–90; 2 Farrand 283–84, 489–92.

Congress is prohibited from increasing or diminishing the compensation of the President during the President's term of office or diminishing the compensation of the judiciary.[41] The Speech or Debate Clause is designed to protect legislators from executive or judicial harassment.[42] The purpose of this clause is to "preserve the constitutional structure of separate, coequal, and independent branches of government."[43]

Every occupant of the White House, after a short time in office, appreciates the degree to which an institutional separation exists, whether Congress is in the hands of the President's party or the opposition party. That is as it should be. The President does not share with Congress his pardoning power, nor does Congress share with the courts its taxing and appropriations powers (although the judiciary is participating in the outer fringes). In 1974 the Supreme Court highlighted the separation that exists in the federal government by stating that the judicial power vested in the federal courts by Article III of the Constitution "can no more be shared with the Executive Branch than the Chief Executive, for example, can share with the Judiciary the veto power, or the Congress share with the Judiciary the power to override a Presidential veto."[44]

The Durability of the Doctrine

Has the balance among political institutions, as fashioned by the framers, failed to meet the test of time? Have events overtaken theory? Tocqueville, quoting with approval a passage from Jefferson, believed that the "tyranny of the legislature" in America would continue for a number of years before being replaced by a tyranny of the executive.[45] Yet presidential power, after cresting with Abraham Lincoln, subsided in the face of a determined and resurgent Congress. Writing in 1885, Woodrow Wilson believed that Congress had become the dominant branch. He said that the Constitution of 1787 was a form of government in name rather than in reality, "the form of the Constitution being one of nicely adjusted, ideal balances, whilst the actual form of our present government is simply a scheme of congressional supremacy."[46]

Two decades later, glancing with covetous eyes toward the White House, Wilson predicted that the President "must always, henceforth, be one of the

41. For a case on judicial salaries and the No-Diminution Clause, see United States v. Will, 449 U.S. 200 (1980).
42. United States v. Johnson, 383 U.S. 169, 177 (1966).
43. United States v. Helstoski, 442 U.S. 477, 491 (1979).
44. United States v. Nixon, 418 U.S. at 704.
45. 1 Tocqueville, Democracy in America 280 (1945 ed.).
46. Woodrow Wilson, Congressional Government 6 (1885).

great powers of the world. . . . We have but begun to see the presidential office in this light; but it is the light which will more and more beat upon it."[47] The new wellspring of presidential power, according to his analysis, was the burden of international responsibilities thrust upon the United States. The Great Depression of the 1930s, joined with the personal qualities of Franklin D. Roosevelt, gave further impetus to executive power.

The reputation of Congress plummeted with such swiftness that Samuel P. Huntington, in an influential study published in 1965, suggested that unless Congress drastically altered its operation it should abandon its legislative role and concentrate on serving constituents and overseeing the agencies.[48] The condition of Congress appeared to deteriorate even further, for in 1968 Philip B. Kurland charged that it did not have the "guts to stand up to its responsibilities." Congress was prostrate, the President transcendent. Kurland invited us to visit the "sickbed of another constitutional concept—the notion of separation of powers." Not only was the patient diseased; the affliction seemed terminal. Theoretically a cure was possible, but Kurland saw no grounds for optimism. The patient had lost the will to live.[49]

These dire predictions suggest that the imbalance between President and Congress is chronic and permanent. At no time, however, has either branch been as all-powerful or as defective as critics have claimed. The political system has shown a capacity for self-correction. Lyndon Johnson and Richard Nixon, testing the limits of presidential power during the 1960s and 1970s, were driven from office. Congress, flexing its muscles during this time of reassertion, ran into barriers erected by the courts. In 1976 the Supreme Court ruled against the Federal Election Commission because Congress had staked out a role for itself in the appointment of four of the commission's six members. The Court held that this procedure was contrary to the separation doctrine. Congress could not both legislate and enforce.[50]

Between 1983 and 1986, the Court flirted with a rigid and impractical notion of separation of powers, suggesting that once Congress legislated, it could not participate in any way in the administration of a law.[51] Although not directly overruling those decisions, the Court in 1988 and again in 1989

---

47. Woodrow Wilson, Constitutional Government in the United States 78 (1908).
48. Samuel P. Huntington, "Congressional Responses to the Twentieth Century," in David B. Truman, ed., The Congress and America's Future 5–31 (1965). Writing a year later, however, Ralph K. Huitt argued that Congress played a more important part in legislation than its critics realized. See his "Congress, the Durable Partner," originally published in 1966 and reprinted in Ralph K. Huitt and Robert L. Peabody, Congress: Two Decades of Analysis 209–29 (1969).
49. Philip B. Kurland, "The Impotence of Reticence," 1968 Duke L. J. 619, 621.
50. Buckley v. Valeo, 424 U.S. 1 (1976).
51. INS v. Chadha, 462 U.S. 919 (1983); Bowsher v. Synar, 478 U.S. 714 (1986).

issued rulings more favorable toward the overlapping of powers, emphasizing checks and balances over a pure separation of powers.[52]

The separation doctrine, subjected to ridicule for much of the twentieth century, still retains vitality. A longer view of American history provides room for optimism. Senator George Wharton Pepper offered this perspective: "If the geometers of 1787 hoped for perfect peace and if the psychologists of that day feared disastrous conflicts, history, as so often happens, has proved that hopes were dupes and fears were liars. There has not been perfect peace; but the conflicts have not proved disastrous."[53]

Implied Powers

In civics courses we are taught that the American Constitution is one of enumerated powers. This is satisfactory only if we stay within the classroom. Once we venture out and observe the actual workings of government, we confront a perplexing array of powers that are not expressly stated. They parade under assorted names: implied and inherent, incidental and inferred, aggregate, powers created by custom and acquiescence, and delicate "penumbras," "interstices," "emanations," and "glosses" that add strange new qualities to the Constitution. Whatever the name, the result is identical: the conferral of a power that is neither expressly stated in the Constitution nor specifically granted by Congress.

The "genius and spirit of our institutions are hostile to the exercise of implied powers." Thus spake the Supreme Court in 1821. After making the appropriate gesture it proceeded to deal amicably with these hostile forces. It was utopian, said the Court, to believe that government could exist without allowing the exercise of discretion somewhere. In this particular case the Court recognized that Congress possessed powers not expressly granted by the Constitution: the power to issue warrants to compel a party's appearance and the power to punish for contempt.[54]

If a constitution is intended to limit power, and if we admit powers that are not expressly stated, can government be kept within bounds? Let the imagination run to far corners, and the answer is no. Let experience be our guide (the framers' preference), and the prospect is more reassuring. The American Constitution cannot survive purely on the basis of express powers or "strict

52. Morrison v. Olson, 487 U.S. 654 (1988); Mistretta v. United States, 488 U.S. 361 (1989).

53. George Wharton Pepper, Family Quarrels: The President, the Senate, the House viii (1931).

54. Anderson v. Dunn, 6 Wheat. 204, 225 (1821).

constructionism," a phrase made popular by recent administrations. Implied powers are required for any government. As Madison noted in Federalist 44, "No axiom is more clearly established in law, or in reason, than that whenever the end is required, the means are authorized; whenever a general power to do a thing is given, every particular power necessary for doing it is included."

The debate in 1789 on the Bill of Rights settled the need to grant implied powers to government. Members of the First Congress proposed that the Tenth Amendment be so worded that all powers not "expressly delegated" to the federal government would be reserved to the states. Madison immediately objected, insisting that it was impossible to limit a government to the exercise of express powers. There "must necessarily be admitted powers by implication, unless the Constitution descended to recount every minutiae." After elimination of the word "expressly," the Tenth Amendment was adopted with this language: "The powers not delegated to the United States by the Constitution, nor prohibited by it to the States, are reserved to the States respectively, or to the people."[55]

Chief Justice Marshall cited this debate when he ruled on the implied power of Congress to establish a national bank, even though that power is not expressly authorized by the Constitution. Marshall observed that there was no phrase in the document that (like the Articles of Confederation) "excludes incidental or implied powers; and which requires that everything granted shall be expressly and minutely described."[56] A constitution represented a general structure, not a detailed instruction manual:

> A constitution, to contain an accurate detail of all the subdivisions of which its great powers will admit, and of all the means by which they may be carried into execution, would partake of the prolixity of a legal code, and could scarcely be embraced by the human mind. It would, probably, never be understood by the public. Its nature, therefore, requires, that only its great outlines should be marked, its important objects designated, and the minor ingredients which compose those objects, be deduced from the nature of the objects themselves.[57]

In interpreting the Constitution it is important to understand that government is created to carry out certain functions required for the people. A number of essential activities find no ready reference in the Constitution. As Marshall remarked: "All admit, that the government may, legitimately, punish

---

55. 1 Annals of Congress 761 (August 18, 1789).
56. McCulloch v. Maryland, 17 U.S. (4 Wheat.) 315, 404 (1819).
57. Id. at 406.

any violation of its laws; and yet, this is not among the enumerated powers of Congress."[58]

The debate on implied powers is frequently sidetracked by partisan and policy motivations. Although Marshall upheld the U.S. Bank partly on the strength of Madison's reasoning on the Tenth Amendment, Madison strongly *opposed* the bank in 1791. This time he spoke against implied powers, insisting that the Constitution was not "a general grant, out of which particular powers are excepted; it is a grant of particular powers only, leaving the mass in other hands."[59] Despite Madison's opposition, the bill for a national bank passed the House of Representatives by a vote of 39 to 20.

Two years later Madison again assumed a partisan stance on implied powers. After President Washington issued what is now known as the Neutrality Proclamation, his administration was subjected to bitter attacks from those who sympathized with France. Alexander Hamilton, writing under the pseudonym "Pacificus," denied that the proclamation had been issued without authority. Hamilton derived the power to issue proclamations from the general clause of Article II of the Constitution: "The executive Power shall be vested in a President of the United States of America." He believed that it was unsound to limit the executive power to the particular items enumerated in subsequent sections. They should not derogate from the "comprehensive grant" of power in the general clause "further than as it may be coupled with express restrictions or limitations." With the exception of the Senate's participation in the appointment of officers and in the making of treaties, and Congress's power to declare war and to grant letters of marque and reprisal, all other executive powers were lodged solely in the President.[60]

Jefferson, outraged by this doctrine, wrote to Madison: "For God's sake, my dear Sir, take up your pen, select the most striking heresies and cut him to pieces in the face of the public."[61] Madison produced five articles under the name "Helvidius," charging that Hamilton's reading of the Constitution must be condemned "as no less vicious in theory than it would be dangerous in practice." The expansive interpretation of executive power would mean that "no citizen could any longer guess at the character of the government under which he lives; the most penetrating jurist would be unable to scan the extent of constructive prerogative."[62]

Madison indulged in hyperbole, as did Hamilton. We could scarcely expect much else in the supercharged political atmosphere of 1793, heightened as

58. Id. at 415.
59. 2 Annals of Congress 1945 (February 2, 1791).
60. 4 The Works of Alexander Hamilton 437–39 (Lodge ed.).
61. 6 The Writings of Thomas Jefferson 338 (Ford ed.).
62. 6 The Writings of James Madison 152 (Hunt ed.).

it was by the intense rivalry between Hamilton and Jefferson in the Cabinet. But the issue they raised was to remain active. By the end of the nineteenth century the issue of implied powers for the President reached the Supreme Court in the case of *In re Neagle* (1890). Justice Stephen Field, serving as circuit justice in California, had his life threatened by two people he had sent to jail, David and Sarah Terry. David Neagle, a U.S. deputy marshal, was assigned to ride circuit to offer protection. One morning during breakfast, Field was assaulted by David Terry. Neagle, after identifying himself, shot and killed Terry. No statute authorized the President to appoint a deputy marshal for the purpose of protecting a Supreme Court Justice traveling in his circuit.

The Court, split 6 to 2, upheld the assignment of Neagle and his immunity from state law. His attorney acknowledged that there was no single specific statute making it a duty to furnish protection to a Supreme Court Justice. To the attorney, however, whatever was "necessarily implied is as much a part of the Constitution and statutes as if it were actually expressed therein."[63] Justice Miller, announcing the opinion for the Court, agreed: "In the view we take of the Constitution of the United States, any obligation fairly and properly inferrible from that instrument, or any duty of the marshal to be derived from the general scope of his duties under the laws of the United States, is 'a law' within the meaning of this phrase."[64]

The two dissenting Justices did not dispute the proposition that "whatever is necessarily implied in the Constitution and laws of the United States is as much a part of them as if it were actually expressed." But they related implied powers to the clause in Article I that augments the powers of Congress: "Congress shall have power . . . to make all laws which shall be necessary and proper for carrying into execution the foregoing powers, and all other powers vested by this Constitution in the government of the United States, or in any department or office thereof." Finding no such law and believing that the federal government was powerless to try to punish a man charged with murder in this offense, they would have had Neagle placed in the custody of the sheriff of San Joaquin, California, to be tried by the courts of that state.[65]

Theodore Roosevelt and William Howard Taft, in their debate on the boundaries of presidential authority, appear to have held diametrically opposed positions on implied power. Roosevelt asserted that it was the President's right and duty to do "anything that the needs of the Nation demanded, unless such action was forbidden by the Constitution or by the laws."[66] His

63. In re Neagle, 135 U.S. 1, 27 (1890).
64. Id. at 59.
65. Id. at 77–78, 83. See also In re Debs, 158 U.S. 1 (1895), which supported the President's use of military force to break a railroad strike.
66. 20 The Works of Theodore Roosevelt 347 (1926).

argument follows the one presented in Hamilton's "Pacificus" writings. Taft maintained that the President "can exercise no power which cannot be fairly and reasonably traced to some specific grant of power or justly implied and included within such express grant as proper and necessary to its exercise. Such specific grant must be either in the Federal Constitution or in an act of Congress passed in pursuance thereof."[67]

Use of the words "express" and "specific" appears to put Taft in the camp of those who believe in enumerated powers. But it is clear that he recognized the need for implied powers—powers that can be "fairly and reasonably traced" or "justly implied." He even adds to the Constitution a "necessary and proper" clause for the President. When Taft's study is read in full, it is evident that he believed in a generous interpretation of executive power: incidental powers to remove officers, inferable powers to protect the lives and property of American citizens living abroad, powers created by custom, and emergency powers (such as Lincoln's suspension of the writ of habeas corpus during the Civil War). Summing up, Taft said that executive power was limited "so far as it is possible to limit such a power consistent with that discretion and promptness of action that are essential to preserve the interests of the public in times of emergency, or legislative neglect or inaction."[68]

Custom and Acquiescence

The Supreme Court often discourages the idea that a precedent, even when repeated, represents an adequate basis for authority. In *Powell v. McCormack* (1969), the Court stated that because "an unconstitutional action has been taken before surely does not render that same action any less unconstitutional at a later date."[69] For example, "local tradition" is insufficient justification for the systematic exclusion of blacks or other minorities from jury service.[70] Fifty years of relying on the legislative veto did not save it from being held unconstitutional by the Supreme Court in 1983, although this method of congressional control persists.[71]

67. William Howard Taft, Our Chief Magistrate and His Powers 139–40 (1916), available in paperback under the title The President and His Powers (1967).

68. For specific references in Taft's 1916 edition, see pp. 56 and 76 on removal powers, p. 95 on inferable powers, p. 135 for powers created by custom, p. 147 for suspension of habeas corpus, and p. 156 for the need for executive discretion and promptness of action. A comparison between Roosevelt and Taft appears in Fisher, President and Congress, at 33–37.

69. Powell v. McCormack, 395 U.S. 486, 546–47 (1969).

70. Eubanks v. Louisiana, 356 U.S. 584 (1958).

71. INS v. Chadha, 462 U.S. 919 (1983); Louis Fisher, "The Legislative Veto: Invalidated, It Survives," 56 Law & Contemp. Prob. 273 (1993).

Still, an action based on usage may acquire legitimacy. Practice and acquiescence for a number of years can be instrumental in fixing the meaning of the Constitution.[72] To the extent that an action is favorably exposed to popular judgment, custom does expand power. The Supreme Court, upholding the President's removal power in a 1903 decision, based its ruling largely on the "universal practice of the government for over a century."[73] Here constitutional law is made not by the courts but by the conduct of the executive and legislative branches.

Taft, often identified with a strict reading of the Constitution and presidential power, recognized that executive authority is based partly on custom: "So strong is the influence of custom that it seems almost to amend the Constitution."[74] A specific example dates from his own administration. After Congress had opened public lands in the West to encourage oil exploration, settlers began to extract oil rapidly, fearing that entrepreneurs on adjacent lots might tap from the same source. Because of the limited supply of coal on the Pacific coast for the navy, it appeared that the federal government might have to purchase from the private sector the very oil it had given away.

Taft issued a proclamation to withdraw the affected lands from private exploration. In the Supreme Court, it was argued that the President could not suspend a statute or withdraw land that Congress had thrown open to acquisition. The Court declined to approach the controversy from the standpoint of abstract constitutional theory. The President's action, it said, was based on and supported by years of precedents. Although it was true that the President had acted without statutory authority (and in fact had acted against it), the Court held that "nothing was more natural than to retain what the Government already owned. And in making such orders, which were thus useful to the public, no private interest was injured. . . . The President was in a position to know when the public interest required particular portions of the people's lands to be withdrawn from entry or location."[75] It was not until 1976 that Congress reversed this interpretation of presidential power.[76]

Justice Frankfurter described the cumulative impact of uncontested executive actions in these words: "A systematic, unbroken executive practice, long pursued to the knowledge of the Congress and never before questioned, engaged in by Presidents who have also sworn to uphold the Constitution, making as it were such exercise of power part of the structure of our government,

72. Stuart v. Laird, 5 U.S. (1 Cr.) 299, 309 (1803).

73. Shurtleff v. United States, 189 U.S. 311, 316 (1903). Additional commentary on custom and acquiescence appears in 16 American Jurisprudence 264–70 (1964).

74. Taft, Our Chief Magistrate and His Powers, at 135.

75. United States v. Midwest Oil Co., 236 U.S. 459, 471 (1915).

76. 90 Stat. 2792, sec. 704(a) (1976).

may be treated as a gloss on 'executive Power' vested in the President by §1 of Art. II."[77] In that same decision—the Steel Seizure Case of 1952—Justice Jackson spoke of a "zone of twilight" in which the distribution of power between Congress and the President is uncertain and "congressional inertia, indifference or quiescence may sometimes, at least as a practical matter, enable, if not invite, measures on independent presidential responsibility. In this area, any actual test of power is likely to depend on the imperatives of events and contemporary imponderables rather than on abstract theories of law."[78] Justice Brennan later noted, "The more longstanding and widely accepted a practice, the greater its impact upon constitutional interpretation."[79] Custom is a source of executive power—particularly when Congress fails to challenge and check.

Acquiescence has been part of Congress's record in permitting the war power to drift to the executive branch. In 1969 the Senate Foreign Relations Committee tried to explain this tendency by saying that Congress was unprepared for America's new role as a world power and the extraordinary demands placed on the Constitution. An atmosphere of real or contrived urgency encouraged legislative passivity. Congress was also overawed by the "cult of executive expertise." In addition, a legacy of guilt remained in the Senate after its rejection of the Covenant of the League of Nations in 1919. Senators practiced a form of penance that has "sometimes taken the form of overly hasty acquiescence in proposals for the acceptance of one form or another of international responsibility."[80]

Legislators are said to acquiesce because of the superior information and technical knowledge available to the executive branch. This attitude conceals a hidden motivation: an unwillingness to be held responsible for issues of national security and military preparedness. Delegation and acquiescence are natural by-products of the better-safe-than-sorry philosophy. In the years following World War II, the executive branch has repeatedly displayed its capacity to act on false information in both domestic policy and national security. No one need be awed by announcements from Presidents or executive officials.

The principles cited in this chapter provide the broad framework for the creation and protection of constitutional rights in America. The Constitution supplies a general structure for the three branches of government, assigns

---

77. Youngstown Co. v. Sawyer, 343 U.S. 579, 610–11 (1952).

78. Id. at 637. Footnote omitted.

79. Walz v. Tax Commission, 397 U.S. 664, 681 (1970) (Brennan, J., concurring). See also Payton v. New York, 445 U.S. 573, 600 (1980), and Marsh v. Chambers, 463 U.S. 783, 790 (1983). An excellent critique of the reliance on custom is by Michael J. Glennon, "The Use of Custom in Resolving Separation of Powers Disputes," 64 B. U. L. Rev. 109 (1984).

80. S. Rept. No. 129, 91st Cong., 1st Sess. 15–16 (1969).

specific functions and responsibilities to each, and reserves certain rights to the people. Armed with powers of self-defense, the branches of government intersect in various patterns of cooperation and conflict. Strong public pressures beat against the branches, raising new constitutional issues and influencing their eventual resolution by legislators, executive officials, and judges.

2

APPOINTMENT POWERS

After Congress creates an office, three steps are required to fill it: nomination by the President, confirmation by the Senate, and commissioning of the appointee by the President. For lesser or "inferior officers," Congress may forgo the confirmation requirement and place the power of appointment directly in the President, the courts, or department heads.

Nomination (at least in theory) is the President's prerogative. In practice it is shared with members of the executive branch, with legislators and judges, and with representatives from the private sector, all subject to various statutory limitations. After submitting a name the President may, and often does, withdraw it. Once the nomination has gone forward, the decision to advise and consent is a privilege reserved to each Senator, but many outside interests offer advice and try to influence the consent. Presidents also make recess and temporary appointments, opening up a vast range of discretionary action that Congress attempts to restrict with statutory guidelines.

Basic Principles

The British monarch not only appointed officers but also created the offices. The framers rejected this concentration of power, with its potential for abuse, by giving Congress the power to create offices and joining the Senate with the President in making appointments. The Constitution allows Congress to vest the appointment of "inferior officers . . . in the President alone, in the Courts of Law, or in the Heads of Departments." For all other offices (except temporary appointments during Senate recesses) the President nominates an individual and seeks the advice and consent of the Senate.

The initial draft presented at the Philadelphia convention (the Virginia Plan) lodged in Congress the responsibility for choosing an executive and the members of a national judiciary. The executive would have been empowered "to appoint to offices in cases not otherwise provided for" by the Constitution. James Wilson, one of the ablest members of the convention, objected to the appointment of judges by a legislature: "Experience shewed the impropriety of such appointmts. by numerous bodies. Intrigue, partiality, and concealment were the necessary consequences. A principal reason for unity in the Executive was that officers might be appointed by a single, responsible person." However, some delegates feared that vesting such power in a single person would be "leaning too much toward Monarchy."[1]

James Madison offered a compromise: Let the Senate (not as numerous as the House, yet more numerous than the executive) appoint the judges. His plan was tentatively agreed to in mid-June. A month later delegates remained divided on the issue. Some worried that the executive, armed with the power to appoint, might favor one region of the country over another. Others, such as Luther Martin of Maryland, argued that the Senate would be "best informed of characters & most capable of making a fit choice." Madison came up with a new plan, allowing the executive to appoint judges with the concurrence of some fraction of the Senate. He thought this had the advantage of uniting the responsibility of the executive with the security afforded by Senate opposition to "incautious or corrupt" nominations. On July 21, however, the convention voted to have judges appointed solely by the Senate. The delegates adopted a different approach for appointments to the executive branch. The President retained power "to appoint to offices in cases not otherwise provided for" in the Constitution.[2]

As the debate continued, the delegates dropped the idea of allowing Congress to choose the President and judicial officers. The concept of three separate and distinct branches took shape, as well as the system of using electors from the states to choose the President.

In early September the convention gave the President authority to nominate and—by and with the advice and consent of the Senate—appoint ambassadors, other public ministers and consuls, judges of the Supreme Court, and all other federal officers. A few days later the convention allowed the President to fill all vacancies that "may happen" during the Senate's recess. It added the phrase "and which shall be created by Law" (to prevent appointments to positions unauthorized by Congress) and reserved to Congress the right to vest the appointment of inferior officers in the President, the courts, or department heads.[3]

The President's appointment power under Article II extends to "Officers of the United States," a term given meaning by several court decisions. The Supreme Court has defined an office as "a public station, or employment, conferred by the appointment of government. The term embraces the ideas of tenure, duration, emolument, and duties." The duties of an officer are "continuing and permanent, not occasional or temporary."[4] Occasional or intermittent duties are carried out by agents, not officers.[5] Unless a person holds his or her

1. 1 Farrand 21, 63, 119.
2. Id. at 119–28, 232–33; 2 Farrand 41–44, 80–83, 121.
3. 2 Farrand 498–99, 533, 627–28.
4. United States v. Hartwell, 73 U.S. (6 Wall.) 385, 398 (1868).
5. United States v. Germaine, 99 U.S. (9 Otto.) 508, 511–12 (1879); Auffmordt v. Hedden, 137 U.S. 310, 326–27 (1890).

position by virtue of a presidential appointment, or by an appointment from the courts or department heads as authorized by law, that person is not an officer of the United States.[6] Any appointee exercising "significant authority" pursuant to a federal statute is an officer of the United States.[7]

The category "inferior officers" was clarified by the Court in 1988 when it upheld the constitutionality of the independent counsel, which Congress had created to investigate and prosecute high-level executive officials. If the Attorney General believed that an independent counsel should be appointed, he would go to a special federal court to have that officer appointed. Opponents of the law argued that the independent counsel was not an "inferior officer" to be appointed by the courts but rather a "principal officer" who must be selected by the President with the advice and consent of the Senate.

Writing for a 7-to-1 Court, Chief Justice Rehnquist admitted that the line between inferior and principal officers "is far from clear" and that the framers provided little guidance. Without attempting a precise definition of the two officers, Rehnquist concluded that the independent counsel was an inferior officer for several reasons: the independent counsel could be removed from office by the Attorney General, implying that the office was to some degree inferior in rank and authority; the independent counsel had statutory authority to perform only certain, limited duties; the office of independent counsel was limited in jurisdiction by statute and by the grant of authority conferred by the special federal court; and the independent counsel was limited in tenure, even though the "temporary" nature of this office could last for several years.[8] After reauthorizing the independent counsel several times, Congress allowed the position to expire in 1999.

To preserve the separation between the executive and legislative branches, the Constitution prohibits Senators and Representatives from being appointed to any federal office created—or to any federal office increased in salary—during their terms of office (the Ineligibility Clause). Furthermore, no officer of the United States "shall be a Member of either House during his Continuance in Office" (the Incompatibility Clause).[9] These provisions reflected the framers' belief that elected officials in England had been corrupted through appointments to office by the Crown.[10]

6. United States v. Mouat, 124 U.S. 303, 307 (1888).
7. Buckley v. Valeo, 424 U.S. 1, 126 (1976).
8. Morrison v. Olson, 487 U.S. 654, 671–72 (1988).
9. Art. I, Sec. 6, Cl. 2.
10. Reservists Committee to Stop the War v. Laird, 323 F.Supp. 833, 835–37 (D.D.C. 1971), aff'd without published opinion, 495 F.2d 1075 (D.C. Cir. 1972), reversed and remanded, 418 U.S. 208 (1974). For additional information on incompatible offices, see 1 Hinds' Precedents, ch. 16; 6 Cannon's Precedents, ch. 158; 40 Op. Att'y Gen. 301 (1943); and 1 O.L.C. 242 (1977).

The meaning of the Ineligibility and Incompatibility Clauses has been shaped much more by Congress and the President than by the courts. The Incompatibility Clause has been difficult to litigate. In 1974 the Supreme Court denied standing to plaintiffs who challenged the right of members of Congress to hold a commission in the armed forces reserves.[11] With regard to the Ineligibility Clause, Congress has at times reduced the salary of an executive position to permit someone from Congress to be appointed to the post. During the administration of William Howard Taft, Congress had increased the salary of the Secretary of State, but Taft wanted to name Senator Philander Knox to that position. Legislation was passed to reduce the compensation of the Secretary of State to the original figure.[12]

This same process has been used in more recent decades. In 1973 Congress enacted legislation to keep the compensation of the Attorney General at the previous level so that President Nixon could nominate Senator William Saxbe. Similarly, Congress passed legislation in 1980 to permit Senator Ed Muskie to become Secretary of State, and in 1993 comparable legislation was passed to allow President Clinton to nominate Senator Lloyd Bentsen for the position of Secretary of the Treasury.[13]

The courts have done little to clarify the boundaries of the Ineligibility Clause. Senator Hugo Black was nominated to the Supreme Court in 1937, even though a retirement system for the judiciary had been enacted that year while Black served in the Senate. The Court avoided the issue by holding that the plaintiff lacked standing to bring the suit.[14] During the Carter administration, the nomination of Congressman Abner Mikva to the D.C. Circuit was challenged because the salaries of federal judges had been increased during Mikva's term in Congress. Once again, the suit was tossed out because of lack of standing. The court said that opponents of Mikva had an opportunity to defeat the nomination, but that Senators on the losing side could not then ask the judiciary to reverse the Senate's action.[15]

The Power to Nominate

In *Marbury v. Madison,* Chief Justice Marshall called the nomination process the "sole act of the president" and "completely voluntary."[16] Marshall was

---

11. Schlesinger v. Reservists to Stop the War, 418 U.S. 208 (1974).
12. 35 Stat. 626 (1909).
13. 87 Stat. 697 (1973); 94 Stat. 343 (1980); 107 Stat. 4 (1993).
14. Ex parte Levitt, 302 U.S. 633 (1937).
15. McClure v. Carter, 513 F.Supp. 265 (D. Idaho 1981), aff'd sub nom. McClure v. Reagan, 454 U.S. 1025 (1981). For additional information on the Ineligibility Clause, see 33 Op. Att'y Gen. 88 (1922) and 42 Op. Att'y Gen. 381 (1969).
16. 5 U.S. (1 Cr.) 137, 155 (1803).

technically correct. The President is the only one who may nominate executive officers and federal judges. The Constitution is express on that point: "he shall nominate." However, there is a world of difference between what is technically required and how political circumstances determine a President's decision. Presidents who initially insist on some type of monopoly over the submission of a nomination quickly learn that political reality compels them to share that choice with others. Here we have a situation in which something appears to be exclusive in terms of the express language in the Constitution but is made far more complex by the need to accommodate representative government and political pressures.[17]

The Court has held that although Congress creates offices, it cannot, "by law, designate the person to fill those offices."[18] That principle was buttressed in 1871 by Attorney General Akerman, who reviewed a proposal that permitted a civil service board to designate a single person for appointment. To him it was "inadmissible" to have a method of selection that gave no room for the exercise of judgment and will by the President. To require the President to appoint a person judged by examiners as the fittest was no different in constitutional principle from insisting that "he shall appoint John Doe to that office."[19]

The Civil Service Act of 1883 allowed the President some latitude by restricting appointments to those "among" the highest grades in competitive examinations. The first rules promulgated by President Arthur provided that four names would be considered for each vacancy. In 1888 the number was lowered to three. Present law provides that a nominating or appointing official will be furnished at least three names from the top of the list of those eligible for each vacancy.[20] When a vacancy occurs in the office of Comptroller General or Deputy Comptroller General, a commission of members of Congress recommends at least three individuals to the President, and the President may ask the commission to recommend additional names.[21]

The President's authority to nominate is curbed in numerous ways. In creating an office, Congress may stipulate the qualifications of appointees. Justice Brandeis once prepared a long list of requirements that Congress had imposed on the President's selection of nominees, including citizenship; being a resident of the United States, a state, a particular state, a particular district, a

---

17. Mitchel A. Sollenberger, "The President 'Shall Nominate': Exclusive or Shared Constitutional Power?" 36 Pres. Stud. Q. 714 (2006).

18. United States v. Ferreira, 54 U.S. (13 How.) 39, 50–51 (1852). See also Myers v. United States, 272 U.S. 52, 128 (1926).

19. 13 Op. Att'y Gen. 516 (1871).

20. 5 U.S.C. 3317–18 (2000). See 22 Stat. 404 (1883) and Civil Service Commission, Biography of an Ideal: A History of the Federal Civil Service 47 (1973).

21. 31 U.S.C. 703(a)(3) (2000).

particular territory, the District of Columbia, or a particular foreign country; specific professional attainments or occupational experience; test by examinations; requirements of age, sex, race, property, or habitual temperance in the use of intoxicating liquors; selection on a nonpartisan basis; and representation by industrial or geographic criteria.[22]

On October 4, 2006, President Bush signed an appropriations bill but objected to the following statutory qualifications for the Administrator of the Federal Emergency Management Agency (FEMA): the Administrator "shall be appointed from among individuals who have (A) a demonstrated ability in and knowledge of emergency management and homeland security; and (B) not less than 5 years of executive leadership and management experience in the public or private sector."[23] The purpose was to avoid a recurrence of the amateurish response by FEMA officials to the Hurricane Katrina disaster in New Orleans. Bush insisted that the qualifications ruled out "a large portion of those persons best qualified by experience and knowledge to fill the office" and announced that the executive branch would construe the statutory language "in a manner consistent with the Appointments Clause of the Constitution."[24]

What is the constitutional argument here? Is it that Congress cannot require that an individual nominated for the position of Surgeon General be a medical doctor? Or that Congress is prohibited from requiring that people nominated to serve on the Council of Economic Advisers be economists? It is true that a President might decide to ignore statutory qualifications, but the Senate can then reject a nominee who falls short of those qualifications. The result is a stalemate and an empty office, perhaps prompting litigation. No matter what objections a President raises in a signing statement, the likely resolution is for the President to comply with the statutory requirements while simultaneously claiming some sort of abstract and impractical independence.

The mere fact that the President submits a name for consideration does not obligate the Senate to act promptly. Particularly toward the end of a President's term, Congress may prefer to let his successor do the nominating. In 1976 dozens of nominations sent to Congress by President Ford were sidetracked in committee, left there to die quietly. The jobs included judges, U.S. attorneys, U.S. marshals, and regulatory commissioners.[25] President Carter received the same treatment in 1980 when Republicans sensed (correctly) that they would soon have their own man in the White House.[26] Predictably,

22. Myers v. United States, 272 U.S. at 265–74 (dissenting opinion).
23. Section 503(c)(2) of H.R. 5441, 109th Congress.
24. 42 Wkly Comp. Pres. Doc. 1742 (2006).
25. Washington Post, August 26, 1976, at A5, and October 3, 1976, at A8.
26. Washington Post, October 16, 1980, at A4.

Democratic Senators in 1988 showed little interest in acting on nominations submitted by President Reagan. President Bush, in 1992, and President Clinton, in 1996 and 2000, experienced the same fate.

Although there is some discretion on the part of the Senate, the President cannot decline to nominate. Once an office is authorized by Congress, it must be filled. A President may frustrate this purpose for a time—as Franklin D. Roosevelt did in the 1930s by delaying the nomination of a Comptroller General—but at some point a name must go forward.

This principle was underscored in 1973 by a court decision against President Nixon. His budget recommended the rescission of $18 million in American Indian educational funds.[27] The administration impounded the money pending congressional action on the rescission request. Private parties brought suit to require the President to appoint members to the National Advisory Council on Indian Education. The Justice Department suggested that the action be dismissed because of the separation of powers doctrine, but District Judge June L. Green denied the motion. Her opinion noted that implementation of the Indian Education Act would apparently be "impossible or impracticable unless the Council is constituted by the President."[28] She also stated that although the President "clearly has discretion to choose whom to appoint to the Council, he apparently has no discretion to decide if the Council should or should not be constituted." On May 5, 1973, about two weeks after Judge Green's opinion, President Nixon appointed fifteen individuals to the council. Further orders by the same judge forced the release of the $18 million and required the appointment of a Deputy Commissioner of Indian Education.[29]

In the Indian education example, Nixon's power to nominate had to be balanced against his constitutional duty under Article II to "take care that the laws be faithfully executed." Failure to appoint would have effectively nullified the law. But when an agency consists of several members at the top (such as commissioners of independent regulatory bodies), there are precedents for not filling every office. Although the Interstate Commerce Commission (ICC) was authorized eleven commissioners, President Carter deliberately kept it to seven by not filling all the vacancies. The reduced size did not prevent the agency from functioning.

Several trucking companies filed a lawsuit, claiming that the ICC was illegally constituted and had taken actions without a quorum. In one of the

27. Budget of the United States Government, Fiscal Year 1974, Appendix, at 1074.
28. Minnesota Chippewa Tribe v. Carlucci, 358 F.Supp. 973, 975 (D.D.C. 1973). This was Civ. Action No. 175-73.
29. Minnesota Chippewa Tribe v. Carlucci (Civ. Action No. 628-73, D.D.C. 1973), memorandum form.

contested actions only five commissioners had voted; in another decision only four commissioners had voted. The trucking companies argued that the Interstate Commerce Act required action by six commissioners (a majority of the statutorily prescribed eleven). In 1980 an appellate court decided that a quorum under the act was a majority of the existing commission rather than a majority of the full complement of eleven.[30] As part of the shift toward deregulation, Congress passed legislation in 1982 to reduce the number of ICC commissioners to seven by January 1, 1983, and to five by January 1, 1986.[31] Legislation in 1995 terminated the ICC and shifted some of its functions to a newly created board within the Department of Transportation.[32]

Participants in the Nominating Process

The selection of a nominee is supposedly a presidential matter. As Alexander Hamilton stated in Federalist 66, there would be "no exertion of *choice* on the part of the Senate. They may defeat one choice of the Executive, and oblige him to make another; but they cannot themselves *choose*—they can only ratify or reject the choice of the President." But this is by no means the practice. Senators from the same party as the President often "nominate" judges, U.S. attorneys, and marshals who serve from their states. When Senator John W. Warner submitted three names to President Bush for a vacant federal judgeship in Virginia's Western District and two names for a vacancy in the Eastern District, a headline in one newspaper read: "Warner Nominates 5 for Judgeships."[33]

Under these circumstances, it is the President who is placed in the position of giving his "advice and consent." If he and his advisers object to a Senator's recommendation, they can offer suggestions in the hope of receiving a more acceptable name. Criteria can be established by executive officials to guide the Senate's choice. Teddy Roosevelt entered the White House declaring: "The Senators and Congressmen shall ordinarily name the *man,* but I shall name the *standard;* and the men have got to come up to it."[34]

Beginning with the Truman administration, the American Bar Association (ABA) formalized its influence in selecting federal judges by setting up a special committee to determine the professional qualifications of judicial candidates. Acting only on names submitted by the Attorney General, the committee informs the chairman of the Senate Judiciary Committee whether,

---

30. Assure Comp. Transp., Inc. v. United States, 629 F.2d 467 (7th Cir. 1980), cert. denied, 449 U.S. 1124 (1981).

31. 96 Stat. 806, sec. 502 (1982).

32. 109 Stat. 803 (1995).

33. Washington Post, March 12, 1989, at B3.

34. 2 George H. Haynes, The Senate of the United States 741 n.1 (1938).

in its judgment, a nominee for the Supreme Court fits the category of "well qualified," "not opposed," or "not qualified." The term "not opposed" means minimally qualified and not among the best available. The ABA categories for the lower courts are "exceptionally well qualified," "well qualified," "qualified," and "not qualified."[35] Because of the crucial role played by the ABA in the appointment process, especially in the 1987 defeat of Judge Robert H. Bork's nomination to the Supreme Court (to be discussed later), the ABA committee has come under intense scrutiny and criticism.[36]

In 1977 President Carter sought greater independence from the Senate by establishing panels to recommend nominees to the appellate courts. The President's constitutional authority to nominate was protected by requiring the panels to recommend five candidates for each vacancy. This arrangement is politically feasible (with regard to the Senate's stake in the procedure) because appellate courts overlap several states. Nominations for district courts, located within a state, are still strongly influenced by individual Senators. When President Reagan took office, he abolished the judicial nominating commissions for appellate judges. During the Bush and Clinton administrations, the nominating process for selecting federal judges followed a variety of practices: screening committees or panels to help Senators choose a nominee, recommendations from the state bar or lawyer associations, and an informal structure for interviewing and recommending candidates for judgeships.

Although many of these factors crowd upon the President's constitutional authority to nominate, some actions are plainly forbidden. Statutory qualifications may curb a President's discretion; they may not eliminate it altogether. In the words of Attorney General Akerman in 1871: "This right to prescribe qualifications is limited by the necessity of leaving scope for the judgment and will of the person or body in whom the Constitution vests the power of appointment." Nor may Congress, as the Supreme Court noted in 1947, violate the Bill of Rights by enacting legislation to provide that "no Republican, Jew or Negro shall be appointed to federal office."[37]

In 1976 the Supreme Court reviewed a lower court decision that upheld the power of Congress to appoint four members to the Federal Election Commission. All six voting members of the commission (including two nominated

---

35. Standing Committee on Federal Judiciary (American Bar Association, 1983). See also Joel B. Grossman, Lawyers and Judges: The ABA and the Politics of Judicial Selection 62–81 (1965); Harold W. Chase, Federal Judges: The Appointing Process (1972).

36. Public Citizen v. U.S. Dept. of Justice, 491 U.S. 440 (1989); Washington Legal Foundation v. U.S. Dept. of Justice, 691 F.Supp. 483 (D.D.C. 1988); Washington Legal Foundation v. American Bar Ass'n, 648 F.Supp. 1353 (D.D.C. 1986).

37. 13 Op. Att'y Gen. 516, 520 (1871); United Public Workers v. Mitchell, 330 U.S. 75, 100 (1947).

by the President) required confirmation by the majority of *both* houses of Congress. The lower court reasoned that Congress possessed the constitutional authority (by way of the "Necessary and Proper" Clause) to appoint members to carry out appropriate legislative functions, even though the commission performed "quasi-executive" and "quasi-judicial" functions as well.[38]

The Supreme Court reversed this judgment. Although it agreed that the "Necessary and Proper" Clause empowered Congress to create the commission, the language could not be read so expansively as to permit Congress to appoint its members. The clause had to be read in concert with other constitutional provisions. For example, Congress could not, merely by concluding that a measure was "necessary and proper," pass a bill of attainder or an ex post facto law. Nor could it violate other portions of the Constitution, such as the Appointments Clause, especially when a commission created by Congress was designed to discharge more than legislative functions. The powers conferred on the Federal Election Commission could be exercised only by "Officers of the United States" appointed pursuant to Article II, Section 2, Clause 2. For the Court, this meant one of two constitutional options: nomination by the President, subject to the advice and consent of the Senate; or vesting the appointment power in the President alone, in the courts of law, or in department heads. Congress chose the first option when it rewrote the act in 1976.[39]

In the Federal Election Commission case, the Court noted that if an agency's powers are "essentially of an investigative and informative nature," Congress could appoint the agency officials. In reauthorizing the Civil Rights Commission in 1983, Congress passed legislation that gave it the right to appoint four of the eight members of the commission. The remaining four members would be appointed by the President. In signing the bill, President Reagan acknowledged that Congress operated within its powers because the essential functions of the Civil Rights Commission were investigative.[40]

Although Congress may not appoint agency officials who discharge executive functions, it can authorize private parties to select members of federal policymaking agencies. The Federal Open Market Committee, which exercises important powers over monetary policy, consists of seven members of the Board of Governors (presidential appointees) and five representatives of the Federal Reserve Banks. The latter are elected annually by the boards of directors of the banks. Members of Congress and private citizens, challenging the constitutionality of this procedure, have been denied standing by the courts to

38. Buckley v. Valeo, 519 F.2d 821, 890–92 (D.C. Cir. 1975).
39. Buckley v. Valeo, 424 U.S. 1, 133–43 (1976); 90 Stat. 475, sec. 101 (1976).
40. 97 Stat. 1301 (1983); Public Papers of the Presidents, 1983 (II), at 1634–35.

have their case heard.[41] Of course, Congress can rewrite the statute governing the appointment procedure at any time.

Senate Advice and Consent

On the question of nominations and appointments, the President and the Senate were originally on equal footing. In an early communication to the Senate, President Washington stated that just as he had "a right to nominate without assigning his reasons, so has the Senate a right to dissent without giving theirs." Washington not only sought the advice of the Senate on nominations but also depended on the judgment of friends in other quarters. Recommendations by members of the House of Representatives, excluded by the Constitution in the appointment process, carried considerable weight.[42]

During the first year of Washington's administration, the Senate rejected Benjamin Fishbourn as naval officer at Savannah, Georgia. It was rumored that the two Senators from that state opposed the nomination because they had someone else in mind for the post. Washington, stung by this rebuff, advised the Senate that prior to voting down a nominee it should first inquire as to the qualifications and reasons in support of the nominee.[43]

In 1813 President Madison bridled at a Senate resolution that authorized a committee to confer with him on the nomination of a minister to Sweden. He declined to meet with it on the ground that the Constitution recognized only two types of action: the Senate could request information from the President or it could designate a committee to communicate with a department head. The appointment of a Senate committee "to confer immediately with the Executive himself appears to lose sight of the coordinate relation between the Executive and the Senate which the Constitution has established, and which ought therefore to be maintained."[44] Madison's successors have not reacted with such ruffled dignity at the thought of meeting with committees or individual lawmakers.

---

41. Melcher v. FOMC, 836 F.2d 561 (D.C. Cir. 1987), cert. denied, 486 U.S. 1042 (1988); Committee for Monetary Reform v. Board of Governors, 766 F.2d 538 (D.C. Cir. 1985); Riegle v. FOMC, 656 F.2d 873 (D.C. Cir. 1981), cert. denied, 454 U.S. 1082 (1981); Reuss v. Balles, 584 F.2d 461 (D.C. Cir. 1978), cert. denied, 439 U.S. 997 (1978).

42. 30 The Writings of Washington 374 (Fitzpatrick ed.). See Roy Swanstrom, The United States Senate, 1789–1801, S. Doc. No. 64, 87th Cong., 1st Sess. 93–95, 101–2 (1962); and Dorothy Gansfield Fowler, "Congressional Dictation of Local Appointments," 7 J. Pol. 25 (1945).

43. 30 The Writings of Washington 370–71.

44. 2 Richardson 516 (July 6, 1813).

Senatorial Courtesy

It has become an accepted practice to defer to Senators' judgments about the merits of appointees from their own states. "Senatorial courtesy" is consistent with the expectation of the framers that Senators would be well suited to determine the fitness of candidates from their constituencies. Madison, in the First Congress, noted that Senators had been joined with the President in the appointment power because they were, "from their nature, better acquainted with the character of the candidates than an individual." A few weeks later Congressman Benjamin Goodhue reinforced the same point by observing that it was "more probable that the Senate may be better acquainted with the characters of the officers that are nominated than the President himself."[45]

To come within the scope of senatorial courtesy, a nominee must be from the state of the Senator, and the appointment must be to a position within that state rather than to a national office, such as the Cabinet. The custom is further refined by requiring that the objecting Senator be from the same party as the President. Although a number of nominations have been defeated because they were "personally offensive" to a Senator, senatorial courtesy has not prevailed in every instance.[46]

The reach of senatorial courtesy is broader than its formal dimensions. In 1970 Senator Barry Goldwater blocked an appointment to a national office (the State Department) that was not even subject to Senate advice and consent. Goldwater advised the Secretary of State that the individual, Arthur J. Olsen, was "personally obnoxious" because of an article he had written in 1964 linking Goldwater—at that time the Republican candidate for President—with right-wing elements in Germany. The Nixon administration, warned by Goldwater that there would be "trouble," withdrew the appointment.[47] Senators from the opposite party can also bargain for power over patronage. During the Nixon years, Senators Alan Cranston and John Tunney of California (both Democrats) were able to work out an agreement that gave every third federal judgeship in that state to a Democrat.[48] Similar accommodations have been reached in subsequent administrations.

During the first year of the Reagan administration, Senator Jesse A. Helms of North Carolina put "holds" on four of the five key regional bureau jobs

45. 1 Annals of Congress 380 (May 19, 1789) and 534 (June 18, 1789).
46. Riddick's Senate Procedure: Precedents and Practices, S. Doc. No. 101-28, 101st Cong., 2d Sess. 951–52 (1992). See also Joseph P. Harris, The Advice and Consent of the Senate 215–37 (1953).
47. Washington Post, August 31, 1970, at A1, and September 1, 1970, at A2.
48. Nina Totenberg, "Will Judges Be Chosen Rationally?" 60 Judicature 93, 95 (1976). See also G. Calvin MacKenzie, The Politics of Presidential Appointments 121–24 (1981).

in the State Department. Operating from a position of strength as the third-ranking Republican member of the Senate Foreign Relations Committee, Helms also functioned as a guardian of conservative values for the Reagan administration and its foreign policy. During the Clinton administration, Helms served as chairman of the Foreign Relations Committee beginning in 1995 and used that leverage and the mechanism of holds to force major reorganizations within the foreign policy agencies.

Senatorial courtesy, in the sense of a Senator objecting to a nominee from his or her state as "personally obnoxious," is not the custom today, but it has been replaced by other legislative techniques that are just as effective. A Senator can block a nominee by threatening a filibuster, indicating opposition through the "blue slip" method used by the Senate Judiciary Committee, and placing a "hold" on a nomination. For the last option, the objecting Senator does not have to be from the state of the nominee.[49]

Supreme Court Nominees

The Senate is especially vigilant in reviewing nominations to the Supreme Court, rejecting approximately one out of five. Many of the rejections stem from partisan considerations, not individual qualifications.[50] Despite this record, the Senate's rejection of two of President Nixon's nominations to the Court seemed to many Senators a bold, if not unconstitutional, course of action. No matter how poorly the President may have made his selections, members of the Senate appeared uncertain and uncomfortable in exercising their prerogative. Acceptance of the third name submitted by President Nixon seemed inevitable. Why this uneasiness and sense of impropriety? A Senator is not obligated to vote for a nominee who appears unsuited for office.

A Senate study in 1976 tried to sharpen the criteria for Supreme Court nominees. The study regarded lawyers with broad experience in their discipline, including political experience, as best suited to handle the responsibilities thrust on members of the Court. Senators, for their part, are justified in considering not merely a nominee's political and constitutional philosophy but also other appointments by the President, particularly when the balance of views on the Court is at stake.[51]

49. Madeleine Scinto and Elana Schor, "Sens. Still Hold out over Holds," The Hill, September 27, 2006, at 1; 152 Cong. Rec. S8955-56 (daily ed., September 5, 2006; statement by Senator Wyden).

50. Henry J. Abraham, Justices and Presidents 8 (1985); Laurence H. Tribe, God Save This Honorable Court 142–51 (1985).

51. Senate Committee on the Judiciary, "Advice and Consent on Supreme Court Nominations," 94th Cong., 2d Sess. (Comm. Print 1976); 121 Cong. Rec. 37650–52 (1975); and 117 Cong. Rec. 39778–83 (1971).

That potential issue took concrete form in 1987 when President Reagan submitted to the Senate the name of Robert H. Bork to be Associate Justice of the Supreme Court. Although Reagan had clearly taken into account Bork's personal beliefs when making his choice, he told the Senate that it should ignore a nominee's philosophy and concentrate solely on questions of quali-fication.[52] Instead, Senators dismissed Reagan's advice and rejected Bork by a vote of 58 to 42, largely because of Bork's views.

Critics of the Senate claimed that the Bork nomination permanently politi-cized the judicial selection process, but in fact the process has always been in-tensely political, although the Bork campaign was extraordinary for the amount of private funds raised and spent in opposition to his nomination.[53] The charge of permanent politicization is overdrawn when one thinks of the Senate's ac-tion a few months later in unanimously confirming Anthony M. Kennedy to the Court with little friction or turmoil. Bork's problem was unique in part because he had spoken and written for decades on controversial issues, giving his opponents a ready supply of ammunition. These voluminous and provocative writings, as Bork later admitted, meant that he could not duck substantive issues raised during the hearings, as did most nominees.[54]

Supreme Court nominations since Bork's defeat have been smoother be-cause Presidents have taken greater care in selecting people who could appeal to a broader community. Anthony Kennedy was confirmed unanimously, 97 to 0. President Bush's nomination of David Souter sailed through, 90 to 9. President Clinton selected two centrists who were confirmed easily: Ruth Bader Ginsburg by a vote of 96 to 3, and Stephen Breyer by a vote of 87 to 9. The exception was President Bush's nomination of Clarence Thomas, a selec-tion that was divisive when first announced and became more so as hearings continued. He was confirmed by the narrow margin of 52 to 48.

During the administration of George W. Bush, it was argued repeatedly by the executive branch that the Senate has an obligation to take a floor vote on a President's nominee to the federal courts. That position was advanced by President Bush, White House Counsel Alberto Gonzales, and other adminis-tration officials. Although, as a matter of comity between the branches, there is a custom and a record of taking floor votes on judicial nominees, there is no constitutional obligation. When a nominee is referred to a committee of jurisdiction, the committee does not even have to hold hearings. It can ignore the nominee and return the name to the administration at the end of the ses-sion. The decision to hold hearings, report a nominee, and take a floor vote

52. Public Papers of the Presidents, 1987 (II), 943, 1057, 1104.
53. William G. Ross, "Participation by the Public in the Federal Judicial Selection Process," 43 Vand. L. Rev. 1 (1990).
54. Robert H. Bork, The Tempting of America 278–79 (1990).

is entirely within the prerogative of the Senate as a separate branch of government.[55] The best method of ensuring committee and floor action is for the President and the White House to work closely with the Senate during the pre-nomination process, meeting with Senators from both parties.

Executive Officials

More circumspect and deferential is the Senate's behavior toward Cabinet officers and other departmental positions. The doctrine that the President is entitled to a Cabinet of his own choice is broadly supported. Some Senators find this submissive attitude offensive and degrading. Senator Charles McC. Mathias Jr. asked in 1977:

> Does it simply mean that after the President has had an opportunity to exercise the broad and plenary power to choose from among 215 million Americans, that we then merely have to ascertain whether his choice is a convicted felon or a committed lunatic, and if we find that that is not the case, we then have to automatically grant confirmation?
> Well, I would say certainly not.[56]

The Senate's reluctance to contest presidential choices for departmental officials was anticipated by Alexander Hamilton, writing in Federalist 76: "As their dissent might cast a kind of stigma upon the individual rejected, and might have the appearance of a reflection upon the judgment of the Chief magistrate, it is not likely that their sanction would often be refused, where there were not special and strong reasons for the refusal." Joseph Story, one of the more distinguished commentators on the Constitution, correctly predicted that Senate rejections would be rare: "The more common error, (if there shall be any) will be too great a facility to yield to the executive wishes, as a means of personal, or popular favor."[57] If the nomination can be killed outright, Senators may encourage one another to mass for the attack. But a Senator may hesitate to step forward against a nominee who faces only minimal opposition.

Only on rare occasions has the Senate rejected a Cabinet nomination, the most recent example being the disapproval of John G. Tower in 1989 for Secretary of Defense. In 1959 the Senate rejected Lewis L. Strauss for Secretary of Commerce. Prior to these two rejections, only seven other Cabinet nomi-

55. Mitchel A. Sollenberger, "Must the Senate Take a Floor Vote on a Presidential Judicial Nominee?" 34 Pres. Stud. Q. 420 (2004).
56. 123 Cong. Rec. 2076 (1977).
57. 3 Joseph Story, Commentaries §1526 (1833).

nees had been rejected, some of them several times. In 1843 the Senate rejected Caleb Cushing three straight times as Secretary of Treasury, the margin against him increasing with each vote. Charles B. Warren was turned down twice in 1925 for the post of Attorney General.[58]

Of eleven department heads submitted by President Carter in 1977, the Senate confirmed eight merely by voice vote. The Senate's perfunctory investigation and approval of Bert Lance as Director of the Office of Management and Budget (OMB), a position considered more powerful than any Cabinet office, became deeply embarrassing for the Senate when Lance resigned amidst serious charges about his past financial dealings. In 1981, roll-call votes were taken for all thirteen Cabinet nominees submitted by President Reagan.

The Senate periodically reexamines its responsibility for reviewing nominees to executive offices. To defer to the President, on the principle that he has a right to select his own assistants, makes a nullity of the Senate's advice-and-consent role. Department heads and their assistants are not mere staff support for the President. They are called on to administer programs that Congress has enacted into law. A lack of interest by an administrator or overt hostility to a legislative program can eviscerate the policies that Congress has taken pains to announce as national goals. Administrators so disposed can shatter agency morale and create uncertainty for career personnel, who may not know whether they are supposed to implement statutory objectives or sabotage them.

Although the record demonstrates that the Senate only infrequently rejects a nomination to an executive position, statistics do not reveal the candidates who are eliminated as a result of a preliminary canvass among Senators, people who decline an offer rather than submit to the glare of Senate publicity, those who are not even seriously considered by the executive branch because of the likelihood of Senate opposition, and the names withdrawn by the President after confirmation becomes hopeless.[59]

Ambassadors

The Constitution requires the Senate's advice and consent for two classes of public office: Justices of the Supreme Court and "Ambassadors, other public Ministers and Consuls."[60] Senate confirmation for all other officers depends on statutory conditions set by Congress.

58. Louis C. James, "Senatorial Rejections of Presidential Nominations to the Cabinet: A Study in Constitutional Custom," 3 Ariz. L. Rev. 232 (1961).
59. See MacKenzie, The Politics of Presidential Appointments, at 174–81.
60. Art. II, Sec. 2.

The special attention accorded diplomatic officers flows from the Senate's responsibility in treaty matters. During the early years, the act of confirming ambassadors often overlapped with substantive questions on treaties. Senators voted not merely on the fitness of a nominee but also on the instructions he had received to negotiate with a foreign country.[61] Presidents have also appointed agents and special envoys without submitting their names to the Senate. The claim is that because their appointments are temporary, they are technically not "officers," even though they discharge diplomatic duties.[62]

The Senate's responsibility for confirming presidential nominees, although fixed firmly in the Constitution, remains unsettled in its application. The Senate was not meant to be a passive participant. Delegates to the Philadelphia convention believed that the Senate would be knowledgeable about nominees and capable of voting wisely. Yet for the most part, it has acted cautiously, uncertain of the scope of its own constitutional power. The source of this uncertainty is not the Constitution. Nowhere in that document, or in its history, is there an obligation on the part of the Senate to approve a nomination. On the contrary, the burden should be on the President to select and submit a nominee with acceptable credentials.

Recess Appointments

The framers of the Constitution recognized that the Senate would not always be in session to give advice and consent to presidential nominations. To cover these periods the President is authorized to make recess appointments: "The President shall have Power to fill up all Vacancies that may happen during the Recess of the Senate, by granting Commissions which shall expire at the End of their next Session."[63] This provision was adopted at the Constitutional Convention without a dissenting vote[64] and with virtually no record to fix its intent and scope.[65] A loose interpretation would jeopardize the Senate's role in the appointment process.

Two words have been most in dispute: "happen" and "recess." Does "happen" mean "happen to take place" during the recess (the literal meaning)? A long list of opinions by Attorneys General has interpreted the language more broadly to mean

61. Harris, The Advice and Consent of the Senate, at 281–84.

62. Henry M. Wriston, "The Special Envoy," 38 Foreign Affairs 219 (1960); Elmer Plischke, Diplomat in Chief 63–118 (1986). For distinctions between "officer" and "rank," see Wood v. United States, 15 Ct. Cl. 151 (1879), aff'd in Wood v. United States, 107 U.S. 414 (1882).

63. Art. II, Sec. 2, Cl. 3.

64. 2 Farrand 540.

65. Id. at 574, 600, 660; 3 Farrand 421. Federalist 67, written by Hamilton, adds little to the intent of the Recess Clause.

"happen to exist" at the time of a recess, including vacancies that occur while the Senate is in session and available to give advice and consent. Attorney General Wirt claimed that the second meaning satisfied the reason, spirit, and purpose of the Constitution (which to Wirt was keeping offices filled).[66] Through various statutes, to be discussed later, Congress has limited the reach of Wirt's opinion.

The word "recess" also requires interpretation. It means more than final adjournment at the end of a session or the end of a Congress. A temporary recess of the Senate, "protracted enough to prevent that body from performing its functions of advising and consenting to executive nominations," permits the President to make recess appointments.[67] Senate adjournment from July 3 to August 8, 1960, constituted a "Recess of the Senate" as interpreted by the Justice Department.[68] When the Senate temporarily adjourned in the middle of this session and reconvened, it continued the same session. It did not commence the "next session" in the meaning of the Recess Clause.[69] Short adjournments "for 5 or even 10 days" do not "constitute the recess intended by the Constitution," according to another Attorney General's opinion.[70] A Justice Department brief in 1993 suggested that recess appointments might be justified for recesses in excess of three days, but the litigation that prompted that analysis was not decided on that ground.[71]

Statutory Restrictions

For more than a century, Congress has experimented with statutory restrictions on the President's power to make recess appointments. If Congress be-

66. 1 Op. Att'y Gen. 631 (1823). For other Justice Department opinions along this line, see Taney at 2 Op. Att'y Gen. 525 (1832); Mason at 4 Op. Att'y Gen. 523 (1846); Bates at 10 Op. Att'y Gen. 356 (1862); Stanbery at 12 Op. Att'y Gen. 32, 38 (1866); Evarts at 12 Op. Att'y Gen. 455, 457 (1868); Devans at 16 Op. Att'y Gen. 522, 524 (1880); Brewster at 18 Op. Att'y Gen. 29 (1884); Miller at 19 Op. Att'y Gen. 261, 262 (1889); Gregory at 30 Op. Att'y Gen. 314, 315 (1914); Daugherty at 33 Op. Att'y Gen. 20, 23 (1921); and Walsh at 41 Op. Att'y Gen. 463, 465–66 (1960). A federal circuit court concurred with the Attorney General opinions from 1823 to 1880 in In re Farrow, 3 F. 112, 113–15 (C.C. N.D. Ga. 1880).

67. 41 Op. Att'y Gen. 463, 466 (1960).

68. Id. The Comptroller General had adopted a similar interpretation; 28 Comp. Gen. 30 (1948).

69. 41 Op. Att'y Gen. 463, 477 (1960); see also 23 Op. Att'y Gen. 599, 604 (1901).

70. 33 Op. Att'y Gen. 20, 25 (1921). See also 3 O.L.C. 311, 314 (1979). A Justice Department brief in 1993 suggested that recess appointments might be justified for recesses in excess of three days, but this particular dispute was not decided on that ground. Memorandum of Points and Authorities in Support of Defendants' Opposition to Plaintiffs' Motion for Partial Summary Judgment, at 24–26, Mackie v. Clinton, Civ. Action No. 93-0032-LFO (D.D.C.).

71. Memorandum of Points and Authorities in Support of Defendants' Opposition to Plaintiffs' Motion for Partial Summary Judgment, at 24–26, Mackie v. Clinton, Civ. Action No. 93-0032-LFO (D.D.C.).

lieves that the exercise of that power undermines the Senate's authority to confirm appointments, it can retaliate by withholding funds to pay the salaries of recess appointees. As Senator Fessenden remarked in 1863: "It may not be in our power to prevent the [recess] appointment, but it is in our power to prevent the payment; and when payment is prevented, I think that will probably put an end to the habit of making such appointments."[72]

Fessenden's comment came after the Senate had asked the Judiciary Committee to explore this question: Did the practice of appointing officers to fill vacancies that existed *prior* to a recess, while the Senate was in session, conflict with the Constitution? The committee rejected Attorney General Wirt's position that a recess appointee can fill a vacancy that occurs during a session. To the committee, a reading of the constitutional language "may happen during the Recess of the Senate" as including what happened before the recess seemed "a perversion of language." Such reasoning tilted the balance of power toward the President and placed excessive emphasis on the filling of a vacancy. Of equal importance was the need to protect the Senate's opportunity to pass judgment on the qualification of an officeholder. Unless Congress placed some constraint on the power to make recess appointments, an "ambitious, corrupt, or tyrannical executive" could nullify the Senate's constitutional function.[73]

Congress passed legislation in 1863 to prohibit the use of funds to pay the salary of anyone appointed during a Senate recess to fill a vacancy that existed "while the Senate was in session and is by law required to be filled by and with the advice and consent of the Senate, until such appointee shall have been confirmed by the Senate."[74] Under this statute an officer had to serve without pay (relying on savings or loans) until the Senate consented to the nomination.

The harshness of this law is illustrated by an issue during the administration of Woodrow Wilson. George Rublee, nominated to the Federal Trade Commission in March 1915, served for more than a year as a recess appointee. After the Senate voted to reject him, he continued to serve (at Wilson's request) the balance of his recess commission until September 1916, when Congress adjourned. Under the 1863 law, Rublee was not entitled to any remuneration. Congress had to pass a special appropriation that paid his salary for fourteen months, from the date his service began to the date the Senate rejected him.[75]

72. Cong. Globe, 37th Cong., 3d Sess. 565 (1863).
73. S. Rept. No. 80, 37th Cong., 3d Sess. (1863). Quotations from the report appear at pp. 5 and 6.
74. 12 Stat. 646 (1863). For the restrictive effect of this statute, see 16 Op. Att'y Gen. 522, 531 (1880); 26 Op. Att'y Gen. 234, 235 (1907); 32 Op. Att'y Gen. 271, 272 (1920); and 41 Op. Att'y Gen. 463, 473–74 (1960).
75. 39 Stat. 801 (1916); see 2 Haynes, The Senate of the United States 776–77.

A House committee in 1940 concluded that the 1863 statute was excessively burdensome. It seemed particularly inequitable when a vacancy arose shortly before a recess, with insufficient time for Senate action, and when a session terminated before the Senate acted on a nomination that had been pending for months. The committee, supported by the Attorney General and the Budget Bureau, recommended changes to make the law "more flexible."[76] Congress revised the 1863 law to permit three exceptions. First, payments may be made if a vacancy arises within 30 days before the end of the session of the Senate. Given the paucity of time, nominations submitted during this period are unlikely to receive the Senate's approval. Second, payments may be made if, at the end of the session, a nomination was pending before the Senate (other than for someone appointed during a preceding recess). This provision has two purposes: it protects the Senate from successive recess appointees, and it protects nominees whose names went forward in a timely manner. Third, payments may be made if a nomination is rejected by the Senate within 30 days before the end of the session and an individual (other than the one rejected) receives a recess appointment. This exception takes care of possible cases of rejection on the eve of a recess. The statute also contains an important limitation: a nomination to fill a vacancy referred to in the three exceptions must be submitted to the Senate no later than 40 days after the Senate's next session begins.[77] "Next session" has been interpreted in a nontechnical way to mean the return of the Senate from its recess, not the next session of Congress.[78]

Like other statutes, this one is not self-executing. It must be constantly monitored by Congress to prevent abuse. Presidents may let a position remain unfilled for months without submitting a name to the Senate and then, just before a recess, forward a name to be covered under the second exception. For example, the office of OMB Deputy Director became vacant on March 24, 1978. President Carter did not submit the name of John White until October 7, making it "pending" at the time of the recess and therefore within the guidelines of the law. By resubmitting White's name within 40 days after the Senate reconvened, Carter stayed within the letter of the law, but his initial delay of six months helped circumvent the statutory requirement for Senate confirmation, which did not occur until April 10, 1979.

The scope of recess appointments is complicated by the presence of "holdover" clauses in federal statutes. For example, a member of the Federal Elec-

---

76. H. Rept. No. 2646, 76th Cong., 3d Sess. (1940). See also S. Rept. No. 1079, 76th Cong., 1st Sess. (1939).

77. 54 Stat. 751 (1940); 5 U.S.C. 5503 (2000). For commentary on the hardship experienced by appointees who had to serve without compensation, see 28 Comp. Gen. 30, 37 (1948), and 41 Op. Att'y Gen. 463, 479–80 (1960).

78. 41 Op. Att'y Gen. 463, 477 (1960).

tion Commission may serve after the expiration of that member's term "until his successor has taken office as a member of the Commission." The statute is ambiguous because it does not define *how* the successor takes office: by Senate confirmation (required for new members) or as a recess appointee.

The statute says that any vacancy in the membership of the commission "shall be filled in the same manner as in the case of the original appointment" (presumably by Senate confirmation). Nevertheless, on October 25, 1978, President Carter made John McGarry a recess appointee to the seat held by Neil Staebler, who was serving in a holdover capacity. Staebler refused to leave office, arguing that McGarry had not been confirmed by the Senate and therefore no vacancy existed for Carter to fill.

A federal district judge, deciding against Staebler, pointed to many inconsistencies in the statute. If a vacancy existed only at the point of confirmation of a successor, would this place an unmanageable task on the President? How could he recruit someone for the office and submit a nomination if, in theory, no vacancy existed? Such a scheme, the court argued, would also disrupt the statutory design of staggered, six-year terms for the six commissioners. Under Staebler's interpretation, would the statutory dates for these terms shift to take account of holdovers, creating a "baggage of peculiar practical difficulties"?[79] The court could find no clear evidence that Congress had tried to restrict the President's power to make recess appointments.[80] If the Senate wanted to protect its right to advise and consent, it could have rejected McGarry's nomination when Carter first submitted it on September 27, 1977, and then again on April 10, 1978. It was only after two sessions of Senate inaction that Carter made the recess appointment.[81]

The district court's decision is not altogether convincing. No one doubts that a President can search for a candidate to replace someone serving in a holdover capacity and have the candidate confirmed by the Senate. Moreover, it does not follow that holdovers would disrupt the statutory design of staggered six-year terms. The terms would not change. Once a nominee had been confirmed by the Senate, that person would serve out the remainder of the six-year term.

President Reagan provoked a battle with the Senate in 1984 when he gave a recess appointment to Martha Seger, placing her on the Federal Reserve Board a few days after Congress began a three-week recess. The Senate Banking Committee had approved her nomination by the narrow margin of 10 to 8. The Senate Majority Leader, Robert C. Byrd, introduced a Senate resolution

79. Staebler v. Carter, 464 F.Supp. 585, 589 (D.D.C. 1979). On appeal, the D.C. Circuit dismissed the case as moot on May 17, 1979, remanding it to the district court.

80. Id. at 592.

81. Id. at 601. For the Senate's record on McGarry, see id. at 587.

stating that the power to make recess appointments should be confined to situations in which the Senate has formally terminated a session or in which the Senate will be in recess for longer than 30 days.[82] The resolution was never put to a vote. However, a year later the Senate passed Byrd's resolution, expressing the Senate's opinion that recess appointments should not be made to the Federal Reserve Board except under unusual circumstances and only for the purpose of fulfilling "a demonstrable and urgent need" in the administration of the board's activities. The Senate also agreed to consider nominations to the board in an expeditious manner.[83] When President Reagan continued to use his recess appointment power freely, Senator Byrd retaliated late in 1985 by holding up action on presidential nominations.[84]

Congress can force a recess appointee to resign by rejecting the nomination. Because of language in a rider attached to the annual Treasury–Postal Service appropriations bill, a rejection can have the effect of eliminating the appointee's compensation.[85] The language reads as follows: "No part of any appropriation for the current fiscal year contained in this or any other Act shall be paid to any person for the filling of any position for which he or she has been nominated after the Senate has voted not to approve the nomination of said person."[86]

The power to make recess appointments has been a major issue in the life of the Legal Services Corporation (LSC). Through the use of holdover provisions and recess appointments, Presidents Reagan and Bush were able to largely circumvent the Senate's power of confirmation. Several recent court decisions may restrict the President's power to make recess appointments not only to the LSC but to other agencies as well.[87]

Recess Appointments of Judges

The use of recess appointments for federal judges has significant implications for judicial independence. The issue became pronounced in the 1950s when

82. 130 Cong. Rec. 23234–36, 23341 (1984).

83. 131 Cong. Rec. 17622–24, 17679 (1985).

84. "Recess Appointments Raise Senators' Anger," Washington Post, September 26, 1985, at A23; Public Papers of the Presidents, Ronald Reagan, 1985 (II), at 1209; "White House Asks End of Appointee 'Backlog,'" Washington Post, October 9, 1985, at A17.

85. 3 O.L.C. 314, 317 (1979).

86. For example, 108 Stat. 2418, sec. 610 (1994).

87. Wilkinson v. Legal Services Corp., 865 F.Supp. 891 (D.D.C. 1994), reversed on other grounds, Wilkinson v. Legal Services Corp., 80 F.3d 535 (D.C. Cir. 1996); Mackie v. Clinton, 827 F.Supp. 56 (D.D.C. 1993); McCalpin v. Durant, 766 F.2d 535 (D.C. Cir. 1985); McCalpin v. Dana, No. 85-542 (D.D.C. October 5, 1982). See "An LSC Dispute May Take Power from President," National Law Journal, February 19, 1996, at A1. These decisions often

President Eisenhower placed three men on the Supreme Court after the Senate had recessed: Earl Warren, William J. Brennan Jr., and Potter Stewart. All three joined the Court and participated in decisions before the Senate had an opportunity to review their credentials. The Senate confirmed them, but the experience convinced most Senators that the procedure was defective both for the Senate and for the judiciary.

In 1960 Senator Philip A. Hart introduced a resolution to discourage this practice. As a Senate resolution, it had no legally binding effect but was meant to express the view of the Senate and to guide executive action. The Senate labored under unique difficulties when called on to confirm a recess appointee who already sat on the Supreme Court. In this situation, a negative vote by the Senate would represent more than the rejection of a nominee; it would remove a sitting Justice. Recess appointments also conflicted with the principle of judicial independence. Should Senators take into account any decisions rendered during the appointment period? If so, Justices might hedge their decisions to please the President or the Senate, leaving disappointed litigants wondering whether the outcome of their case turned on the uncertain status of recess appointees.

Opponents of Hart's resolution argued that the President needed to exercise his constitutional power to make recess appointments because of the heavy workload of the Court. They also objected to ambiguities in the language of the resolution and the fact that it had not been referred to the Department of Justice or the Judicial Conference for comment. Nor had there been any hearings. The Senate passed the resolution 48 to 37, essentially along party lines.[88] The resolution, after a preamble that details the disadvantages of making recess appointments to the Supreme Court, reads as follows:

> *Resolved,* That it is the sense of the Senate that the making of recess appointments to the Supreme Court of the United States may not be wholly consistent with the best interests of the Supreme Court, the nominee who may be involved, the litigants before the Court, nor indeed the people of the United States, and that such appointments, therefore, should not be made except under unusual circumstances and for the purpose of preventing or ending a demonstrable breakdown in the administration of the Court's business.

turn on statutory issues. Is the holdover limited to one year (Mackie)? Does the statute say the holdover "shall" or "may" continue to serve (Wilkinson)?

88. 106 Cong. Rec. 18145 (1960). See also House Committee on the Judiciary, "Recess Appointments of Federal Judges," 86th Cong., 1st Sess. (Comm. Print January 1959); Note, "Recess Appointments to the Supreme Court—Constitutional But Unwise?" 10 Stan. L. Rev. 124 (1957).

Although legally nonbinding, the resolution had its intended effect. No President since Eisenhower has made a recess appointment to the Supreme Court.

The President's constitutional authority to make recess appointments to the federal courts was upheld by the Second Circuit in 1962.[89] However, in 1983 a panel of the Ninth Circuit held that the President's constitutional power under Article II to make recess appointments could not supplant the lifetime tenure guaranteed to judges by Article III. Federal judges serving under a recess appointment lacked the independence required by the Constitution. A judge receiving his commission under the Recess Appointment Clause "may be called upon to make politically charged decisions while his nomination awaits approval by popularly elected officials. Such a judge will scarcely be oblivious to the effect his decision may have on the vote of these officials."[90]

The decision by the three-judge panel was overturned by the full Ninth Circuit, sitting en banc. Divided 7 to 4, the court held that there was no reason to favor the constitutional provision for lifetime tenure for federal judges over the constitutional provision for recess appointments. Moreover, Presidents have been making judicial recess appointments since 1789, totaling approximately 300 such appointments. Although historical acceptance alone cannot conclusively establish the constitutionality of a practice, the court decided that the recess provision to appoint federal judges "has been inextricably woven into the fabric of our nation."[91] The dissenters denied the permanence of this pattern, noting that with one exception (the appointment prompting this case), the federal courts had functioned since 1964 without the assistance of recess appointees.[92]

The fact that federal courts sanctioned the use of judicial recess appointments did not require the political branches to accept the practice as constitutionally acceptable. Both branches appear to understand that judicial recess appointments pose a substantial risk to the independence of the judiciary and to the constitutional rights of litigants. The decision of the Ninth Circuit, en banc, operates more like an advisory opinion: it is constitutional if you want to do it. The final word on whether it is actually done lies with the President and the Senate.

On December 27, 2000, President Clinton selected Roger L. Gregory as a recess appointee to the Fourth Circuit, the first time since 1980 that a President had named an Article III judge as a recess appointee. President Bush submitted Gregory's name on May 9, 2001, for a lifetime appointment, which the Senate approved by a vote of 93 to 1. Bush made two other recess

89. United States v. Allocco, 305 F.2d 704 (2d Cir. 1962), cert. denied, 371 U.S. 964 (1963).
90. United States v. Woodley, 726 F.2d 1328, 1330 (9th Cir. 1983).
91. United States v. Woodley, 751 F.2d 1008, 1012 (9th Cir. 1985), cert. denied, 475 U.S. 1048 (1986).
92. United States v. Woodley, 751 F.2d at 1024.

appointments to the federal courts in early 2004: Charles W. Pickering for the Fifth Circuit and William H. Pryor for the Eleventh Circuit. After Pickering's recess appointment expired, he announced that he would not seek a lifetime position. His appointment came between the first and second sessions of the 108th Congress and was thus an *intersession* action.

Pryor's appointment was more controversial because it was *intrasession,* and the Senate recess was short (February 12 to 23, 2004). Of the more than 300 recess appointments to Article III courts, only 14 have been intrasession. The Senate was in recess 145 days for one appointee, 112 days for two, 79 days for two, 73 days for one, 64 days for three, 35 days for four, and 10 days for Pryor.[93] The seemingly technical distinction between inter- and intrasession recess appointments has a practical effect. Someone who receives an intersession appointment serves until the end of the next session, or about a year. An individual with an intrasession appointment made early during the session serves close to two years. An effort to disqualify Pryor in a case because he sat as a recess appointee was unsuccessful.[94]

Temporary Appointments

In addition to the power to make recess appointments, Presidents make other temporary or interim appointments. When the head of an executive department dies, resigns, or is sick or absent, the next in command may perform the duties until a successor is appointed or the absence ceases. As an alternative, the President may direct someone else (previously appointed with the advice and consent of the Senate) to perform the duties. These acting officials were once restricted by law to a period not to exceed 30 days, but that limit was violated with such frequency that in 1988 Congress increased it to 120 days and in 1998 to 210 days.[95]

As an example of earlier practices, L. Patrick Gray was named Acting Director of the Federal Bureau of Investigation in May 1972, upon the death of Director J. Edgar Hoover, and he continued to serve in that capacity for almost a year. President Nixon did not submit Gray's name to the Senate for confirmation until February 21, 1973. With the Senate clearly opposed to Gray, Nixon withdrew the nomination on April 17, and Gray resigned shortly thereafter.[96]

---

93. Henry B. Hogue, "Recess Appointments to Article III Courts," 34 Pres. Stud. Q. 656 (2004).

94. Evans v. Stephens, 387 F.3d 1220 (11th Cir. 2004), cert. denied, 125 S.Ct. 1640 (2005), but see also the separate statement by Justice Stevens at 125 S.Ct. 2244 (2005).

95. 5 U.S.C. 3345–48 (2000); 102 Stat. 988, sec. 7 (1988). For earlier versions, see 12 Stat. 656 (1863); 15 Stat. 168 (1868); 26 Stat. 733 (1891). See also 2 O.L.C. (1978).

96. In a letter to Senator William Proxmire on February 22, 1973, Comptroller General Staats concluded that Gray was subject to the thirty-day limit in 5 U.S.C. 3348 and that his

Acting officials frequently served for more than the 30 days allowed under the previous Vacancy Act. That situation was tolerated by Congress if the President had forwarded the person's name to the Senate for confirmation. But when the President failed to send a name forward, Senate prerogatives were directly threatened. That was the situation in 1973 when President Nixon planned to dismantle the Office of Economic Opportunity (OEO). Instead of nominating a Director and seeking the advice and consent of the Senate, he appointed Howard J. Phillips as Acting Director. The administration asserted that the President had the constitutional power to appoint officers temporarily without Senate confirmation, drawing that power from the President's obligation under Article II, Section 3, to "take Care that the Laws be faithfully executed." It was a bizarre argument: the administration ignored a number of laws in order to do what no law permitted.

A district court denied that the President possessed an inherent (or derivative) power to make interim appointments unless in an emergency, and the court found no emergency in this situation. The appointment was invalid because it did not satisfy the statute (requiring the Senate's advice and consent), nor was it made during a Senate recess.[97] As an emergency measure to permit the OEO to function, the court allowed Phillips's successor, Alvin J. Arnett, to assume control as Acting Director. Arnett was later nominated and confirmed as OEO Director.

A different dilemma arose on February 15, 1972, when John Mitchell announced his resignation as Attorney General effective March 1, 1972. President Nixon submitted Deputy Attorney General Richard Kleindienst's name to Congress as his nominee for Attorney General. Kleindienst assumed the duties on March 1, and on June 8 he was confirmed. During this interim he authorized several wiretaps. The question was whether the wiretaps were valid, since Kleindienst had served for more than the 30 days permitted under the Vacancy Act. A district court upheld the wiretaps, pointing out that his name had been sent to the Senate for confirmation even before he assumed the duties of Attorney General: "Had the President been dilatory in sending a name to Congress, perhaps a different situation would be present."[98] In a separate decision, a district court held that Robert Bork became Acting Attorney General in 1973 under a statute other than the Vacancy Act and therefore was not subject to the 30-day limit.[99]

---

continued service was prohibited by law (B-150136). The Justice Department maintained that Gray became Acting Director under a different law (28 U.S.C. 508–10).

97. Williams v. Phillips, 360 F.Supp. 1363 (D.D.C. 1973). The D.C. Court of Appeals denied Phillips's motion for a stay, pending appeal, because he failed to show sufficient likelihood of success on the merits; Williams v. Phillips, 482 F.2d 669 (D.C. Cir. 1973).

98. United States v. Lucido, 373 F.Supp. 1142, 1151 (E.D. Mich. 1974).

99. United States v. Halmo, 386 F.Supp. 593, 595 (E.D. Wis. 1974).

Presidents have created other problems related to temporary appointees by dispatching agents on diplomatic missions without seeking the advice and consent of the Senate. Since the appointments were of a temporary nature, it could be argued that they did not satisfy the legal meaning of an "office," including such qualities as tenure and duration. But Congress can use its appropriations power to rein in appointments to nonambassadorial posts. Teddy Roosevelt created a stir by appointing extralegal, unsalaried commissions to study social and economic issues. When he asked Congress for $25,000 to publish a commission study, Congress retaliated by prohibiting the appointment of commissions that lacked legislative authority. Although Roosevelt protested that Congress had no right to pass such restrictions and threatened to ignore the proscription, he had to seek private funds to publish the study.[100]

His cousin, Franklin D. Roosevelt, created agencies by executive order and used appropriations to finance agency activities that lacked legislative support. Congress passed the "Russell Rider" in 1944 to prohibit the use of any appropriations for an agency unless Congress had specifically authorized it.[101] Toward the end of the administration of Lyndon Johnson, Congress prohibited the use of funds for interdepartmental boards, commissions, councils, committees, or similar groups that did not have prior and specific congressional approval. That prohibition has been repeated each year in appropriations bills.[102]

The appointment power operates in a framework of studied ambiguity, its limits established for the most part not by court decisions but by imaginative accommodations between the executive and legislative branches. The actual power of nominating officials has been parceled out to interest groups, legislators, judges, and party leaders, with the White House trying to coordinate and centralize the decisions. For its part, the Senate is often hesitant in challenging and rejecting the names submitted by the President, especially candidates for executive departments. Each Senator has a widely different interpretation of the appropriate degree of deference. Largely uncharted is the realm of recess and temporary appointments, an area of vast presidential discretion. Congress polices the borders of this power by imposing statutory constraints and conditions, producing a compromise that appears to meet the needs and interests of both branches.

100. 20 The Works of Theodore Roosevelt 416–17 (1926); 35 Stat. 1027, sec. 9 (1909).

101. 58 Stat. 387, sec. 213 (1944), codified at 31 U.S.C. 1347 (2000). See 90 Cong. Rec. 6021–39 for the legislative history. The restriction applies to "action agencies" that perform governmental functions, not to advisory bodies; 3 Op. O.L.C. 263 (1979).

102. Action under Johnson had its origin in 1968; see S. Rept. No. 1275, 90th Cong., 2d Sess. 2–3, and H. Rept. No. 1348, 90th Cong., 2d Sess. 8. For contemporary language, see 118 Stat. 3274, sec. 610 (2004).

3

THEORY IN A CRUCIBLE: THE REMOVAL POWER

Occasionally a statement in the *Federalist Papers* is so wide of the mark, at such odds with events to come, that it has an abrupt and startling effect. So it is with the breezy claim of Alexander Hamilton, in Federalist 77, that the consent of the Senate "would be necessary to displace [public officials] as well as to approve."

The issue that Hamilton resolved so nonchalantly produced deep divisions among the members of the First Congress. The question of who should remove executive officials overshadowed most of the matters that pressed upon the fledgling legislative body in 1789. From May 19 through June 24 the House of Representatives explored the removal power in all its nuances. The debate, occupying almost 200 pages of the record, represents one of the most thorough expositions on the nature of implied powers. In contrast to many members of Congress today, who let constitutional issues slide by to be disposed of by the courts (if at all), those of the First Congress faced the constitutional issue with a deep sense of responsibility.

The members of the First Congress explored four schools of thought: (1) the Senate, because of its role in appointments, must have equal participation in removals; (2) removals may be made only by the constitutional process of impeachment; (3) Congress, since it creates an office, may attach to it any condition that it deems proper for tenure and removal; and (4) the power of removal belongs exclusively to the President as an incident of the executive power.[1] Even those four categories fail to do justice to the wide-ranging nature of the debate, the complexity of the issues, or the shifting tide of opinion that advanced and receded each day as the deliberation continued.[2]

The "Decision of 1789"

James Madison precipitated the debate on the removal power by proposing three executive departments: Foreign Affairs, Treasury, and War. At the head

---

1. Ex parte Hennen, 13 Pet. 230, 233 (1839), argument of Mr. Coxe for plaintiff; 2 George H. Haynes, The Senate of the United States 786–87 (1938); Edward S. Corwin, The President 87 (1957).

2. The House debate in 1789, on all three executive departments, appears in 1 Annals of Congress 368–83 (May 19), 384–96 (May 20), 396 (May 21), 455–79 (June 16), 479–512

of each department would be a Secretary appointed by the President with the advice and consent of the Senate "and to be removable by the President." William Smith of South Carolina immediately objected to giving the President the sole power of removal. Madison countered by saying that the removal power would make the President responsible for the conduct of department heads. His fellow Virginian, Theodorick Bland, wanted the removal power shared with the Senate to make it consistent with the Constitution's appointment process, but the House rejected Bland's motion to add the words "by and with the advice and consent of the Senate." John Vining, opposing the motion, pointed out that the Senate could not serve as an impartial judge in impeachment proceedings if it had already rendered a judgment in a removal case. As the first day's debate drew to a close, the House by a "considerable majority" declared that the removal power lay with the President.

Two days later the House considered a resolution to make the heads of the three executive departments "removable by the President." Eleven members, Madison among them, were appointed to draw up a bill. When the House next took up the topic on June 16, William Smith clarified his position by identifying two choices: either the Constitution gave the President the power of removal (in which case it was nugatory for Congress to repeat it) or else it was not given to him (and therefore improper for Congress to confer it). He also cautioned that competent people would be reluctant to accept a position and risk their reputation if the President could remove them at will. Smith wanted the language eliminated and the question left to the judiciary. This represents a fifth school of thought on the removal issue and an early inclination, long before *Marbury v. Madison* (1803), toward judicial review.

Madison, after taking a few days to reexamine the Constitution, conceded that it did not "perfectly correspond with the ideas I entertained of it from the first glance." Precisely how he had adjusted his opinion is not evident from his remarks. The Constitution, he said, vested the executive power in the President subject to certain exceptions, such as the Senate's participation in the appointment process. He believed that Congress could not extend the exceptions or modify in any way the President's authority. Therefore it was improper to associate the Senate with the President in the removal process. Yet to strike the clause might imply that Congress doubted whether the President had the removal power. It was better, Madison concluded, to retain the language.

Other legislators objected to letting Congress amend the Constitution by statutory construction whenever the document was silent on a question.

(June 17), 512–52 (June 18), 552–77 (June 19), 578–85 (June 22), 590–92 (June 24), 592–607 (June 25), 611–14 (June 27), 614–15 (June 30), and 615 (July 1).

Samuel Livermore acknowledged that Congress had authority to create an office and to attach to it whatever limitations and restrictions it thought appropriate, but he considered it very improper to say that the power of giving birth to a creature permitted Congress to "bring forth a monster." Since he feared that a President might remove someone on mere caprice to make room for a favorite, he wanted every person "to have a hearing before he is punished." Here enters a sixth school: procedural due process.

On June 17 the House resumed debate on the motion to make the Secretary of Foreign Affairs "removable by the President." Thomas Hartley from Pennsylvania denied that officials had a property in their office and could be removed only for criminal conduct. That doctrine "may suit a nation which is strong in proportion to the number of dependents upon the Crown, but will be very pernicious in a Republic like ours." Some officers held their commissions during good behavior; others, like the Secretary, served at the pleasure of the President.

George Clymer of Pennsylvania had no doubt that the removal power belonged to the executive. Even if the Constitution had been silent on the power of appointment, he reasoned, the executive would have had that power as well. The Constitution mentioned appointment only to "give some further security against the introduction of improper men into office. But in cases of removal there is not such necessity for this check." One of the more active participants in the debate, Roger Sherman of Connecticut, said that an officer existed as a creature of Congress. Depending on the statute creating the office, the person might hold office during good behavior, be elected every year, be displaced for negligence of duty, or be subjected to any other provision without calling on the President or the Senate.

Madison abhorred this theory of government. He considered it fundamental that the Constitution vested the executive power in the President and required him to take care that the laws were faithfully executed. If the President wantonly removed a meritorious officer, that would "subject him to impeachment and removal from his own high trust." Madison wanted to protect the responsibility of the President: "Vest this power in the Senate jointly with the President, and you abolish at once that great principle of unity and responsibility in the Executive department, which was intended for the security of liberty and the public good."

Debate continued on June 18. The idea of deriving the removal power from the general nature of "executive power," as Madison had suggested, elicited a challenge from Alexander White of Virginia, who said that such a doctrine could be supported only by examples "brought from beyond the Atlantic." This is an amusing twist. Madison advanced essentially the same argument in 1793 while trying to refute Hamilton in the celebrated Pacificus-Helvidius exchange.

Still another Virginian, John Page, objected to joining the Senate with the President in the removal power. In nine cases out of ten, he predicted, in which the President was convinced that someone must be removed, it would be impossible to produce the necessary evidence. Could the Senate proceed without evidence? If not, should such a man "be saddled upon the President, who had been appointed for no other purpose but to aid the President in performing certain duties?" James Jackson denied that the heads of departments were necessarily dependent on the President. The Constitution itself "specifically points them out." Benjamin Goodhue blunted the force of that argument. He explained that even though Senators played an important role in confirming an officer, since they might be better acquainted with the nominee than the President, the man's *performance in office* could be better judged by the President. Livermore believed that Congress should not interfere with the executive departments by including language on removals: "Leave them to do their duty, and let us do ours."

June 19 arrived and the House still did not know whether to strike the words "to be removable by the President." Peter Silvester of New York helped crystallize the issue: Congress had to give its opinion either by declaration or by implication. If the Constitution lodged the removal power in the President, it was useless for Congress to interfere by making an express declaration. If the Constitution did *not* leave the power with the President, could Congress give it? Although the Constitution did not expressly grant the power, there was nothing "in contradiction to it." The problem was compounded, Sherman added, by the fact that the words "to be removable by the President" might imply that the President lacked the removal power and had to have it granted by law. The motion to strike the language was rejected, 20 to 34.

By June 22 the House was headed in the direction of treating the removal power by implication, not declaration. Egbert Benson moved that the bill provide that the chief clerk (second in command in the Foreign Affairs Department) take charge of all records whenever the Secretary "shall be removed from office" by the President. His motion avoided the problem posed by the phrase "to be removable by the President," which appeared to be a grant of power by Congress. The new language met opposition from Smith, who preferred that Congress express itself in "more candid and manly" terms by declaration, not implication. Benson's motion carried, however, 30 to 18. Benson then moved to strike the phrase "to be removable by the President," to which the House agreed, 31 to 19.

In the Senate, the proposal to delete the President's power to remove the Secretary of Foreign Affairs resulted in a tie vote (9 to 9). Vice President Adams broke the tie by voting against the motion.[3] A few days later, during

3. 1 Journal of the First Session of the Senate 42 (1820). The vote occurred on July 18, 1789.

House action on the bill to establish a War Department, Benson offered language to give the President removal power by implication. Although the identical principle and language were at issue, his motion carried by the smaller margin of 24 to 22. On a motion in the Senate to strike the President's power to remove the Secretary of War, the effort failed by a close vote of 9 to 10.[4]

The Foreign Affairs and War Departments had been regarded as "executive departments" in part because of their origin and evolution during the Continental Congress. No such concession was made for Treasury.[5] One would have expected the House, jealous of its control over finances, to challenge the President's power to remove the Secretary of the Treasury. Instead, the challenge came from the Senate, which deleted the President's power to remove the Secretary. Later, on a motion that the Senate recede from its position and accept the House language, another tie vote occurred, 10 to 10. Vice President Adams cast the deciding vote for the motion.[6]

As a result of these actions, Congress passed legislation to adopt the same approach for the Departments of Foreign Affairs, War, and Treasury. The subordinate officers would have charge and custody of all records whenever the Secretary "shall be removed from office by the President of the United States."[7]

The fact that Congress recognized the President's freedom to remove department heads did not mean that the President could remove *all* administrative officials. Congress did not vest the entire removal power with him. When Madison turned his attention to the tenure of the Comptroller of the Treasury, he said that it was necessary "to consider the nature of this office." Its properties were not "purely of an Executive nature," he said. "It seems to me that they partake of a Judiciary quality as well as Executive; perhaps the latter obtains in the greatest degree." Because of the mixed nature of the office, "there may be strong reasons why an officer of this kind should not hold his office at the pleasure of the Executive branch of the Government."[8] Madison's insight would hold the attention of scholars and courts more than a century later.

How did Madison know enough about the Comptroller of the Treasury to comment in such detail on that officer's duties and nature? The answer is that he was familiar with the actions of the Continental Congress in 1781 in creating a Superintendent of Finance, auditors, and the Comptroller, who functioned as a quasi-judicial officer. The Comptroller was responsible for the settlement of public accounts, and on all appeals he "shall openly and publicly

4. Id. at 51 (August 4, 1789).
5. Louis Fisher, President and Congress 86–87 (1972).
6. 1 Journal of the First Session of the Senate 50, 62–63.
7. 1 Stat. 29, 50, 67 (1789).
8. 1 Annals of Congress 611–12 (June 27, 1789).

hear the parties, and his decision shall be conclusive." Madison wanted to preserve the Comptroller's independence, even from the President.

On the removal issue, Hamilton later retreated from the position he had taken in Federalist 77. In 1793, in his Pacificus essays, he advanced a broad interpretation of executive power. With the exception of the Senate's participation in the appointment of officers and in the making of treaties, and the power of Congress to declare war and grant letters of marque and reprisal, Hamilton contended that "the *executive power* of the United States is completely lodged in the President. This mode of construing the Constitution has indeed been recognized by Congress in formal acts, upon full consideration and debate; of which the power of removal from office is an important instance."[9]

Controversies from Jackson to Cleveland

Congress has authority to create an office and specify the term of office. May it also specify the manner in which an incumbent is removed? This issue, presented here as an academic riddle, assumed solid form with Andrew Jackson in the White House.

Jackson's predecessors had used the removal power with restraint. The opportunity for removal, however, expanded considerably in 1820 when Congress passed legislation that limited a large number of federal officers to a term of four years, stipulating that they would be "removable from office at pleasure."[10] Supported by this legislative authority and by his own philosophy favoring the rotation of federal personnel, Jackson removed more officers than all the Presidents who preceded him (252 for Jackson, compared with 193 for his predecessors).[11] These numbers, though large, are less impressive as a proportion of the growing federal bureaucracy and do not constitute anything near the "clean sweep" suggested by some historians.[12]

Congressional opposition to Jackson's policy came to a head in 1833 when he removed the Secretary of the Treasury for refusing to carry out his policy toward the national bank. At issue was more than the removal power. Congress regarded Treasury with proprietary interest, often treating the Secretary as *its* agent. It had, for example, delegated to the Secretary—not the President—the responsibility for placing governmental funds in either national banks or state

9. 4 The Works of Alexander Hamilton 439 (Lodge ed.). Emphasis in original.
10. 3 Stat. 582 (1820).
11. 2 Haynes, The Senate of the United States, at 793; Leonard D. White, The Jacksonians 317–21 (1954).
12. Erik McKinley Eriksson, "The Federal Civil Service Under President Jackson," 13 Miss. Valley Hist. Rev. 517 (1927).

banks. The Senate responded to Jackson's action by passing a resolution of censure: "*Resolved,* That the President, in the late Executive proceedings in relation to the public revenue, has assumed upon himself authority and power not conferred by the Constitution and laws, but in derogation of both."

Jackson, outraged that the Senate should censure him on the basis of unspecified charges and without an opportunity to be heard, in circumvention of the formal constitutional procedure for impeachment, prepared a lengthy and impassioned protest. With great force he argued that the Constitution vested in the President the executive power, requiring him to take care that the laws be faithfully executed. That made him, he said, "responsible for the entire action of the executive department." Following this logic, the President had a right to employ agents of his own choice to aid him. When no longer willing to be responsible for their acts, he could remove them. Jackson regarded the Secretary of the Treasury as "wholly an executive officer."[13] Three years later the Senate ordered its resolution of censure expunged from the record.[14] Millard Fillmore, in his first annual message to Congress in 1850, suggested that in the case of "unfortunate" administrative appointments it would be proper for the President to exercise the power of removal.[15]

The removal power ripened into a poisonous dispute during the administration of Andrew Johnson. Even before he took office, Congress had begun to trench upon the President's removal power. Legislation in 1863 created a Comptroller of the Currency to hold office for a term of five years "unless sooner removed by the President, by and with the advice and consent of the Senate." Two years later Congress passed legislation to authorize military and naval officers, upon dismissal by the President, to apply for a trial.[16]

Congress continued this policy in 1867 by passing the Tenure of Office Act. Every person holding civil office with the advice and consent of the Senate became entitled to hold office until the President appointed a successor, with the advice and consent of the Senate. The bill further provided that the Secretaries of State, Treasury, War, Navy, and Interior; the Postmaster General; and the Attorney General should hold office during the term of the President who appointed them and for one month thereafter, "subject to removal by and with the advice and consent of the Senate." During Senate recesses the

13. 3 Richardson 1288–1312 (April 15, 1834). Jackson also rebuffed the Senate's effort to obtain "copies of the charges, if any," relating to the removal of a federal employee. He said that in cases of this nature, the President possessed the "exclusive power of removal from office." Id. at 1352.

14. Register of Debates, 24th Cong., 2d Sess. 379–418, 427–506 (1837); S. Journal, 24th Cong., 2d Sess. 123–24 (January 16, 1837).

15. 6 Richardson 2616 (December 2, 1850).

16. 12 Stat. 666, sec. 1 (1863); 13 Stat. 489, sec. 12 (1865).

President could suspend an official but would have to report to the Senate, upon its return, the evidence and reasons for the suspension. If the Senate concurred in his action the suspended officer would be removed. If the Senate refused to concur, the suspended officer would resume the functions of his office.[17]

Here was a frontal challenge to presidential control over his own officers. Johnson vetoed the bill, claiming that it violated the Constitution and the construction placed upon it by the debate of 1789. His message was well reasoned and fully documented, but Congress, caught up in the fierce politics of that time, was receptive to neither facts nor argument. Both houses promptly overrode his veto.[18]

Johnson had hoped that the disruptive voice in his Cabinet, Secretary of War Edwin M. Stanton, would resign. He did not. As the months rolled by and the political crisis deepened, Johnson decided to suspend Stanton. The Senate returned from its recess and refused to concur in the suspension. Johnson upped the ante by *removing* Stanton, with the expectation that the constitutionality of the Tenure of Office Act would be tested in the courts. Yet because of the actions of Ulysses S. Grant, installed by Johnson as War Secretary ad interim, and Lorenzo Thomas, Grant's successor, the tactic backfired. Stanton was able to regain his office. Johnson's strategy merely fanned the fire of impeachment that had been smoldering for a year, a movement that fell one vote short in the Senate.[19]

President Grant, in his first annual message in 1869, recommended that Congress repeal the Tenure of Office Act. To him the law was inconsistent with efficient administration: "What faith can an Executive put in officials forced upon him, and those, too, whom he has suspended for reason?" Congress revised the act that year, softening the suspension section but retaining the Senate's involvement in the removal process.[20]

Congress continued to expand the Senate's role. Legislation in 1872 required the Postmaster General and his three assistants to be appointed by the President, by and with the advice and consent of the Senate, and provided that they might be "removed in the same manner." In 1876 Congress required the Senate's advice and consent for the removal of all first-, second-, and third-class postmasters.[21]

17. 14 Stat. 430 (1867).
18. 8 Richardson 3690–94 (March 2, 1867); 14 Stat. 430 (1867).
19. Lately Thomas, The First President Johnson 484–618 (1968); Raoul Berger, Impeachment 252–96 (1973); Harold M. Hyman, "Johnson, Stanton, and Grant: A Reconsideration of the Army's Role in the Events Leading to Impeachment," 66 Am. Hist. Rev. 85 (1960).
20. 9 Richardson 3992 (December 6, 1869); 16 Stat. 6 (1869).
21. 17 Stat. 284, sec. 2; 19 Stat. 80, sec. 6.

A new confrontation over the removal power occurred from 1885 to 1886, after Grover Cleveland suspended several hundred officials and refused to deliver certain papers and documents to the Senate. Cleveland declared that the power to remove or suspend executive officials was vested solely in the President by the Constitution, particularly by the "Executive Power" and "Take Care" Clauses. He also noted that the law governing suspensions, as amended in 1869, did not justify the Senate's request for documents. Because of this dispute, Congress repealed the Tenure of Office Act in 1887.[22]

Court Interpretations: 1789 to 1926

Myers v. United States (1926) represents the first full-scale judicial decision on the removal power, but the issue had been explored by courts throughout the nineteenth century. In *Marbury v. Madison,* Chief Justice Marshall noted that the President had discretion over an office until an appointment was made. Thereafter, "his power over the office is terminated in all cases, where by law the officer is not removable by him. The right to the office is *then* in the person appointed, and he has the absolute, unconditional power of accepting or rejecting it."[23] Marshall reasoned that since Congress had given Marbury's office a tenure of five years, he had a right to serve for that duration. Of course, Marshall's decision did nothing to secure the job for Marbury, but it suggested that Congress could circumscribe the President's removal power by statute.

In 1839 the Supreme Court gave its first full attention to the nature of the removal power. *Ex parte Hennen* concerned the removal of a clerk by a new federal judge. A unanimous Court said that the power to appoint a clerk had been vested exclusively in the lower court. The Court had no control over the appointment or removal, nor could it entertain any inquiry into the grounds for removal. If the judge had abused his power, the plaintiff was advised to seek relief elsewhere—just how or where, the Court did not say.[24]

In 1854 the Court ruled on President Pierce's authority to remove Aaron Goodrich as Chief Justice of the Supreme Court for the territory of Minnesota. The Attorney General had advised the President that he possessed the power

22. 10 Richardson 4960–68 (March 1, 1886); 16 Stat. 7, sec. 2 (1869); 24 Stat. 500 (1887). This incident is described in detail in Grover Cleveland, The Independence of the Executive 25–82 (1913), and Louis Fisher, "Grover Cleveland Against the Senate," 7 Cong. Studies 11 (1979).

23. Marbury v. Madison, 5 U.S. (1 Cr.) 137, 162 (1803). Emphasis in original. In Myers v. United States, 272 U.S. 52, 139–42 (1926), Chief Justice Taft stated that the President's removal power had not been before the Court in *Marbury.* Justice McReynolds, dissenting in the *Myers* case, argued (at 201–2) that *Marbury* had expressly repudiated the claim that the President could remove officials contrary to congressional directives.

24. Ex parte Hennen, 13 Pet. 230 (1839).

to remove territorial judges "for any cause that may, in your judgment, require it."[25] This was a novel and sensitive issue: the President's removal power directed against a sitting judge (not a potential member of the judiciary, as in *Marbury*). Still, it did not create a direct clash between the President and the judiciary. Territorial judges were not judges within Article III of the Constitution and therefore were not entitled to hold their offices "during good Behaviour." Goodrich served as judge of a "legislative court," established to carry out Article I duties, not a constitutional court.

Justice Daniel, delivering the opinion of the Court, said that the true question related neither to the tenure of the judicial office nor to the powers and functions of the President. Instead, the question was whether a court could command the withdrawal of money from the Treasury to settle Goodrich's claim. The particular facts of the case convinced the Court that the President's action was executive in nature, requiring judgment and discretion, and could not be reviewed and countermanded by the courts.[26]

Justice McLean dissented. He agreed that the removal power, as applied to executive officers, "has been, perhaps, too long established and exercised to be now questioned." But extending it to judicial officers was another matter. The presidential duty to see that the laws were faithfully executed and the President's responsibility over administrators related to political, not judicial, officers of the government. Justice McLean warned that whenever "any portion of the judicial power shall become subject to the executive, there will be an end to its independence and purity."[27] He regarded the payment of money to Goodrich as a ministerial act and therefore subject to mandamus proceedings.

A removal case in 1886 involved the discharge of a naval cadet who sued for his pay. The Court of Claims upheld his position without passing judgment on the President's removal power (the cadet had been removed by the Secretary of the Navy). The court stated that when Congress, by law, vests the appointment of officers in the heads of departments, "it may limit and restrict the power of removal as it deems best for the public interest." Since the naval officer had not been found deficient at any examination, had not been dismissed for misconduct under the provisions of law, and had not been sentenced by court-martial (also pursuant to law), he was still in office and entitled to the pay attached to it. The Supreme Court unanimously affirmed the judgment of the Court of Claims.[28]

25. 5 Op. Att'y Gen. 288, 291 (1851).

26. United States v. Guthrie, 58 U.S. (17 How.) 284, 305 (1854).

27. Id. at 310. For a later decision upholding the right of the President to suspend a territorial judge and replace him with someone else before the completion of his term of office, see McAllister v. United States, 141 U.S. 175 (1891).

28. United States v. Perkins, 116 U.S. 483, 485 (1886).

In 1897 the Court reviewed President Cleveland's removal of a U.S. attorney who argued that his commission for a four-year term had been illegally abridged. After reviewing many precedents, including repeal of the Tenure of Office Act, the Court unanimously concluded that the President may remove an officer "when in his discretion he regards it for the public good, although the term of office may have been limited by the words of the statute creating the office."[29]

A decision in 1903, also unanimous, dealt with the important issue of the degree to which Congress can specify the cause for removal. Congress had specified "inefficiency, neglect of duty, or malfeasance in office" as the statutory grounds for removing a customs official. President McKinley removed a customs official without relying on any of those causes. The Court acknowledged that Congress can restrict the President to specified causes, but only if the statute used "plain language" to limit the President's general power of removal.[30]

A 1922 case focused on President Wilson's dismissal of an officer from the Quartermaster Corps. Chief Justice Taft, writing for a unanimous Court, concluded that the legislative restrictions imposed on the President's power to remove an Army officer did not apply, since the President had submitted the name of another officer to take the place of the one dismissed and the Senate had given its consent. Taft presumed that the Senate knew that its confirmation would fill the legal complement of such officers and lend support to the President's removal.[31]

The Myers Case and Its Progeny

Up to this point, the Supreme Court's record on the removal power, marked largely by unanimous holdings, had avoided many of the central questions. Fundamental issues were finally addressed in the celebrated case of *Myers v. United States* (1926). Since the litigation resulted from Woodrow Wilson's action, his earlier pronouncements on the removal power need to be reviewed.

In 1920 Wilson opposed a section of the budget and accounting bill that reserved to Congress a role in the removal of the Comptroller General and the

---

29. Parsons v. United States, 167 U.S. 324, 343 (1897). For an earlier opinion by Attorney General Roger B. Taney supporting the President's power to remove a district attorney, see 2 Op. Att'y Gen. 482, 489 (1831).

30. Shurtleff v. United States, 189 U.S. 311, 316 (1903). Also regarding the right of Congress to limit presidential removals to causes prescribed by law, see Reagan v. United States, 182 U.S. 419 (1901). For other statutory restrictions on removals, see Blake v. United States, 103 U.S. (13 Otto.) 227 (1881), and Burnap v. United States, 252 U.S. 512 (1920).

31. Wallace v. United States, 257 U.S. 541, 545–46 (1922).

Assistant Comptroller General. They could be taken from office by impeachment, concurrent resolution, "and in no other manner." A concurrent resolution, which requires the consent of the House and Senate, is not sent to the President for his signature. Wilson vetoed the bill, expressing his conviction that Congress lacked constitutional power to "limit the appointing power and its incident, the power of removal derived from the Constitution."[32] Congress revised the bill to require a joint resolution (which would go to the President), and President Harding signed the bill into law. But even as modified, the bill allowed Congress to *initiate* a removal.[33]

The case that reached the Supreme Court resulted from the appointment of Frank S. Myers, postmaster at Portland, Oregon, to a four-year term in 1917. Prior to the expiration of his term, the Postmaster General removed him, an action concurred in by President Wilson. The removal violated legislation that required the Senate's advice and consent for the removal of all first-, second-, and third-class postmasters. Myers sued to recover his salary. Attorneys for Myers argued that the appointment of postmasters derived from a statute passed pursuant to a power specifically granted to Congress by the Constitution ("to establish post offices and post roads"). Congress could therefore attach to that office any conditions it desired. Solicitor General Beck, arguing for the administration, maintained that the legislative condition requiring the Senate's advice and consent for removals could be held unconstitutional "without assuming the absolute power of the President to remove any executive officer."[34]

Chief Justice Taft, writing for a 6-to-3 majority, opted for a broader interpretation of presidential power—too broad, in fact, to withstand scholarly analysis and subsequent Court holdings. Taft even parted company from his own reasonable position in *Wallace* (1922), where he had held that "*at least in absence of restrictive legislation,* the President, though he could not appoint without the consent of the Senate, could remove without such consent in the case of any officer whose tenure was not fixed by the Constitution."[35] In *Myers,* Taft claimed an unrestricted power of removal for the President, even in the presence of statutory limitations. From the congressional debates of 1789 he decided that there was not the "slightest doubt" that the power to remove officers appointed by the President and the Senate is "vested in the President alone."[36] However, the record in 1789 reveals deep divisions among members of the House and extremely close votes on the Senate side. Moreover, many of

32. H. Doc. No. 805, 66th Cong., 2d Sess. (1920).
33. 42 Stat. 24, sec. 303 (1921).
34. Myers v. United States, 272 U.S. 52, 61, 98 (1926).
35. Wallace v. United States, 257 U.S. 541, 544 (1922). Emphasis added.
36. Myers v. United States, 272 U.S. at 114.

the legislators supported presidential power because the office in question was Secretary of Foreign Affairs, an agent of the President and executive in nature. There was no reason why that principle had to be extended to postmasters.

Taft recognized that the Court had agreed in *Shurtleff* that Congress might restrict the President's power by specifying causes for removal. He realized also that Congress, in establishing regulatory agencies (beginning with the Interstate Commerce Commission in 1887), had specified causes for removal: inefficiency, neglect of duty, or malfeasance in office. Still, he held that the postmaster law requiring the Senate's advice and consent for removals was "in violation of the Constitution, and invalid."[37] In a significant passage, Taft acknowledged that "there may be duties so peculiarly and specifically committed to the discretion of a particular officer as to raise a question whether the President may overrule or revise the officer's interpretation of his statutory duty in a particular instance."[38] Taft must have been referring to executive, not adjudicatory, duties, because in the very next sentence he writes: "Then there may be duties of a quasi-judicial character imposed on executive officers and members of executive tribunals whose decisions after hearing affect interests of individuals, the discharge of which the President can not in a particular case properly influence or control."[39]

In the first of three dissents, Justice Holmes called the Chief Justice's arguments "spider's webs inadequate to control the dominant facts." Justice McReynolds's dissent identified many of the statutes that prescribed restrictions on removals. Protected by those restrictions were members of the Interstate Commerce Commission, the Board of General Appraisers, the Federal Reserve Board, the Federal Trade Commission, the Tariff Commission, and the Shipping Board, among others.[40]

The third dissenter, Justice Brandeis, conceded that the power to remove (or suspend) a high political officer "might conceivably be deemed indispensable to democratic government and, hence, inherent in the President." But he flatly denied that the President's ability to remove an inferior administrative officer, such as a postmaster, was essential to the workings of government.[41]

Taft's decision provoked immediate criticism from the academic community. The most devastating rebuke came from Edward S. Corwin, whose monograph *The President's Removal Power Under the Constitution* appeared in 1927. Corwin did not object too strongly to the proposition that when an executive officer is appointed by the President, with the advice and consent of

37. Id. at 171, 176.
38. Id. at 135.
39. Id.
40. Id. at 177, 181.
41. Id. at 241, 247.

the Senate, the removal power belongs to the President alone. Such a conclusion, although "decidedly vulnerable on both historical and logical grounds, is not improbably supported by practical considerations."[42]

What Corwin found intolerable was the more sweeping proposition that *any* executive officer could be removed by the President. Such a notion denied Congress the right to determine the tenure of an officer. A balance had to be reached, said Corwin, between the President's removal power and the power of Congress to create an office under the "Necessary and Proper" Clause. To Corwin, this balance depended on the nature of the office involved. For example, he believed that a member of the Interstate Commerce Commission did not exercise power that resulted from presidential authority, either constitutional or statutory. The commissioner's powers derived from a delegation by Congress of its own express power under the Constitution.[43] But this distinction does not resolve the issue; officers in the executive departments also derive their powers and duties from Congress.

Corwin said that Presidents had been able to live with a number of statutory restrictions on their removal power. Procedural safeguards existed for personnel in the classified civil service. They could not be removed "except for such cause as will promote the efficiency of said service and for reasons given in writing, and the person whose removal is sought shall have notice of the same and of any charges preferred against him." Federal employees had the right to join unions; no postal employee could be reduced in rank or dismissed for joining such an organization. Civil service employees had the right to petition Congress without fear of removal. Congress had passed many other statutes to specify the causes for removal from regulatory commissions. Corwin's reading of the debates of 1789 led him to reject Taft's conclusion that a vast majority of the members of the House believed that removal was an incident of the executive power. Instead, Corwin said, Congress found that those who held to that theory "were a fraction of a fraction, a minority of a minority."[44] Somewhere between Corwin's and Taft's views on the debates of 1789 lies the truth.

Corwin could not delineate with any precision the boundaries between executive-legislative prerogatives over the removal power. He asserted that the power of Congress was not absolute, any more than the President's was; it was "conditioned in each case by the nature of the office being dealt with as shown particularly by the source and nature of its powers."[45] But who decides "nature," and with what criteria?

42. Edward S. Corwin, The President's Removal Power Under the Constitution vi (1927).
43. Id. at v–viii; reproduced with little change as "Tenure of Office and the Removal Power Under the Constitution," 27 Colum. L. Rev. 353 (1927).
44. Corwin, The President's Removal Power Under the Constitution, at 4, 22–23.
45. Id. at 66.

Independent Commissions

That issue reached the Supreme Court in 1935 in *Humphrey's Executor v. United States*. William E. Humphrey, nominated by President Hoover for the Federal Trade Commission (FTC) in 1931, had been confirmed by the Senate. The FTC Act allowed the President to remove a commissioner for "inefficiency, neglect of duty, or malfeasance in office." On July 25, 1933, President Roosevelt asked Humphrey to resign, explaining that the "aims and purposes of the Administration with respect to the work of the Commission can be carried out most effectively with personnel of my own selection." The following month he wrote to Humphrey: "I do not feel that your mind and my mind go along together on either the policies or the administering of the Federal Trade Commission." The bitterness of the conflict was foreshadowed by Humphrey's letter to Roosevelt, in which he described unnamed enemies who came with "slanderous and polluted lips and spew their putrid filth upon you under the pledge of secrecy." Humphrey railed against "mental perverts who glorify treachery and intellectual dishonesty."[46] When Humphrey refused to resign, Roosevelt removed him for policy reasons rather than those specified in the FTC Act.[47]

Justice Sutherland, delivering a unanimous opinion, described the FTC as charged with the enforcement of "no policy except the policy of the law. Its duties are neither political nor executive, but predominantly quasi-judicial and quasi-legislative." "Quasi," of course, is no more precise a term than Corwin's "nature," but Sutherland felt confident that a distinction could be drawn between the executive duties of a postmaster (the *Myers* case) and the duties of an FTC commissioner. The FTC "cannot in any proper sense be characterized as an arm or an eye of the executive."[48] Of course, it is a stretch to call a postmaster an arm or eye of the President.

Corwin applauded the narrowing of Taft's holding but did not like Sutherland's classification of the FTC. If an FTC commissioner was not in the executive department, Corwin asked, "where is he? In the legislative department; or is he, forsooth, in the uncomfortable halfway situation of Mahomet's coffin, suspended 'twixt Heaven and Earth?" Instead of conjuring up a fourth branch, floating independently, Corwin wanted to preserve the existing three branches of government. He regarded all nonjudicial agencies established to

---

46. William E. Leuchtenburg, "The Case of the Contentious Commissioner: Humphrey's Executor v. U.S.," in Harold M. Hyman and Leonard W. Levy, eds., Freedom and Reform: Essays in Honor of Henry Steele Commager 289 (1967).

47. Humphrey's Executor v. United States, 295 U.S. 602, 618–19 (1935).

48. Id. at 624, 627–28.

carry out the law as being "executive" in the sense of the Constitution.[49] Justice Jackson, in a later case, also voiced exasperation with the location of regulatory agencies in our tripartite system: "The mere retreat to the qualifying 'quasi' is implicit with confession that all recognized classifications have broken down, and 'quasi' is a smooth cover which we draw over our confusion as we might use a counterpane to conceal a disordered bed."[50]

In his closing paragraph, Sutherland admitted that there existed a "field of doubt" between *Myers* and *Humphrey's*: "We leave such cases as may fall within it for future consideration and determination as they may arise."[51] The "field of doubt" was soon in the courts because of a bitter, long-festering, and frustrating disagreement that threatened to paralyze the Tennessee Valley Authority (TVA). Arthur E. Morgan, chairman of the Board of Directors, was locked in a nasty feud with his fellow directors. He resisted President Roosevelt's effort to negotiate a settlement, claiming that Congress alone was the proper party to investigate the dispute. The President, after weeks of discussion, told Morgan either to withdraw publicly the charges he had made against his colleagues or to resign. When Morgan chose to do neither, Roosevelt removed him.[52]

The TVA Act required that appointments and promotions be made on the basis of "merit and efficiency." Any member of the Board of Directors found by the President "to be guilty of a violation of this section shall be removed from office by the President." The act also made board members subject to removal at any time by concurrent resolution. (Woodrow Wilson vetoed the budget and accounting bill because it permitted removal by that very instrument.)

Morgan's complaint was dismissed by a district court. Although admitting that FDR's action was not specifically based on statutory considerations, the court did not find in the TVA Act a clear enough intent by Congress to limit the executive power over removals. Echoing the holding in *Shurtleff*, it stated that there had to be "plain language" in a statute to take away that power.[53] The district court's opinion was upheld by the Sixth Circuit. While the case was pending in the district court, the Senate confirmed the appointment of James P. Pope to succeed Morgan, implying that at least one house of

---

49. Corwin, The President, at 93, 378–79.

50. FTC v. Ruberoid Co., 343 U.S. 470, 487–88 (1952).

51. Humphrey's Executor v. United States, 295 U.S. at 632.

52. For background on Morgan's removal, see C. Herman Pritchett, The Tennessee Valley Authority 203–15 (1943). A transcript of White House hearings, conducted by President Roosevelt in the presence of Chairman Morgan and the other two directors of the TVA, is reprinted in S. Doc. No. 155, 75th Cong., 3d Sess. (1938). Acting Attorney General Robert H. Jackson had advised FDR that the TVA was an executive agency and its members could be removed by the President; 39 Op. Att'y Gen. 145 (1938).

53. Morgan v. TVA, 28 F.Supp. 732 (E.D. Tenn. 1939).

Congress did not oppose Morgan's removal. The appellate court also regarded the TVA as predominantly an administrative arm of the executive branch and therefore distinguishable from the regulatory commission involved in *Humphrey's*.[54]

More akin to *Humphrey's* was President Eisenhower's removal of a member of the War Claims Commission. The enabling statute, anticipating a short-lived agency, made no provision for removal. Eisenhower removed an official on the ground that the act should be administered "with personnel of my own selection." The Court of Claims dismissed the plaintiff's suit, but a unanimous Supreme Court held that the President had no power under the Constitution or statute to remove a member from the commission. The agency's task, said the Court, had an "intrinsic judicial character." Congress had explicitly rejected a legislative option that would have placed responsibility with the administration. Therefore, Congress could not have wanted to hang "the Damocles' sword of removal" over the head of the commission for no other reason than that the President wanted his own man.[55]

Disloyalty Dismissals and Procedural Safeguards

As a result of congressional action and various executive orders, federal employees have been removed from office on the charge that they represented a security risk. One of the more flagrant legislative efforts came in 1943 when the chairman of the House Un-American Activities Committee (HUAC) announced that 39 federal employees were "irresponsible, unrepresentative, crackpot radical bureaucrats" and affiliates of "Communist-front organizations." A special subcommittee, created to examine his allegations, subsequently accused three of the employees of engaging in "subversive activity." By attaching an amendment to an appropriations bill, Congress prohibited the use of public funds to pay the salaries of the three individuals. Counsel for Congress contended that congressional power over appropriations was plenary and not subject to judicial review.[56] In 1946, however, in *United States v. Lovett,* the Supreme Court struck down the legislative language because it inflicted punishment without a judicial trial and therefore violated the Constitution's prohibition against bills of attainder.[57]

---

54. Morgan v. TVA, 115 F.2d 990 (6th Cir. 1940), cert. denied, 312 U.S. 701 (1941); Arthur Larson, "Has the President an Inherent Power of Removal of His Non-Executive Appointees?" 16 Tenn. L. Rev. 259 (1940).

55. Wiener v. United States, 357 U.S. 349 (1958).

56. 89 Cong. Rec. 4583 (1943); United States v. Lovett, 328 U.S. 303, 306–7 (1946).

57. United States v. Lovett, 328 U.S. 303 (1946).

Congressional use of purse strings to remove "disloyal" workers from federal employment was rebuffed again in 1982. Language in an appropriations bill stated that "none of the funds appropriated or otherwise made available by the Act may be used, pursuant to the Comprehensive Employment Training Act (CETA), for the participation of individuals who publicly advocate the violent overthrow of the Federal Government, or who have within the past five years, publicly advocated the violent overthrow of the Federal Government." This language, as amplified by the legislative history, was meant to exclude from the CETA program Dorothy Blitz, a member of the Communist Workers Party. She challenged the language as a violation of her right of free speech under the First Amendment and a violation of the Bill of Attainder Clause. A federal court in 1982 agreed that the "Blitz Amendment" failed to draw a line between mere advocacy (protected by the Constitution) and advocacy that incites and is likely to produce violent action. Finding the statutory language contrary to the First Amendment, the court did not address the bill of attainder question.[58]

Congress has adopted more general standards to regulate federal workers suspected of disloyalty. In 1950 it passed legislation to permit certain agencies to suspend civilian employees whenever "necessary in the interest of national security."[59] As later rewritten, the authority was extended to the Departments of State, Commerce, Justice, and Defense; the military departments; the Coast Guard; the Atomic Energy Commission (whose duties were later assigned to the Energy Department and to the Nuclear Regulatory Commission); the National Aeronautics and Space Administration; and any "such other agency of the Government of the United States as the President designates in the best interests of national security." If the agency head determines that the "interests of national security permit," he or she may notify the employee of the reasons for the suspension.[60]

Once suspended, an employee has access to procedural safeguards before being removed. An employee with a permanent or indefinite appointment, who has completed a probationary or trial period and who is a citizen of the United States, is entitled to the following protections before removal: (1) a written statement of the charges within 30 days after suspension, stated as specifically as security considerations permit; (2) an opportunity to answer the charges and submit affidavits; (3) a hearing (at the employee's request) by an agency authority constituted for that purpose; (4) a review of the case by

58. Blitz v. Donovan, 538 F.Supp. 1119 (D.D.C. 1982).
59. 64 Stat. 476 (1950).
60. 64 Stat. 476 (1950), modified by 80 Stat. 529 (1966) and codified at 5 U.S.C. 7531–32 (2000).

the agency head or designee before a decision adverse to the employee is made final; and (5) a written statement of the decision.

Administrative actions can be challenged in the courts. An appellate court decision in 1950 concerned the removal of Dorothy Bailey from her federal job on the ground of disloyalty. Although she was given notice, an opportunity for a hearing, and access to an appeal, the agency did not permit her to confront and cross-examine her secret accusers. The court rejected her plea for trial-type procedures, concluding that compliance with the Sixth Amendment was not a prerequisite for dismissing civil service employees. "Even in normal times," observed the court, "and as a matter of ordinary internal operation, the ability, integrity and loyalty of purely executive employees is exclusively for the executive branch of Government to determine, except in so far as the Congress has a constitutional voice in the matter." The court also noted that disloyalty in the government service "under present circumstances" (the Cold War) was a matter of great public concern.[61]

Judge Edgerton, dissenting, demonstrated an appreciation for individual rights and procedural due process that would later find expression in Supreme Court rulings. He noted that Bailey occupied a "wholly nonsensitive position," that the informants had not been identified to her or even to the Regional Loyalty Board responsible for investigating her case, and that the informants did not make their statements under oath. In contrast, Bailey had denied under oath any membership in or relationship or sympathy with the Communist Party, any activities connected with it or with communism, and any affiliation with any organization that advocated the overthrow of the United States government.

Edgerton believed that the executive order providing standards for Bailey's dismissal required that employees have an opportunity to cross-examine opposing witnesses. If secret accusers wanted to preserve their anonymity, the accused should be cleared or the proceedings dropped. Although Edgerton agreed that most dismissals from government employment were not punitive, did not require a judicial trial, and were within the authority of the executive, Dorothy Bailey's dismissal constituted punishment—not for wrong conduct but for "wrong views." Dismissal for disloyalty was punitive in nature, as in the *Lovett* case, and the right of confrontation and cross-examination was essential for nonsensitive positions. The government had not demonstrated that the suspicion of disloyalty indicated a security risk: "*Appellant's dismissal for wrong thoughts has nothing to do with protecting the security of the United States.*"[62]

61. Bailey v. Richardson, 182 F.2d 46, 51, 64 (D.C. Cir. 1950), aff'd per curiam by an equally divided Supreme Court, 341 U.S. 918 (1951).
62. Bailey v. Richardson, 182 F.2d at 70. Emphasis in original.

Corwin did not believe that federal employees dismissed for loyalty reasons were entitled to procedural safeguards. Even in cases of disloyalty, it was "plausible doctrine that the President enjoys an overriding power of removal."[63] What did Corwin cite to support his position? None other than the majority opinion in *Myers!* The particular page of the decision cited by Corwin contains this statement by Chief Justice Taft: "The power to remove inferior executive officers, like that to remove superior executive officers, is an incident of the power to appoint them, and is in its nature an executive power." Corwin had excoriated that opinion when it first appeared. Why did he invoke it three decades later to support his argument? In his own value system the stigma of disloyalty did not have constitutional significance for the removal issue. To him it was a "unique proposition" that a court should stand in judgment against the determination of an executive official that someone is disloyal.[64] But why was it "unique" for a court to insist on procedural standards and constitutional rights for those accused of betraying their country? Why take the word of anonymous accusers?

Within a few years the Supreme Court began to place restrictions on administrative removals of so-called security risks. A leading case involved Kendrick Cole, removed from his position with the Department of Health, Education, and Welfare (HEW) after an administrative investigation disclosed that he had associated with groups on the Attorney General's "subversive list." The Court decided that the term "national security," as used in the statute supporting the removal, related only to activities directly concerned with the nation's safety. Whereas the federal government could summarily suspend employees who occupied "sensitive" positions, this power did not extend to other positions. In view of the "stigma attached to persons dismissed on loyalty grounds," the need for procedural safeguards seemed even greater than in other cases.[65]

Members of Congress tried to override the decision by specifically extending summary suspension powers to nonsensitive federal jobs, but the effort failed. In other cases the Supreme Court insisted that individuals whose employment status had been jeopardized and injured by the federal government were entitled to confront and cross-examine their "faceless informers." When administrators were legally unable to remove employees for loyalty reasons, they switched to grounds of "suitability" as established by civil service regulations.[66]

63. Corwin, The President, at 104, footnote omitted. Footnote 109, on p. 385 of Corwin's work, refers to *Myers,* at 161.
64. Id. at 108, 110.
65. Cole v. Young, 351 U.S. 536, 546 (1956).
66. For congressional override efforts, see Walter F. Murphy, Congress and the Court 174–75, 218–19, 236 (1962). For other cases on employment rights, see Service v. Dulles, 354

Through a series of holdings from the late 1960s to the early 1970s, the Supreme Court insisted that individuals could not be deprived of "property" or "liberty" without the protection of fundamental procedural safeguards, including notice and a hearing. That pattern was interrupted in 1974 when a sharply divided (5 to 4) Court decided that a nonprobationary employee in the competitive civil service had been adequately protected by hearing procedures made available *after* his dismissal.[67]

The employee claimed that the standards and procedures established by the Lloyd-LaFollette Act interfered with his freedom of expression and denied him procedural due process of law. Lloyd-LaFollette permitted the removal or suspension of employees in the competitive service "for such cause as will promote the efficiency of the service." An employee was entitled to reasons given in writing; notice of the action and of any charges preferred against her or him; a copy of the charges and reasonable time to file an oral or written answer to them, with affidavits; representation by an attorney; and a written decision at the earliest practicable date.[68]

A concurring opinion by Justice Powell, joined by Justice Blackmun, formed the 5-to-4 majority. Justice Powell balanced the government's interest against that of the employee, giving particular weight to the government's interest in removing employees whose conduct "hinders efficient operation and to do so with dispatch." Requirement of a prior evidentiary hearing, Powell said, "would impose additional administrative costs, create delay, and defer warranted discharges."[69]

The goal of governmental efficiency, used in this case to *remove* an employee, was later invoked by the Court to *protect* officeholders. Through a series of rulings, the Court has attempted to limit the use of patronage dismissals at the local level. The general pattern of those decisions is to protect public

U.S. 363 (1957); Vitarelli v. Seaton, 359 U.S. 535 (1959); Greene v. McElroy, 360 U.S. 474 (1959); and Cafeteria Workers v. McElroy, 367 U.S. 886 (1961). In Peters v. Hobby, 349 U.S. 331 (1955), the Court held that the Loyalty Review Board exceeded its delegated jurisdiction. For further discussion, see C. Herman Pritchett, Congress Versus the Supreme Court 96–106 (1961). For "suitability" grounds, see H. Rept. No. 1637, 92d Cong., 2d Sess. 61 (1973).

67. Arnett v. Kennedy, 416 U.S. 134 (1974). For "property" and "liberty" issues, see Sniadach v. Family Finance Corp., 395 U.S. 337 (1969); Goldberg v. Kelly, 397 U.S. 254 (1970); Bell v. Burson, 402 U.S. 535 (1971); Lynch v. Household Finance Corp., 405 U.S. 538 (1972); and Perry v. Sindermann, 408 U.S. 593 (1972).

68. 37 Stat. 555, sec. 6 (1912), as amended by 62 Stat. 354 (1948), and codified at 5 U.S.C. 7501 (1994). Rewritten by the Civil Service Reform Act of 1978 and codified at 5 U.S.C. 7501–14 (1994).

69. Arnett v. Kennedy, 416 U.S. at 168. See also Bishop v. Wood, 426 U.S. 341 (1976), for lack of a pretermination hearing. In 1985 the Court held that a public employee was entitled to a hearing *before* termination; Cleveland Board of Education v. Loudermill, 470 U.S. 532 (1985).

employees in nonpolicymaking, nonconfidential positions so that they cannot be fired solely on the ground of political belief or affiliation.[70] These cases apply primarily to state and local governments, not to the federal government.

Public employees have a constitutional right under the First Amendment to comment on matters "of public concern."[71] However, in 1983 the Court upheld the removal of public employees who object to internal office conditions and attempt to organize opposition to superiors, even when the reasons for dismissal are alleged to be mistaken or unreasonable.[72] In 1987 a 5-to-4 decision by the Court overturned the removal of a public employee who had remarked to a coworker after learning of the assassination attempt on President Reagan, "If they go for him again, I hope they get him." Justice Powell explained that the offhand remark by a clerical employee was insufficiently disruptive of the office to justify dismissal.[73] When federal employees are removed for "national security" concerns, the Court is still prone to defer to executive branch decisions to protect classified and sensitive information.[74]

Removal Actions from Nixon to Bush I

Although a large number of federal employees are formally protected from summary removal procedures, informal political pressures are sometimes used to force civil servants from office or place them in undesirable assignments. Punishment is often applied to employees who draw attention to deficiencies within the executive agencies (whistleblowers). John M. McGee offended his superiors in the Navy Department during the late 1960s by talking about lax inspection procedures that permitted the theft of millions of gallons of fuel in Thailand. For his outspokenness the Navy reprimanded him and denied him an in-grade salary increase.[75]

The Air Force meted out stiffer punishment to Ernest Fitzgerald, a procurement specialist. In response to Senator William Proxmire's question in 1968 about whether the C-5A cargo aircraft was running $2 billion above initial cost estimates, Fitzgerald called the figure "approximately right." The Pentagon, which had yet to acknowledge the cost overrun, took away Fitzgerald's

70. Rutan v. Republican Party of Illinois, 497 U.S. 62 (1990); Branti v. Finkel, 445 U.S. 507 (1980); Elrod v. Burns, 427 U.S. 347 (1976).
71. Pickering v. Board of Education, 391 U.S. 563 (1968).
72. Connick v. Myers, 461 U.S. 138 (1983).
73. Rankin v. McPherson, 483 U.S. 378 (1987).
74. Department of Navy v. Egan, 484 U.S. 518 (1988).
75. 115 Cong. Rec. 11045–48 (1969). See General Accounting Office, "Investigation in Thailand of the Systems for Distributing Petroleum, Oil, and Lubricants and for Processing Related Documentation," Report No. B-163928 (January 9, 1969).

civil service protection, assigned him menial tasks, searched into his private life for incriminating evidence, and eventually fired him.[76] After more than a decade of arduous litigation, Fitzgerald won back his old job and, in 1982, was awarded legal fees and even gained a promotion. Former President Nixon, who, in a taped White House conversation, said of Fitzgerald, "Get rid of that son of a bitch," agreed in 1981 to pay Fitzgerald $142,000 to avoid a public trial.[77]

Fitzgerald's case has certain parallels with that of Gordon Rule, a naval procurement official who antagonized his superiors. In testimony before the Joint Economic Committee in 1972, he delivered his views with customary bluntness and spent the next day in bed recovering from laryngitis. There he received a visit from an admiral who asked him to sign a request for retirement. Rule, recipient of the Navy's highest civilian award the previous year, refused. His superiors tried to detail him to a training school to update its curriculum and had other pedestrian tasks lined up for him after that, but Rule fought successfully to retain his procurement responsibilities.[78]

The "Saturday Night Massacre" of 1973 catapulted the removal issue back into the courts. Archibald Cox, after pursuing presidential documents too assiduously for President Nixon's safety, was dismissed as Watergate special prosecutor. As an official in the executive branch, he normally would have been subject to presidential removal, but Nixon had relinquished that authority when the Justice Department released an order conferring an unusual degree of autonomy on the special prosecutor. The order gave Cox the "greatest degree of independence that is consistent with the Attorney General's statutory accountability. . . . The Attorney General will not countermand or interfere with the Special Prosecutor's decisions or actions." According to the order from the Justice Department, the special prosecutor would not be removed "except for extraordinary improprieties on his part." Otherwise, he was to carry out his responsibilities "until such time as, in his judgment, he has completed them or until a date mutually agreed upon between the Attorney General and himself."[79]

76. For more on the McGee and Fitzgerald incidents, see Senator William Proxmire, Report from Wasteland 25–47 (1970); "The Dismissal of A. Ernest Fitzgerald by the Department of Defense," hearings before the Joint Economic Committee, 91st Cong., 1st Sess. (1969).

77. Washington Post, August 14, 1981, at A1, A11, and June 16, 1982, at A3; 128 Cong. Rec. 27150 (1982). In 1982 the Supreme Court held that Nixon, as a former President, was entitled to absolute immunity from damages related to the firing of Fitzgerald; Nixon v. Fitzgerald, 457 U.S. 731 (1982). For the extension of a qualified immunity to presidential aides involved in the Fitzgerald dismissal, see Harlow v. Fitzgerald, 457 U.S. 800 (1982).

78. "The Acquisition of Weapons Systems" (part 6), hearings before the Joint Economic Committee, 92d Cong., 2d Sess. 1821–1924, 2205–44 (1973).

79. 38 Fed. Reg. 14688 (1973).

Ralph Nader and several members of Congress brought suit against Robert Bork, Acting Attorney General, for discharging Cox. The administration made no claim that Cox had been removed for "extraordinary improprieties." A district court did not agree with Bork that the congressional plaintiffs lacked standing. Nor was the controversy moot because Cox had returned to Harvard University and a new special prosecutor had been sworn in. The issue was still alive. Legislation had been introduced relating to Watergate, and the new special prosecutor might be dismissed, as the court noted, "if he presses too hard." The court held that Cox had been illegally discharged from office.[80]

The Carter administration offered several proposals designed to insulate the Justice Department from political pressures. One idea was to prevent the removal of the Attorney General except on a stated, rational basis. Carter's Attorney General, Griffin Bell, explained in an interview, "We would like to put a system in place where anybody that is Attorney General would have a feeling of independence, even though he might not be completely independent under the Constitution."[81] The Ethics Act of 1978 prohibited the removal of a special prosecutor except for extraordinary impropriety, physical disability, mental incapacity, or "any other condition that substantially impairs the performance of such special prosecutor's duties."[82]

When Congress rewrote the Ethics Act, it changed the name of the special prosecutor to independent counsel and used "good cause" as a reason for removal rather than "extraordinary impropriety." The statute was challenged as unconstitutional in part on the ground that the good-cause provision interfered with the President's ability to control the independent counsel. Although in 1986 the Court had denied that Congress could vest executive functions in an officer removable by Congress (the Comptroller General),[83] in 1988 the Court pointed out that Congress had no role in the removal of the independent counsel. In that sense, the removal provisions of the Ethics Act were similar to those of *Humphrey's Executor v. United States* (1935) and *Wiener v. United States* (1958).[84] The Court conceded that the latter two cases involved officials with "quasi-legislative" and "quasi-judicial" duties, whereas the independent counsel carried out executive, law enforcement functions. But it concluded: "We simply do not see how the President's need to control the exercise of that discretion is so central to the functioning of the Executive Branch as to require as a matter of constitutional law that the counsel be terminable at will by the President."[85]

80. Nader v. Bork, 366 F.Supp. 104 (D.D.C. 1973).
81. Washington Post, November 9, 1977, at A2:2.
82. 92 Stat. 1869, sec. 596 (1978).
83. Bowsher v. Synar, 478 U.S. 714 (1986).
84. Morrison v. Olson, 487 U.S. 654, 686 (1988).
85. Id. at 691–92.

The independent counsel statute was scheduled for reauthorization in 1992, but the Republicans blocked action partly because of their anger with the investigation of independent counsel Lawrence E. Walsh into the Iran-Contra affair. After the election of Bill Clinton, when questions were raised about his involvement in an Arkansas land development venture (Whitewater Development Company), Republicans now swung around to support reauthorization. However, because the law had lapsed, Attorney General Janet Reno had to rely on her own authority when, on January 20, 1994, she named a special prosecutor, Robert B. Fiske Jr., to investigate Whitewater and the July 1993 suicide of Vincent Foster, who had worked in the White House Counsel's office.

The independent counsel law was enacted on June 30, 1994 (P.L. 103-270). It reauthorized the independent counsel for five years, added new guidelines to control expenditures, required periodic court review to determine whether an independent counsel's office should be terminated because its work was substantially complete, directed independent counsels to avoid making conclusory statements in their final reports that unindicted individuals were guilty of criminal misconduct, and clarified the Attorney General's authority to use independent counsels in cases involving members of Congress. The new law gave the federal court panel the option of reappointing Fiske or selecting someone else. The panel decided on a replacement, former Republican Solicitor General Kenneth W. Starr. When the statute expired in 1999, Congress decided not to renew it.

Some attempts by Congress to limit the President's removal power have been rebuffed. The Nixon administration was able to resist an effort by Congress to remove the Director and Deputy Director of the Office of Management and Budget (Roy Ash and Frederick Malek). Congress wanted to abolish the two offices and reestablish them subject to Senate confirmation. Nixon vetoed the bill in 1973 because it required "forced removal by an unconstitutional procedure." He did not dispute the authority of Congress to abolish an office but said that the exercise of such power "cannot be used as a backdoor method of circumventing the President's power to remove." Congress, unable to override the veto, passed new legislation in 1974 that applied the confirmation process only to future OMB Directors and Deputy Directors.[86]

In 1978 Congress passed legislation requiring the President, when removing an Inspector General from office, to communicate the reasons to both houses of Congress. The Office of Legal Counsel in the Justice Department considered this provision "an improper restriction on the President's exclusive

---

86. 88 Stat. 11 (1974). Veto message: Public Papers of the Presidents, 1973, at 539. See also Louis Fisher, Presidential Spending Power 51–55 (1975).

power to remove Presidentially appointed executive officers."[87] In 1981 Reagan removed a dozen Inspectors General governed by the 1978 statute but did not submit reasons to Congress other than a general desire to have nominees of his own choosing.[88]

Three other Reagan efforts were turned back by court action. In 1981 his removal of a member of the D.C. Judicial Nomination Commission was struck down by a federal judge, who ruled that the commission's sole function and duty were to exercise independent decision-making on merit qualifications. These duties were confined exclusively to local District of Columbia matters in which Congress, under the Constitution, had special supervisory responsibilities.[89] Reagan also tried to remove Democratic members of the U.S. Parole Commission but backed off after one member went to court and legislators from both houses criticized his effort to interfere with the commission's independence.[90]

In 1983 President Reagan fired three Carter holdovers on the Commission on Civil Rights and nominated replacements who shared his positions on quotas, affirmative action, and busing. After a prolonged battle in the courts and in Congress, the commission was reconstituted to give the President authority to appoint only four of its eight members. The other four, including two of the Carter holdovers, would be named by Congress. Language was also added to allow the President to remove members "only for neglect of duty or malfeasance in office." The previous statute contained no provision for removal.[91]

Several other Reagan removals survived court challenges. Upon entering office, President Reagan imposed a hiring freeze on individuals who had been selected for federal jobs between November 5, 1980, and January 20, 1981. His order affected approximately 20,000 people. Some had quit their former jobs in anticipation of a position with the federal government. An appellate court upheld his action by labeling most of the individuals "federal appointees" rather than federal employees. They therefore lacked the usual procedural safeguards against removal. In a few cases, individuals had access to possible remedies if their appointments had been improperly revoked.[92]

President Reagan triggered a court test in August 1981 because of his response to a strike by the Professional Air Traffic Controllers Organization (PATCO). He announced that any controllers who failed to report for duty

87. 1 O.L.C. 18 (1977).
88. 92 Stat. 1103, sec. 3(b) (1978); Public Papers of the Presidents, 1981, at 24–25.
89. Borders v. Reagan, 518 F.Supp. 250, 268 (D.D.C. 1981).
90. Stephen Gettinger, "The Power Struggle over Federal Parole," 8 Corrections Magazine 41 (1982).
91. Berry v. Reagan, Civ. Action No. 83-3182 (D.D.C. November 14, 1983); 97 Stat. 1301 (1983).
92. National Treasury Employees Union v. Reagan, 663 F.2d 239 (D.C. Cir. 1981).

within 48 hours would forfeit their jobs. About 11,400 PATCO members were subsequently discharged and told that they would not be rehired. The government's action found support in the courts, but the discharge could be interpreted not as an act of presidential discretion but rather an obligation to enforce antistrike legislation passed by Congress.[93]

Reagan's Secretary of Labor removed two members of the Benefits Review Board in 1982 without specifying his reasons or providing them with a hearing. Although the board performed adjudicatory duties, it was not an Article III court whose members were entitled to lifetime tenure. The statute establishing the board addressed neither the members' tenure nor the terms of their removal. The Secretary's action was upheld by an appellate court on the ground that in the face of statutory silence, the officers served at the discretion of the appointing officer.[94]

An effort by President George H. W. Bush to use the removal power was also blocked in court. The dispute began with litigation between the U.S. Postal Service and the Postal Rate Commission. The Postal Service has a Board of Governors consisting of nine members who are appointed by the President and who may be removed only for cause. The commission is a five-member body that holds hearings to consider proposed rate increases. Commissioners are appointed by the President and also can be removed only for cause.

President Bush threatened to remove any member of the Board of Governors who refused to withdraw from the litigation. The objective was to protect the authority of the Justice Department to litigate, rather than to have such decisions exercised by independent agencies such as the Postal Service. A bare majority of five governors rejected his appeal. To gain a majority in his favor, Bush used his recess appointment power to replace someone whose term had expired but still remained on the board. That tactic backfired when federal courts held that because of a holdover provision in the statute governing the Postal Service, there was no vacancy to fill. Moreover, the Postal Service was allowed to appear in court without Justice Department approval.[95]

Clinton's Travelgate

In what could have been a routine operation without political cost, use of the removal power in 1993 severely damaged the credibility of President Clinton and

93. United States v. PATCO, 524 F.Supp. 160 (D.D.C. 1981).

94. Kalaris v. Donovan, 697 F.2d 376 (D.C. Cir. 1983), cert. denied, 462 U.S. 1119 (1983).

95. Mail Order Ass'n v. U.S. Postal Service, 986 F.2d 509 (D.C. Cir. 1993); Mackie v. Clinton, 827 F.Supp. 56 (D.D.C. 1993); Mackie v. Bush, 809 F.Supp. 144 (D.D.C. 1993); Neal

his White House. All seven employees of the White House Travel Office—who admittedly served at the pleasure of the President—were dismissed. Although Clinton had full authority to fire these employees, investigations by Congress, the press, and independent counsels raised serious questions that would plague the administration for years to come. Why did this action, securely grounded in the President's removal power, create such havoc for the Clinton White House?

On May 19, 1993, the employees of the Travel Office were dismissed with the charge that they had followed poor management practices. Dee Dee Myers, President Clinton's press secretary, also stated that the FBI had been asked to examine the records in the Travel Office, suggesting that the employees might have been guilty of criminal actions as well. Catherine Cornelius, Clinton's 25-year-old third cousin who had handled travel operations for his 1992 campaign, had been hired to run the office.[96] Even before Clinton's inauguration, she had prepared memos indicating how travel might be handled in the new administration. On April 12, a month before the firings, she began work at the Travel Office and was told to keep her eyes and ears open for improper activities.[97]

Two other outsiders, also with financial interests, were involved. Harry Thomason, a Hollywood producer, close friend of Clinton, and co-owner of an airplane charter company, helped spur the White House inquiry that led to the dismissals. With a White House office and a pass that gave him free access to the building, Thomason was well positioned to promote economic opportunities for his colleagues in the travel business.[98] After the firings, Penny Sample was brought in to handle press charters. She was the Clinton-Gore campaign's charter broker and a close associate of Darnell Martens, another co-owner (along with Dan Richland) of Thomason's airplane charter company.[99] The developing scandal was quickly dubbed "Travelgate."

Why did this exercise of the removal power backfire on Clinton? From the start, members of Congress and reporters challenged the rationale for the dismissals. The White House did an internal review, and Congress directed the General Accounting Office to conduct a separate inquiry. House Republicans tried to obtain documents through a resolution of inquiry, but that effort was

Devins, "Tempest in an Envelope: Reflections on the Bush White House's Failed Takeover of the U.S. Postal Service," 41 UCLA L. Rev. 1035 (1994).

96. "White House Ousts Its Travel Staff," New York Times, May 20, 1993, at A1.

97. White House Travel Office Management Review (prepared by the White House), July 2, 1993, at 6 (hereafter referred to as Travel Office Management Review).

98. "Complaint by Clinton Friend Led to Ouster of Travel Staff," New York Times, May 21, 1993, at A1.

99. Travel Office Management Review, at 5, 20.

blocked by the House Judiciary Committee (controlled by Democrats).[100] After the Republicans gained control of Congress in the 1994 elections, the House Committee on Government Reform and Oversight, chaired by William Clinger, launched a vigorous investigation that helped flush out key documents. Four main issues emerged.

First, the manner of the dismissals offended Congress and the press. Having worked in the White House for at least 8 years—and some for as many as 30 years—the employees could have been given several weeks' notice and then eased out gently. Instead, they were abruptly fired with a cloud over their heads and no opportunity to rebut charges of incompetence or possible illegality. Six weeks later an internal review by the White House conceded that the employees should have been treated "with more sensitivity" and with an opportunity "to hear the reasons for their termination, especially the allegations of wrongdoing, and should have been afforded an opportunity to respond."[101]

Two of the employees retired. The White House, embarrassed by its ineptitude, found federal jobs for the others. Billy Dale, who had headed the Travel Office, was indicted on charges of embezzlement. In November 1995 a federal jury took less than two hours to acquit him. Dale later explained that although he had been willing to admit that he had mingled public and private funds, he had not spent the money on himself.[102] Legislation was enacted to reimburse the White House Travel Office employees for the legal expenses related to their firings.[103]

Second, the involvement of Cornelius, Thomason, and Sample invited charges of nepotism and cronyism. Transferring the operation of the Travel Office to an outside, independent agency might have been justified, but not to a cousin, a Hollywood friend, and a business associate, each with financial interests. The White House review acknowledged that it had been a mistake to let "people with personal interests in the outcome to be involved in evaluating the Travel Office" and that the White House had not been sufficiently sensitive "to the appearance of favoritism toward friends."[104] World Wide Travel of Little Rock, hired on May 19, 1993 (on a no-bid basis), to handle White House travel arrangements, had made financial contributions to Clinton dur-

100. H. Rept. No. 103-183, 103d Cong., 1st Sess. (1993).
101. Travel Office Management Review, at 2, 15.
102. "Stop Lying About My Record," Washington Post, January 21, 1996, at C4.
103. The House passed this legislation by a vote of 350 to 43; 142 Cong. Rec. 5253–59, 5301 (1996). The funds were added to an omnibus appropriations bill; 1996 CQ Almanac 1–48. Congress had previously provided $150,000 to cover legal expenses for five former employees of the White House Travel Office; 107 Stat. 1198 (1993).
104. Travel Office Management Review, at 3.

ing the 1992 campaign. On May 21, after extensive press criticism, the White House and World Wide Travel agreed that "it would be desirable for World Wide to leave." A temporary contract was awarded to American Express.[105]

Third, President Clinton claimed that the FBI had been brought in not for a criminal probe but to use the bureau's auditing capability: "The FBI was called in to look at the auditor's report, not to accuse any of these people of doing anything criminal. . . . And the FBI sounds like a huge deal to you, but when you're in Washington and you're the President, you can't call the local police or the local prosecutor; that's who you call."[106] But an independent audit could have been obtained from federal agencies that have no role in criminal inquiries, such as the Office of Management and Budget.[107]

Finally, the Travel Office affair was a factor in the July 1993 suicide of Vincent Foster, who worked in the White House Counsel's office. Why this incident weighed so heavily on his mind has never been adequately explained. The criticism that followed the dismissals seemed to hit him hard. Associate White House Counsel William Kennedy talked to Foster about the Travel Office, and Foster expressed concern that evidence of possible wrongdoing might be tampered with or destroyed. FBI agents also talked with Foster about the Travel Office. He agreed that Peat Marwick should do an audit of the Travel Office before the employees were fired. Hillary Clinton told Foster that she had heard about problems in the Travel Office, and Foster told David Watkins (who headed the White House Office of Management and Administration) to keep her updated about the situation. At the time of the dismissals, Foster and Kennedy told Watkins to delete any reference to an FBI investigation.[108]

A June 30, 1994, report by Independent Counsel Robert B. Fiske Jr. on Foster's suicide provides further details. Those close to Foster said that the "single greatest source of his distress was the criticism he and others within the Counsel's Office received" following the firing of the seven Travel Office employees. When the White House prepared its internal report, there was some discussion about reprimanding Foster, but that did not happen. Foster's wife believed that the Travel Office matter was the greatest cause of stress and anxiety in the weeks prior to his death. Shortly before his death Foster consulted an attorney about the likelihood of congressional hearings into the Travel Office firings. A torn note made public six days after Foster's death indicates his preoccupation with the Travel Office affair and his expectation that he would

105. Id. at 13.
106. Public Papers of the Presidents, 1993 (I), at 747.
107. Travel Office Management Review, at 7–8, 17, Exhibit H.
108. Id. at 7–11.

have to defend himself at congressional hearings. Of the ten separate entries in the note, five appear to relate to the Travel Office.[109]

Whatever questions remain unanswered about Travelgate, several lessons stand out. Even when the President operates on full constitutional authority through his removal power, political miscalculations and poor judgment can yield deep wounds and personal tragedies. In the hands of inexperienced, partisan, and ambitious aides, the White House remains a source for political abuse and embarrassments.

George W. Bush

In the first year of the Bush II administration, a dispute arose over whether the President had the authority to replace an existing member of the Civil Rights Commission with someone of his own choice. The heart of the controversy centered on the statutory meaning of the six-year term given to commissioners. Congress created the commission in 1957 to investigate allegations of discrimination on the basis of color, race, religion, sex, age, disability, or national origin. At first, the commission consisted of six members serving open-ended terms. In 1983, after President Reagan attempted to remove five members to produce a balance that was more favorable to his conservative policies, Congress amended the statute to provide for eight members with staggered six-year terms. The amendment also prohibited the President from removing members except for neglect of duty or malfeasance in office. The purpose was to structure the commission to foster independence and nonpartisanship, and staggered terms were a means of insulating the commission from abrupt White House pressures.

On November 30, 1995, President Clinton appointed retired Judge A. Leon Higginbotham to the commission, with a six-year term set to expire on November 29, 2001. On December 14, 1998, Higginbotham died in office. Clinton appointed Victoria Wilson to the vacancy on January 13, 2000, noting in his appointment certificate that the appointment was "for the remainder of the term expiring November 29, 2001." On December 6, 2001, President Bush appointed Peter N. Kirsanow to take the seat once filled by Higginbotham and Wilson. Kirsanow was sworn in on December 7; however, when he appeared at a scheduled commission meeting the next day, the commission chair refused to recognize him, and the commission voted 5 to 3 not to seat him.

---

109. Report of the Independent Counsel In Re Vincent W. Foster, Jr., June 30, 1994, at 10–14.

The administration went to court to seek a declaratory judgment that Kirsanow was a member of the commission upon his December 6 appointment and that Wilson was no longer empowered to serve because her commission had expired on November 29, 2001. A district judge, without written opinion, ruled that Bush could not appoint Kirsanow because there was no vacancy to fill, since Wilson was entitled to a full six-year term. The legal conflict had important political consequences. Wilson supported many of the goals of the liberal, Democratic-controlled commission. In one of its most recent actions, the commission had issued a report on the 2000 presidential election, charging that Bush had gained his victory in Florida through "a pattern and practice of injustice, ineptitude and inefficiency" by disenfranchising black voters. Kirsanow, a black attorney from Cleveland, had been critical of the traditional civil rights leadership and would have tilted the commission from a 5-to-3 liberal majority to a deadlocked 4-to-4 balance.[110]

The D.C. Circuit reversed the district court on May 9, 2002. Though acknowledging that amendments enacted in 1994 had introduced some ambiguities, the court held that Congress had intended the commission to operate with eight members serving staggered six-year terms. The timing and expiration of those terms ensured that the commission would maintain a better political balance. Allowing Wilson to serve a full six-year term would disrupt the fixed and staggered terms and undermine the intended nonpartisan nature of the commission. The court stated that the commissioners' terms "run with the calendar, rather than with the person." Kirsanow had therefore been validly appointed to a vacant seat.[111]

The Congressional Presence

As originally justified, the removal power was intended to protect the unity and responsibility of the executive. Because of the authority of Congress to create an office and attach conditions to it—especially regarding tenure and cause for dismissal—the removal power has been limited by legislative action over the years.

110. Neil A. Lewis, "No Room for Bush's Civil Rights Appointee," New York Times, February 5, 2002, at A21; Neely Tucker, "Judge Rejects Bush Pick for Civil Rights Agency," Washington Post, February 5, 2002, at A1.

111. United States v. Wilson, 290 F.3d 347, 356 (D.C. Cir. 2002), cert. denied, 537 U.S. 1028 (2002). See "Bush Wins Rights Panel Case," Washington Post, November 19, 2002, at A23, and Morton Rosenberg, "Tenure of Members of the Civil Rights Commission," Congressional Research Service memorandum to the House Subcommittee on the Constitution, Committee on the Judiciary, December 14, 2001.

Congress may remove an individual by abolishing the office. A term of office created by one statute can be reduced or eliminated by a subsequent statute, requiring the discharge of a federal employee.[112] Congress has a wide assortment of tools to force federal workers out of office, even at the top policymaking level. One scholar estimated that congressional pressure is responsible for more firings and reassignments of executive branch personnel than is presidential action.[113]

Although the President remains theoretically responsible for the operation of the executive branch, this expectation has become increasingly unrealistic with the growth of the federal bureaucracy, the creation of agencies and commissions charged with legislative and judicial functions, civil service reform, and procedural safeguards imposed by Congress and the courts. With each development, the President's removal power suffered some shrinkage until it now applies, in general, only to major officials on whom the president depends to carry out policies.[114]

Although members of Congress participate extensively in the removal power, Presidents draw the line on certain tactics. President Hoover repulsed the Senate's effort to remove members of the Federal Power Commission that it had already confirmed. Finding fault with the decisions of the commission, the Senate voted to reconsider its confirmation of three of the commissioners and asked Hoover to return their nominations. Hoover insisted that the appointments had been made constitutionally and would not "admit the power in the Senate to encroach upon the Executive functions by removal of a duly appointed executive officer under the guise of reconsideration of his nomination." If the House of Representatives believed that the commissioners had been derelict in the performance of their duties, the "orderly and constitutional manner" of proceeding would be by impeachment.[115] The Senate proceeded to vote on the three commissioners, reconfirming two and rejecting George Otis Smith. It then instituted a court action to test Smith's right to hold office. A unanimous Supreme Court held that after the Senate confirms a nomination and the appointee takes the oath and enters into the duties of office, the Senate may not reconsider and possibly reject the nomination.[116]

Congress, restricted in frontal attacks, can use other methods to dislodge federal employees. Either house of Congress can pass a simple resolution, or

112. Crenshaw v. United States, 134 U.S. 99 (1890).
113. Harold Seidman, Politics, Position, and Power 54 (1980).
114. The courts continue to recognize the President's authority to remove purely executive officers; Martin v. Tobin, 451 F.2d 1335 (9th Cir. 1971); Martin v. Reagan, 525 F.Supp. 110 (D. Mass. 1981).
115. Public Papers of the Presidents, 1931, at 12, 15. Hoover's position had been supported by the Attorney General; 36 Op. Att'y Gen. 383 (1931).
116. 74 Cong. Rec. 3939–40 (1931); United States v. Smith, 286 U.S. 6 (1932).

both houses can pass a concurrent resolution, expressing the view that the President should remove an executive official. These resolutions are purely hortatory and have no legal effect, but they generate pressure for removal or resignation. In 1924 the Senate, after investigating the Teapot Dome scandal, passed a resolution stating that "it is the sense of the United States Senate that the President of the United States immediately request the resignation of Edwin Denby as Secretary of the Navy." On the day the resolution passed, President Coolidge announced that no official recognition could be given to it. The dismissal of an officer, "other than by impeachment, is exclusively an Executive function." Nevertheless, Denby offered his resignation several days later.[117]

Through the pressure of the investigative power, congressional committees can precipitate resignation or removal. In 1924 a special committee under Senator Burton K. Wheeler investigated the failure of Attorney General Harry Daugherty to prosecute people implicated in the Teapot Dome scandal. Daugherty resigned within a matter of weeks.[118] In 1958, after hearings by a House oversight subcommittee publicized the financial operations of the Federal Communications Commission, commissioner Richard A. Mack resigned.[119] Veterans Administration chief Robert P. Nimmo resigned in 1982 following detailed congressional investigations into his expenditure of funds.[120] A top official in the Interior Department resigned in 1989 when Senator J. Bennett Johnston, chairman of the Committee on Energy and Natural Resources, threatened to delay confirmation votes on all Interior Department nominees until the official quit.[121] In 1998 the Inspector General of the Treasury Department resigned following charges by a Senate subcommittee that she had violated federal procurement rules and given contradictory testimony to Congress.[122]

Congress also intervenes to *protect* incumbents and ensure their tenure. It does this partly by specifying grounds for removal and by establishing procedural safeguards for federal employees facing dismissal or disciplinary action. In 1978, as part of the Civil Service Reform Act, Congress created a special counsel to protect the rights of whistleblowers. It has long been in the interest of Congress to prevent the top layer of the bureaucracy from penalizing federal employees who disclose agency wrongdoing or ineptitude. Congress

117. Debate on the Denby resolution appears at 65 Cong. Rec. 2223–45 (1924); Coolidge announcement, id. at 2335.

118. Hasia Diner, "Teapot Dome, 1924," in Arthur M. Schlesinger Jr. and Roger Bruns, eds., Congress Investigates 210–11 (1975).

119. Congressional Quarterly Almanac, 1958, at 687–90.

120. "Embattled VA Chief Steps Down," Washington Post, October 4, 1982, at A1.

121. "Interior Official Resigns Under Fire," Washington Post, May 27, 1989, at A7.

122. Stephen Barr, "Treasury Inspector General to Resign," Washington Post, January 17, 1998, at A10.

depends on these employees to call attention to waste, corruption, and other practices that agencies like to conceal. Civil service employees who are fired for circulating a petition to Congress can be reinstated through court action.[123] But if their communications to Congress contain false or irresponsible information, protection from the judiciary may not be available.[124] Members of Congress resort to hearings, letters to agency heads, and other tactics to prevent an employee's removal or to press for reinstatement. Members intervene for reasons of simple justice and to keep open the channels of communication between agencies and Congress.

The case of Ernest Fitzgerald, a hero to liberal critics of military spending, has already been discussed. Members of Congress also defend agency employees identified with conservative causes. In 1963 the State Department informed Otto Otepka, a security officer, that he was being dismissed for giving classified information to the Senate Internal Security Subcommittee. Otepka found himself caught between conflicting loyalties. Departmental procedures restricted the disclosure of information; statutory provisions encouraged civil service employees to furnish information to Congress and its committees. After the subcommittee held hearings on his dismissal and issued a lengthy report critical of the State Department, many of the initial charges against Otepka were dropped. Instead of dismissal, he was demoted and reprimanded.[125]

Frances Knight, longtime director of the Passport Office, solidified her position over the years by forging close ties with Capitol Hill. Providing overnight passport service for Senators, Congressmen, and their constituents was one way to nurture congressional support. When Abba Schwartz, chief of the State Department's Bureau of Security and Consular Affairs from 1962 to 1966, tried to reorganize Knight out of a job, congressional defenders helped defeat the proposal. Within a few years Schwartz lost his own job through a reorganization plan; Knight remained head of the Passport Office until 1977.[126]

Because of a fundamental interest in program implementation, the operation of the civil service, and access to agency information, members of Con-

---

123. Steck v. Connally, 199 F.Supp. 104 (D.D.C. 1961).

124. Turner v. Kennedy, 332 F.2d 304 (D.C. Cir. 1964).

125. "State Department Security—1963–65," prepared by the Senate Committee on the Judiciary, 90th Cong., 1st Sess. (Comm. Print December 15, 1967). For congressional supporters of Otepka, see William J. Gill, The Ordeal of Otto Otepka (1969).

126. Sanford J. Ungar, "J. Edgar Hoover Leaves the State Department," 28 Foreign Policy 11–16 (1977); and "Frances Knight Ouster Tarnishes Carter Image," Human Events, July 16, 1977, at 1, 9–10.

gress will always be concerned about the suspension and removal of federal employees. Some past congressional techniques are off-limits today: allowing the Senate to act jointly with the President (such as under the Tenure of Office Act), using the power of the purse to remove named employees, abolishing a position to put someone else in place, and permitting the Senate to reconsider the nomination of an official who has already been confirmed and appointed. But Congress can abolish offices through reorganization and program cutbacks, provided it does not violate the Bill of Attainder Clause or First Amendment freedoms, and it can apply irresistible pressure both for and against agency employees through its investigative power.[127]

127. See Louis Fisher, "Congress and the Removal Power," in James A. Thurber, ed. Divided Democracy 255–74 (1991).

4

LEGISLATIVE POWERS

Article I of the Constitution provides that "all legislative Powers herein granted shall be vested in a Congress of the United States." In one of the most restrictive opinions ever written on the President's role, Justice Black held that the Constitution "limits his functions in the lawmaking process to the recommending of laws he thinks wise and the vetoing of laws he thinks bad."[1] Black's theory, whatever its merits, ignores the vast scope of presidential legislative power that exists today and even in much earlier periods.

The theory of constitutional limits—of powers enumerated and clearly defined—has lost ground to a number of stubborn forces. Even at the outset, more than two centuries ago, the lines between the three branches of the federal government were not crisp demarcations. Madison admitted that the boundaries between executive, legislative, and judicial powers, "though in general so strongly marked in themselves, consist in many instances of mere shades of difference."[2] In Federalist 37 he paused to acknowledge the inherent limitations of our language. Just as naturalists had difficulty defining the exact line between vegetable life and the animal world, it was an even greater task to draw the boundary between the departments of government, or "even the privileges and powers of the different legislative branches."

Madison could not foresee the vast quantity of legislative power to be delegated to the President, to executive agencies, and later to independent regulatory commissions. Delegations are supposed to be accompanied by legislative standards that protect the essential lawmaking function of Congress, but standardless delegations are common. They survive court scrutiny because of procedural safeguards, guidelines placed in the legislative history of a statute, and various customs and traditions that help confine executive discretion.

In addition to statutory grants of powers, other forms of "administrative legislation" include presidential proclamations, executive orders, agency regulations, and White House supervision of the rulemaking process. To retain some semblance of control, Congress has evolved a highly sophisticated set of tools, many of them of a nonstatutory nature. An important statutory control, the legislative veto, is treated in the next chapter.

1. Youngstown Co. v. Sawyer, 343 U.S. 579, 587 (1952).
2. 5 The Writings of James Madison 26 (Hunt ed.).

Delegation

It is a fundamental principle of constitutional government that the legislature may not delegate its power to another branch. John Locke said that the legislature "cannot transfer the power of making laws to any other hands, for it being but a delegated power from the people, they who have it cannot pass it over to others."[3] This concept is embodied in the ancient maxim *delegata potestas non potest delegari* ("delegated power cannot be delegated").[4]

Although Congress cannot surrender the basic legislative power entrusted to it by the Constitution, it may give substantial discretionary authority to the executive branch and the independent regulatory commissions. The tension between these two competing values is relieved by some judicial tightrope walking. One author suggested this humorous but accurate syllogism: *Major Premise:* Legislative power cannot be constitutionally delegated by Congress. *Minor Premise:* It is essential that certain powers be delegated to administrative officers and regulatory commissions. *Conclusion:* Therefore, the powers thus delegated are not legislative powers.[5]

This kind of circular logic reappears in many decisions on delegation. Typically the Supreme Court declares that it would be a breach of the Constitution for Congress to transfer its legislative power to the President. After genuflecting to the theory of separated powers, the Justices regularly uphold the delegation in question.[6] Statutory language is sanctioned even when it is vague and ill defined, such as general guidelines based on "excessive profits," "reasonable rates," "unjust discrimination," and the "public interest." The courts tolerate this kind of legislation not because the language is specific, which is far from the case, but because Congress supplies standards of due process to guide officials in administering the statute. Agencies are required by law to give notice and a hearing prior to issuing a rule or regulation. Findings of fact are supplied for the record; procedures exist for appeal. The Administrative Procedure Act (APA) of 1946 established various standards for agency rulemaking in order to guarantee fairness and equitable treatment. Through such procedural standards Congress tries to minimize the opportunity for executive caprice and arbitrariness.

3. John Locke, Second Treatise on Civil Government, §141.
4. Patrick W. Duff and Horace E. Whiteside, "Delegata Potestas Non Potest Delegari: A Maxim of American Constitutional Law," 14 Corn. L. Q. 168 (1929); Horst P. Ehmke, "'Delegata Potestas Non Potest Delegari,' a Maxim of American Constitutional Law," 47 Corn. L. Q. 50 (1961).
5. Robert E. Cushman, The Independent Regulatory Commissions 429 (1941).
6. For example, Field v. Clark, 143 U.S. 649, 692 (1891), and Hampton & Co. v. United States, 276 U.S. 394, 406 (1928).

Vague and general grants of legislative power are criticized from various perspectives. Some scholars insist that political accountability and democratic values depend on the establishment of clear guidelines for administrators.[7] Vague statutes also make it difficult to conduct program evaluation, stressed in such statutes as the Legislative Reorganization Act of 1970, the Congressional Budget and Impoundment Control Act of 1974, and the Government Performance and Results Act of 1993.[8] How can Congress determine whether programs are being carried out effectively unless the original legislative goals are clearly stated? Unless statutory standards exist, how can courts judge whether agency actions are faithful to legislative intent?

The Impulse for Broad Delegation

From the first year of its existence, Congress has found it necessary to set general goals and give executive officials broad discretion in carrying out legislative policy. In 1789 the House of Representatives debated a bill to establish a permanent seat of government. The bill authorized the President to appoint a certain number of commissioners who would report recommendations for the best location and, with the President's advice, purchase the property and construct the necessary buildings for Congress and the rest of government.

Representative Thomas Tucker of South Carolina objected to the delegation as "totally inadmissible" because it gave a discretionary power "which no body of men ought to exercise but ourselves with the other branch of the Legislature. . . . Were we sent here to give such powers to any men?" Tucker proposed that the commissioners report to Congress, not the President, requiring Congress at a later session to pass legislation for the nation's capital. His motion lost, 21 to 29. A year later Congress delegated the responsibility to the President and the commissioners.[9]

The avoidance of clear and explicit statutory language is sometimes rooted in a genuine dilemma: the problem of legislating for future events. William Blackstone, the eighteenth-century English jurist, observed that the "manner, time, and circumstances of putting laws in execution must frequently be left to the discretion of the executive magistrates."[10] Despite his strictures against delegation, Locke recognized that the legislature could not always be in session, nor could it provide laws to cover every conceivable contingency.[11]

7. Theodore J. Lowi, The End of Liberalism 298 (1969); David Schoenbrod, Power Without Responsibility: How Congress Abuses the People Through Delegation (1993).
8. 84 Stat. 1168, sec. 204 (1970); 88 Stat. 325, Title VII (1974); 107 Stat. 285 (1993).
9. 1 Annals of Congress 879 (September 5, 1789); 1 Stat. 130 (1790).
10. William Blackstone, Commentaries, Book 1, 270.
11. Locke, Second Treatise on Civil Government, §153.

Contingent (or conditional) legislation has had a long tradition in America. An early legal test involved a trade act directed against Britain. After the legislation lapsed in 1810, Congress let the President renew the trade restrictions at his discretion. A merchant complained that these presidential actions had the force of law and were thus legislative in nature, violating the separation doctrine. The Supreme Court rejected this contention, affirming that Congress could legislate conditionally and leave to others the task of ascertaining the facts that bring its declared policy into operation.[12]

Courts recognize that it is essential to phrase statutes in general terms when events are "future and impossible to be fully known." Many subjects of government depend on legislation that cannot be known to the lawmaking power "and must, therefore, be a subject of inquiry and determination outside of the halls of legislation."[13] The nature of government often requires Congress to pass general legislation and leave to other branches the responsibility to "fill in the details."[14]

Over time, conditions in the economy requiring regulation became increasingly complex, interrelated, and subject to change. Administrators could not resolve problems while operating in a legislative straitjacket. They needed an opportunity to experiment and learn. Courts accepted broadness and generality in statutes as unavoidable qualities of legislation. Congress need only declare a general policy and leave to administrative officers the duty of applying the statute to particular circumstances.[15]

Especially in the case of the independent regulatory commission, the courts sanctioned vague statutory language. When Congress looked at the industries to be regulated after the Civil War and saw the turbulent, almost revolutionary changes in progress, it decided that commissions run by experts offered a more hopeful instrument than legislators periodically passing statutes that needed regular revision. A commission, operating under a general charter, could respond more effectively to economic and technological change.

The judiciary consistently rejected challenges to these broad delegations, upholding the power of the Interstate Commerce Commission to protect the "public interest," accepting the guideline of "unfair method of competition" for the Federal Trade Commission, the standard of "public convenience, interest, or necessity" for the Federal Communications Commission, and the ability of the Securities and Exchange Commission to ensure that corporations do not

12. Brig Aurora v. United States, 11 U.S. (7 Cr.) 382 (1813).
13. Locke's Appeal, 72 Pa. St. 491, 498–99 (1873).
14. Wayman v. Southard, 10 Wheat. 1, 46 (1825).
15. For example, Buttfield v. Stranahan, 192 U.S. 470, 496 (1904); Union Bridge Co. v. United States, 194 U.S. 364, 386 (1907); Monongahela Bridge Co. v. United States, 216 U.S. 177 (1910); and United States v. Grimaud, 220 U.S. 506, 516 (1911).

"unduly or unnecessarily complicate the structure" or "unfairly or inequitably distribute voting power among security holders."[16]

The commissions offer some built-in safeguards to protect against abuse. They operate on a multimember (collegial) basis, in contrast to executive departments headed by a single administrator. This structure creates a capacity for self-checking and self-correction, limiting the abuse of delegated power and patterning the plural-member commissions more along the organizational lines of appellate courts. The terms of commissioners are lengthy and staggered, insulating them somewhat from presidential transitions and the pressure of biennial elections. Statutory restrictions are placed on the number of commissioners who may belong to the same political party (although this safeguard is neutralized when the President selects nominal members of a political party or when members classify themselves as Independents).[17]

Broad delegations result from other circumstances. Lawmakers, agency heads, and their staffs may decide that they lack the expertise to draft specific language. Agencies are reluctant to press for the adoption of strict standards. When an assistant general counsel in the Department of Health, Education, and Welfare expressed misgivings about the lack of clarity in legislation being drafted for social services, his boss, HEW Secretary Wilbur Cohen, offered this advice: "Put it in regulations . . . do it later. I can't think of an answer."[18] Even at that point an agency may find it difficult to place in a regulation all the factors needed to guide governmental action. In 1981 the Department of Justice canceled a proposed rule after concluding that "it is impossible to foresee and enumerate all of the favorable or adverse factors which may be relevant and should be considered in the exercise of administrative discretion."[19]

These circumstances, faced by legislators and administrators alike, invite vague formulations of objectives. Furthermore, specificity of language may undermine the consensus needed to pass legislation. A ban on "sex discrimination" can attract a majority of votes in Congress. Working out precisely what the phrase means in terms of father-son banquets or boy choirs might fracture the coalition required for passage.

16. For examples of the "public interest" guideline, see ICC v. Goodrich Transit Co., 224 U.S. 194, 214–15 (1912); Intermountain Rate Cases, 234 U.S. 476, 486–88 (1914); Avent v. United States, 266 U.S. 127, 130 (1924); and N.Y. Central Securities Co. v. United States, 287 U.S. 12, 24–25 (1932). For "unfair method of competition," see FTC v. Gratz, 253 U.S. 421, 427–28 (1920). For the "public convenience" standard, see FCC v. Pottsville Broadcasting Co., 309 U.S. 134, 137–38 (1940). For the Securities and Exchange Commission, see American Power Co. v. SEC, 329 U.S. 90, 104–6 (1946).

17. Louis Fisher, The Politics of Shared Power: Congress and the Executive 146–76 (1998).

18. Martha Derthick, Uncontrollable Spending for Social Services Grants 8–9 (1975).

19. 46 Fed. Reg. 9119 (1981).

Congress may also find a responsibility so vexing, so lacking in political rewards, that it tries to shift the chore elsewhere. General tariff-making exposed Congress to such ridicule that it delegated the bulk of that task to the executive branch and the Tariff Commission (now the International Trade Commission). As one study concluded, "Every favor which can be conferred is also a danger, because it must sometimes be refused. Responsibility involves blame. And, if the demands exceed what the congressman can effectively handle, then he may happily yield up a significant portion of his power. This is what happened with the tariff."[20]

As much as Congress tries to rid itself of unwanted tasks, it has difficulty breaking free entirely. In the case of international trade, industries and labor unions appealed to Congress for protection from foreign competition. Legislation soon appeared, providing federal assistance payments for dislocated industries and a variety of nontariff barriers. The Trade Act of 1974 marked a reassertion of Congress in this area. Trade legislation is now a regular part of the congressional agenda, but it is frequently done under a "fast-track" procedure. The President negotiates a trade package, with members of Congress as participants, and the President's proposal is then submitted in the form of a bill that cannot be amended by Congress and cannot be buried in committee. Under the terms of fast-track legislation, Congress must vote on the bill and either pass it or defeat it. This procedure was used in 1993 to pass President Clinton's North American Free Trade Agreement (NAFTA).

The prohibition on amendments for fast-track legislation is somewhat misleading. Although the President's implementing bill cannot be amended in committee or on the floor, a draft bill is freely circulated and subject to congressional pressure for changes.[21] In fact, NAFTA passed only with the understanding that Clinton would negotiate side agreements with Mexico regarding the enforcement of labor and environmental laws in that country.

The history of federal pay adjustments illustrates the frustration of trying to delegate an intrinsically political issue. Prior to 1967 Congress determined the rate of compensation for Senators and Representatives by a separate statute, setting forth the specific dollar amounts paid to legislators. In that year, as part of the Postal Revenue and Salary Act, Congress established a commission to recommend every four years the rates of compensation for members of Congress, Justices of the Supreme Court, federal judges, and certain high-ranking government officials. The President, after receiving these recommendations, would submit to Congress his own proposals for salaries. They took

20. Raymond P. Bauer et al., American Business and Public Policy 37 (1963). For delegation of the tariff power, see Louis Fisher, President and Congress 133–55 (1972).

21. Harold Hongju Koh, "The Fast Track and United States Trade Policy," 18 Brook. J. Int'l L. 143 (1992).

effect within 30 days unless disapproved by either house or replaced by a different salary schedule enacted into law. The Federal Pay Comparability Act of 1970 relied on a similar procedure.[22]

Through such mechanisms Congress hoped to remove "politics" from pay adjustments, but the issue continued to bounce around as a political football. When President Nixon refused to submit an alternative pay plan, an appellate court held that his action violated the law.[23] Members of Congress, responding to what they thought their constituents wanted, frustrated the policy of comparability by blocking salary increases.

Some members of Congress went to court, claiming that the system of automatic pay increases without affirmative action by Congress violated the Constitution's Ascertainment Clause: "The Senators and Representatives shall receive a Compensation for their Services, to be ascertained by Law" (Article I, Section 6). The courts held that the meaning of "ascertains" does not require Congress to vote for specific salary adjustments.[24] Existing procedure allowed congressional salaries to be increased unless Congress passed a joint resolution of disapproval within a 30-day period.[25] Failure to act during that time allowed the increase to take effect.

The pay issue continued to dog Congress. In 1989, in one of his last official actions, President Reagan recommended a 51 percent salary hike for members of Congress. The increase was scheduled to take place on February 8 unless both houses voted to block it. It looked as though legislators would get a huge pay increase by not acting during the 30-day review period, but Congress was condemned for wanting a salary boost without actually voting on it. Having absorbed a public beating for several weeks, members created the worst of all worlds by voting on February 7 to kill the pay raise. So much for clever delegations and deft parliamentary maneuvers! Legislation enacted at the end of 1989 required Congress to approve, by recorded vote, pay increases.[26]

The Domain of Foreign Affairs

The delegation of legislative power sometimes draws its force from an effort to distinguish between domestic and foreign affairs. In *United States v.*

22. 84 Stat. 1946 (1970).
23. National Treasury Employees Union v. Nixon, 492 F.2d 587 (D.C. Cir. 1974).
24. Humphrey v. Baker, 848 F.2d 211 (D.C. Cir. 1988), cert. denied, 488 U.S. 966 (1988); Pressler v. Blumenthal, 434 U.S. 1028 (1978), aff'g Pressler v. Simon, 428 F.Supp. 302 (D.D.C. 1976) (three-judge court).
25. 2 U.S.C. 351–61 (1988). See also Louis Fisher, "History of Pay Adjustments for Members of Congress," in Robert W. Hartman and Arnold R. Weber, eds., The Rewards of Public Service (1980).
26. 103 Stat. 1765 (1989); 2 U.S.C. 359 (2000).

Curtiss-Wright Corp. (1936), Justice Sutherland wrote eloquently about "this vast external realm, with its important, complicated, delicate and manifold problems." As a consequence, he said, legislation over the international field must often accord to the President "a degree of discretion and freedom from statutory restrictions which would not be admissible were domestic affairs alone involved."[27]

Curtiss-Wright is used to justify not only broad grants of legislative authority to the President but also the exercise of inherent and extraconstitutional presidential power. Because of the "very delicate, plenary and exclusive power of the President as the sole organ of the federal government in the field of international relations," Sutherland argued that the exercise of presidential power does not depend solely on an act of Congress.[28] Indeed, some of the powers are not even inherent in the Constitution, for Sutherland searched for powers outside the Constitution.[29]

His remarks in *Curtiss-Wright* went far beyond the necessities of the case, echoing positions he had taken as a U.S. Senator and member of the Foreign Relations Committee. The decision closely tracks his article "The Internal and External Powers of the National Government" (printed as a Senate document in 1910) and his book *Constitutional Power and World Affairs* (1919).[30] Every judge carries predilections to the bench, but few use a Supreme Court case to disseminate a personal position written decades before on an issue not at all essential to the dispute before the Court.

Sutherland believed that foreign and domestic affairs differed "both in respect of their origin and their nature" because the powers of external sovereignty "passed from the Crown not to the colonies severally, but to the colonies in their collective and corporate capacity as the United States of America."[31] Scholars, pointing out that the states in 1776 operated as sovereign entities and not as parts of a collective body, have repudiated Sutherland's thesis. The creation of the Continental Congress did not interrupt the sovereign power of the states to make treaties, borrow money, solicit arms, lay embargoes, collect tariff duties, and conduct separate military campaigns.[32] The Supreme Court

27. United States v. Curtiss-Wright Corp., 299 U.S. 304, 319, 320 (1936).
28. Id. at 320.
29. Louis Henkin, Foreign Affairs and the Constitution 22 (1972).
30. S. Doc. No. 417, 61st Cong., 2d Sess. (1910). See also Joel Francis Paschal, Mr. Justice Sutherland: A Man Against the State 93 (1951).
31. United States v. Curtiss-Wright Corp., 299 U.S. at 315–16.
32. Charles Lofgren, "United States v. Curtiss-Wright Export Corporation: An Historical Reassessment," 83 Yale L. J. 1 (1973); David M. Levitan, "The Foreign Relations Power: An Analysis of Mr. Justice Sutherland's Theory," 55 Yale L. J. 467 (1946); Claude H. Van Tyne, "Sovereignty in the American Revolution: An Historical Study," 12 Am. Hist. Rev. 529 (1907).

has recognized that the American colonies, upon their separation from England, exercised the powers of a sovereign and independent government.[33]

Even if the power of external sovereignty had somehow passed intact from the Crown to the "United States," the Constitution divides that power between Congress and the President. The President and the Senate share the treaty power. The President receives ambassadors from other countries, but U.S. ambassadors must be approved by the Senate. Congress has the power to declare war, to raise and support the military forces, to make rules for their regulation, to provide for calling up the militia to suppress insurrections and repel invasions, and to provide for the organization and disciplining of the militia. The Constitution explicitly grants to Congress the power to lay and collect duties on foreign trade, to regulate commerce with foreign nations, and to establish a uniform rule of naturalization.

Moreover, world events since Sutherland's opinion have increased the degree of overlap between foreign and domestic affairs.[34] In 1991 President Bush was criticized for spending too much time traveling abroad while neglecting domestic problems. He replied that his efforts to promote trade agreements with other nations would benefit U.S. exports: "I guess my bottom line . . . is you can't separate foreign policy from domestic."[35] President Clinton made a similar comment in 1993: "There is no longer a clear division between what is foreign and what is domestic."[36]

Nevertheless, the Supreme Court looks more sympathetically upon delegation that involves external affairs. Even Chief Justice William Rehnquist, a strong advocate of the nondelegation doctrine, held to a different standard for international crises, "the nature of which Congress can hardly have been expected to anticipate in any detail."[37] Rehnquist agreed that Congress "is permitted to legislate both with greater breadth and with greater flexibility" when a statute governs military affairs.[38] *Curtiss-Wright* is frequently cited to support broad delegations of legislative power to the President and even the existence of independent, implied, and inherent powers for the President.[39]

33. United States v. California, 332 U.S. 19, 31 (1947); Texas v. White, 74 U.S. (7 Wall.) 700, 725 (1869); M'Ilvaine v. Coxe's Lessee, 8 U.S. (4 Cr.) 209, 212 (1808); Ware v. Hylton, 3 U.S. (3 Dall.) 199, 222–24 (1796).

34. Bayless Manning, "The Congress, the Executive, and 'Intermestic' Affairs: Three Proposals," 55 Foreign Affairs 306 (1977).

35. Public Papers of the Presidents, 1991 (II), 1629.

36. Id. 1993 (I), 2.

37. Dames & Moore v. Regan, 453 U.S. 654, 669 (1981). See also his comment at 678.

38. Rostker v. Goldberg, 453 U.S. 57, 66 (1981), quoting Parker v. Levy, 417 U.S. 733, 756 (1974).

39. For broad-delegation arguments, see Ex parte Endo, 323 U.S. 283, 298 n.21 (1944); Zemel v. Rusk, 381 U.S. 1, 17 (1965); Goldwater v. Carter, 444 U.S. 996, 1000 n.1 (1979). Inherent pow-

During the Iran-Contra hearings in 1987, several officials of the Reagan administration defended their actions partly based on what they believed to be the Court's doctrine in *Curtiss-Wright*.[40] In particular, they relied on Sutherland's description of the President as the "sole organ" in foreign affairs, a phrase taken from John Marshall during a debate in 1800 in the House of Representatives. The reference to Marshall seems impressive, given his later elevation to Chief Justice of the Supreme Court, but the full context of Marshall's remark makes it clear that he understood that foreign policy was made *jointly* by the President and the Senate (for treaties) or by the President and Congress (for statutes). Only after the policy had been formulated and announced through this joint action did the President become the "sole organ" in *implementing* national policy.[41] Although Sutherland falsely represented Marshall's meaning, his dictum in *Curtiss-Wright* continues to be used by others to promote inherent and extraconstitutional powers for the President in external affairs.[42]

Subdelegation

The problem of delegation is compounded when the agent of Congress transfers the responsibility to a subordinate. The Supreme Court has been as lenient toward subdelegation as it has been toward delegation, recognizing that the President and department heads cannot personally discharge all the statutory tasks assigned to them. It is unreasonable to assume that every statute imposes on the President a personal, nondelegable duty to review the decisions of subordinates. Such an interpretation would place "a burdensome, if not impossible, personal duty on the President" and could not be accepted as legislative intent unless Congress so stated.[43]

After World War II Congress enacted legislation to specifically recognize the President's need to subdelegate some of the functions invested in him by law. A survey disclosed that President Truman had to act, either expressly or

ers are discussed in United States v. Pink, 315 U.S. 203, 229 (1942); Knauff v. Shaughnessy, 338 U.S. 537, 542 (1950); and United States v. Mazurie, 419 U.S. 544, 566–67 (1975).

40. "Iran-Contra Investigation," joint hearings before the Senate and House Iran-Contra committees, 100th Cong., 1st Sess., vol. 100-7 (part 2), 38–39, 133–34 (testimony of Oliver L. North); vol. 100-5, 419–21, 426 (testimony of Bretton G. Sciaroni) (1987).

41. Annals of Congress, 6th Cong., 613 (1800). See also Louis Fisher, "Foreign Policy Powers of the President and Congress," 499 Annals 148 (1988).

42. Richard A. Posner, Not a Suicide Pact: The Constitution in a Time of National Emergency 4, 39, 70 (2006).

43. French v. Weeks, 259 U.S. 326 (1922). "Obviously all the functions of his great office cannot be exercised by the President in person"; United States v. Chemical Foundation, 272 U.S. 1, 13 (1926).

by inference, under at least 1,100 statutes. In 1950, on the basis of that study, Congress authorized the President to subdelegate functions to his department heads or agency officials on the condition that the officer discharging those tasks be someone who had been confirmed by the Senate. In this way Congress hoped to maintain some system of accountability to elected representatives.[44]

Checks on Delegated Power

Not since 1935 has the Supreme Court struck down a delegation of power to the executive branch because of inadequate legislative guidelines. In that year delegations of power were twice overruled. Both decisions involved the National Industrial Recovery Act (NIRA), which gave industrial and trade associations the responsibility for drawing up codes to minimize competition, raise prices, and restrict production. If the President found the codes unacceptable, he could prescribe his own and enforce them by law.

Those who drafted the NIRA, under heavy pressure from Roosevelt to produce a bill, gave scant thought to constitutional questions of delegation or procedural safeguards. Congress felt equally pressured to rush the bill to enactment. General Hugh Johnson, administrator of the National Recovery Administration (NRA), cared little for procedural niceties and his attorneys operated under impossible deadlines. They processed hundreds of codes under the worst of conditions, including having to deal with an array of industry and trade association officials who dominated the drafting sessions. A coherent strategy for litigation was overshadowed by persistent conflicts between NRA attorneys and U.S. attorneys, Interior Department lawyers, and the Antitrust Division of the Justice Department.[45]

In the first NRA case, the Court struck down a section of the statute governing controls on petroleum production because it failed to establish a "criterion to govern the President's course." The Court said that Congress "has declared no policy, has established no standard, has laid down no rule."[46] Justice Cardozo, dissenting in this case because he found that Congress had supplied adequate standards, exclaimed in the second case: "This is delegation running riot."[47]

---

44. 64 Stat. 419 (1950), codified at 3 U.S.C. 301 (2000). See Glendon A. Schubert Jr., "Judicial Review of the Subdelegation of Presidential Power," 12 J. Pol. 668 (1950); Glendon A. Schubert Jr., "The Presidential Subdelegation Act of 1950," 13 J. Pol. 647 (1951); Eli G. Nobleman, "The Delegation of Presidential Functions: Constitutional and Legal Aspects," 307 Annals 134 (1956); and Nathan Grundstein, Presidential Delegation of Authority in Wartime (1961).

45. Peter H. Irons, The New Deal Lawyers 22–107 (1982).

46. Panama Refining Co. v. Ryan, 293 U.S. 388, 415, 430 (1935).

47. Schechter Corp. v. United States, 295 U.S. 495, 553 (1935). A year later an appellate court struck down an emergency appropriations bill because it unconstitutionally delegated

The Court's decisions were handed down in a climate increasingly hostile to agency rulemaking. The scope of agency discretion and procedural irregularities were constant sore points. A Committee on Administrative Law, established by the American Bar Association in May 1933, viewed with anxiety the creation of the New Deal agencies, objected to the "haphazard bedlam" of administrative practice, and advocated more uniformity and due process.[48]

The furious legislative pace of the Roosevelt administration overburdened an administrative system that was already strained and deficient. During his first 15 months in office FDR issued 674 executive orders. In its first year the NRA approved hundreds of codes and released 2,998 administrative orders that approved or modified the codes. Almost 6,000 NRA press releases, some of them having legislative effect, were issued during this period.[49] Department officials were sometimes unaware of their own regulations. As the Court discovered in *Panama Refining,* the government brought an indictment and took an appeal to the Court before discovering that the regulation on which the proceeding was based had been eliminated by an executive order.[50] These embarrassments led to the creation of the *Federal Register,* which published presidential and agency documents that were legislative in effect.

In neither NRA case did the Supreme Court object to delegation as a general principle. The Constitution did not deny to Congress "the necessary resources of flexibility and practicality, which will enable it to perform its function in laying down policies and establishing standards—while leaving to selected instrumentalities the making of subordinate rules within prescribed limits and the determination of facts to which the policy as declared by the legislature is to apply."[51]

The "Schechter Rule," with its insistence on statutory standards, is rarely followed by either Congress or the courts. Standardless delegations have been upheld for many reasons, including the accumulated customs of a regulated industry and the practices developed by states that help narrow the discretion of a federal agency.[52] Standardless delegations have been considered acceptable when the legislative history leading to the enactment of a "facially standardless" statute supplies guidelines for administrative action.[53] The judiciary

legislative power to the President; Franklin Tp. in Somerset County, N.J. v. Tugwell, 85 F.2d 208, 218–20 (D.C. Cir. 1936).

48. 58 A.B.A. Rep. 201 (1933).

49. 59 A.B.A. Rep. 553–54 (1934).

50. Panama Refining Co. v. Ryan, 293 U.S. at 412–13.

51. Id. at 421; Schechter Corp. v. United States, 295 U.S. at 529–30.

52. Fahey v. Mallonee, 332 U.S. 245, 250, 253 (1947), concerning the Home Owners' Loan Act of 1933 and the Federal Home Loan Bank Board.

53. Carl McGowan, "Congress, Court, and Control of Delegated Powers," 77 Colum. L. Rev. 1119, 1128 n.33 (1977).

recognizes that circumstances may require Congress to delegate broadly so that it can encompass those who might otherwise, through technicalities available in a statute, try to evade the purpose of federal regulation.[54] When Congress delegates the power to tax, it is not obliged to supply stricter standards to guide administrators.[55] Efforts in recent years to resurrect the nondelegation doctrine have been consistently unsuccessful.[56] In 1999 the D.C. Circuit held that language in the Clean Air Act resulted in an unconstitutional delegation of legislative power. When the Supreme Court decided the case in 2001, it ruled that the transfer of authority to the agency was not an unconstitutional delegation.[57]

A separate question concerns the delegation of legislative power to *private* groups. In 1936 the Supreme Court struck down a statute in part because it delegated power to representatives of the coal industry to set up a code of mandatory regulations: "This is legislative delegation in its most obnoxious form; for it is not even delegation to an official or an official body, presumptively disinterested, but to private persons whose interests may be and often are adverse to the interests of others in the same business."[58] The Court considered such statutes an unconstitutional interference with personal liberty and private property and a denial of rights safeguarded by the Due Process Clause of the Fifth Amendment.

A few years later, however, the Court allowed Congress to give farmers a veto power over marketing proposals made by the Secretary of Agriculture, and in subsequent years it upheld the delegation of legislative power to private associations that possess attributes of sovereignty over their members.[59]

The breadth of contemporary delegation is underscored by the Economic Stabilization Act of 1970, which authorized the President "to issue such orders and regulations as he may deem appropriate to stabilize prices, rents, wages, and

54. Mourning v. Family Publications Service, Inc., 411 U.S. 356, 365–66, 371 (1973), concerning the Federal Reserve Board and the Truth in Lending Act.

55. Skinner v. Mid-America Pipeline Co., 490 U.S. 212 (1989).

56. Loving v. United States, 517 U.S. 748 (1996); Touby v. United States, 500 U.S. 160 (1991); Skinner v. Mid-America Pipeline Co., 490 U.S. at 218–24; Mistretta v. United States. 488 U.S. 361 (1989); Bowsher v. Synar, 478 U.S. 714, 720 (1986).

57. American Trucking Associations v. U.S. E.P.A., 175 F.3d 1027 (D.C. Cir. 1999); Whitman v. American Trucking Associations, 531 U.S. 457 (2001).

58. Carter v. Carter Coal Co., 298 U.S. 238, 311 (1936). In an earlier case the Court held that Congress had invalidly delegated to the states its power over maritime law; Knickerbocker Ice Co. v. Stewart, 253 U.S. 149, 163–66 (1920).

59. Currin v. Wallace, 306 U.S. 1 (1939). United States v. Mazurie, 419 U.S. 544 (1975), permitted a delegation of legislative power to Indian tribal councils. In Larkin v. Gendel's Den, Inc. 459 U.S. 116 (1982), the Court declared unconstitutional the delegation of state power to churches to veto liquor-license applications in their vicinity. For the broad scope of participation by private groups in the administration of federal laws, see George W. Liebmann, "Delegation to Private Parties in American Constitutional Law," 50 Ind. L. Rev. 650 (1975).

salaries at levels not less than those prevailing on May 25, 1970." The remaining sections of the act failed to provide procedural safeguards—for example, giving notice prior to issuing orders, providing a hearing for affected parties, and establishing machinery for judicial review.[60] President Nixon invoked that authority in 1971 to place a 90-day freeze on all prices, rents, wages, and salaries.[61]

Private parties appealed to the courts to have the act struck down as an invalid delegation of legislative power. In one of the principal cases, a three-judge court upheld the legislation by noting that some of the legislative guidelines had been included in committee reports and the legislative history of the act: "Whether legislative purposes are to be obtained from committee reports, or are set forth in a separate section of the text of the law, is largely a matter of drafting style."[62] Yet it is more than that. Agencies are bound by law; they are not bound as tightly by nonstatutory controls (a point pursued in the next section). Congress subsequently amended the 1970 statute to provide more explicit standards and guidelines.[63]

The scope of delegated power was at issue in 1975 when President Ford responded to the Arab oil embargo by placing a fee on imported oil. After an initial fee of a dollar per barrel, imposed on January 23, 1975, the plan called for additional dollar increases on March 1 and April 1. The Ford administration acknowledged that taxes and tariffs are legislative prerogatives, requiring specific authorization by statute, but argued that a "fee" on imported material "may be set for non-revenue purposes and need not be legislated."[64] For those who criticized that position as an undue delegation of legislative authority, a federal judge observed that the "non-delegation doctrine is almost a complete failure."[65] An appellate court reversed the decision, holding that there was no statutory authority for the fees imposed by President Ford. The fees would have generated an estimated $4.8 billion a year, which exceeded the total amount of revenue derived from customs in 1974.[66]

---

60. 84 Stat. 799 (1970).

61. 36 Fed. Reg. 15727 (1971).

62. Amalgamated Meat Cutters & Butcher Workers v. Connally, 337 F.Supp. 737, 750 (D.D.C. 1971) (three-judge court).

63. The 1970 act was extended by 84 Stat. 1468, 85 Stat. 13, and 85 Stat. 38 before being fundamentally rewritten by legislation in 1971 (85 Stat. 743), which provided for more specific standards, procedural safeguards, and judicial review. For critiques of the 1970 act, see Stanley H. Friedelbaum, "The 1971 Wage-Price Freeze: Unchallenged Presidential Power," 1974 Sup. Ct. Rev. 33.

64. Algonquin Sng., Inc. v. FEA, 518 F.2d 1051, 1060 (D.C. Cir. 1975).

65. Commonwealth of Massachusetts v. Simon, Civ. Action No. 75-0129, and Algonquin Sng., Inc. v. Simon, Civ. Action No. 75-0130 (D.D.C. February 21, 1975), reprinted at Algonquin Sng., Inc. v. FEA, 518 F.2d at 1064.

66. Algonquin Sng., Inc. v. FEA, 518 F.2d at 1056, 1061.

The Supreme Court, in upholding the fees, did not analyze the fee versus duty distinction. A unanimous Court held that the fees were within the scope of the Trade Expansion Act and its legislative history. The legislative standards "are clearly sufficient to meet any delegation doctrine attack."[67]

The Supreme Court has never discarded the nondelegation doctrine, but Justices who raise that banner usually do so in dissenting opinions, not opinions for the majority. The majority uses the doctrine indirectly to restrict the reach of a statute until Congress deliberately, consciously, and explicitly expands its coverage. For example, in 1958 the Court decided that Congress had not intended to give the Secretary of State the discretion he claimed: the power to deny passports to persons with alleged communist beliefs and associations. Referring to *Panama Refining,* the Court said that it would "construe narrowly all delegated powers that curtail or dilute" such basic freedoms as the right to travel.[68]

A similar approach was used by the Court in 1980 to invalidate a safety standard promulgated by the Secretary of Labor. Justice Stevens, joined by Chief Justice Burger and Justice Stewart, agreed that the construction placed on the statute by the government would have represented an unconstitutional delegation of legislative power. Justice Rehnquist, in a separate opinion, wrote an even stronger critique of the delegation.[69] The nondelegation doctrine has appeared in several dissents.[70]

Restrictions are more likely to come from the guidelines furnished by administrators who implement the programs rather than from more stringent legislative standards. As agencies gain experience, they should be able to generalize from this knowledge and announce rules for future actions.[71] Congress may intervene to control administrative action by changing authorization language or by placing limitations in appropriations bills.[72] If the President is-

67. FEA v. Algonquin Sng., Inc., 426 U.S. 548, 559 (1976).

68. Kent v. Dulles, 357 U.S. 116, 129 (1958).

69. Industrial Union v. American Petroleum, 448 U.S. 607, 646, 671–88 (1980). Justice Powell, joining the majority, withheld opinion on the delegation issue (at 664 n.1). See National Cable Television Assn. v. United States, 415 U.S. 336, 341–42 (1974), and FPC v. New England Power Co., 415 U.S. 345 (1974), where the Court read narrowly a congressional statute to avoid constitutional problems of delegation.

70. American Textile Mfrs. Inst. v. Donovan, 452 U.S. 490, 543–48 (1981) (Rehnquist, J., and Burger, C.J.); McGautha v. California, 402 U.S. 183, 251–52 (1971) (Brennan, J.); California Bankers Assn. v. Shultz, 416 U.S. 21, 90–93 (1974) (Douglas and Brennan, JJ.); Zemel v. Rusk, 381 U.S. 1, 21–22 (1965) (Douglas, J.); Arizona v. California, 373 U.S. 546, 624–27 (1963) (Harlan, Douglas, and Stewart, JJ.).

71. Henry J. Friendly, The Federal Administrative Agencies: The Need for Better Definition of Standards 14, 142–46 (1962); Kenneth Culp Davis, "A New Approach to Delegation," 36 U. Chi. L. Rev. 713 (1969); Kenneth Culp Davis, Discretionary Justice (1969).

72. Eisenberg v. Corning, 179 F.2d 275 (D.C. Cir. 1949).

sues an executive order pursuant to delegated authority and Congress wants to revoke the order, such action is well within its power.[73] Congress may decide to delegate with a shorter leash by including a termination date in a statute (so-called sunset or self-destruct provisions). One of the most effective checks on delegated authority results from the exercise of nonstatutory controls.

Nonstatutory Controls

Vagueness in legislation is partially remedied by details that appear in the legislative history, such as committee reports, committee hearings, floor debates, and correspondence from review committees. This material considerably narrows the range of agency discretion. For example, the Consolidated Appropriations Act for fiscal year 2005 contained what appeared to be an extraordinary grant of power: a lump sum of $1.8 billion for construction by the Corps of Engineers. But the two houses of Congress had quite specific projects in mind when arriving at that sum. The projects appeared in the conference report, organized state by state, so that each member knew the projects to be carried out.[74]

Nonstatutory controls meet the needs of both branches. Neither Congress nor the agencies are always certain of the specifics to be included in a statute. When judgments and predictions are wrong, the statute has to be rewritten. Putting guidelines and details in nonstatutory sources adds valuable flexibility to the legislative and administrative process. If an adjustment is necessary after a law is passed, committees and agencies can depart from the nonstatutory scheme without having to pass new legislation.

The system of nonstatutory controls is fragile. Much depends on a "keep the faith" attitude among agency officials. They must want to maintain the integrity of their budget presentations and preserve a relationship of trust and confidence with congressional committees. Violation of that trust may result in budget cutbacks, restrictive language in statutes, and itemized appropriations. The House Appropriations Committee has reminded the Pentagon that regardless of the lump-sum nature of defense appropriations, the department is expected to spend funds in accordance with its detailed budget justifications:

> In a strictly legal sense, the Department of Defense could utilize the funds appropriated for whatever programs were included under the individual appropriation accounts, but the relationship with the Con-

73. Feliciano v. United States, 297 F.Supp. 1356, 1358 (D. Puerto Rico 1969), aff'd, 422 F.2d 943 (1st Cir. 1970), cert. denied, 400 U.S. 823 (1970).

74. 118 Stat. 2935–36 (2004); H. Rept. No. 108-792, 108th Cong., 2d Sess. 887–95 (2004).

gress demands that the detailed justifications which are presented in support of budget requests be followed. To do otherwise would cause Congress to lose confidence in the requests made and probably result in reduced appropriations or line item appropriation bills.[75]

The evolution of nonstatutory controls is reflected in the history of "reprogramming" of funds by the Defense Department. Reprogramming consists of the shift of funds *within* an appropriations account (for example, within "Aircraft Procurement, Navy"). Shifting money from one account to another (such as from "Aircraft Procurement, Navy" to "Weapons Procurement, Navy") is called a "transfer" and requires statutory authority. Reprogramming is essentially a nonstatutory development. Control is exercised for the most part through committee reports, agency directives, and a complicated set of understandings between the two branches.

Several decades ago the extent of legislative control over defense reprogramming consisted basically of review by two members from each of the appropriations committees: the chairman of the defense appropriations subcommittee and the ranking minority member. Often the review was by staff members. Gradually the subcommittee began to place restrictions in the committee reports. The Defense Department incorporated these restrictions in its directives and instructions for agency officials. Congressional review began to include a greater number of committee members (extending to the full subcommittee and sometimes to the full committee) and eventually the authorization committees (Armed Services). On occasion the committees agreed that the decision was of such fundamental importance that it should be made on the floor of Congress rather than worked out as an agency-subcommittee agreement.[76]

Although the procedure has worked well, members of Congress uncovered attempts to circumvent the understandings. Particularly serious to Congress was a practice followed by some defense agencies. When funds for a program were not granted, other funds would be reprogrammed to it. This practice made a mockery of congressional action on the budget. After warnings were issued by the committees having jurisdiction (both Appropriations and Armed Services), a restriction was placed in the defense appropriations bill. For a number of years it has been the practice of Congress to insert this language: "no part of the funds in this Act shall be available to prepare or present a request to the Committees on Appropriations for reprogramming of funds,

75. H. Rept. No. 662, 93d Cong., 1st Sess. 16 (1973). For a general treatment of nonstatutory controls, see Michael W. Kirst, Government Without Making Laws (1969).

76. On the development of reprogramming, see Louis Fisher, Presidential Spending Power 80–98 (1975).

unless for higher priority items, based on unforeseen military requirements, than those for which originally appropriated and in no case where the item for which reprogramming is requested has been denied by the Congress."[77] Congress included the clause concerning "higher priority items" to discourage agencies from applying surplus funds to marginal and low-priority programs.

The tenuous nature of nonstatutory controls is underscored by an incident that occurred in 1975. The conference report on the defense appropriations bill directed the Navy Department to produce as its air combat fighter a derivative of the plane selected by the Air Force. The purpose was to increase commonality between the two services. Instead, the Navy picked an aircraft that was not a derivative. A contractor who had bid on the project with the expectation that the Navy would follow the understanding in the conference report lodged a formal protest with the General Accounting Office (GAO), claiming that the contract was null and void. The contractor insisted that directives placed in a conference report were binding on an agency.

The GAO disagreed. The Comptroller General ruled that such directives have legal force only when some ambiguity in the language of a public law requires recourse to the legislative history. Otherwise, agencies follow nonstatutory controls for practical, not legal, reasons. Agencies may ignore nonstatutory controls, but only "at the peril of strained relations with the Congress." To be legally binding, the directive on the Navy aircraft had to appear in the public law.[78]

Nonstatutory controls are weak when Congress sends contradictory signals, such as adopting one policy in an authorization bill while expressing something else in a committee report that accompanies an appropriations bill. In 1978 the Supreme Court declined to give preference to the latter: "Expressions of committees dealing with requests for appropriations cannot be equated with statutes enacted by Congress, particularly not in the circumstances presented by this case."[79] Two years later an appellate court held that statements in a conference report, suggesting that Congress did not contemplate the use of certain statutory authority, cannot negate that authority when Congress grants it with unambiguous statutory language.[80]

Nonstatutory controls play an especially binding role in the annual authorization bill that covers the U.S. intelligence community. Instead of publicly disclosing the amounts spent for these agencies, the House committee report

77. 118 Stat. 969, sec. 8005 (2004).

78. 55 Comp. Gen. 307, 319, 325–26 (1975). See also 55 Comp. Gen. 812 (1976) and 1 O.L.C. 133 (1977).

79. TVA v. Hill, 437 U.S. 153, 191 (1978). See also Demby v. Schweiker, 671 F.2d 507 (D.C. Cir. 1981), which favored statutory requirements over contrary instructions in a subsequent conference report and its legislative history.

80. Nat'l Small Shipments v. CAB, 618 F.2d 819 (D.C. Cir. 1980).

explains that a classified schedule ("directly incorporated into, and integral to, the bill itself") identifies the dollar amounts and personnel ceilings for all programs included in the bill.[81] Failure by the administration to honor the numbers in the classified schedule would destroy the agreement between the executive and legislative branches to maintain secret budgets for the Central Intelligence Agency (CIA) and other components of the intelligence establishment.

Administrative Legislation

Presidents are obligated under the Constitution to take care that the laws are "faithfully executed." The often conflicting and ambiguous passages within a law must be interpreted by executive officials to construct the purpose and intent of Congress. As important as intent is the *extent* to which a law is carried out. President Taft once remarked, "Let any one make the laws of the country, if I can construe them."[82]

To carry out the laws, administrators issue rules and regulations of their own. The courts long ago appreciated this need. Rules and regulations "must be received as the acts of the executive, and as such, be binding upon all within the sphere of his legal and constitutional authority."[83] Current law authorizes the head of an executive department or military department to prescribe regulations "for the government of his department, the conduct of its employees, the distribution and performance of its business, and the custody, use, and preservation of its records, papers, and property."[84]

These duties, primarily of a "housekeeping" nature, relate only distantly to the citizenry. Many regulations, however, bear directly on the public. It is here that administrative legislation must be restricted in its scope and application. Regulations are not supposed to be a substitute for the general policymaking that Congress enacts in the form of a public law.[85] Although administrative regulations are entitled to respect, the authority to prescribe rules and regulations is not an independent source of power to make laws. Agency rulemaking must rest on authority granted directly or indirectly by Congress.[86]

81. For example, H. Rept. No. 215 (part 1), 101st Cong., 1st Sess. 3 (1989).
82. William Howard Taft, Our Chief Magistrate and His Powers 78 (1916).
83. United States v. Eliason, 41 U.S. (16 Pet.) 291, 301 (1842). See also Boske v. Comingore, 177 U.S. 459 (1900).
84. 5 U.S.C. 301 (2000).
85. 6 Op. Att'y Gen. 10 (1853).
86. Chrysler Corp. v. Brown, 441 U.S. 281, 306–8 (1979). See also Lincoln Electric Co. v. Commissioner of Int. Rev., 190 F.2d 326, 330 (6th Cir. 1951); American Broadcasting Co. v. United States, 110 F.Supp. 374, 384 (S.D. N.Y. 1953), aff'd, 347 U.S. 284 (1954); and Independent Meat Packers Ass'n v. Butz, 526 F.2d 228, 234–36 (8th Cir. 1975), cert. denied, 424 U.S. 966 (1976).

Substantive policies must be published in the *Federal Register* or in the *Code of Federal Regulations,* not in internal agency manuals.[87] Unless agencies articulate and publish the standards and procedures that govern their decisions, the public is denied an opportunity for meaningful response and courts are unable to review the validity of agency actions.[88] Agencies may not legally ignore or depart from the policies and procedures that they promulgate.[89] They cannot violate their own regulations.

In theory, agency regulations carry into effect the will of Congress as expressed in a statute: "A regulation which does not do this, but operates to create a rule out of harmony with the statute, is a mere nullity."[90] In practice, ambiguities and vagueness in statutes create opportunities, if not the necessity, for creative rulemaking by agencies. When a statute contains contradictory demands, the courts have sanctioned the adoption of rules that "harmonize" the competing provisions.[91]

Presidential Proclamations

Proclamations by the President take two forms. Some are merely declaratory in effect, such as those issued to designate Earth Week, Law Day, National Farm Safety Week, and other issues of general interest. Other proclamations have substantive impact.

The first venture into presidential lawmaking occurred in 1793, when the Washington administration debated the merits of proclaiming America's neutrality in the war between England and France. In English law, proclamations had been used to give public notice of anything the king thought fit to advertise to his subjects. The issue was a delicate one for the Washington administration. Would a proclamation encroach on the power of Congress to decide questions of war and peace? George Washington asked his Cabinet whether he should call Congress back in special session, but they advised against it.[92] Relying for authority on the "law of nations," President Washington warned Americans to avoid any involvement in the war and instructed law officers to prosecute all persons who violated his proclamation.

87. Morton v. Ruiz, 415 U.S. 199 (1974).
88. Environmental Defense Fund v. Ruckelshaus, 439 F.2d 584, 598 (D.C. Cir. 1971); Historic Green Springs, Inc. v. Bergland, 497 F.Supp. 839, 854–57 (E.D. Va. 1980).
89. Vitarelli v. Seaton, 359 U.S. 535 (1959); Note, "Violations by Agencies of Their Own Regulations," 87 Harv. L. Rev. 629 (1974).
90. Manhattan Co. v. Commissioner, 297 U.S. 129, 134 (1936). See Ernst & Ernst v. Hochfelder, 425 U.S. 185, 213–14 (1976), and Batterton v. Francis, 432 U.S. 416, 425 n.9 (1977).
91. Citizens to Save Spencer City v. EPA, 600 F.2d 844 (D.C. Cir. 1979).
92. 32 The Writings of George Washington 420–21 n. 14.

Washington's attempt at lawmaking had a built-in limitation: enforcing the proclamation needed statutory backing. When Gideon Henfield was prosecuted for violating the proclamation, he was acquitted because jurors rebelled against the idea of convicting someone for a crime established by a proclamation.[93] With no statute to cite, the government dropped other prosecutions.[94] After Congress returned in December, Washington told the two houses that it rested with "the wisdom of Congress to correct, improve, or enforce" the policy his proclamation had established.[95] In short, he needed law from the legislative branch. Congress responded by passing the Neutrality Act of 1794, giving the administration the firm legal footing it needed to prosecute violators.

Recent decades have witnessed frequent use of proclamations to announce major initiatives in the field of international trade. President Nixon's "New Economic Policy," unveiled in 1971, included a 10 percent surcharge placed on articles imported into the United States.[96] Importers turned to the Customs Court for relief, contending that the surcharge went beyond the scope of any authority delegated to the President by Congress. The Customs Court, in 1974, agreed with the importers and declared the surcharge invalid. The proclamation "arrogated unto the President a power beyond the scope of any authority delegated to him by the Congress."[97] Had this decision stood, the federal government would have had to repay about $500 million it had collected.[98]

A year later, however, the Court of Customs and Patents Appeals reversed the decision, concluding that the President had acted within the power delegated to him by the Trading with the Enemy Act (TWEA). Neither Proclamation 4074 nor the administration's legal defense (opinion of the General Counsel of the Treasury, September 29, 1971) had referred to the TWEA. Furthermore, nothing in the TWEA specifically authorized a surcharge. The appeals court was not surprised that Congress "did not *specify* that the President could use a surcharge in a national emergency. Having left the battlefield, it would hardly do to dictate all the weapons to be used in the fight." It was also "self-evident" to the court that the surcharge had overtones of foreign

93. Francis Wharton, State Trials of the United States During the Administrations of Washington and Adams 84–85, 88 (1849).

94. 2 John Marshall, The Life of George Washington 273 (1832).

95. Annals of Congress, 3d Cong., 1–2 Sess. 11 (1793).

96. Public Papers of the Presidents, 1971, at 889. Proclamation 4074, 36 Fed. Reg. 15724 (1971). The surcharge was terminated December 20, 1971; Proclamation 4098, 36 Fed. Reg. 24201 (1971).

97. Yoshida Int'l, Inc. v. United States, 378 F.Supp. 1155, 1167 (Cust. Ct. 1974).

98. Washington Post, July 9, 1974, at A1:5.

relations and foreign policy, invoking *Curtiss-Wright* for congressional authority to delegate more broadly in foreign affairs than in domestic affairs.[99]

This reliance was misplaced. *Curtiss-Wright* involved a specific delegation
of authority to prevent arms shipments to other regions. The TWEA, as the
court acknowledged, did not specifically delegate authority to impose a surcharge. Moreover, imposition of a surcharge is peculiarly within the province
of Congress to levy tariffs and regulate foreign commerce.[100]

Less successful was Proclamation 4744, issued by President Carter in 1980
to impose a fee on imported oil. This action, which would have increased the
price of gasoline by ten cents a gallon, was meant to lower domestic gasoline
consumption. A district court ruled that the proclamation "does not fall within
the inherent powers of the President, is not sanctioned by the statutes cited by
Defendants [the Department of Energy], and is contrary to manifest Congressional intent." At the time the court handed down its decision, Congress was about
to strip Carter of his authority to impose fees or quotas on imported oil.[101]

Executive Orders

A more far-reaching instrument for administrative legislation is the executive order. No one knows how many have been issued; in the early years they
were not numbered. In 1907 the State Department began assigning each
order a number and filing it in chronological order. By October 13, 2006,
the numbered series had reached 13,412. That total is understated, however,
since an administration that discovered executive orders from prior decades
had to shoehorn them into the existing series by using letters or fractions (for
example, Executive Order 106½, Executive Order 103A). Estimates of the
unnumbered executive orders range from 15,000 to as high as 50,000.[102]

99. United States v. Yoshida Int'l, Inc., 526 F.2d 560, 576, 580–82 (Ct. Cust. and Pat. App.
1975); see p. 572 and n. 13 for the lack of inherent presidential power to regulate commerce or
to set tariffs. In a separate action (*Alcan Aluminum Corp. v. United States*), challenging the appellate court decision in *Yoshida*, the Supreme Court denied certiorari; 429 U.S. 986 (1976).

100. When a statute prescribes a specific procedure and the President elects to follow a different course, a presidential proclamation is illegal and void. Pritchard & Co. v. United States,
167 F.Supp. 272 (Cust. Ct. 1958); Carl Zeiss, Inc. v. United States, 76 F.2d 412 (Cust. and
Pat. App. 1935).

101. Independent Gasoline Marketers Council v. Duncan, 492 F.Supp. 614, 620–21
(D.D.C. 1980); "Oil Import Fees: The Administration of the Program and Its Impact," hearings before the House Committee on Ways and Means, 96th Cong., 2d Sess. (1980).

102. On the numbering of executive orders, see "Presidential Executive Orders," compiled
by WPA Historical Records Survey (2 vols., 1944), at viii. On the estimates, see "Executive
Orders and Proclamations: A Study of a Use of Presidential Power," printed for the House
Committee on Government Operations, 85th Cong., 1st Sess. 37 (1957). A partial list of unnumbered orders appears in "List and Index of Presidential Executive Orders (Unnumbered

In June 1941, before the attack on Pearl Harbor and America's entry into World War II, President Roosevelt resorted to executive orders to seize North American Aviation's plant in California. He based his action not on statutory authority but on the general powers vested in him "by the Constitution and laws of the United States, as President of the United States of America and Commander in Chief of the Army and Navy of the United States." He invoked those same powers when he seized shipbuilding companies, a cable company, a shell plant, and almost 4,000 coal companies.[103] Not until 1943 did Congress pass the War Labor Disputes Act to provide statutory authority for the presidential seizure of plants, mines, and other facilities. Congress invoked its power of the purse in 1944 by passing the "Russell Amendment" to prevent Presidents from using appropriated funds to finance agencies created by executive order unless Congress had specifically appropriated for the agency or specifically authorized the expenditure of funds by it.[104]

Beginning with Franklin Roosevelt, Presidents used executive orders to articulate and implement an antidiscrimination policy. Roosevelt threatened to withhold contracts from employers that failed to satisfy equal employment provisions in federal contracts. His executive order prohibited discrimination in the employment of workers in "defense industries or government because of race, creed, color, or national origin." Presidents Truman and Eisenhower continued that policy, and Kennedy threatened to cancel contracts as a means of forcing compliance with federal equal employment standards. Executive Order 11246, issued by President Johnson, established the administrative structure for carrying out the nondiscrimination clause.[105]

Opponents of Executive Order 11246 objected that it violated statutory policy. In Title VII of the Civil Rights Act of 1964, Congress prohibited employment discrimination on the basis of race, color, religion, sex, or national origin. During the Nixon administration, the "Philadelphia Plan" (promul-

Series), 1789–1941," New Jersey Historical Records Survey, Work Projects Administration (1943). Under Title 3 of the *Code of Federal Regulations,* five-year compilations are published containing the full text of all proclamations and executive orders issued from 1936 to the present.

103. See 6 Fed. Reg. 2777 (1941) and John L. Blackmun Jr., Presidential Seizure in Labor Disputes (1967).

104. 58 Stat. 387, sec. 213 (1944); 31 U.S.C. 1347 (2000). This restriction applies to "action agencies" that exercise governmental power, not to advisory bodies; 3 Op. O.L.C. 263 (1979). The "Russell Amendment" was severely weakened by legislation passed in 2000; see 5 U.S.C. 3161 (2000).

105. Executive Order (hereafter E.O.) 8802, 6 Fed. Reg. 3109 (1941); E.O. 10308, 16 Fed. Reg. 12303 (1951); E.O. 10479, 18 Fed. Reg. 4899 (1953); E.O. 10925, 26 Fed. Reg. 1977 (1961); E.O. 11246, 30 Fed. Reg. 12319 (1965). See also James E. Remmert, "Executive Order 11,246: Executive Encroachment," 55 Am. Bar Asso. J. 1037 (1969), and Ruth H. Morgan, The President and Civil Rights: Policy-Making by Executive Order (1970).

gated pursuant to Executive Order 11246) required contractors to set specific goals for hiring members of minority groups as a condition for working on federally assisted projects. The Comptroller General decided that the plan conflicted with Title VII. To the Comptroller General, it was immaterial whether the administration designated the hiring commitment as a "goal" or a "quota." Whatever the name, the practice violated the 1964 act.[106]

The Secretary of Labor disagreed. He said that interpretation of the Civil Rights Act had been vested by Congress in the Department of Justice, which had approved the plan as consistent with the act. The Secretary also claimed that the Comptroller General failed to recognize executive orders "as an independent source of law."[107] Certain members of Congress declared their opposition to the plan. A Senate subcommittee charged in 1971 that it was a "blatant case of usurpation of the legislative function by the executive branch."[108]

Federal courts upheld the legality of the plan as well as the executive order that placed it in operation. This use of presidential power was supported partly by the chief executive's implied power—as it relates to procurement policy—to ensure that "the largest possible pool of qualified manpower be available for the accomplishment" of federal projects.[109] However, a number of decisions handed down since that time have circumscribed the reach of Executive Order 11246.[110]

Encroaching on Congress's prerogative of the purse was an executive order by President Kennedy in 1961 establishing the Peace Corps. Seven months went by before Congress appropriated funds for the agency. In the meantime, Kennedy financed the agency by drawing on contingency funds made available by the Mutual Security Act.[111]

---

106. 49 Comp. Gen. 59 (1969).

107. 115 Cong. Rec. 23740 (1969); 42 Op. Att'y Gen. 402 (1969).

108. See "Congressional Oversight of Administrative Agencies: The Philadelphia Plan," report of the Senate Judiciary Committee prepared by its Subcommittee on Separation of Powers, 92d Cong., 1st Sess. 13 (Comm. Print 1971).

109. Contractors Ass'n of Eastern Pa. v. Secretary of Labor, 442 F.2d 159, 171 (3d Cir. 1971), cert. denied, 404 U.S. 854 (1971). See also Contractors Ass'n of Eastern Pa. v. Secretary of Labor, 311 F.Supp. 1002 (E.D. Pa. 1970), and Robert P. Schuwerk, "The Philadelphia Plan: A Study in the Dynamics of Executive Power," 39 U. Chi. L. Rev. 723 (1972).

110. United States v. East Texas Motor Fr. System, 564 F.2d 179 (5th Cir. 1977); Chrysler Corp. v. Brown, 441 U.S. 281 (1979); Liberty Mutual Insurance Co. v. Friedman, 639 F.2d 164 (4th Cir. 1981). See also "Committee Analysis of Executive Order 11246 (The Affirmative Action Program)," prepared by the Senate Committee on Labor and Human Resources, 97th Cong., 2d Sess. (Comm. Print April 1982), and Andrée Kahn Blumstein, "Doing Good the Wrong Way: The Case for Delimiting Presidential Power Under Executive Order No. 11,246," 33 Vand. L. Rev. 921 (1980).

111. E.O. 10924, 26 Fed. Reg. 1789 (1961). Appropriation: 75 Stat. 721 (1961). See also H. Rept. No. 1115, 87th Cong., 1st Sess. 66 (1961).

Another controversial executive order involved the Subversive Activities Control Board (SACB), established by President Truman in 1950 to investigate communist activities. The board required the public registration of "communist-action" and "communist-front" organizations. Once stigmatized in this fashion, members of such organizations became subject to various penalties. A series of court decisions held that the registration feature violated the Fifth Amendment prohibition against self-incrimination. Congress rejuvenated the board in 1968 by authorizing it to determine, through hearings, whether individuals and organizations were communist. The following year an appellate court declared that the new procedure violated the First Amendment freedom of association. After the Supreme Court refused to review this decision, the board faced extinction.[112]

The SACB gained a new lease on life in 1971 when President Nixon issued an executive order expanding the board's power and field of inquiry.[113] Senator Sam Ervin, challenging the order, introduced a resolution stating that the President had no power "to alter by Executive order the content or effect of legislation enacted by Congress." The Senate adopted Ervin's amendment to prohibit the use of appropriated funds to implement the executive order. Congressman Don Edwards attempted to instruct House conferees to accept the Ervin amendment, but his motion was tabled.[114]

The dispute continued the next year when the House passed a bill to legitimate the executive order. Senator Proxmire offered an amendment to delete $450,000 of the SACB's funds (its entire budget). During debate on the amendment, Senator Ervin remarked that the board had held hearings on 111 cases the previous year, devoting about 48 seconds to each case. "That is all they did last year," Ervin said, "except draw their breath and their salaries."[115] After the Senate adopted the Proxmire amendment, House and Senate conferees compromised by providing the board with $350,000 but expressly pro-

112. The SACB, created by 64 Stat. 997 (1950), was rejuvenated by 81 Stat. 765 (1968). For court cases on the SACB, see Communist Party of the United States v. SACB, 367 U.S. 1 (1961); Albertson v. SACB, 382 U.S. 70 (1965); United States v. Robel, 389 U.S. 258 (1967); and Boorda v. SACB, 421 F.2d 1142 (D.C. Cir. 1969), cert. denied, 397 U.S. 1042 (1970).

113. E.O. 11605, 36 Fed. Reg. 12831 (1971). A federal court, without deciding the issue, noted that there was no precedent for a President "delegating to an independent, quasi-judicial body far-reaching responsibilities different in form and effect from those specifically given that body when created by the Congress"; American Servicemen's Union v. Mitchell, 54 F.R.D. 14, 17 (D.D.C. 1972).

114. Ervin: S. Res. 163, 92d Cong., 1st Sess. (1971), and 117 Cong. Rec. 30248 (1971). Adoption of his amendment: 117 Cong. Rec. 25898–902 (1971). Edwards: id. at 27305–12. A Proxmire amendment to delete $450,000 for the SACB was rejected, 41 to 47; id. at 25888–98.

115. House passage: 118 Cong. Rec. 19075–103 (1972). Proxmire amendment: id. at 21053–74. Ervin remark: id. at 21063–64.

hibiting it from using any of the funds to carry out the executive order.[116] Beginning with the fiscal year 1974 budget, the administration did not even bother to request funds for the SACB.

Executive orders are a source of law only when they draw upon the constitutional powers of the President or powers expressly delegated by Congress. Actions that exceed those bounds have been struck down by the courts. When executive orders lack statutory support, they have been held by the courts to be without the force and effect of law. Executive orders may not supersede a statute or override contradictory congressional expressions.[117]

The major example of the judiciary striking down an executive order is the Steel Seizure Case of 1952, which held that President Truman's attempt to seize the steel mills of the nation to prosecute the war in Korea had no statutory or constitutional basis.[118] When departmental policies are contrary to due process, they have been held invalid. For instance, in *Cole v. Young* (1956), the Supreme Court decided that the standard prescribed by an executive order—directed against "disloyal" civilian employees in the Department of Health, Education, and Welfare—did not conform to statutory provisions.[119]

In 1994 President Clinton tried to enact legislation that would ban employers from replacing striking workers. The measure, blocked by a Republican-led filibuster in the Senate, was set aside for later action. However, when Republican victories in the fall elections gave them control of Congress, the administration became convinced that legislative action would be impossible. On March 8, 1995, acting administratively rather than legislatively, Clinton issued Executive Order 12954 to declare that it was the policy of the executive branch "in procuring goods and services that, to ensure the economical and efficient administration and completion of Federal Government contracts, contracting agencies shall not contract with employers that permanently replace lawfully striking employees."[120] The order applied to all federal contracts over $100,000.

116. 86 Stat. 1134, sec. 706 (1972). See also "President Nixon's Executive Order 11605 Relating to the Subversive Activities Control Board," hearings before the Senate Committee on the Judiciary, 92d Cong., 1st Sess. (1971).

117. Lack of statutory support: Manhattan-Bronx Postal Union v. Gronouski, 350 F.2d 451 (D.C. Cir. 1965), cert. denied, 382 U.S. 978 (1966); Stevens v. Carey, 483 F.2d 188 (7th Cir. 1973); Independent Meat Packers Ass'n v. Butz, 526 F.2d 228, 234–36 (8th Cir. 1975), cert. denied, 424 U.S. 966 (1976). Conflicts with statutory policy: Marks v. CIA, 590 F.2d 997, 1003 (D.C. Cir. 1978); Weber v. Kaiser Aluminum & Chemical Corp., 563 F.2d 216, 227 (5th Cir. 1977), rev'd on other grounds, Steelworkers v. Weber, 443 U.S. 193 (1979).

118. Youngstown Co. v. Sawyer, 343 U.S. 579 (1952).

119. Cole v. Young, 351 U.S. 536, 555 (1956). Other executive orders or proclamations were struck down in Little v. Barreme, 2 Cr. 170 (1804); United States v. Symonds, 120 U.S. 46 (1887); Panama Refining Co. v. Ryan, 293 U.S. 388, 433 (1935); and Schechter Corp. v. United States, 295 U.S. 495, 525–26 (1935).

120. 60 Fed. Reg. 13023 (1995).

The Republicans proposed legislation that would let companies continue to hire permanent replacements for striking workers and introduced an amendment to prohibit the Labor Department from spending appropriated funds to enforce the executive order. Another filibuster, this time by Senate Democrats, prevented action on the legislation to authorize the hiring of permanent replacements, and Clinton said that he would veto any bill that attempted to overturn his order. Meanwhile, the Chamber of Commerce had taken the issue to court to challenge the legality of Clinton's order. On February 2, 1996, the D.C. Circuit held that the order was an improper attempt to set broad labor policy and violated the National Labor Relations Act by interfering with the right of private employers to hire replacements.[121]

On May 14, 1998, President Clinton issued Executive Order 13083, setting forth principles of federalism to be followed by executive departments and agencies. The order identified nine conditions to justify federal intervention or preemption.[122] A number of state and local governmental organizations objected to the principles expressed in the order and asked that it be withdrawn. The White House offered to do some rewriting, with state and local input, but later withdrew the order. By a vote of 417 to 2, the House passed an amendment to prohibit the use of any funds to implement the order.[123] The funds cutoff became law in an omnibus appropriations bill.[124] Also in 1998, a House effort to block funding of a Clinton executive order to prohibit discrimination based on "sexual orientation" in the federal civilian workforce failed by a vote of 176 to 252.[125]

An effort to use litigation to stymie another Clinton executive order was unsuccessful. In 1997 Clinton issued Executive Order 13061, announcing a national policy to restore and protect America's rivers. Legislative initiatives taken in each house to challenge the order were never completed. In 1998 a federal court tossed out a case brought by several members of Congress, who charged that the order violated the Constitution by attempting to create legislation without an express delegation by Congress. The court held that the lawmakers had not alleged sufficient concrete injury to establish standing to maintain the suit. The injuries were "clearly institutional, rather than personal," and the quality of their injury was "too abstract and not sufficiently specific to support a finding of standing."[126] That decision was upheld on appeal.[127]

121. Chamber of Commerce v. Reich, 74 F.3d 1322 (D.C. Cir. 1996).
122. 63 Fed. Reg. 27651 (1998).
123. 144 Cong. Rec. 18950–58, 18967 (1998).
124. 112 Stat. 2681-116, sec. 623 (1998).
125. 144 Cong. Rec. 18959–65, 18966–67 (1998).
126. Chenoweth v. Clinton, 997 F.Supp. 36, 38, 39 (D.D.C. 1998).
127. Chenoweth v. Clinton, 181 F.3d 112 (D.C. Cir. 1999).

Congressional and scholarly interest in executive orders and proclamations has increased dramatically over the past decade. Two House committees held hearings in 1999 to explore the impact of these executive instruments on legislative prerogatives,[128] and several books have taken a close look at how executive orders, proclamations, national security directives, and presidential signing statements influence executive power, the legislative process, the system of checks and balances, and constitutional government.[129]

The intense legislative scrutiny of Clinton's executive orders and proclamations did not carry over into the administration of George W. Bush. The two houses of Congress, both Republican controlled, exercised much less oversight of his presidential initiatives. Some legislative interest was directed toward Executive Order 13233, which made extensive changes to the Presidential Records Act of 1978. The effect of the order was to decrease the statutory authority of the archivist to permit access to presidential records.[130] Congressional scrutiny occurred mainly in the House, where the Government Reform Committee held extensive hearings and reported legislation (H.R. 4187) in 2002 to supersede the executive order.[131] The full House never acted on the bill, and the Senate showed little interest in the controversy. A district court decided part of the dispute in 2004, but glacial progress characterized efforts to litigate the legal and constitutional questions.[132]

Secret Executive Directives

The Iran-Contra hearings in 1987 called attention to a significant number of secret executive directives called National Security Decision Directives (NSDDs).

128. "Congressional Limitation of Executive Orders," hearing before the Subcommittee on Commercial and Administrative Law of the House Committee on the Judiciary, 106th Cong,, 1st Sess. (1999); "Executive Orders," hearing before the Subcommittee on Legislative and Budget Process of the House Committee on Rules, 106th Cong., 1st Sess. (1999).

129. Kenneth R. Mayer, With the Stroke of a Pen: Executive Orders and Presidential Power (2001); Phillip J. Cooper, By Order of the President: The Use and Abuse of Executive Direct Action (2002); William G. Howell, Power Without Persuasion: The Politics of Direct Presidential Action (2003); and Adam L. Warber, Executive Orders and the Modern Presidency: Legislating from the Oval Office (2006).

130. 66 Fed. Reg. 56025 (2001).

131. H. Rept. No. 107-790, 107th Cong., 2d Sess. (2002).

132. American Historical Assn. v. National Archives and Records Administration, 310 F.Supp.2d 216 (D.D.C. 2004). See Jonathan Turley, "Presidential Papers and Popular Government: The Convergence of Constitutional and Property Theory in Claims of Ownership and Control of Presidential Records," 88 Corn. L. Rev. 651 (2003); Stephen H. Yuhan, "The Imperial Presidency Strikes Back: Executive Order 13,233, the National Archives, and the Capture of Presidential History," 79 N.Y.U. L. Rev. 1570 (2004).

Unlike proclamations and executive orders, they are not published in the *Federal Register,* even though they often have a direct impact on employees of the federal government and on private citizens. Some of the directives are publicly released; others remain confidential and classified. A study by the GAO in 1988 determined that at least 1,042 presidential directives had been issued since 1961, and only 247 of those had been publicly released. NSDDs allow the executive branch to set policy while skirting public, congressional, and judicial review.[133]

Under the 1980 Intelligence Oversight Act, Presidents were required to make a confidential "finding" that a covert operation was necessary. During the Iran-Contra affair, President Reagan issued an "oral" finding and tried to retroactively authorize what the CIA had done. In 1991, after an extensive investigation of Iran-Contra, Congress rewrote the Intelligence Oversight Act to tighten the procedures for findings. They must now be in writing, cannot have retroactive effect, and may not authorize any action that violates federal law or the Constitution. Findings are submitted to the intelligence committees or to a select group of eight members of Congress for review.[134] The purpose of these changes was to subject presidential orders in the field of covert operations to adequate checks, but the history of recent decades demonstrates the potential for executive abuses and the need for vigilant congressional oversight. Chapter 9 discusses how President Bush secretly ordered the National Security Agency to eavesdrop on international telephone calls after 9/11, with only a few members of Congress briefed about the program.

Procedural Controls

Because of the ubiquity and necessity of administrative regulations, they must be reconciled to the rule of law. Unlike legislatures, agencies are not representative bodies. They are not created to formulate and express a will. It is their duty to carry out the will announced by the legislative body. Agency officials may have greater expertise than legislators because of their opportunity to specialize, but this capability introduces a weakness into the administrative process: narrowness of view. Procedures are needed to bring forth, in systematic fashion, the full information and facts required for fair and intelligent rulemaking.[135]

Procedural safeguards are basic to the maintenance of a legal system. Yet throughout the nineteenth century and well into the twentieth, due process

133. General Accounting Office, "The Use of Presidential Directives to Make and Implement U.S. Policy," GAO-NSIAD-89-31 (December 1988); Eve Pell, "The Backbone of Hidden Government," Nation, June 19, 1989.

134. 105 Stat. 441–45 (1991).

135. "Report of the Attorney General's Committee on Administrative Procedure," S. Doc. No. 8, 77th Cong., 1st Sess. 101–2 (1941).

in administrative matters depended on voluntary agency actions and scattered statutory directives. It is remarkable that not until the 1930s were administrative regulations required to be published in a central document. The House Judiciary Committee in 1935 spoke of "utter chaos" regarding the publication and distribution of administrative rules and pronouncements.[136]

Congress passed legislation in 1935 to provide for the custody of federal documents and their publication in the *Federal Register.* Included among the documents to be published are all presidential proclamations and executive orders that have general applicability and legal effect and all documents or orders that prescribe a penalty. Based partly on the statutory authority vested in him by the Federal Register Act, President Roosevelt issued an executive order in 1936 that gave the Bureau of the Budget (now the Office of Management and Budget) the responsibility for reviewing all proposed executive orders and proclamations.[137]

Additional steps were needed to improve the process for drafting rules. In a major study published in 1937 for the Brownlow Committee, James Hart supported the use of advisory committees as one way to present administrators with the views of organized (and unorganized) interests. Other basic procedural safeguards to be used in the formulation of regulations were notice of a proposed regulation, formal hearings, publication of draft regulations, informal conferences with affected groups, and progression from voluntary to mandatory standards.[138] The Walter-Logan Bill, vetoed by President Roosevelt in 1940, represented the first general legislative effort to impose a uniform procedural standard on administrative agencies. Roosevelt vetoed it partly because he believed that legislation should await the report of the Attorney General's Committee on Administrative Procedure, which was released in 1941.

These studies, reinforced by congressional hearings, culminated in the Administrative Procedure Act (APA) of 1946, a landmark effort to guarantee fairness by establishing procedures and uniform standards for rulemaking. Some of the major features of the act include adequate notice to concerned parties, an opportunity for interested persons to submit material, and publication of the rule no less than 30 days before its effective date. The APA relies on the doctrine of separated powers by prohibiting investigative or prosecutorial personnel from participating in an agency's decision. Judicial review is available. Courts may find unlawful any agency action that is "arbitrary, capricious,

136. H. Rept. No. 280, 74th Cong., 1st Sess. 1–2 (1935). See also Erwin N. Griswold, "Government in Ignorance of the Law—A Plea for Better Publication of Executive Legislation," 48 Harv. L. Rev. 198 (1934).

137. 49 Stat. 500, sec. 5 (1935). Roosevelt's Executive Order 7298, February 18, 1936, appeared too early for the first volume of the *Federal Register.* It is reprinted in James Hart, "The Exercise of Rule-Making Power," The President's Committee on Administrative Management 355 (1937).

138. Hart, President's Committee, at 339–42.

an abuse of discretion, or otherwise not in accordance with law" and "contrary to constitutional right, power, privilege, or immunity."[139] Agencies may circumvent the notice-and-comment requirement of the APA by issuing "interpretive rules" and "general statements of policy," but these actions lack the force and effect of law.[140]

Although executive orders and proclamations are published in the *Federal Register,* their announcement is not expected to be preceded by formal notice, hearings, or other APA procedures required for agency regulations.[141] Draft copies are sometimes made available to Congress and the public for notice and comment, but such initiatives are voluntary on the part of the President.[142] Recent case law suggests that Congress can impose notice-and-comment requirements on presidential proclamations and executive orders that are issued to implement statutory policy, provided Congress does so explicitly.[143]

The ambiguity of "enumerated" and "separated" powers is nowhere more evident than in the assignment of the legislative power. Much of the original legislative power vested in Congress is now exercised, as a practical matter, by executive agencies, independent commissions, and the courts. The President's legislative power, invoked on rare occasions in the early decades, is now discharged on a regular basis throughout the year in the form of executive orders, proclamations, and other instruments of executive lawmaking. In self-defense, Congress has developed a complex system that depends on procedural guidelines for agency action, judicial review, committee and subcommittee oversight, and a constantly evolving structure of informal, nonstatutory controls.

139. 60 Stat. 237, sec. 10(e) (1946); 5 U.S.C. 500–706 (2000).

140. Chrysler Corp. v. Brown, 441 U.S. 281, 313–15 (1979).

141. Metzenbaum v. Edwards, 510 F.Supp. 609, 611 (D.D.C. 1981). See also Harold H. Bruff, "Judicial Review and the President's Statutory Powers," 68 Va. L. Rev. 1, 18–24 (1982).

142. A rare, if not unprecedented, example of an executive order published in draft form in the *Federal Register* for notice and comment was an order by President Carter to improve federal regulations. It was first printed at 42 Fed. Reg. 59740 (1977), and 43 Fed. Reg. 12661 (1978) included an analysis of public comments; it was published in final form as Executive Order 12044 four months after its original publication.

143. In United States v. Wayte, 549 F.Supp. 1376, 1389–91 (C.D. Cal. 1982), a district judge held that President Carter's Proclamation 4771 on draft registration was invalid for failure to comply with notice-and-comment requirements of the Military Selective Service Act. Although reversed in United States v. Wayte, 710 F.2d 1385, 1388–89 (9th Cir. 1983), both decisions recognize the authority of Congress to make such a requirement. In United States v. Martin, 557 F.Supp. 681 (N.D. Iowa 1982), concerning the same issue, another district judge said that statutes enacted by Congress "are not subjected to notice and comment periods and no reason appears why the same should not be true for presidential proclamations" (at 690). This analogy ignores the constitutional grant of legislative power to Congress and the checks that operate on that power, including bicameralism and the presidential veto, which are not available to constrain presidential proclamations and executive orders.

5

VETOES: PRESIDENTIAL AND LEGISLATIVE

It is customary today to associate the veto with executive power, but the veto has played a more general role in government. Roman tribunes uttered "veto" to protect the plebs from injustice at the hands of the patricians.[1] Seventeenth-century Poland adopted a *liberum veto,* permitting a single deputy of the legislature to exclaim, "I disapprove." The New York Constitution of 1777 lodged the veto power in a Council of Revision consisting of the governor, chancellor, and judges of the supreme court.[2] The framers of the American Constitution debated (and rejected) the idea of a joint revisionary power, to be shared between the President and the Supreme Court, as a way to preserve their independence from Congress.[3]

The veto, as an instrument to prevent or postpone governmental action, is exercised today on many fronts: the executive veto provided in the Constitution, the ability of courts to strike down legislative and executive actions as invalid, statutes that vest in governors and private parties a veto power, and Senate vetoes of treaties and appointments. The "item veto" remains a topic of perennial interest. A "legislative veto" was available to Congress until the Supreme Court declared it unconstitutional in 1983, but functional equivalents persist. Presidential signing statements, which date back at least to the 1830s, have attracted new interest in recent decades.

The Presidential Veto

The framers of the Constitution gave short shrift to the proposal for an absolute executive veto. They had only to recall the first charge leveled against King George III in the Declaration of Independence: "He has refused his Assent to Laws, the most wholesome and necessary for the common good." James Wilson and Alexander Hamilton thought that an absolute veto would be acceptable for the American Presidency, but delegates at the Philadelphia convention rejected the proposal, ten states against and not a single one in

1. Charles J. Zinn, The Veto Power of the President 1 (1951), a committee print for the use of the House Committee on the Judiciary.
2. Federalist 73; Charles C. Thach Jr., The Creation of the Presidency 35–41 (1923).
3. 1 Farrand 105, 108, 139; 2 Farrand 77.

favor. The President received a qualified veto, subject to an override by a two-thirds majority of each house of Congress.[4]

Some of the Antifederalists, espousing a literalist view of the separation doctrine, regarded the executive veto as an encroachment on the legislature. One critic of the Constitution called it "a political error of the greatest magnitude, to allow the executive power a negative, or in fact any kind of control over the proceedings of the legislature."[5] To this kind of criticism Hamilton replied, in Federalist 73, that the veto was necessary to protect the President against the "depredations" of the legislature: "He might gradually be stripped of his authorities by successive resolutions or annihilated by a single vote. And in the one mode or the other, the legislative and executive powers might speedily come to be blended in the same hands."

The Purpose of the Veto

Hamilton identified one of the principal objectives of the veto: to protect the executive from legislative encroachment. Use of the veto for other reasons has produced periodic waves of censure. Edward Pessen, professor of history at Baruch College, concluded that the veto power exercised by Ford, Nixon, Johnson, and almost all Presidents since Andrew Jackson has been "utterly at odds" with the intentions of the framers. Madison and Hamilton, he said, believed that the veto would be used for limited purposes: "protection of the integrity of the Presidential office and rejection of flagrantly unconstitutional legislation."[6]

Charles L. Black Jr., professor of law at Yale University, also argued that President Ford misused the veto. This power may be applied "only rarely, and certainly not as a means of systematic policy control over the legislative branch, on matters constitutionally indifferent and not menacing the President's independence."[7] According to Black, the early vetoes mainly protected the integrity of the President's office.

Should the veto be used sparingly and invoked primarily to protect the President's office? These assertions are not well-founded. With regard to the

4. 1 Farrand 96–104. George Reed of Delaware later proposed that the President be given an absolute veto; his motion was rejected, 1 to 9 (2 Farrand 200). The delegates voted on August 15 to require a three-fourths majority for an override, voting 6 to 4 (id. at 301), but reversed themselves on September 12 by an identical vote in support of the two-thirds requirement (id. at 582–83, 585–87).

5. Anonymous "William Penn" writing in the *Philadelphia Independent Gazetteer*, January 3, 1788, cited by Morton Borden, ed., The Antifederalist Papers 210 (1965).

6. Edward Pessen, "The Arrogant Veto," Nation, August 30, 1975, at 133–37.

7. Charles L. Black Jr., "Some Thoughts on the Veto," 40 Law and Contemp. Prob. 87, 90 (1976).

frequency of vetoes, the framers could not have anticipated the vast range of activities to be carried out by the federal government, the outpouring of legislation that resulted, and the great mass of private bills. On a single day in 1886 President Cleveland received nearly 240 private bills granting new pensions for veterans, increasing their benefits, or restoring old names to the list. Many of the bills were so indefensible that they invited a veto.[8] Private bills did not bombard the early Presidents. Although congressional efforts to override vetoes of public bills are common, Congress generally concedes vetoes of private bills without a vote.[9]

The framers did not foresee the emergence of party politics, the possibility that different parties could control Congress and the White House, and how this would encourage vetoes. Congress has also provoked numerous vetoes by passing hundreds of measures in the closing days of a session.[10] Another stimulus for vetoes is the congressional practice of tacking irrelevant amendments ("riders") onto appropriations bills. Since appropriations are necessary for the operation of government, members use riders in the hope of gaining passage of a legislative idea that might not survive on its own merits. Rutherford B. Hayes vigorously opposed this tactic, which he regarded as a coercive measure designed to strip him of the veto power.[11] After a series of vetoes he prevailed, but Presidents continue to receive omnibus bills that are amalgams of disparate elements. These factors help explain the growth in the number of presidential vetoes.

What of the second proposition: that vetoes should be used primarily to protect the President's office? Justice White, in a 1976 opinion, claimed that the veto's principal aim was not to provide "another check against poor legislation" but rather to protect the executive against legislative encroachments.[12] Some delegates to the Philadelphia convention, including Elbridge Gerry, did regard the veto primarily as an instrument to defend the executive branch, not the general interest. But Madison viewed the power in more generous terms. The veto existed "to restrain the Legislature from encroaching on the other co-ordinate Departments, or on the rights of the people at large; or from passing laws unwise in their principle, or incorrect in their form."[13] Hamilton, in Federalist 73, defended the veto as necessary not only to protect the President but also to furnish "an additional security against the enaction of improper

---

8. 10 Richardson 5001–2 (May 8, 1886) and 5020–40 (June 21–23, 1886).

9. Clarence A. Berdahl, "The President's Veto of Private Bills," 52 Pol. Sci. Q. 505 (1937).

10. John D. Long, "The Use and Abuse of the Veto Power," 4 Forum 253 (1887).

11. 9 Richardson 4475, 4488, 4494 (April 29, May 29, and June 23, 1879); T. Harry Williams, ed., Hayes: The Diary of a President 193–234 (1964).

12. Buckley v. Valeo, 424 U.S. 1, 285 (1976), concurring in part and dissenting in part.

13. 2 Farrand 586; 1 Farrand 139. See also 2 Farrand 74, 587, and 4 Farrand 81.

laws. It establishes a salutary check upon the legislative body, calculated to
guard the community against the effects of faction, precipitancy, or of any
impulse unfriendly to the public good, which may happen to influence a
majority of that body." The veto would protect the community from the passage of "bad laws, through haste, inadvertence, or design." This larger view of
Madison and Hamilton has prevailed.

It is interesting that Gerald Ford's critics placed such heavy emphasis on the
use of the veto to protect the President's office. The historical record is quite to
the contrary. George Washington vetoed two bills—the first on constitutional
grounds (an apportionment bill) and the second because he thought the bill
so carelessly drafted and so unwise in substance that it should not become
law.[14] Neither bill affected the President's office. Professor Black suggested
that the second bill, involving the military, "may have been seen as a dangerous weakening of the country's military force, connected with the Commander-in-Chief power, so that the veto may well be thought to fall within
the category of defense of the presidential office."[15] This analysis depends on
too many "mays." The evidence is straightforward: Washington thought it a
bad bill.

John Adams and Thomas Jefferson did not use the veto power. The next
President, James Madison, relied on it five times for regular (as opposed to
pocket) vetoes. Four were for constitutional reasons (one involving trials in
district courts, one having to do with internal improvements, and two concerning church-state separation). The fifth bill, regarding the national bank,
seemed to Madison too poorly designed to accomplish its purpose.[16] Professor
Black stated that Madison vetoed the bank bill because it failed to provide
adequately for circulating money in time of war: "Perhaps, without stretching too much, such a veto may (like Washington's second veto) be connected
with protection of the President's role as Commander-in-Chief, and with the
effective execution of that power."[17] Again, too much stretching.

During this initial period of 28 years, covering four Presidents and seven
administrations, there were seven regular vetoes, five of them for constitutional reasons. Only one affected the independence of the executive: the district courts bill, which Madison vetoed in part because he thought it usurped
his appointment power.[18]

Ironically, the critics of the Ford administration borrowed unwittingly
from Whig theories of the nineteenth century. Increased use of the veto by

14. 1 Richardson 116, 203.
15. Black, "Some Thoughts on the Veto," at 90.
16. 1 Richardson 496, 569, 474, 475, 540 (in order of my discussion).
17. Black, "Some Thoughts on the Veto," at 90–91.
18. 2 Richardson 496.

Presidents Jackson and Tyler produced this basic complaint: the veto's limited purpose (to defend the Constitution) had been ignored by Presidents. Members of Congress tried to reduce the vote needed for an override from two-thirds to a simple majority, but all such proposals failed.[19]

During this period a number of chief executives announced their philosophy of the veto power. In 1841 President William Henry Harrison recommended a restrained use of the veto, for it was "preposterous" to believe that the President could better understand the wishes of the people than their own representatives. He conceded that Presidents were more independent of sectional pulls, however, and might have to veto legislation of a strongly local nature. Harrison justified vetoes to protect the Constitution, to defend the people from hasty legislation, and to preserve the rights of minorities from the effects of combinations.[20]

Harrison's successor, John Tyler, exercised the veto so frequently that his opponents in Congress introduced a resolution to impeach him. Among the grounds was this: "I charge him with the high crime and misdemeanor of withholding his assent to laws undispensable [sic] to the just operations of government, which involved no constitutional difficulty on his part."[21]

The Democratic Party supported a less restrictive view of the veto power. President Polk, in a detailed analysis in 1848, denied that the obligations of the President were "in any degree lessened by the prevalence of views different from his own in one or both Houses of Congress." The President had to do more than check hasty and inconsiderate legislation. If Congress, after full deliberation, agreed to measures that the President regarded as "subversive of the Constitution or of the vital interests of the country, it is his solemn duty to stand in the breach and resist them."[22] The Democratic platforms of 1844, 1848, 1852, and 1856 placed the party on record as being "decidedly opposed" to taking from the President his qualified veto power to suspend the passage of bills that lacked a two-thirds majority in each house. The veto power, claimed the platforms, had saved the American people from the "corrupt and tyrannical domination" of the U.S. Bank and the "corrupting system of general interest improvements."[23]

Zachary Taylor, who followed Polk to the White House, adhered to the Whig interpretation. He viewed the veto as "an extreme measure, to be resorted to only in extraordinary cases, as where it may become necessary to

19. Edward Campbell Mason, The Veto Power 133–37 (1890).
20. 3 Richardson 1866.
21. Cong. Globe, 27th Cong., 3d Sess. 144 (1843).
22. 6 Richardson 2512 (December 5, 1848).
23. Kirk H. Porter and Donald Bruce Johnson, National Party Platforms 4, 11, 17, 24 (1956).

defend the executive against the encroachments of the legislative power or to prevent hasty and inconsiderate or unconstitutional legislation."[24] The personal opinion of the President "ought not to control the action of Congress upon questions of Domestic policy; nor ought his opinion & objections to be interposed when questions of Constitutional power have been settled by the various Departments of government and acquiesced in by the people." On such subjects as the tariff, the currency, and internal improvements, "the will of the people as expressed through their Representatives in Congress ought to be . . . carried out and respected by the Executive."[25] That is essentially the position of Democrats who criticized Ford's veto record. Little did they know that they followed in the footsteps of Zachary Taylor.

Constitutional Procedures

If the President decides to withhold his signature from a bill, he is directed by Article I, Section 7, of the Constitution to return it "with his Objections to that House in which it shall have originated, who shall enter the Objections at large on their Journal, and proceed to reconsider it." If "two thirds of that House" agree to pass the bill, it is reconsidered by the other house, "and if approved by two thirds of that House, it shall become a Law." The ambiguities of this language were later clarified by legislative precedents and judicial decisions.

Must Congress immediately proceed to reconsider a veto? That was the practice under the early Presidents, when vetoes were rare, but Congress eventually adopted the practice of delaying a vote to permit the committees of jurisdiction to report their recommendations. If Congress decides not to contest a veto, it need not be reconsidered at all. It is established today that if a President vetoes a bill, Congress may schedule an override vote anytime during the two years of a Congress.[26]

What is meant by "two thirds of that House"—two-thirds of the total membership of each house, or merely two-thirds of a majority present? The House of Representatives decided on two-thirds of the members present, provided they formed a quorum.[27] This ruling was liberalized in 1912 when Speaker Champ Clark held that an override required two-thirds of the mem-

24. 6 Richardson 2561 (December 4, 1849).

25. Taylor's first "Allison letter," April 22, 1848, to his brother-in-law, John Stadler Allison, reprinted in Arthur M. Schlesinger Jr., ed., 2 History of American Presidential Elections 913–14 (1971).

26. "Pocket Veto Legislation," hearing before the House Committee on the Judiciary, 101st Cong., 2d Sess. 95–114 (1990).

27. 4 Hinds' Precedents §§3537–38 n.2.

bers present *and voting.* On this particular override attempt there were 174 yeas, 80 nays, and 10 present. The 174 did not represent two-thirds of the 264 present, but it did constitute two-thirds of the 254 voting. The override therefore carried.[28]

In 1919 the Supreme Court, referring to precedents established by Congress, decided that two-thirds of a quorum sufficed for an override. Two-thirds of "that House" meant a house organized and entitled to exert legislative power (a quorum).[29] The practice of Congress has been to require two-thirds of the members present and voting.

Another issue: Can a President sign a bill after Congress has recessed? If presidential approval of a bill is not strictly an executive function, being legislative in nature, must approval occur only when both houses are actually sitting for legislative functions? The Court in 1899 refused to accept that construction. If a President decides to sign a bill, no further action by Congress is required, so there is no need for it to sit.[30]

Taking this a step further, can a President sign a bill after the final adjournment of Congress? For much of our history, Presidents accepted the theory that they were a constituent part of Congress with respect to the lawmaking process and therefore could sign legislation only while Congress was in session. For that purpose, they would come to a special room in the Capitol and sign hundreds of bills in the remaining days of a Congress. President Cleveland challenged that practice and refused to go to the Capitol but relented a year later upon the advice of his Attorney General.[31] In 1920 and again in 1931, two Attorneys General argued that a President had constitutional authority to sign a bill after the final adjournment of Congress.[32] In 1932 the Supreme Court agreed. Important for the Court was the constitutional right of the President to take up to ten days (Sundays excepted) to consider the merits of bills presented to him. The Court pointed out that during the last 24 hours of the 71st Congress, 184 bills were presented to President Hoover—a burden that required the full ten days for him to act responsibly. Furthermore, the holding of the Court in 1899 that no action by Congress was required for the signing of a bill after a recess applied equally well to final adjournment.[33]

28. Id. §1111.

29. Missouri Pac. Ry. Co. v. Kansas, 248 U.S. 276 (1919).

30. La Abra Silver Mining Co. v. United States, 175 U.S. 423, 451–55 (1899).

31. E. I. Renick, "The Power of the President to Sign Bills After the Adjournment of Congress," 32 Am. L. Rev. 208 (1898).

32. 32 Op. Att'y Gen. 225 (1920) and 36 Op. Att'y Gen. 403 (1931). See Lindsay Rogers, "The Power of the President to Sign Bills After Congress Has Adjourned," 30 Yale L. J. 1 (1920).

33. Edwards v. United States, 286 U.S. 482 (1932).

A remaining question concerns the meaning of "presentation." The Constitution provides that any bill not returned by the President within the ten-day period "after it shall have been presented to him" shall be a law, as if he had signed it, unless a congressional adjournment prevented its return. Must Congress present the bill to him personally ("presented to him"), or may it leave the bill with an agent at the White House? If the President is traveling outside Washington, D.C., but within the United States, presentation to the White House has been considered adequate. But what if the President is traveling abroad?

That issue reached the Court of Claims in 1964. Congress had delivered a bill to the White House on August 31, 1959, after President Eisenhower had departed for a trip to Europe. He did not return until September 7 and vetoed the bill on September 14. Congress did not attempt an override. Had he acted within the ten-day period? The Court of Claims held that a President about to travel abroad had three choices. He could demand that Congress personally present bills to him abroad, ask that they be delayed until his return, or direct that bills be accepted at the White House as though he were present. If Congress disliked the second option, it could send the bill abroad and present it to the President ("who has to make himself reasonably available for that purpose").[34] In this case, Eisenhower had advised Congress that he was selecting the second option and Congress had acquiesced. The veto was therefore valid.

Most of the controversies over the veto power have been resolved politically rather than through litigation. James Monroe alarmed some members of Congress in 1817 by signaling in advance his opposition to contemplated legislation. He announced his "settled conviction" that Congress lacked the constitutional authority to appropriate money for internal improvements. A House committee, established to review his message, reacted with indignation. The committee's report said that the President's message should not be permitted to have any influence on Congress's disposition to legislate on the subject. Nothing should restrain the ability of Congress to express its will. If Congress, deferring to the President's opinion, refrained from action, "it might happen that the opinion of the President would prevent the enaction of a law, even though there should be the Constitutional majority of two-thirds of both Houses in its favor." Such a practice should not go uncontested, for otherwise, the presidential veto "would acquire a force unknown to the Constitution, and the legislative body would be shorn of its power from a want of confidence in its strength, or from indisposition to exert it."[35] Today, such "interference" by the President is commonplace.

---

34. Eber Bros. Wine & Liquor Corporation v. United States, 337 F.2d 624, 630 (Ct. Cl. 1964), cert. denied, 380 U.S. 950 (1965). See also 2 Op. O.L.C. 383 (1977).

35. Annals of Congress, 15th Cong., 1st Sess. 451–52 (1817). For Monroe announcement, see id. at 18.

Other practices broadened the scope of presidential action. The Constitution provides for three forms of action: the President may sign a bill, veto it, or allow it to lapse by using a "pocket veto." Custom soon extended the range of choices, such as letting a bill become law without the President's signature. Grover Cleveland took this course in 1894 to dissociate himself from the Wilson-Gorman Tariff Act. To veto the bill would have offended his party (in control of both houses of Congress and therefore responsible for the measure), yet Cleveland did not want his name on the bill. He believed that it contained provisions "which are not in line with honest tariff reform, and it contains inconsistencies and crudities which ought not to appear in tariff laws or laws of any kind."[36]

In 1995 President Clinton decided to let the defense appropriations bill become law without his signature. Although the bill contained $7 billion more than he had requested, he intended to ask Congress to rescind (terminate) some of the funds. Moreover, he planned to use some of the excess funds to finance his deployment of U.S. troops to Bosnia, a commitment that Congress had not authorized or approved.[37]

Signing Statements

When a President signs a bill, what effect does his accompanying statement have on the meaning and intent of the bill? In interpreting a statute, should courts look to signing statements as they do to the legislative history prepared by Congress? Those questions have triggered a substantial amount of debate.[38] A President's signing statement is more likely to influence executive officials and members of Congress than the courts.

Andrew Jackson sparked a controversy in 1830 when he signed a bill and simultaneously sent to Congress a message that restricted the reach of the statute.[39] The House, which had recessed, was powerless to act on the message. A House report later interpreted his action as constituting, in effect, an item veto of one of the bill's provisions.[40] President Tyler continued the custom by advising the House in 1842 that after signing a bill he had deposited with the

36. Robert McElroy, 2 Grover Cleveland 116 (1923).
37. Public Papers of the Presidents, 1995 (II), at 1813.
38. Frank B. Cross, "The Constitutional Legitimacy and Significance of Presidential 'Signing Statements,'" 40 Admin. L. Rev. 209 (1988); Brad Waites, "Let Me Tell You What You Mean: An Analysis of Presidential Signing Statements," 21 Ga. L. Rev. 755 (1987); Marc N. Garber and Kurt A. Wimmer, "Presidential Signing Statements as Interpretations of Legislative Intent: An Executive Aggrandizement of Power," 24 Harv. J. on Legis. 363 (1987).
39. 3 Richardson 1046 (May 30, 1830).
40. H. Rept. No. 909, 27th Cong., 2d Sess. 5–6 (1842).

Secretary of State "an exposition of my reasons for giving to it my sanction." He expressed misgivings about the constitutionality and policy of the entire act.[41] A select committee of the House issued a spirited protest, claiming that the Constitution gave the President only three options upon receiving a bill: a signature, a veto, or a pocket veto. To sign a bill and add extraneous matter in a separate document could be regarded "in no other light than a defacement of the public records and archives."[42]

A more obvious form of item veto developed with regard to public works legislation when Presidents decided to carry out certain projects while ignoring others. Senator Stephen Douglas of Illinois explained how an appropriations act of 1857 had failed to benefit his state. President Buchanan, after quarreling with Congressmen from Illinois, penalized them by withholding funds from their districts. The funds had been scheduled for post offices and other public buildings.[43] In 1876, while signing a river and harbor bill, President Grant objected to certain projects and announced that he would refuse to spend funds on projects that were "of purely private or local interest."[44]

These early disputes over signing statements provided Presidents with some latitude in deciding how much of a bill to enforce. Could a President, through a signing statement, nullify or dilute a bill that both houses had passed and presented to him? Does that technique create, in effect, a form of item veto? What happened to the President's constitutional obligation to "take Care that the Laws be faithfully executed"? If he found a bill constitutionally or politically repugnant, why not veto it and give Congress a chance to repair the offending passages?

The attention given to signing statements is somewhat overblown. The important focus is not on what the President says at the time of a signing statement but what he does afterward. On the one hand, if he assures that a bill is faithfully carried out, what he says is of little interest. On the other hand, if the President says nothing in a signing statement and then proceeds to direct an agency to sabotage a statutory directive, the constitutional violation is just as plain. Remedies could then be pursued in court or in Congress.

During the Clinton administration, Assistant Attorney General Walter Dellinger prepared several memos on signing statements, concluding that they "may on appropriate occasions perform useful and legally significant functions." He singled out three benefits: "(1) explaining to the public, and particularly to constituencies interested in the bill, what the President believes to be the likely effects of its adoption; (2) directing subordinate officers within

41. 5 Richardson 2012 (June 25, 1842).
42. H. Rept. No. 909, 27th Cong., 2d Sess. 2 (1842).
43. Cong. Globe, 36th Cong., 2d Sess. 1177 (1861).
44. 9 Richardson 4331 (August 14, 1876).

the executive branch how to interpret or administer the enactment; and (3) informing Congress and the public that the Executive believes that a particular provision would be unconstitutional in certain of its applications, or that it is unconstitutional on its face, and that the provision will not be given effect by the executive branch to the extent that such enforcement would create an unconstitutional condition."[45] Regarding the first two categories as generally uncontroversial, Dellinger analyzed the third. He thought that a President's refusal to enforce a provision was particularly justified when it encroached on his constitutional powers, although he recognized that the regular veto power was also available for that purpose.

A second Dellinger memo referred to a number of examples in which Presidents, by refusing to carry out a law, had triggered litigation that helped clarify the reach and meaning of a statute. A prominent case involved presidential opposition to the Tenure of Office Act and its limitation on the removal power of the President. The standoff between the branches on this issue led to the Court's decision in *Myers v. United States* (1926), upholding the President's authority to remove officials who carry out purely executive duties.[46] Dellinger also called attention to the obligation of the executive branch to identify unconstitutional provisions in pending bills and communicate its concerns to Congress so that drafting issues could be corrected. To announce a problem only at the signing stage undercuts the credibility of executive objections.

In 2006 the Justice Department testified before the Senate Judiciary Committee on the controversy over signing statements. The Bush administration justified presidential objections to provisions in bills that required agencies to seek the approval of designated committees before attempting to complete administrative actions. This type of legislative veto, said the department, was invalid under the Supreme Court's decision in *INS v. Chadha* (1983). Thus, in signing statements, Presidents would order executive officials to merely "notify" the committees of pending agency actions rather than seek their approval.[47] In fact, agencies continued to seek committee approval regardless of what the Court decided or the White House directed. In this case, two levels of the executive branch took fundamentally different positions. The President, the White House, and the Justice Department insisted on what would be acceptable under *Chadha*. Executive departments and agencies entered into political accommodations with committees as part of a practical, pragmatic arrangement. The matchup here is between theory and practice, and in the case of post-*Chadha* activity, practice wins.

45. 17 Op. O.L.C. 131 (1993). Also available at http://usdoj.gov/olc/signing.htm.
46. 18 Op. O.L.C. 199 (1994).
47. Hearing on June 27, 2006, available at http://judiciary.senate.gov/print_testimony.cfm?id=1969&wit_id=5479.

Pocket Vetoes

The Constitution provides that any bill not returned by the President "within ten Days (Sundays excepted)" shall become law "unless the Congress by their Adjournment prevent its Return, in which Case it shall not be a Law." This instrument, known as the "pocket veto," was first used in 1812 by President Madison. From Madison through Andrew Johnson, Presidents who used the pocket veto generally prepared a memorandum giving the reasons for their disapproval. This practice lapsed from Grant through Hoover but was reinstated by Franklin D. Roosevelt.[48]

The Supreme Court did not address the pocket veto issue until 1929. A bill had been presented to President Coolidge less than ten days before Congress adjourned at the end of its first session. The adjournment lasted from July to December. The Supreme Court unanimously upheld the pocket veto, concluding that the adjournment prevented the President from returning the bill. The critical issue was not whether an adjournment was final or interim but whether it "prevented" the bill's return. The Court also decided that "ten Days" meant calendar days, not legislative days.[49]

Other questions were resolved in 1938 involving a period during which Congress had not adjourned. The Senate alone had recessed for three days. The Supreme Court considered the time so short that the Senate could act with "reasonable promptitude" on the veto. Also, the Secretary of the Senate had been functioning during the recess and was able to receive (and did receive) the bill. The Court emphasized that the veto procedure serves two fundamental purposes: (1) to give the President an opportunity to consider a bill presented to him and (2) to give Congress an opportunity to consider his objections and override them. Both objectives require protection. To allow the pocket veto power to expand without limit would create a kind of absolute veto emphatically rejected by the framers.[50]

There the matter rested until December 14, 1970, when the Family Practice of Medicine Bill was presented to President Nixon. It had passed by such overwhelming majorities (64 to 1 in the Senate and 346 to 2 in the House) that a veto would have met an almost certain override. Both houses adjourned on December 22 for the Christmas holidays. The Senate returned on December 28, the House the following day. Not counting December 27 (a Sunday),

48. Clement E. Vose, "The Memorandum Pocket Veto," 26 J. Pol. 397 (1964).

49. The Pocket Veto Case, 279 U.S. 655 (1929). See also Abram R. Serven, "The Constitution and the 'Pocket Veto,'" 7 N.Y.U.L. Q. Rev. 495 (1929).

50. Wright v. United States, 302 U.S. 583, 589–90, 596–97 (1938). For an Attorney General's opinion upholding a pocket veto after Congress had adjourned in 1943 for two months, see 40 Op. Att'y Gen. 274 (1943).

the Senate was absent for four days and the House for five. Despite the brief interval and the Senate's designation of an officer to receive messages from the President, Nixon pocket vetoed the bill on December 24.[51]

Unlike the 1929 case, Nixon's action involved a short adjournment *during* a session rather than a lengthy adjournment at the end of a session. This distinction was of pivotal importance to the judiciary. A district court held that the Christmas adjournment had not prevented Nixon from returning the bill to Congress as a regular veto. The bill therefore became law, said the court, on December 25, 1970.[52]

The manner in which the appellate court upheld this decision the next year cast doubt on pocket vetoes during *any* intrasession adjournment, no matter how long. An intrasession adjournment of Congress "does not prevent the President from returning a bill which he disapproves so long as appropriate arrangements are made for the receipt of presidential messages during the adjournment."[53] This reasoning could be carried a step further. Because of the often brief interval between the first and second sessions (which can be shorter than an intrasession adjournment), it is logical to prohibit *inter*session pocket vetoes as well. This reasoning would restrict the use of the pocket veto to one occasion: final adjournment at the end of the second session.

The Nixon administration did not carry this case to the Supreme Court.[54] What was left hanging as a legal issue was soon resolved by a political accommodation. The Ford administration, communicating its views through House Minority Leader John Rhodes, decided not to use the pocket veto during intersession adjournments. In 1975 Rhodes announced, "he will either sign it or veto it in the ordinary way, which would preserve the right of this House and of the other body to either sustain or override those vetoes when we come back after the sine die adjournment."[55]

The determination of Senator Ted Kennedy to settle the matter in the courts resulted in a further announcement from the Justice Department on April 13, 1976. It stated that President Ford would use the return veto rather than the pocket veto during both intrasession and intersession recesses and adjournments of Congress, provided that the house of Congress to which the bill was returned had specifically authorized an officer or other agent to receive return vetoes during that period.[56]

51. Public Papers of the Presidents, 1970, at 1156. The pocket veto was dated December 24 and released December 26.
52. Kennedy v. Sampson, 364 F.Supp. 1075, 1087 (D.D.C. 1973).
53. Kennedy v. Sampson, 511 F.2d 430, 437 (D.C. Cir. 1974).
54. Arthur John Keeffe, with John Harry Jorgenson, "Solicitor General Pocket Vetoes the Pocket Veto," 61 Am. Bar Assn. J. 755 (1975).
55. 121 Cong. Rec. 41884 (1975).
56. 122 Cong. Rec. 11202 (1976); Kennedy v. Jones, 412 F.Supp. 353 (D.D.C. 1976).

The accommodation announced by the Ford administration on the pocket veto was honored by President Carter. Nevertheless, after Congress adjourned at the end of the first session of the 97th Congress (to return in about six weeks), President Reagan pocket vetoed a special relief bill for a bankrupt Florida firm.[57] At the end of the first session of the 98th Congress, Reagan again exercised his pocket veto power between sessions. On November 30, 1983, he pocket vetoed a bill to require the certification of human rights practices in El Salvador as a precondition for sending military aid. The House had adjourned sine die on November 18 and did not return until January 23, 1984—nine weeks later. A bipartisan group of 33 members of the House of Representatives filed suit to require that the bill be published as a public law. A district judge upheld President Reagan's action. The judge reasoned that the case most pertinent was the Pocket Veto Case of 1929, which also involved a multimonth sine die adjournment between the first and second sessions. Although the 1929 decision had been shaken by *Wright* in 1938 and the *Kennedy* cases, the judge felt obliged to follow the single holding of the Supreme Court that seemed to him most relevant.[58]

That decision was overturned by the D.C. Circuit, which pointed out that both the House and the Senate, before adjourning, had expressly arranged for an agent to receive veto messages from the President: "It is difficult to understand how Congress could be said to have prevented return of H.R. 4042 simply by adjourning. Rather, by appointing agents for receipt of veto messages, Congress affirmatively *facilitated* return of the bill in the eventuality that the President would disapprove it."[59] The appellate court also noted that "the line that divides the first session of a Congress from the second has ceased to have any practical significance."[60]

It appeared that the pocket veto issue might finally be resolved in the courts, but in 1987 the Supreme Court held that the dispute was moot because the bill had expired by its own terms, regardless of whether it had previously been enacted into law. The mootness argument was not persuasive. The issue was a live case in the sense that the pocket veto exercised by President Reagan was "capable of repetition" and therefore proper for a court to decide.[61] The Court might have used mootness to duck an even more troublesome issue: whether members of Congress have standing to sue in court.[62]

57. Public Papers of the Presidents, 1981, at 1208. President Reagan abided by *Kennedy v. Sampson* to the extent that he did not exercise the pocket veto during intrasessions; Public Papers of the Presidents, 1984 (II), at 1205.

58. Barnes v. Carmen, 582 F.Supp. 163 (D.D.C. 1984).

59. Barnes v. Kline, 759 F.2d 21, 30 (D.C. Cir. 1985). Emphasis in original.

60. Id. at 38.

61. Burke v. Barnes, 479 U.S. 361 (1987).

62. Id. at 366 (Stevens, J., dissenting).

The Court's decision not to decide tossed the issue back to the two political branches for possible resolution, which may have been another reason for the Court's action. In 1990 the House Rules Committee reported legislation to restrict the pocket veto to the end of a Congress (adjournment sine die).[63] The bill was referred to the House Judiciary Committee, which favorably reported the bill later that year,[64] but no further action was taken by the House. The Bush Justice Department claimed that the President can pocket veto a bill anytime Congress adjourns for more than three days, a period of time it borrowed from the constitutional provision in Article I, Section 5, that requires either house to obtain the consent of the other when it adjourns for more than three days.[65] However, there is no relationship at all between that provision and the veto power.[66]

The Pocket Veto Case of 1929 stands on a fragile foundation. It has been the practice of each house of Congress to authorize an official to receive messages from the President anytime that house is not in session. The President is therefore not "prevented" from returning a bill. Congressional recesses and adjournments are of much shorter duration than in 1929. More important, allowing pocket vetoes during intrasession recesses and between sessions would give the President an absolute veto that the framers deliberately withheld. This result is tolerable if it can be shown that a multimonth adjournment within or between sessions somehow threatens the fundamental powers of the President. The reasoning in *Wright* and *Kennedy* seems more persuasive than the Pocket Veto Case of 1929. The veto procedure must serve two purposes: allowing the President an opportunity to consider a bill, and giving Congress an opportunity to consider presidential objections and vote to override. Until the issue is finally resolved, Congress can avoid pocket vetoes by remaining in session for ten days, excluding Sundays, after presenting the last bill of the first session to the President or by delaying presentment of the bill until the beginning of the next session (but within the same Congress).

During the Bush I and Clinton administrations, the pocket veto adopted an odd form. On November 30, 1989, President Bush exercised what appeared to be a pocket veto of a bill providing emergency relief for Chinese immigration. He said that the adjournment of Congress had "prevented my return of H.R. 2712 within the meaning of Article I, section 7, clause 2 of the Constitution," citing the Pocket Veto Case as controlling law. However, because of questions raised by *Kennedy v. Sampson,* he sent the bill with his objections to the Clerk

63. H. Rept. No. 417 (part 1), 101st Cong., 2d Sess. (1990).

64. H. Rept. No. 417 (part 2), 101st Cong., 2d Sess. (1990).

65. "H.R. 849," hearing before the House Committee on Rules, 101st Cong., 1st Sess. 57–58 (1989).

66. Barnes v. Kline, 759 F.2d at 39–41.

of the House of Representatives.[67] Thus, although the President claimed the constitutional power to exercise a pocket veto, he handled the dispute as a return veto. On January 23, 1990, the House published Bush's veto message in the *Congressional Record* and made it plain that this was a regular veto subject to congressional override. On the following day, the House voted 390 to 25 to override the veto. A day later, by a vote of 62 to 37, the Senate failed in its override attempt. The Senate Library recorded the veto as a regular veto.[68]

President Clinton also returned some "pocket vetoes" to Congress. On August 5, 2000, he used what he called the "protective return" to veto the Marriage Tax Relief Reconciliation Bill, claiming that Congress's summer break (from July 27 to September 6) "prevented my return" of the bill within the meaning of the Constitution as interpreted by the Pocket Veto Case. Yet he added this qualification: "In addition to withholding my signature and thereby invoking my constitutional power to 'pocket veto' bills during an adjournment of the Congress, to avoid litigation, I am also sending H.R. 4810 to the House of Representatives with my objections, to leave no possible doubt that I have vetoed the measure."[69] Similarly, on August 31, he "pocket vetoed" the Death Tax Elimination Bill and appended the same qualification.[70] Upon its return on September 6, the House treated the two veto messages as return vetoes, not pocket vetoes. The following day the House voted 274 to 157 to override the veto of the death tax bill, short of the two-thirds majority needed. On September 13 the House voted 270 to 158 to override the marriage tax bill, again less than the required two-thirds.

The Item Veto

Given the omnibus nature of modern legislation, should Presidents be allowed to veto individual items of a bill? Although the courts have never recognized that authority, Presidents have exercised discretion on some occasions. Examples in the previous section on signing statements illustrate the growing tendency of Presidents to selectively enforce certain statutes. Discretionary enforcement of legislation has received support from influential legislators. In 1896 Senator John Sherman, second-ranking Republican on the Finance Committee, expressed regret that President Cleveland had vetoed a rivers and harbors bill. Sherman regarded the appropriations bill as permissive in nature:

67. Public Papers of the Presidents, 1989 (II), at 1612.
68. Presidential Vetoes, 1989–1996, S. Pub. 105-22, at 2.
69. Public Papers of the Presidents, 2000 (II), at 1564.
70. Id. at 1742–43.

"If the President of the United States should see proper to say, 'That object of appropriation is not a wise one; I do not concur that the money ought to be expended,' that is the end of it. There is no occasion for the veto power in a case of that kind."[71]

This practice of impounding funds, which gained momentum under Franklin D. Roosevelt, allowed Presidents to negate part of an appropriations act. Most of the impoundments by Roosevelt, Truman, Eisenhower, and Kennedy were directed at military programs. Lyndon Johnson moved against domestic programs, but only temporarily, for he backtracked in the face of opposition from Congress and the states. The spate of Nixon's impoundments caused Congress to pass the Impoundment Control Act of 1974, which directed the President to report two types of impoundments: a permanent cancellation of funds (rescission), which required the approval of both houses of Congress within 45 days of continuous session, and a temporary withholding of funds (deferral), which could be disapproved by either house at any time.[72]

Because of the Supreme Court's decision in *INS v. Chadha* (1983), the one-house legislative veto over deferrals was no longer available to Congress. For a few years the Reagan administration and Congress agreed to restrict the use of deferral authority because of the Court's decision, but after passage of the Gramm-Rudman-Hollings Act in 1985, the administration relied heavily on deferrals to curb spending. The result was a court ruling that held the one-house legislative veto and the deferral authority to be inseverable. If the legislative veto fell because of *Chadha,* the deferral authority fell with it.[73]

In addition to impoundment actions, Presidents have attempted to nullify sections of authorization bills. Woodrow Wilson signed a merchant marine bill in 1920, ignoring one section that he found unconstitutional. On the basis of advice from the State Department, Wilson refused to carry out the provisions of that section because it "would amount to nothing less than the breach or violation" of 32 treaties.[74]

President Nixon, upon signing a military authorization bill in 1971, said that one of the sections (the "Mansfield Amendment" dealing with Southeast Asia) did not represent the policy of his administration. He regarded that section as "without binding force or effect."[75] A federal court in 1972 disputed

71. 28 Cong. Rec. 6031 (1896).

72. 88 Stat. 332–39 (1974). See also Louis Fisher, Presidential Spending Power 147–201 (1975).

73. City of New Haven, Conn. v. United States, 809 F.2d 900 (D.C. Cir. 1987). This decision limited deferrals to routine actions, a policy that Congress promptly enacted into law; 101 Stat. 785, sec. 206 (1987).

74. 17 Richardson 8871–72 (September 24, 1920).

75. Public Papers of the Presidents, 1971, at 1114.

his position: "No executive statement denying efficacy to the legislation could have either validity or effect."[76]

However, Presidents since Nixon have frequently used signing statements to single out provisions that they find constitutionally defective. Through such statements they attempt to nullify or modify an objectionable section. Rarely are these remarks litigated. The Reagan administration provoked a court battle when the President signed the Competition in Contracting Act (CICA) of 1984 but objected because the bill attempted to give the Comptroller General unconstitutional powers. Attorney General William French Smith and Office of Management and Budget (OMB) Director David Stockman instructed agencies not to comply with that part of the statute. The Reagan administration thus exercised the functional equivalent of an item veto. A series of court rulings in the Third Circuit and the Ninth Circuit upheld the section conferring power on the Comptroller General. One of the decisions made this observation:

> Art. I, § 7 is explicit that the President must either sign or veto a bill presented to him. Once signed by the President, as CICA was on July 18, 1984, the bill becomes part of the law of the land and the President must "take care that [it] be faithfully executed." Art. I, § 7 does not empower the President to revise a bill, either before or after signing. It does not empower the President to employ a so-called "line item veto" and excise or sever provisions of a bill with which he disagrees. . . . The "line item veto" does not exist in the federal Constitution.[77]

Some writers argue that a separate veto of a rider might be upheld in the courts if the rider bore no relationship to the legislation. An article in the *Wall Street Journal* in 1987 argued that the President may exercise the item veto to defend his office against omnibus bills passed by Congress. That claim of an "inherent" item veto has been thoroughly examined and rejected.[78] Although some officials in the Bush I administration thought the idea had merit and was worth using to provoke a court test, President Bush concluded otherwise and in 1990 submitted to Congress language that would amend the Constitution to give the President item veto authority.[79]

76. DaCosta v. Nixon, 55 F.R.D. 145, 146 (E.D. N.Y. 1972).

77. Lear Siegler, Inc., Energy Products Div. v. Lehman, 842 F.2d 1102, 1124 (9th Cir. 1988). For other CICA cases, see the series of *Ameron* rulings at 607 F.Supp. 962 (D. N.J. 1985), 610 F.Supp. 750 (D. N.J. 1985), 787 F.2d 875 (3d Cir. 1986), and 809 F.2d 979 (3d Cir. 1986).

78. Pork Barrels and Principles: The Politics of the Presidential Veto (Washington, D.C.: National Legal Center, 1988).

79. H. Doc. 179, 101st Cong., 2d Sess. (1990).

In 1992, in the midst of a presidential election year, Bush was tempted once again to claim that an inherent item veto existed, allowing him to invoke that power without seeking either statutory authority or a constitutional amendment. An opinion from the Department of Justice had examined that claim in 1988 in a lengthy and detailed memo and had repudiated it.[80] Bush finally dropped the idea, making this statement:

> Some argue that the President already has that authority, the line-item veto authority, but our able Attorney General [William Barr], in whom I have full confidence, and my trusted White House Counsel [C. Boyden Gray], backed up by legal opinions from most of the legal scholars, feel that I do not have that line-item veto authority. And this opinion was shared by the Attorney General in the previous administration.[81]

The item veto continues to attract support, but misconceptions are widespread. The public assumes that it would be a helpful weapon in combating "logrolling" and "pork-barrel" politics in Congress. In his State of the Union Message in 1984, President Reagan appealed for line-item authority as "a powerful tool against wasteful or extravagant spending."[82] Closer examination, however, punctures some of the emotional appeal of the item veto.

First, President Reagan pointed out that most states have granted their governors an item veto: "It works in 43 States. Let's put it to work in Washington for all the people." This argument might carry weight if Congress resembled state legislatures and if presidential power were analogous to gubernatorial power. Yet the parallels in each case are weak. Governors were originally granted item vetoes because state legislatures were in session for only brief periods, usually meeting once every other year. This part-time status placed a heavy premium on responsible action by the governor and necessitated substantial delegation of budget authority to him. Item vetoes were also used to comply with balanced budget requirements in state constitutions. Neither condition applies to the federal government.

Second, governors can exercise an item veto because appropriations at the state level are highly itemized, descending to such minutiae as $2,000. Congress does not itemize appropriations bills. Funds are included in broad, lump-sum accounts, such as $5 billion for one program or $10 billion for another. Without itemized appropriations, the President would have no items to veto.

---

80. 12 Op. O.L.C. 128 (1988).
81. Public Papers of the Presidents, 1992 (I), at 479.
82. Public Papers of the Presidents, 1984 (I), at 89.

That fact escaped President Reagan in 1988 when he claimed that item veto authority would have allowed him to eliminate from a bill such projects as "cranberry research, blueberry research, the study of crawfish, and the commercialization of wildflowers."[83] But the bill he signed did not mention those four projects; they were mentioned only in the conference report accompanying the bill.[84] The veto power applies to bills, not reports.

Congress could itemize appropriations bills the way the states do, but that would deprive agency officials of the latitude and discretion they now have (and want to retain) with regard to lump-sum amounts. Itemizing appropriations would lock every project and program into public law, leaving executive departments with a detailed statutory menu of how funds are to be spent. If circumstances and public needs change, what then? Even the smallest change would force officials to return to Congress and redo the legislation. Neither branch wants that kind of inflexibility and added workload.

Third, it is widely assumed that logrolling is a peculiar trait of the legislature, yet it is no less characteristic of the executive branch. The Blue Ribbon Defense Panel, in its report to President Nixon in 1970, concluded that the frequent unanimity of the Joint Chiefs could not be interpreted simply as subjugation of particular service views. Such unanimity could just as "cogently support a conclusion that the basis of such recommendations and advice is mutual accommodation of all Service views, known in some forums as 'log rolling,' and a submergence and avoidance of significant issues or facets of issues on which accommodations of conflicting Service views are not possible."[85] The Senate Armed Services Committee made the same point in 1985.[86] It is unrealistic to think that the executive branch is uniquely blessed with a penchant for economy or coherence.

Fourth, allowing the President to veto a portion of a bill may upset the original design of the legislation. Deletion of some sections may make the remainder contrary to legislative intent, in terms of not only technical and substantive questions but also political balance (trade-offs and compromises).

Fifth, who would define "item"? Would it embrace restrictive language and provisos or only dollar amounts? Would it apply only to entire appropriation accounts or to earmarking of specific programs within an account as well? One of the most difficult issues litigated in state courts is the governor's power to veto not merely dollar amounts but also provisos and conditions attached

83. Public Papers of the Presidents, 1988 (I), at 86.

84. H. Rept. No. 498, 100th Cong., 1st Sess. 1099–1100 (1987). The "study of crawfish" shows up only by implication on p. 1100 as $200,000 for "research in Louisiana."

85. Report to the President and the Secretary of Defense on the Department of Defense by the Blue Ribbon Defense Panel 33 (July 1, 1970).

86. S. Prt. No. 86, 99th Cong., 1st Sess. 5 (1985).

to the money. Can governors, with an item veto, convert a conditional appropriation into an unconditional appropriation? Can they strike legislative language from a dollar amount, or are they forced to treat the two as a single item to be accepted or vetoed in whole? Those issues have bedeviled state courts and are unlikely to be resolved by federal courts.[87]

Sixth, Congress could easily neutralize the theoretical advantage of the item veto. State legislatures have become adroit at combining within a single item a program that the governor dislikes and one that he supports. The availability of an item veto would trigger a new round of budgetary legerdemain and political unaccountability.

Seventh, an item veto might make Congress more irresponsible. To satisfy constituent demands, even of the most indefensible nature, a member need only add extraneous material to a bill with the understanding among his colleagues that the President will probably strike the offending amendment. Instead of adopting a reform to control logrolling, the problem might be exacerbated.

Eighth, the item veto would magnify the stature of the President's budget. When first initiated under the Budget and Accounting Act of 1921, the executive budget was nothing more than a proposal to be amended (up or down) as Congress decided. The final judgment lay with Congress, subject to presidential veto. The President, armed with an item veto, could strike from an appropriations bill the programs that Congress had added or augmented. Rarely could Congress attract a two-thirds majority in each house to override him. Administration officials who advocate item veto authority are very candid in admitting that congressional initiatives and add-ons would be the targets.[88] The President's budget should be a starting point, not a fixed ceiling, for congressional action (a point discussed in chapter 7).

Presidents and White House aides could easily use item veto authority to control the votes of members of Congress. A particular project in a member's district or state could be held hostage in return for that member's support for a nominee or some other objective of the White House.[89] Coercion could be quite subtle. A presidential aide advises a member of Congress that the OMB is questioning a project in a bill before the President and then asks, as an aside, how the member plans to vote on the administration's bill (or nominee or treaty) scheduled for the following week.

87. Louis Fisher and Neal Devins, "How Successfully Can the States' Item Veto Be Transferred to the President?," 75 Geo. L. J. 159, 169–73 (1986).

88. Economic Report of the President, 1985, at 96; "Item Veto," hearings before the House Committee on the Judiciary, 85th Cong., 1st Sess. 24 (1957).

89. "Item Veto," hearings in 1957, at 94 (statement by Senator Paul H. Douglas). See also the objections against the line-item veto by Congressman Clarence Cannon; 106 Cong. Rec. 9767–68 (1960).

Members of Congress have experimented with various forms of line-item authority. In February 1995 the House passed language to change the President's power to rescind funds—a step that occurs *after* a bill becomes law. The Impoundment Control Act of 1974 allowed the President to propose rescissions (cancellations or terminations) of appropriated funds, but unless Congress voted its *approval* within 45 days of continuous session, the funds had to be released and spent. The House bill allowed presidential proposals to rescind funds to become law within 20 days unless Congress *disapproved* them by bill or joint resolution. If the President vetoed the disapproval bill, Congress would need a two-thirds majority in each chamber to override the veto.

This procedure, called "enhanced rescission," would shift substantial power from Congress to the President. The Senate debated enhanced rescission in March 1995, as well as a version called "expedited rescission" that would have surrendered less legislative power to the President. This proposal forced at least one house of Congress to consider and vote on a President's recommendation. (The existing rescission process allowed Congress to ignore presidential proposals.)

Both rescission bills were shelved in favor of a substitute that had been considered and rejected by the Senate ten years before: "separate enrollment." This procedure would convert the 13 appropriations bills into about 10,000 mini-bills. After an appropriations bill had passed both chambers, a clerk would break it into separate paragraphs, sections, and numbers, with each part made into a bill and presented to the President. Separate enrollment would have increased the President's general veto power by giving him greater choice.

In 1996 Congress finally cleared an enhanced rescission bill, and President Clinton signed it. The Republicans delayed its effectiveness until January 1, 1997, to prevent Clinton from using it in the middle of an election year. Under this legislation, the President could propose the cancellation of certain appropriations (discretionary budget authority rather than appropriations for mandatory spending), new direct spending (entitlements), and tax benefits limited to 100 or fewer beneficiaries. The President would be required to submit these proposed cancellations within 5 days after signing a bill, and Congress would have 30 days to disapprove of them; any bill of disapproval had to be presented to the President for his signature or veto. If vetoed, Congress would need a two-thirds majority in each house for an override.

Senator Robert C. Byrd and five other legislators brought suit to challenge the constitutionality of the Line Item Veto Act of 1996. Although Congress had by statute authorized a lawsuit by members of Congress, the Supreme Court unanimously held that they lacked standing. The decision pointed out that Senator Byrd and his five colleagues were simply on the losing end of a vote to give the President greater authority. Moreover, both houses of Congress had filed briefs defending the constitutionality of the statute. The effect of the decision was to advise lawmakers who lose during the legislative process to seek remedies within Congress rather than turn to the courts for relief.[90] A year later, after standing had been established for two private plaintiffs, the Court declared the statute unconstitutional on the ground that the President's cancellation authority violated the Presentation Clause. "In both legal and practical effect," the Court regarded the act of cancellation as an amendment to a statute, and "repeal of statutes, no less than enactment, must conform with Art. I."[91]

In 2006 Congress debated legislation to give the President expedited rescission authority (S. 2381 and H.R. 4890), and hearings were held in each house. The legislation authorized the President to send Congress a special message proposing the cancellation of certain items that had been enacted into law. Unlike the Impoundment Control Act of 1974, Congress could not ignore his recommendations. The bills included a "fast-track" procedure, requiring committee and floor action on presidential proposals. If the committee of jurisdiction failed to act, the President's proposals would be automatically discharged from committee for floor action. No legislative amendments would be allowed, either in committee or on the floor. The house to which the proposals were sent would be required to vote, either for or against. To enact the President's recommendations, both houses would have to give their approval under the expedited process and submit the bill to the President for his signature. If one house rejected the proposals, there would be no purpose in having the other house act. H.R. 4890 passed the House on June 22, 2006, and was referred to the Senate. The Senate did not act on the House measure or report its own version.

The Legislative Veto

The legislative veto emerged in the 1930s as an effort to reconcile two conflicting needs. Executive officials wanted to broaden their discretionary authority, and Congress insisted on a control mechanism without the need to pass another public law. The resulting accommodation permitted Presidents and administrators to make proposals that would become law unless Congress

90. Raines v. Byrd, 521 U.S. 811 (1997).
91. Clinton v. City of New York, 524 U.S. 417, 438 (1998), quoting from INS v. Chadha, 462 U.S. 919, 954 (1983).

disapproved by simple resolution of either house (a one-house legislative veto) or by concurrent resolution (a two-house veto). Neither resolution went to the President for his signature or veto. As it evolved, the legislative veto included requirements for congressional approval as well as disapproval and vested some of the control in congressional committees and subcommittees.

This procedure obviously departs from the customary route of having Congress pass a bill and present it to the President. Article I, Section 7, of the Constitution provides that "every Order, Resolution, or Vote to which the Concurrence of the Senate and House of Representatives may be necessary (except on a question of Adjournment)" shall be presented to the President. The legislative veto reverses the normal order. Under its procedure, the President presents proposals subject to the veto of Congress.

Even before the 1930s, the Constitution permitted some exceptions to the Presentation Clause. Congress adopted constitutional amendments in the form of resolutions and referred them directly to the states (rather than through the President) for ratification. This procedure, sanctioned by Article V of the Constitution, was upheld by the Supreme Court in 1798.[92]

From an early date Congress also passed simple resolutions and concurrent resolutions for internal housekeeping matters. Since these were not regarded as "legislative in effect," there was no need to present them to the President. Many of them were adopted pursuant to congressional powers under Article I to determine procedural rules and to punish or expel members. A Senate report in 1897 concluded that whether a resolution was "legislative in effect" depended not merely on its form but also on its substance. If it contained matter that was "legislative in its character and effect," it had to be presented to the President.[93]

Simple and concurrent resolutions gradually evolved into instruments for controlling executive actions. An important conceptual breakthrough occurred in the nineteenth century when executive officials realized that the legislative effect of such resolutions could be changed fundamentally by having their use sanctioned in a public law. In 1854 Attorney General Caleb Cushing stated that a simple resolution could not coerce a department head "unless in some particular in which a law, duly enacted, has subjected him to the direct action of each; and in such case it is to be intended, that, by approving the law, the President has consented to the exercise of such coerciveness on the part of either House."[94] Specific examples were not long in coming. In 1905 Congress relied on concurrent resolutions to direct the Secretary of War to

92. Hollingsworth v. Virginia, 3 Dall. 378 (1798).
93. S. Rept. No. 1335, 54th Cong., 2d Sess. 8 (1897).
94. 6 Op. Att'y Gen. 680, 683 (1854).

investigate matters relating to rivers and harbors. Two years earlier Congress had resorted to simple resolutions to direct the Secretary of Commerce to make investigations and issue reports.[95]

Reorganization Authority

Although in recent decades the legislative veto has been attacked as a congressional usurpation of executive duties, initially it favored the President. President Hoover wanted to reorganize the executive branch to achieve "economy and efficiency" but doubted whether his proposals would survive the regular legislative process. As a shortcut, he recommended that Congress delegate reorganization authority to him, subject to the approval of a joint committee of Congress.[96] In 1932, in the midst of the Great Depression, Congress gave Hoover the authority he wanted. He could submit reorganization plans to Congress, and they would become law within 60 days unless either house disapproved. In December, after being defeated overwhelmingly for reelection, he issued 11 executive orders consolidating some 58 governmental activities. With a single vote, the House of Representatives rejected all his initiatives.[97]

Despite this rebuff, the procedure clearly favored the President. Hoover did not have to secure the support of both houses, as would have been necessary through the regular legislative process. Instead, the burden was placed on Congress to prevent his plans from taking effect. Other expedited features also benefited the President. The executive orders to reorganize could not be buried in committee, filibustered, or amended by Congress, either in committee or on the floor.

Constitutional doubts were raised about the legislative veto. Hoover's Attorney General, William Mitchell, viewed legislative vetoes as intrusions by Congress on the President's administrative duties.[98] Partly on the basis of that opinion, but also because of greater trust in the new President, Congress in 1933 granted Franklin D. Roosevelt broad-ranging powers of reorganization without the check of a legislative veto. His authority lasted two years.[99]

In 1937 Roosevelt asked Congress to renew the authority to reorganize the executive branch, subject to a joint resolution of disapproval (a form of legislative action that must be submitted to the President for his signature). He advised Congress in 1938 that any action short of a bill or joint resolution, such

95. 33 Stat. 1147, sec. 2 (1905); 32 Stat. 829, sec. 8 (1903). See 2 Hinds' Precedents §§1593–94.
96. Public Papers of the Presidents, 1929, at 432.
97. 76 Cong. Rec. 2125–26 (1933).
98. 37 Op. Att'y Gen. 56 (1933).
99. 47 Stat. 1518, sec. 403(c) (1933); 48 Stat. 16 (1933).

as a simple resolution or concurrent resolution, was merely "an expression of congressional sentiment" and could not "repeal Executive action taken in pursuance of a law."[100] The Senate passed a bill incorporating his principles.

Although Roosevelt said that he would "in the overwhelming majority of cases" sign a joint resolution disapproving his reorganization proposals, members of the House of Representatives were not satisfied. They disliked the prospect of having to locate a two-thirds majority in each house if the President invoked his veto power. In effect, they would have delegated authority by majority vote but could retrieve it only with an extraordinary majority. Realizing that his proposal was dead in the House of Representatives, Roosevelt reversed his constitutional principles within a matter of days. The administration supported an amendment to allow Congress to reject any executive order by a majority vote of both houses (a concurrent resolution).

Arguments were hastily concocted to rationalize the administration's switch. The President would be acting as an "agent" of Congress, subject to the conditions established by the legislative branch. The legislative veto would be the vehicle by which Congress would announce that the President had violated or misused his power of agency. Moreover, administration supporters distinguished between the use of a concurrent resolution applied to past laws (which would have been unconstitutional) and those applied to laws "in the making" (constitutionally acceptable).[101]

By 1939 both branches agreed that any grant of reorganization authority to the President would be accompanied by a two-house veto provision. The House Select Committee on Government Organization defended the concurrent resolution procedure by pointing to a recent Supreme Court decision, *Currin v. Wallace,* which had upheld a delegation of authority to the Secretary of Agriculture to designate tobacco markets. No market could be designated unless two-thirds of the growers voting in a referendum favored it.[102] To the committee, it seemed absurd "to believe that the effectiveness of action legislative in character may be conditioned upon a vote of farmers but may not be conditioned on a vote of the two legislative bodies of the Congress."[103]

As enacted in 1939, the Reorganization Act authorized the President to submit plans for executive reorganization. The plans would take effect after 60 days unless Congress, within that time, disapproved them by concurrent resolution. Extension of the authority in 1949 permitted disapproval by a single house. Congress renewed the President's reorganization authority periodically until 1973, when it lapsed because of opposition to President

100. 83 Cong. Rec. 4487 (1938).
101. Id. at 5004–5.
102. 49 Stat. 732, sec. 5 (1935); Currin v. Wallace, 306 U.S. 1 (1939).
103. H. Rept. No. 120, 76th Cong., 1st Sess. 6 (1939).

Nixon. Congress restored the authority in 1977, but only after a major challenge from Congressman Jack Brooks, who believed that the constitutional process required Congress to vote affirmatively on each reorganization plan. As passed, however, the legislation retained the one-house veto.[104] Brooks described the measure as the "best unconstitutional bill you could draw up."[105]

The Justice Department, having objected to previous legislative vetoes on the ground that they trespassed on presidential authority, made an exception for reorganization authority. Attorney General Griffin Bell argued that since the decision to present a plan lay solely with the President, this freedom not to act was equivalent to a presidential veto.[106] Judging from the record of the executive branch on reorganization authority—proposing a joint resolution in 1938, acceding to a concurrent resolution the next year and a simple resolution a decade later—it appeared that the Justice Department could construct whatever argument was necessary to obtain reorganization authority for the President.

The reorganization authority given to President Carter in 1977 was extended for a year before expiring in April 1981. The Reagan administration, perhaps to maintain a consistent policy against *all* legislative vetoes, did not push hard for renewal of the reorganization authority. The advantages of this delegation had been oversold by its proponents and deserved closer scrutiny by scholars.[107] Reorganization could continue, but through the regular legislative process.

The Spirit of Accommodation

Whatever constitutional misgivings Presidents had about the legislative veto of reorganization acts, they acquiesced because they realized that Congress would not delegate such authority without attaching strings to it. By this reasoning, a constitutional issue was reduced to practical proportions. Presidents who wanted the authority had to be willing to accept the conditions that went with it.

President Roosevelt regarded the Lend Lease Act of 1941 as unconstitutional because Congress could terminate the President's authority by concurrent resolution. The political situation, however, did not permit him to disclose his position. Long-standing political enemies had already opposed the concurrent resolution as unconstitutional; to reveal his attitude would associate the President

---

104. 53 Stat. 561 (1939); 63 Stat. 203 (1949); and 91 Stat. 29 (1977). See also the remarks of Congressman Brooks at 123 Cong. Rec. 9344 (1977).

105. H. Rept. No. 105, 95th Cong., 1st Sess. 43 (1977).

106. 43 Op. Att'y Gen. No. 10 (January 31, 1977).

107. See Louis Fisher and Ronald C. Moe, "Presidential Reorganization Authority: Is It Worth the Cost?" 96 Pol. Sci. Q. 301 (1981).

with the wrong group. His Attorney General, Robert H. Jackson, later explained: "to make public his views at that time would confirm and delight his opposition and let down his friends. It might seriously alienate some of his congressional support at a time when he would need to call on it frequently."[108]

The Nixon administration never uttered a word of protest when the Impoundment Control Act of 1974 authorized the President to defer the spending of funds subject to a one-house veto. It wanted the authority and accepted the condition. No one in the Ford, Carter, or Reagan administrations suggested that the one-house veto over deferrals was in any way unconstitutional.

The War Powers Resolution, passed over Nixon's veto, allowed Congress by concurrent resolution to direct the President to disengage from military operations. Congress never exercised this veto, and legal advisers in the executive branch testified that a President need not honor the legislative veto when his constitutional responsibilities were at stake. But both branches recognized that the legislative veto helped bridge a substantive area that is not exclusively executive or legislative (see chapter 9).

Arms sales, subject to a two-house veto, relied on a legislative veto to accommodate the competing interests of Congress and the President. During a briefing in 1978, Attorney General Bell was asked whether President Carter would feel bound if Congress, by concurrent resolution, vetoed his Middle East arms sale package. Bell replied: "He would not be bound in our view, but we have to have comity between the branches of government, just as we have between nations. And under a spirit of comity, we could abide by it, and there would be nothing wrong with abiding by it. We don't have to have a confrontation every time we can." White House adviser Stuart Eizenstat added: "I think the point the Judge is making is that we don't concede the constitutionality of any of [the legislative vetoes] yet, but that as a matter of comity with certain of these issues where we think the Congress has a legitimate interest, such as the War Powers Act, as a matter of comity, we are willing to forego the specific legal challenge and abide by that judgment because we think it is such an overriding issue."[109]

Committee Vetoes

A committee veto obligates an executive agency to submit its program to designated committees before placing the program in operation. Committee

---

108. Robert H. Jackson, "A Presidential Legal Opinion," 66 Harv. L. Rev. 1353, 1356–57 (1953).

109. Office of the White House Secretary, Briefing by Attorney General Griffin B. Bell, Stuart E. Eizenstat, Assistant to the President for Domestic Affairs and Policy, and John Harmon, Office of Legal Counsel, June 21, 1978, at 4.

vetoes actually predate the legislative vetoes of the reorganization acts. Legislation in 1867 placed the following restriction on appropriations for public buildings and grounds: "To pay for completing the repairs and furnishing the executive mansion, thirty-five thousand dollars: *Provided,* That no further payments shall be made on any accounts for repairs and furnishing the executive mansion until such accounts shall have been submitted to a joint committee of Congress, and approved by such committee."[110] Such were the sad straits of President Andrew Johnson.

President Wilson vetoed a bill in 1920 because it provided that no government publication could be printed, issued, or discontinued unless authorized under regulations prescribed by the Joint Committee on Printing. Wilson said that Congress had no right to endow a joint committee or a committee of either house "with power to prescribe 'regulations' under which executive departments may operate."[111]

The executive branch continued to object to committee involvement in administrative matters. In 1933 Attorney General Mitchell regarded as unconstitutional a bill that authorized the Joint Committee on Internal Revenue Taxation to make the final decision on any tax refund that exceeded $20,000.[112] Previous legislation had allowed the committee to decide all tax refunds over $75,000. Apparently, executive officials had lived with that requirement without objection. By lowering the dollar threshold, an acceptable procedure was transformed into unconstitutional "meddling" with executive detail.[113] At what point on the continuum between $75,000 and $20,000 did the constitutional violation occur? The joint committee presently conducts a review (in effect, a veto) of tax refunds in excess of $2 million.[114]

Many of the committee vetoes originated in the 1940s in response to emergency conditions during World War II. Because of the volume of wartime construction, it was impracticable to follow the customary practice of having Congress authorize each defense installation or public works project. Beginning with an informal system in 1942, all proposals for the acquisition of land and leases were submitted in advance to the Naval Affairs Committees for their approval. On the basis of that understanding, Congress agreed to pass general authorization statutes in lump sums, without specifying individual projects. Two years later Congress incorporated that practice into law. Additional "coming into agreement" provisions were added in 1949 and 1951,

110. 14 Stat. 469 (1867).
111. H. Doc. No. 764, 66th Cong., 2d Sess. 2 (1920).
112. 37 Op. Att'y Gen. 56 (1933).
113. See 76 Cong. Rec. 2448 (1933).
114. 26 U.S.C. 6405 (2000).

requiring the approval of the Armed Services Committees for the acquisition of land and real estate transactions.[115]

Every President from Truman to the present has expressed opposition to committee vetoes. Frequently they signed bills stating that they would not abide by a committee veto provision, but the committee veto became a fixture in an increasing number of statutes. During the Eisenhower administration, Attorney General Herbert Brownell advised that the committee veto represented an unconstitutional infringement on executive duties.[116] Undaunted, Congress created another procedure that yielded precisely the same control. A bill was drafted to prohibit appropriations for certain real estate transactions unless the Public Works Committees first approved the contracts. Eisenhower signed the bill after Brownell assured him that this procedure—based on the authorization-appropriation distinction—was within Congress's power.[117] The form had changed; the committee veto remained.

In addition to committee vetoes provided by statute, Congress has evolved a complex set of committee and subcommittee vetoes that are described in nonstatutory sources, chiefly committee reports and department directives and instructions. Most activity in this area consists of agency proposals to re-program funds within an appropriation account. Depending on the amount of money involved and the nature of the transaction, prior approval by committees and subcommittees may be required.[118]

Legislative Veto of Regulations

Rulemaking represents a fusion of two qualities. It is both legislative (agency regulations have the force of law) and executive (agencies carry out the laws passed by Congress). The extent of lawmaking by federal agencies prompted Congress in the Legislative Reorganization Act of 1946 to make its celebrated plea that each standing committee exercise "continuous watchfulness" over the execution of laws. Senator Robert LaFollette remarked that when Congress "yields up that rulemaking power and delegates it to an executive agency, it is part of the responsibility of Congress to keep informed as to whether the power is being exercised as it intended it should be."[119]

115. See Virginia A. McMurtry, "Legislative Vetoes Relating to Public Works and Buildings," in "Studies on the Legislative Veto," House Committee on Rules, 96th Cong., 2d Sess. 432–514 (1980).

116. 41 Op. Att'y Gen. 230 (1955), reprinted in 60 Dick. L. Rev. 1 (1955). See also 41 Op. Att'y Gen. 300 (1957).

117. Joseph P. Harris, Congressional Control of Administration 230–31 (1964).

118. Fisher, Presidential Spending Power, at 75–98.

119. 92 Cong. Rec. 6446 (1946); 60 Stat. 832, sec. 136 (1946).

Criticism of agency rulemaking, a constant issue over the next few decades, reached a shrill pitch in the 1970s. Constituents reported various "horror stories" of administrative regulations that seemed to be a product of agency confusion, caprice, and plain harassment. Members of Congress vented this frustration by introducing legislation to control the regulatory process. Some of the proposals called for a legislative veto over agency regulations.

In 1976 the House of Representatives voted 265 to 135 in favor of the Administrative Rulemaking Reform Act. Although far in excess of a majority, the vote fell short of the two-thirds needed under the parliamentary procedure used (suspension of the rules). The legislation would have permitted Congress, by concurrent resolution, to disapprove agency rules.[120] In 1982 the Senate voted 69 to 25 for a two-house veto over agency regulations.[121]

Although Congress was never able to pass a generic legislative veto to cover all agency rulemaking, it applied that control selectively to individual agencies. In 1974 it adopted a one-house veto over General Services Administration (GSA) regulations involving President Nixon's papers, a two-house veto over regulations issued by the Commissioner of Education, a two-house veto over passenger restraint rules by the National Highway Traffic Safety Administration, and a one-house veto over Federal Election Commission (FEC) regulations.[122] In 1978 it chose a one-house veto to disapprove incremental pricing regulations proposed by the Federal Energy Regulatory Commission (FERC). In 1980 it decided on a two-house veto for Federal Trade Commission (FTC) rules and renewed that legislative veto two years later.[123]

This extension of the legislative veto to agency rulemaking ruptured the fragile accommodation that had lasted for decades between the two branches. Of special concern to the executive branch was the effort to apply the legislative veto to *all* rulemaking. The Justice Department was prepared to use its influence in court to oppose the legislative veto concept in its entirety.

Court Challenges

Some of the early decisions by federal courts upheld legislative vetoes and found others unconstitutional. Initially, the courts approached the contro-

120. 122 Cong. Rec. 31668 (1976).
121. 128 Cong. Rec. 5116 (1982). The bill, containing the two-house veto, passed the Senate 94 to 0; 128 Cong. Rec. 5297 (1982).
122. General Services Administration: 88 Stat. 1697, sec. 104(b) (1974); Education: 88 Stat. 566, sec. 509 (1974); National Highway Traffic Safety Administration: 88 Stat. 1482, sec. 109 (1974); Federal Election Commission: 88 Stat. 1287, sec. 209 (1974), and 90 Stat. 486, sec. 110 (1976).
123. Federal Energy Regulatory Commission: 92 Stat. 3372, sec. 202(c) (1978); Federal Trade Commission: 94 Stat. 393, sec. 21(a) (1980), and 96 Stat. 1870 (1982).

versy with great caution and circumspection. They limited their holdings to the specific statutes before them and often avoided, on procedural grounds, any decision at all. As Congress broadened the use of the legislative veto, attempting to implement generic statutes to control all agency rulemaking, court decisions also became more comprehensive in analyzing the legislative veto.

The constitutionality of legislative vetoes reached the Supreme Court obliquely in 1976. The Federal Election Campaign Act had been challenged on a number of grounds, especially the limitations placed on private campaign contributions and Congress's participation in the appointment of FEC members. The statute also allowed either house of Congress to veto regulations proposed by the FEC. Having struck down the manner in which the commission was appointed (and therefore its ability to issue rules as constituted), the Court declined to pass judgment on the legislative veto.[124] Justice White, however, suggested in a separate opinion that the legislative veto had constitutional support. The one-house veto, he said, "no more invades the President's powers than does a regulation not required to be laid before Congress." White indicated, however, that legislative vetoes might be invalid if Congress tried to usurp "the functions of law enforcement, to control the outcome of particular adjudications, or to pre-empt the President's appointment power."[125]

Several decisions appeared in 1977. An appellate court ruled that the issue of a one-house legislative veto over FEC regulations was not ripe for judicial determination because Congress had yet to exercise the veto.[126] In the same year the Court of Claims considered a challenge to the one-house veto in the Federal Salary Act. The court held that the President had an opportunity to exercise his veto when the bill containing the legislative veto was first presented to him. Under the court's ruling, Congress had a right to delegate conditionally, and if it exercised its disapproval power to keep federal salaries as before, no further participation by the President was required.[127]

In a third decision in 1977, the Supreme Court reviewed a statute that allowed either house of Congress to disapprove regulations issued by the GSA concerning President Nixon's tape recordings and other materials. Although not ruling squarely on the legislative veto, the Court remarked: "Whatever are the future possibilities for constitutional conflict in the promulgation of regulations respecting public access to particular documents, nothing in the

124. Buckley v. Valeo, 424 U.S. 1, 140 n.176 (1976).
125. Id. at 284–85, 285–86.
126. Clark v. Valeo, 559 F.2d 642 (D.C. Cir. 1977), aff'd sub nom., Clark v. Kimmitt, 431 U.S. 950 (1977).
127. Atkins v. United States, 556 F.2d 1028, 1063–65 (Ct. Cl. 1977), cert. denied, 424 U.S. 1009 (1978).

Act renders it unduly disruptive of the Executive Branch and, therefore, unconstitutional on its face."[128]

These rulings approached the legislative veto with great circumspection. In the FEC case, the appellate court warned that the "question of legislative review of Executive and administrative agency actions is a sweeping subject to be treated in gingerly fashion by the courts." Judicial review "ought at an absolute minimum be informed by experience and not depend solely on abstract analysis or speculation."[129] In the federal salary case, the Court of Claims expressed no interest in considering "the general question of whether a one-House veto is valid as an abstract proposition, in all instances, across-the-board, or even in most cases." It was imperative for courts to consider a specific mechanism in a specific statute and to concentrate on "how it works, what it involves, what values and interests are implicated—not on an overarching attempt to cover the entire problem of the so-called legislative veto, or even a large segment of it."[130]

The same caution appears in a 1980 decision by the Ninth Circuit striking down a legislative veto in a deportation case. Acting under statutory authority, the House of Representatives disapproved 6 of 340 requests by the Attorney General to suspend the deportation of aliens. The Ninth Circuit held that the legislative veto violated the doctrine of separated powers and intruded impermissibly upon the executive and judicial branches. Still, it was careful to circumscribe the reach of its decision, which was directed against legislative vetoes affecting individual, adjudicative determinations. It emphasized that it was not faced with a legislative veto used in situations in which "the unforseeability of future circumstances" (as with the Nuclear Nonproliferation Act and its two-house veto) or "the broad scope and complexity" of an agency's rulemaking authority prevented Congress from establishing specific statutory guidelines.[131]

The incremental, case-by-case approach to legislative vetoes stopped abruptly in 1982 when the D.C. Circuit struck down a one-house veto of FERC regulations, a two-house veto of FTC regulations, and a committee veto of Housing and Urban Development (HUD) reorganizations. The broad basis of those rulings implied that all legislative vetoes, of whatever character, were unconstitutional because they failed to follow the established course for lawmaking.[132] In the HUD case, two appellate judges cautioned that

128. Nixon v. Administrator of General Services, 433 U.S. 425, 444–45 (1977).
129. Clark v. Valeo, 559 F.2d at 650 n.10.
130. Atkins v. United States, 556 F.2d at 1059.
131. Chadha v. INS, 634 F.2d 408, 433 (9th Cir. 1980).
132. Consumer Energy Council of America v. FERC, 673 F.2d 425 (D.C. Cir. 1982); Consumers Union, Inc. v. FTC, 691 F.2d 575 (D.C. Cir. 1982); AFGE v. Pierce, 697 F.2d 303 (D.C. Cir. 1982).

the court should rehear the case en banc "because vitally important issues of executive-legislative relations are articulated too broadly and explored inadequately in the panel opinion." They warned of the danger of lumping together as one concept all the legislative vetoes that had been enacted, ranging from rulemaking to war powers.[133] However, the judiciary seemed hell-bent on invalidating the legislative veto on the broadest possible ground, regardless of practical working relationships established over the years by Congress and the executive branch.

Chadha and Beyond

The immigration case decided by the Ninth Circuit in 1980 was argued twice before the Supreme Court. Attorneys representing the House and the Senate explained that this legislative veto originated during the FDR administration to accommodate the interests of both Congress and the President. Many aliens had been subjected to mandatory deportation from the United States, with relief available only in the form of private bills passed by Congress. Because of the hardship on aliens of good character and the Roosevelt administration's desire for discretionary authority, Congress amended the law in 1940 to allow the Attorney General to suspend deportations. In delegating that authority, however, Congress reserved the right to disapprove individual suspensions by a two-house veto.[134] By 1952, Congress decided to rely on a concurrent resolution of approval for certain categories of aliens and a one-house disapproval for others.

In its decision in *INS v. Chadha,* announced on June 23, 1983, the Supreme Court found that the one-house legislative veto in the Immigration and Nationality Act was unconstitutional because it violated both the principle of bicameralism and the Presentation Clause of the Constitution. Chief Justice Burger, joined by five Justices, wrote the opinion for the Court. He said that whenever congressional action has the "purpose and effect of altering the legal rights, duties, and relations of persons" outside the legislative branch, Congress must act through both houses in a bill presented to the President.[135] Justice Powell concurred in the judgment but stated his preference for a more narrowly drawn holding. Justice White delivered a lengthy dissent dissecting

133. AFGE v. Pierce, 697 F.2d at 308–9 (Judges Mikva and Wald).

134. Harvey C. Mansfield, "The Legislative Veto and the Deportation of Aliens," 1 Pub. Adm. Rev. 281 (1940).

135. INS v. Chadha, 462 U.S. 919, 952 (1983). A few weeks later the Court affirmed the opinions of the D.C. Circuit striking down the FERC and FTC legislative vetoes; 463 U.S. 1216 (1983).

the majority's reasoning. Justice Rehnquist also dissented, but only on the question of severability. To Rehnquist, the legislative history seemed persuasive that Congress had delegated the authority to suspend deportations only on the condition that it retain a one-house veto. If the legislative veto fell, so should the Attorney General's authority, because to Rehnquist they were inseverable. The majority held that it was possible to strike down the legislative veto and preserve the delegated authority.

The majority's opinion raised a host of questions. First, it decided that the legislative veto was severable from the immigration statute, despite clear evidence of a quid pro quo between Congress and the President. If severability could be discovered by the Court from this legislative history, it could be found in many other statutes that delegated authority. As a result, the executive branch was given a one-sided advantage in an accommodation that was meant to be a careful balancing of executive and legislative interests.

Second, the Court claimed that the mere fact that a law or procedure was "efficient, convenient, and useful in facilitating functions of government, standing alone, will not save it if it is contrary to the Constitution. Convenience and efficiency are not the primary objectives—or the hallmarks—of democratic government." Later in the decision, the Court said that although the legislative veto might be a "convenient shortcut" and an "appealing compromise," it was "crystal clear from the records of the Convention, contemporaneous writings and debates, that the Framers ranked other values higher than efficiency."[136]

Here the Court played fast and loose with history, for efficiency was highly valued by the framers. The decade prior to the Philadelphia convention represented an anxious and persistent search for a form of government that would perform more efficiently than that set up by the Articles of Confederation. In deciding the *Chadha* case, the Ninth Circuit treated the efficiency issue more responsibly and with better balance.[137]

Third, the Court described the purpose of the Presentation Clause as a means of giving the President the power of self-defense against an encroaching Congress. The President's veto would check "oppressive, improvident, or ill-considered measures."[138] This argument was misleading because it suggested that the legislative veto, by evading the President's veto, threatened the independence of the executive branch and invited ill-considered measures. In fact, the legislative veto was directed only against measures submitted by the President. He sent them up and retained total control over their contents.

136. INS v. Chadha, 462 U.S. at 944, 958–59.
137. Chadha v. INS, 634 F.2d at 420–25.
138. INS v. Chadha, 462 U.S. at 947–48.

Congress could not amend them; members had to vote yes or no. Even if exercised, a legislative veto simply restored the status quo. For example, if either house defeated a reorganization plan, the structure of government remained as before. The same reasoning applied to the use of legislative vetoes against agency regulations, arms sales, and other actions. The President did not need the veto for purposes of "self-defense."

Fourth, the Court said that the framers wanted congressional power exercised "in accord with a single, finely wrought and exhaustively considered, procedure." The records of the Philadelphia convention and debates in the states preceding ratification provide "unmistakable expression of a determination that legislation by the national Congress be a step-by-step, deliberate and deliberative process."[139] But both houses of Congress regularly used "shortcut" methods that posed no problems under *Chadha:* suspending the rules, asking for unanimous consent, placing legislative riders on appropriations bills, and even passing bills that have never been sent to committee.

Fifth, it was not self-evident that the House of Representatives altered the legal rights of Jagdish Rai Chadha when it disapproved the Attorney General's recommendation for suspended deportation. The Attorney General, acting through the Immigration and Naturalization Service, did not have exclusive authority to determine suspensions. By statute, that authority was conditioned on the availability of a one-house veto.

Sixth, each house of Congress may alter the legal rights and duties of individuals outside the legislative branch without resorting to bicameral action and presentation to the President. Each House may command witnesses to appear before congressional committees and may apply sanctions to those who refuse to cooperate. The Supreme Court has recognized the power of either house to issue subpoenas and to hold uncooperative executive officials in contempt.[140]

Seventh, note 18 of the majority opinion stated that there was no provision "allowing Congress to repeal or amend laws by other than legislative means pursuant to Art. I." In adopting a one-house veto, Congress was not repealing or amending the immigration law. It was fulfilling it. The law was effectively amended when the Supreme Court (without any participation by the other two branches) deleted the legislative veto and allowed the remainder of the statute to remain in force.

Eighth, the ability to "make law" through unilateral executive orders and presidential proclamations was all the more extraordinary in view of the

139. Id. at 951, 959.
140. Subpoena power: Eastland v. United States Servicemen's Fund, 421 U.S. 491, 505 (1975); contempt power: Anderson v. Dunn, 6 Wheat. 204 (1821).

Court's decision in *Chadha* that congressional lawmaking must follow the comprehensive route set forth in the Constitution: action by both houses and presentation of a bill or joint resolution to the President. Under *Chadha*, legislative shortcuts were available only for the President, not for Congress.

The Court's ignorance of history and congressional procedures has produced some strange results. Its theory of government is too much at odds with the practices developed over decades by the political branches. Neither administrators nor legislators want the static model proffered by the Court. The conditions that spawned the legislative veto more than half a century ago have not disappeared. Executive officials still want substantial latitude in administering delegated authority; lawmakers still insist on maintaining control without having to pass another law. The executive and legislative branches will therefore develop substitutes to serve as the functional equivalent of the legislative veto. Forms will change, but not power relationships and the need for a quid pro quo.

The Court never seemed to understand the elementary features of the lawmaking process. Depriving Congress of the legislative veto need not benefit the President. Instead of a one-house veto over executive reorganization proposals, all Congress had to do was insist on a joint resolution of approval, which is precisely what it did in 1984 as one way to comply with *Chadha*.[141] This procedure satisfies the twin tests of bicameralism and presentation, but it requires the President to obtain the support of both houses within a specified number of days. The burden is reversed, placing responsibility on the President to cultivate support in both houses instead of requiring one house to disapprove to stop the President. Under the procedure for a joint resolution of approval, if one house withholds support, the practical effect is a one-house veto. If it wanted to, Congress could extend the joint resolution of approval to arms sales, national emergencies, and other areas it has delegated to the President.

No one should underestimate the ingenuity of Congress or its ability to think up devices that will be more cumbersome for the President than the legislative veto. The temptation will be strong for Congress to grant powers for shorter periods, forcing the President to return to Congress for extensions. Of course, inaction by either house could deny the President the authority.

Internal House and Senate rules offer another alternative. Congress can require that funds be appropriated only after an authorizing committee has passed a resolution of approval. This is essentially a committee veto, but the

---

141. 98 Stat. 3192 (1984). This authority expired a few months later. The administration found the joint resolution of approval so burdensome that it never requested a renewal of reorganization authority.

Justice Department may acquiesce because the process relies on Congress's distinction between authorization and appropriation, and the committee resolution is directed at a stage within Congress rather than outside it.

If an agency adopts a regulation that offends Congress, legislators can attach language to an appropriations bill denying the use of funds to implement the regulation. No constitutional issue arises concerning the right of Congress to do this, although riders to appropriations bills are far from the ideal way to make law. They are added without the hearings, careful consideration, and substantive knowledge that are more likely with the legislative veto process.[142] Since a President would rarely veto an appropriations bill because of an objectionable rider, the practical effect is at least a two-house veto. Because of House-Senate comity, the effect in many instances will be a one-house veto.

Statutes can require that selected committees be notified before an agency implements a program. Notification does not raise a constitutional issue, since it falls within the report-and-wait category already sanctioned by court rulings.[143] But "notification" in a statute can become a code word for prior approval. Only in highly unusual circumstances would an agency defy the expressed wishes of an oversight committee.

Congress has continued to use the legislative veto in the years following *Chadha*. Most of these legislative vetoes require agencies to obtain the approval of the Appropriations Committees. Presidents sign them into law, occasionally objecting that they are invalid under the Court's decision. From the day that *Chadha* was issued on June 23, 1983, to the end of 2006, more than 500 new legislative vetoes had been enacted into law.

A few examples illustrate the persistence of legislative vetoes. In 1984 President Reagan signed a housing appropriations bill but objected that it contained a number of committee vetoes. His signing statement implied that agencies were not bound by the statutory requirements and need only notify their review committees rather than seek their approval.[144] The House Appropriations Committee reacted to this provocation by threatening to repeal the committee vetoes and, at the same time, repeal the discretion and flexibility it had given to agency officials. Instead of receiving some latitude tied to committee approval, agencies in the future would have to comply fully with *Chadha* by obtaining a new public law for midyear adjustments. Agency heads quickly wrote to the Appropriations Committee and suggested that it

142. Appropriations riders and other techniques are carefully examined by Frederick M. Kaiser, "Congressional Action to Overturn Agency Rules: Alternatives to the 'Legislative Veto,'" 32 Admin. L. Rev. 667 (1980).

143. Sibbach v. Wilson & Co., 312 U.S. 1, 14–15 (1941). See also INS v. Chadha, 462 U.S. at 935 n.9.

144. Public Papers of the Presidents, 1984 (II), at 1056–57.

would be better to take these executive-legislative understandings out of the public law and place them in conference reports. The agencies promised to abide by the committee vetoes.[145] What had been done directly by statute would now be done by informal agreements. *Chadha* does not affect these nonstatutory legislative vetoes.

To take a second example, Congress required the Agency for International Development (AID) to obtain the prior written approval of the Appropriations Committees before transferring funds from one appropriations account to another. In 1987 OMB Director James Miller III advised Congress that the committee veto violated the constitutional principles of *Chadha*. The House Appropriations Committee basically said: "Fine. We'll repeal the committee veto and also your authority to transfer funds." OMB, realizing that its tactic had backfired, retreated. The regular language, including the committee veto, was enacted into law.[146] Two years later, compromise language was adopted, allowing AID to transfer funds provided it adhered to "regular notification procedures."[147] That phrase meant that AID must notify the Appropriations Committees about proposed transfers and wait 15 days. If the committees object during that period, AID could proceed only at great risk to itself.

A final example comes from the Bush I administration. Secretary of State James A. Baker III wrote a letter to Congress in which he agreed to give four committees of Congress and several congressional leaders a veto power over the release of some funds appropriated for the Contras in Nicaragua. Although White House counsel C. Boyden Gray and former federal judge Robert H. Bork claimed that the arrangement constituted a legislative veto forbidden by *Chadha,* Baker went ahead because it seemed both practical and constitutional. In fact, this kind of informal, nonstatutory "side agreement" is not covered by *Chadha*. Four members of the House of Representatives challenged the "Baker Accord" as unconstitutional, but their suit was dismissed by a federal district court.[148]

There are still limits on what Congress can attempt to do under variations of the legislative veto. Congress passed legislation in 1986 giving it a board of review (composed of nine members of Congress) with a veto over decisions

145. H. Rept. No. 916, 98th Cong., 2d Sess. 48 (1984); Louis Fisher, "Judicial Misjudgments about the Lawmaking Process: The Legislative Veto Case," 45 Pub. Adm. Rev. 705, 707 (Special Issue, November 1985).

146. "OMB Objection Raises House Panel's Hackles," Washington Post, August 13, 1987, at A13; 101 Stat. 1329-155, sec. 514 (1987).

147. 103 Stat. 1219, sec. 514 (1989).

148. Burton v. Baker, 723 F.Supp. 1550 (D.D.C. 1990). For the positions of Gray and Bork, see Washington Post, March 26, 1989, at A5, and 135 Cong. Rec. 6528–29, 6534 (1989).

made by a regional authority responsible for two airports serving the District of Columbia. The Supreme Court held that the veto power violated the doctrine of separation of powers.[149] Congress responded with remedial legislation, reconstituting the board of review and giving it the power to recommend but not to veto. The new statute authorized Congress to pass a joint resolution of disapproval to reject actions by the regional authority. Joint resolutions satisfy the requirements of *Chadha* (bicameralism and presentation), but even this new arrangement did not satisfy the courts. In 1994 the D.C. Circuit held that the board of review acted as an agent of Congress and that the power to make "recommendations" was in fact the power to coerce.[150]

Since *Chadha,* Congress has continued to use informal and nonstatutory methods to control the executive branch. Agencies comply because they want to retain administrative flexibility. Because some of these "gentlemen's agreements" are not placed in statutes, they are unaffected by the Court's decision. They are not legal in effect. They are, however, in effect legal. For the committee vetoes placed in statutes, protests in presidential signing statements are unlikely to overcome agencies' desires to comply with procedures agreed to by committees of jurisdiction.

With or without the legislative veto, Congress will remain a partner in "shared administration." It is inconceivable that any court or any President can prevent it. Call it supervision, intervention, interference, or just plain meddling, Congress will find a way.[151] And government is not worse off because of it. For the most part, statutes can define only the broad contours of public policy. The specific application of funds will remain a joint enterprise between executive agencies and congressional committees. Contrary to the Court's doctrine, future legislative control will not be exercised solely through public laws. We should not be too surprised or disconcerted if, after the Court has closed the door to the legislative veto, we hear a number of windows being raised and perhaps new doors being constructed, making the executive-legislative structure as accommodating of shared power as it has been in the past.

149. Wash. Airports v. Noise Abatement Citizens, 501 U.S. 252 (1991).

150. Hechinger v. Metro. Wash. Airports Authority, 36 F.3d 97 (D.C. Cir. 1994), cert. denied, 513 U.S. 1126 (1995).

151. For further details, see my articles "Congress and the President in the Administrative Process: The Uneasy Alliance," in Hugh Heclo and Lester M. Salamon, eds., The Illusion of Presidential Government 21–43 (1981); "Micromanagement by Congress: Reality and Mythology," in L. Gordon Crovitz and Jeremy A. Rabkin, eds., The Fettered Presidency 139–57 (1989); and "The Legislative Veto: Invalidated, It Survives," 56 Law and Contemp. Prob. 273 (1993).

6

POWER OVER KNOWLEDGE: SEEKING AND
WITHHOLDING INFORMATION

The Constitution does not explicitly grant Congress the power to investigate; neither does it give the President the privilege of withholding information. Yet the Supreme Court has held that both powers, when exercised for the proper functioning of each branch, are implied in the Constitution. The Court announced in 1927 that a legislative body "cannot legislate wisely or effectively in the absence of information respecting the conditions which the legislation is intended to affect or change."[1] Investigation is a prerequisite for intelligent lawmaking. In 1974 the Court decided that the President's interest in withholding information for the purpose of confidentiality is implied in the Constitution: "To the extent this interest relates to the effective discharge of a President's powers, it is constitutionally based."[2]

These implied powers collide whenever Congress, in an attempt to carry out its investigative function, is denied information by a President who invokes executive privilege. Which power should yield? It would be satisfying to discover a formula that is both unequivocal and trustworthy, but too much depends on individual circumstances. To subordinate one branch to another would destroy their coequal status and disrupt the system of separated powers. We are left with a search for general boundaries and guideposts that satisfy constitutional principles as well as practical realities.

Congressional Investigations

Congress uses its investigative power to satisfy four main purposes: to enact legislation, to oversee the administration of programs, to inform the public, and to protect its integrity, dignity, reputation, and privileges. To enforce those essential duties, Congress possesses an implied power to punish for contempt.

A study of court cases necessarily distorts the record of Congress and its investigative power. The cases test the outer limits of the power to probe and

1. McGrain v. Daugherty, 273 U.S. 135, 175 (1927).
2. United States v. Nixon, 418 U.S. 683, 711 (1974).

usually place Congress in an unfavorable light. By their very nature, these cases are exceptional. The vast majority of congressional investigations proceed without the need for litigation and without jeopardizing either individual liberties or the separation of powers. Moreover, the investigative power of Congress often enhances individual liberties by curbing executive abuses.

Early Precedents

The House ordered its first major investigation on March 27, 1792. It appointed a committee to inquire into the ill-fated expedition of Major General Arthur St. Clair, whose troops had suffered disastrous losses to the Indians. The committee was empowered "to call for such persons, papers, and records, as may be necessary to assist their inquiries." According to the account of Thomas Jefferson, President Washington convened his Cabinet to consider the extent to which the House could call for papers. The Cabinet considered and agreed,

> first, that the House was an inquest, and therefore might institute inquiries. Second, that it might call for papers generally. Third, that the Executive ought to communicate such papers as the public good would permit, and ought to refuse those, the disclosure of which would injure the public: consequently were to exercise a discretion. Fourth, that neither the committee nor House had a right to call on the Head of a Department, who and whose papers were under the President alone; but that the committee should instruct their chairman to move the House to address the President.

The Cabinet concluded that "there was not a paper which might not be properly produced." The committee examined papers furnished by the executive branch, listened to explanations from department heads and other witnesses, and received a written statement from General St. Clair.[3] Yet the potential for executive privilege had been established. The President could refuse papers "the disclosure of which would injure the public."

The first use of the investigative power to protect the dignity of the House occurred in 1795. William Smith, a Representative from South Carolina, told the House that one Robert Randall had confided to him a plan to obtain from Congress a grant of some 20 million acres, to be divided into 40 shares. More than half would be set aside for members of Congress who supported the scheme. Congressman William Murphy had also been approached by Ran-

---

3. 1 The Writings of Thomas Jefferson 303–5 (Bergh ed. 1903). See also 3 Annals of Congress 490–94, 1106–13 and Appendix (1052–59, 1310–17) (1792).

dall on the attempted bribery. One of Randall's associates, Charles Whitney, contacted Congressman Daniel Buck to curry his favor. The House passed a resolution to direct the Sergeant at Arms, upon the order of the Speaker, to apprehend Randall and Whitney.[4]

On January 6, 1796, the House concluded that Randall was guilty of contempt and a breach of House privileges by attempting to corrupt the integrity of its members. He was brought to the bar, reprimanded by the Speaker, and recommitted to custody. The case against Whitney was handled differently, since he had attempted to bribe a member-elect. The House released Whitney from custody without charging him with contempt, and a week later it voted to release Randall.[5]

The first committee witness punished for contempt of the House was Nathaniel Rounsavell, a newspaper editor charged in 1812 with divulging sensitive information to the press. Although he admitted to a select committee that he had been the source of a published account concerning secret House debates on a proposed embargo, and that he had derived part of the information by overhearing a conversation between members of the House, he refused to identify the members or say where the conversation had occurred. Placed in the custody of the Sergeant at Arms and brought before the bar of the House to be interrogated, he once again declined to identify the legislators.

On the following day, still in custody, Rounsavell prepared a letter disclaiming any intention of showing disrespect to the House. He described the conversation of the members as inadvertent and explained that he had withheld information from the committee only because it might incriminate those who had committed no crime. Only with prior knowledge, obtained from other sources, had he been aware that the subject under discussion was an embargo. At that point, John Smilie of Pennsylvania rose to identify himself as the member from whom Rounsavell had obtained the information. Smilie considered the published information "of no importance." If the House wanted a victim, he said, he offered himself as a substitute for Rounsavell.

Some means had to be found to discharge Rounsavell without compromising the rights and dignity of the House. The Speaker asked him: "Are you willing to answer such questions as shall be propounded to you by order of the House?" Rounsavell answered in the affirmative. The House then moved that the editor, having purged himself of contempt, be discharged from confinement. The motion carried without opposition.[6]

4. Annals of Congress, 4th Cong., 1st Sess. 155–70 (1795).
5. Id. at 171–245, passim. For further details on Congress's power to punish for contempt, see 2 Hinds' Precedents §§1597–1640.
6. Annals of Congress, 12th Cong., 1st Sess. 1255–74. Additional cases in which the House punished witnesses for contempt are described in 3 Hinds' Precedents §§1666–1701.

Judicial Review and the Contempt Power

The British Parliament regarded its contempt power and determination of legislative privileges as wholly immune from review by the courts. Not so with Congress. The authority of Congress to punish citizens for contempt of its authority or for a breach of its privileges, the Supreme Court has ruled, "can derive no support from the precedents and practices of the two Houses of the English Parliament, nor from the adjudged cases in which the English courts have upheld these practices."[7]

The power of Congress to hold an individual in contempt became the subject of judicial scrutiny in *Anderson v. Dunn* (1821). The controversy arose when Congressman Lewis Williams advised the House that a Colonel John Anderson had offered him $500 in return for certain favors and considerations. The House issued a warrant directing the Sergeant at Arms to take Anderson into custody. After being brought to the bar and interrogated by the Speaker, Anderson was declared guilty of contempt and in violation of the privileges of the House. The Speaker reprimanded him and discharged him from custody.[8]

Three questions were before the Supreme Court: Did the House have authority to issue the warrant? Was issuance of a warrant exclusively a judicial power? Did the Constitution require a jury trial for all crimes? The Court upheld the action of the House as a valid exercise in self-preservation. Without the power to punish for contempt, the House would be left "exposed to every indignity and interruption that rudeness, caprice, or even conspiracy, may mediate against it."[9] However, the Court held that the power to punish for contempt was limited. The House had to exercise the least possible power adequate to the end proposed (in this case, the power of imprisonment), and the duration of punishment could not exceed the life of the legislative body (that is, imprisonment had to terminate with adjournment).

Because of this latter restriction, an individual could violate the dignity of the House in the closing days of a Congress and be punished only during that period. Partly for that reason, as well as a desire to delegate such matters to the courts, Congress passed legislation in 1857 to enforce the attendance of witnesses on the summons of either house. Failure to appear or refusal to answer pertinent questions could lead to indictment as a misdemeanor in the courts.[10]

---

7. Kilbourn v. Thompson, 103 U.S. 168, 189 (1881). See also Marshall v. Gordon, 243 U.S. 521, 533–41 (1917), and Watkins v. United States, 354 U.S. 178, 192 (1957).

8. Annals of Congress, 15th Cong., 1st Sess. 580–83, 592–609, 777–90 (1818).

9. Anderson v. Dunn, 6 Wheat. 204, 228 (1821). The Senate, a continuing body, is not limited by the expiration of a Congress; McGrain v. Daugherty, 273 U.S. 135, 181–82 (1927).

10. 11 Stat. 155 (1857), amended by 12 Stat. 333 (1862). The 1857 law, as amended, was upheld by the Supreme Court; In re Chapman, 166 U.S. 661 (1897). The 1857 law, amended in 1936 (49 Stat. 2041) and 1938 (52 Stat. 942), is codified at 2 U.S.C. 192–94 (2000).

The contempt power was narrowed by *Kilbourn v. Thompson* (1881). The House of Representatives had summoned Hallet Kilbourn to answer certain questions and produce papers relating to a real estate partnership. For refusing to comply with the congressional directive, he was judged guilty of contempt and imprisoned for 45 days. The Supreme Court recognized that Congress possessed a number of judicial powers. It could punish its members for disorderly behavior or for failure to attend its sessions. The House could decide cases of contested elections and determine the qualifications of its members. It exercised the sole power of impeachment of officers of the government and in some cases might even fine or imprison a contumacious witness. But neither house possessed a general power to punish for contempt.[11] The constitutional right of a person to life, liberty, or property, unless taken by due process of law, meant "a trial in which the rights of the party shall be decided by a tribunal appointed by law, which tribunal is to be governed by rules of law previously established."[12] The congressional investigation of Kilbourn involved a matter pending in the courts and was thus, to the Court, judicial and not legislative in nature. Subsequent holdings, discussed later, have narrowed the reach of *Kilbourn*.

McGrain v. Daugherty (1927) adopted a more generous view of investigations used to obtain information for a legislative function. A Senate committee, investigating the Teapot Dome scandal, issued a subpoena commanding Mally S. Daugherty to give testimony and bring certain records. He refused to appear for either purpose. The Supreme Court faced this issue: Did either house of Congress have the power to compel a private individual to appear before it, or one of its committees, to give testimony needed for the exercise of its legislative function? The Court decided that the Senate had ordered the investigation for a legitimate object; the witness had wrongfully refused to appear and testify; and the Senate was entitled to have him give testimony pertinent to the inquiry, either at its bar or before a committee.[13] Two years later the Court unanimously supported another phase of the Senate's investigation of the Teapot Dome scandal, this time concerning the president of Mammoth Oil Company.[14] When committees and subcommittees report contempt actions, it is the duty of the Speaker of the House or the President of the Senate to certify the statement of facts reported by a congressional panel.

11. Kilbourn v. Thompson, 103 U.S. at 190.
12. Id. at 182. A 1917 decision held that a letter written to a House committee chairman, though ill-tempered in content, was not of such a character as to threaten the ability of the House to carry out its legislative authority; Marshall v. Gordon, 243 U.S. 521, 545–46 (1917).
13. McGrain v. Daugherty, 273 U.S. at 180.
14. Sinclair v. United States, 279 U.S. 263 (1929).

Committee recommendations are considered by the house involved and may be voted down.[15]

Prior to 1978, Congress had only two methods of enforcing compliance with its power to investigate and to issue subpoenas: an implied power to punish for civil contempt, and the statutory mechanism (adopted in 1857) to punish for criminal contempt.[16] The two methods differ fundamentally in purpose and scope.

Under the first procedure, a witness who refuses to testify can be committed to the Sergeant at Arms of the respective house until the person is purged by supplying the requested information or otherwise satisfying Congress. The objective is to force compliance with the congressional will. Once an individual is purged, the punishment ends. In any event, punishment may not extend beyond that session of Congress.

Under the second procedure, the objective is to punish rather than coerce. Once convicted of criminal contempt, an individual forfeits the opportunity to be purged and escape further punishment. Moreover, punishment may continue beyond that session of Congress (including a fine of not more than $100,000 and imprisonment up to one year).[17] Before an individual is indicted by a grand jury and convicted by a court, it is possible to purge oneself of contempt by cooperating with Congress.[18]

In 1978 Congress adopted a third approach. If an individual refuses, or threatens to refuse, to comply with a Senate subpoena, the Senate may request a court order requiring the individual to comply with the subpoena. Failure to obey a court order may result in a citation for civil contempt. Sanctions imposed under this procedure "shall not abate upon adjournment sine die by the Senate at the end of a Congress if the Senate or the committee or subcommittee of the Senate which issued the subpena [sic] or order certifies to the court that it maintains its interest in securing the documents, answers, or testimony during such adjournment."[19] This procedure does not apply to federal officers. Since the purpose is to coerce rather than punish, sanctions are lifted once the individual complies with the Senate's request.[20]

15. Ansara v. Eastland, 442 F.2d 751 (D.C. Cir. 1971); Wilson v. United States, 369 F.2d 198 (D.C. Cir. 1966).

16. The power of either house to punish for contempt was not impaired by the 1857 statute; Jurney v. MacCracken, 294 U.S. 125, 151 (1935).

17. For the distinction between civil and criminal contempt in congressional investigation cases, see United States v. Fort, 443 F.2d 670, 676–77 (D.C. Cir. 1970), cert. denied, 403 U.S. 932 (1971), and Charles Alan Wright, Federal Practice and Procedure: Criminal §704 (2d ed., 1982).

18. 132 Cong. Rec. 7887–89 (1986).

19. 28 U.S.C. 1365 (2000).

20. Application of U.S. Senate Perm. Subcom. on Invest., 655 F.2d 1232 (D.C. Cir. 1981), cert. denied, 454 U.S. 1084 (1981).

A Supreme Court decision in 1995 had implications for the ability of the Justice Department to prosecute lawmakers and government officials for lying to Congress. Section 1001 of Title 18 criminalized any unsworn false statements in any matter within the jurisdiction of any "department or agency" of the United States. In holding that Section 1001 did not apply to federal courts, the Court overruled a 1955 case that had applied Section 1001 to a former member of Congress who had made a false statement to the Disbursing Office of the House of Representatives. Although Section 1001 was not available for prosecuting individuals who lied to Congress, other statutes were available, including perjury charges for lying under oath.[21] Congress responded to the decision by enacting legislation a year later that reinstated criminal penalties for making false statements to Congress.[22]

In December 1995 the Clinton administration refused to release records subpoenaed by the Senate Whitewater Committee, which was seeking notes taken by then–White House associate counsel William Kennedy during a November 5, 1993, meeting. The meeting had taken place shortly after the administration learned that the Clintons had been named in Resolution Trust Corporation's request to the Justice Department for a criminal investigation of a failed Arkansas savings and loan owned by the Clintons' business partner in the Whitewater land venture. The White House argued that the records were protected under the attorney-client privilege, a claim rarely asserted for a President. It appeared that in order to enforce the subpoena, the committee would have to go to court.[23]

President Clinton believed that a President "ought to have a right to have a confidential conversation with his minister, his doctor, his lawyer" and stated that he should not "be the first president in history to give up his right to attorney-client privilege." However, this had not been a meeting between Clinton and his personal attorney to discuss private legal matters. Government attorneys, supposedly paid to conduct government business, had attended the meeting. After the Senate voted to go to court to enforce the subpoena, the White House surrendered the notes.[24]

---

21. Hubbard v. United States, 514 U.S. 695 (1995).

22. 110 Stat. 3459 (1996).

23. "White House Rejects Subpoena," Washington Post, December 13, 1995, at A1.

24. "Legal Experts Uncertain on Prospects of Clinton Privilege Claim," Washington Post, December 14, 1995, at A14; "Compromise on Notes Rejected," Washington Post, December 15, 1995, at A2; "Whitewater Notes Being Surrendered," Washington Post, December 22, 1995, at A1. For further details on the dispute over the Kennedy notes, see Louis Fisher, The Politics of Executive Privilege 103–6 (2004).

Protection of Individual Rights

The investigative power is interpreted broadly by the courts to permit Congress to carry out its legislative functions. Zealous or careless investigations, however, can violate individual freedoms protected by the Constitution. In 1957 the Supreme Court ruled that certain portions of the Bill of Rights are applicable to congressional investigations: "Witnesses cannot be compelled to give evidence against themselves. They cannot be subjected to unreasonable search and seizure. Nor can the First Amendment freedoms of speech, press, religion, or political belief and association be abridged." These are strong words, yet later in the same decision, the Court used meeker language to warn that Congress cannot "unjustifiably encroach" on First Amendment rights.[25] How far can Congress go?

The Supreme Court has tried to circumscribe the reach of congressional investigations. In *Kilbourn* (1881) the Court stated that congressional investigations must relate to some legislative purpose. Congress could not conduct "fruitless" investigations into the personal affairs of individuals (fruitless in the sense that the investigation "could result in no valid legislation on the subject to which the inquiry referred"). Later the Court rendered a more sympathetic judgment by adopting a presumption in favor of a legislative purpose. Thus, *McGrain* (1927) decided that a "potential" for legislation was sufficient. It was enough that the subject was one that Congress could legislate on and "would be materially aided by the information which the investigation was calculated to elicit."[26]

Even the "potential" theory was too narrow a test for congressional investigations. The courts recognized that committee investigations may take researchers up "blind alleys" and into nonproductive enterprises: "To be a valid legislative inquiry there need be no predictable end result."[27]

One way to limit congressional investigations is to require proper authorization. When a congressional resolution defines the scope of an investigation,

25. Watkins v. United States, 354 U.S. 178, 188, 198–99 (1957). For an earlier decision, sustaining an abridgment of First Amendment rights by the House Committee on Un-American Activities, see Barsky v. United States, 167 F.2d 241 (D.C. Cir. 1948), cert. denied, 334 U.S. 843 (1948). In 1953 the D.C. Circuit held that a search and seizure by a Senate committee violated the Fourth Amendment; Nelson v. United States, 208 F.2d 505 (D.C. Cir. 1953), cert. denied, 346 U.S. 827 (1953). Some portions of the Bill of Rights do not apply to congressional investigations. The Sixth Amendment right of cross-examination need not be granted to a witness; United States v. Fort, 443 F.2d 670, 681–82 (D.C. Cir. 1970), cert. denied, 403 U.S. 932 (1971).

26. Kilbourn v. Thompson, 103 U.S. at 194–95; McGrain v. Daugherty, 273 U.S. at 177.

27. Eastland v. United States Servicemen's Fund, 421 U.S. 491, 509 (1975).

a committee may not go beyond the legislative instruction.[28] Inquiries must be properly authorized by Congress before a committee invokes criminal sanctions to punish a witness for refusing to cooperate.[29] Although the procedural rights required of a criminal trial are not necessary for legislative contempt actions, someone threatened with a contempt citation must be given notice and an opportunity to answer.[30]

Congressional investigations must respect the Fifth Amendment right that protects individuals against self-incrimination. In the *Quinn* and *Emspak* decisions in 1955, the Supreme Court reversed the convictions of individuals who had refused to testify before a House committee regarding their alleged membership in the Communist Party. The Court ruled that even indirect and ambiguous references to the Fifth Amendment afford witnesses the privilege against self-incrimination.[31] But Congress may, through a majority vote of either house or a two-thirds vote of a committee or subcommittee, request a federal court to issue an order that compels witnesses to testify. By surrendering their Fifth Amendment right, witnesses are given partial immunity (their testimony may not be used against them in any criminal case).[32] This partial immunity ("use immunity") provides less protection than "transactional immunity," which offers absolute protection against prosecution for the transaction (offense).[33]

During the Iran-Contra investigation in 1987, Congress offered partial immunity to Colonel Oliver North and several other witnesses. North was later convicted of three felonies: obstructing the investigation by Congress, mutilating government documents, and taking an illegal gratuity. The charges were subsequently dismissed because of his immunized testimony. Under new and more stringent standards imposed by the courts, prosecutors must show that a defendant's testimony could have had no influence on the witnesses called to a trial. Otherwise, the remarks of the witnesses are "tainted" and may not be used to convict.[34]

---

28. United States v. Rumely, 345 U.S. 41 (1953); United States v. Patterson, 206 F.2d 433 (D.C. Cir. 1953).

29. Gojack v. United States, 384 U.S. 702 (1966).

30. Groppi v. Leslie, 404 U.S. 496 (1972).

31. Quinn v. United States, 349 U.S. 155 (1955); Emspak v. United States, 349 U.S. 190 (1955).

32. For immunity procedure, see 18 U.S.C. 6001–5 (2000). Its use as a substitute for the Fifth Amendment has been upheld in Ullmann v. United States, 350 U.S. 422 (1956), which supported the Immunity Act of 1954 (68 Stat. 745); Kastigar v. United States, 406 U.S. 441 (1972); and Application of U.S. Senate Select Com. on Pres. Cam. Act., 361 F.Supp. 1270 (D.D.C. 1973).

33. Brown v. Walker, 161 U.S. 591 (1896); Counselman v. Hitchcock, 142 U.S. 547 (1892).

34. United States v. North, 910 F.2d 843 (D.C. Cir. 1990), cert. denied, 500 U.S. 941 (1991); United States v. Poindexter, 951 F.2d 369 (D.C. Cir. 1991), cert. denied, 506 U.S.

By the early 1950s it was evident that the congressional investigative process had taken a turn for the worse. Most frequently attacked for violating individual rights and freedoms were the House Un-American Activities Committee (HUAC) and the Senate Permanent Investigations Subcommittee, chaired by Joseph R. McCarthy. Members of Congress, bar associations, and civic and political action groups drafted codes of fair procedure. Beginning in 1953 the House Rules Committee held hearings on suggested codes of rules for the committees, and in 1955 the House adopted a set of procedures for committee investigations.[35] Those procedures are now part of the House rules.

Each committee may fix the number of its members that constitutes a quorum for the purpose of taking testimony and receiving evidence, but the number cannot be less than two. The Supreme Court had earlier held that testimony received from a witness before a committee without a quorum could not be regarded as perjury. Under such circumstances the committee is not a "competent tribunal."[36] In the Senate, one-member committees (or subcommittees) may constitute a quorum for the purpose of receiving testimony and even taking sworn testimony, but committees that adopt special rules permitting a one-person quorum must publish the rule in the *Congressional Record* within 30 days.[37]

Due process was at issue in *Watkins v. United States* (1957). John Watkins, a labor organizer, described for HUAC his past participation with the Communist Party. He even agreed to identify current members of the party but objected to committee questions about those who had left the movement. Instead of "taking the Fifth," Watkins considered such questions irrelevant to the committee's work. He believed that the committee had no right to expose people publicly because of their past activities. His refusal to answer certain questions led to his conviction for contempt.

The Supreme Court, in a 6-to-1 decision, agreed with Watkins. Fundamental fairness demanded that a witness be given adequate guidance in deciding the pertinency of questions. Whether in the resolution authorizing the investigation, in the remarks of the chairman or members of the committee, or in the nature of the proceeding, a witness must have an opportunity to make a reasonable judgment about a question's pertinence. The Court ruled that unless the subject matter appears with "undisputable clarity, it is the duty of the investigative

---

1021 (1992). See Ronald F. Wright, "Congressional Use of Immunity Grants After Iran-Contra," 80 Minn. L. Rev. 407 (1995).

35. "Legislative Procedure," hearings before the House Committee on Rules, 83d Cong., 2d Sess. (1953). See Edward J. Heubel, "Congressional Resistance to Reform: The House Adopts a Code for Investigating Committees," 1 Midwest J. Pol. Sci. 313 (1957).

36. Christoffel v. United States, 338 U.S. 84 (1949).

37. United States v. Reinecke, 524 F.2d 435 (D.C. Cir. 1975).

body, upon objection of the witness on grounds of pertinency, to state for the record the subject under inquiry at that time and the manner in which the propounded questions are pertinent thereto." Because HUAC failed to do that, Watkins's conviction violated the Due Process Clause of the Fifth Amendment.[38]

The tone of the *Watkins* decision, containing reprimands aimed at Congress—together with other decisions handed down during that period—produced a groundswell of opposition from legislators. Various bills were introduced to curb the Court.[39] In the face of this political pressure, the Supreme Court retreated from its position two years later.

Lloyd Barenblatt, a college professor, refused to answer certain questions put to him by a subcommittee of HUAC. He maintained that (1) the compelling of testimony by the subcommittee was neither legislatively authorized nor constitutionally permissible because of vagueness in the character of the authority given to the parent committee, (2) he had not been adequately apprised of the pertinency of the subcommittee's questions, and (3) the questions he refused to answer infringed on rights protected by the First Amendment. He expressly disclaimed reliance on the Fifth Amendment privilege against self-incrimination.

The Supreme Court, sharply divided 5 to 4, rejected all three contentions. Borrowing language from *Watkins,* the Court decided that pertinency had been made to appear with "undisputable clarity." As to the constitutional question, the Court acknowledged that in some circumstances the First Amendment protects an individual from being compelled to disclose associational relationships. But the judiciary chose to balance competing private and public interests. In this case the Court struck the balance in favor of the government's interest in self-preservation. Justice Black, in a biting dissent, objected to the "balancing test" because the interest of a solitary individual is not likely to outweigh the alleged interest of the government. To him, the real interest in an individual's right to remain silent is the "interest of the people as a whole in being able to join organizations, advocate causes and make political 'mistakes' without later being subjected to governmental penalties for having dared to think for themselves."[40] The Court remained divided in two 1961

38. Watkins v. United States, 354 U.S. 178, 214–15 (1957). In 1927 the Court had held, on the basis of prior decisions, that a witness "rightfully may refuse to answer where the bounds of the power are exceeded or the questions are not pertinent to the matter under inquiry"; McGrain v. Daugherty, 273 U.S. at 176.

39. For this period, see Walter F. Murphy, Congress and the Court (1962), and C. Herman Pritchett, Congress Versus the Supreme Court (1961).

40. Barenblatt v. United States, 360 U.S. 109, 144 (1959). Contemporary law provides that individuals summoned to testify before Congress shall be deemed guilty of a misdemeanor when they refuse to answer "any question pertinent to the question under inquiry." 2 U.S.C. 192 (2000).

cases that upheld, by a 5-to-4 margin, HUAC's right to question individuals suspected of Communist Party ties.[41]

When the activities of an organization do not raise questions of subversion, at least directly, the rights of association are more likely to find protection in the courts. This is the teaching of *NAACP v. Alabama* (1958), which involved an attempt by a state attorney general (not a legislature) to obtain an organization's membership list. The principles announced gave greater support to the rights to freedom of speech, assembly, and association.[42]

Committees may not intervene in a pending adjudicatory proceeding by focusing on the process used by agency officials to reach a decision. In such cases Congress would be interfering not in an agency's "*legislative* function, but rather, in its *judicial* function."[43] Congressional inquiries into the legislative (rulemaking) function of an agency are more permissible, but even here, a member of Congress may not force an executive official to take into account considerations that Congress had not intended.[44]

For the most part, however, courts assume that agency officials possess the necessary "backbone" to withstand searching inquiries by congressional committees.[45] Even when pressure during a congressional hearing becomes the direct impetus for a change in agency policy, courts treat such influence as "part of the give and take of democratic government."[46]

The Speech or Debate Clause

Article I, Section 6, of the Constitution provides that "for any Speech or Debate in either House," Senators and Representatives "shall not be questioned in any other Place." This clause, adopted at the Constitutional Convention without discussion and without opposition, is almost verbatim from the Articles of Confederation and closely follows language in the English Bill of Rights of 1689.[47] The courts have consistently held that the immunities of the Speech or Debate Clause exist not for the personal or private benefit

41. Wilkinson v. United States, 365 U.S. 399 (1961). A companion case, Braden v. United States, 365 U.S. 431 (1961), also upheld HUAC on a 5-to-4 vote. In McPhaul v. United States, 364 U.S. 372 (1960), the Court split 5 to 4 in upholding a HUAC contempt citation.

42. NAACP v. Alabama, 357 U.S. 449 (1958). See also Gibson v. Florida Legislative Investigation Committee, 372 U.S. 539 (1963).

43. Pillsbury Co. v. FTC, 354 F.2d. 952, 954 (5th Cir. 1966). Emphasis in original.

44. D.C. Federation of Civic Associations v. Volpe, 459 F.2d 1231, 1247 (D.C. Cir. 1972), cert. denied, 405 U.S. 1030 (1972).

45. Gulf Oil Corp. v. FPC, 563 F.2d 588, 610–12 (3d Cir. 1977).

46. United States ex rel. Parco v. Morris, 426 F.Supp. 976, 982 (E.D. Pa. 1977).

47. United States v. Johnson, 383 U.S. 169, 177 (1966).

of members "but to protect the integrity of the legislative process by insuring the independence of individual legislators."[48]

How much can be done under the shield of this clause? In *Kilbourn v. Thompson* (1881), the first case to interpret the Speech or Debate Clause, the Supreme Court read it broadly to include not only "words spoken in debate" but also anything "generally done in a session of the House by one of its members in relation to the business before it."[49] The clause protects members' remarks made in the course of committee hearings or in committee reports. Speeches printed in the *Congressional Record* are covered, whether delivered or not. The acquisition of information by congressional staff, obtained formally or informally, is a necessary stage of legislative conduct generally protected by the Speech or Debate Clause.[50]

A number of other activities, which the courts call "political" rather than "legislative," are not protected: contacts with executive agencies, assistance to individuals who seek federal contracts, preparing news releases and newsletters for constituents, and speeches delivered outside Congress.[51] Nor is there any legislative immunity when disseminating documents and information outside Congress.[52]

In some early cases the courts afforded legislators more protection under the Speech or Debate Clause than their aides received.[53] *Gravel* (1972), however, treated members of Congress and their aides "as one" when an aide carries out a task that would have been a legislative act if performed personally by the member. When performing these tasks, aides become members' "alter egos."[54] But even in the case of legislative acts, the Speech or Debate Clause does not extend a privilege to members or aides who "violate an otherwise valid criminal law in preparing for or implementing legislative acts."[55]

How these principles work in practice can be seen from the *Eastland* and *McSurely* decisions. In the first, the Supreme Court in 1975 upheld an investigation by a Senate subcommittee that threatened an organization's First

48. United States v. Brewster, 408 U.S. 501, 507 (1972).
49. Kilbourn v. Thompson, 103 U.S. 168, 204 (1881). For early decisions on the Speech or Debate Clause as supportive of a far-reaching legislative investigative power, see Tenney v. Brandhove, 341 U.S. 367 (1951), and Nelson v. United States, 208 F.2d 505 (D.C. Cir. 1953), cert. denied, 346 U.S. 827 (1953).
50. Committee hearings and reports: Doe v. McMillan, 412 U.S. 306, 311–13 (1973); *Congressional Record:* Hutchinson v. Proxmire, 433 U.S. 111, 116 n.3 (1979); legislative staff: Tavoulareas v. Piro, 527 F.Supp. 676, 680 (D.D.C. 1981).
51. United States v. Brewster, 408 U.S. at 513; Hutchinson v. Proxmire, 443 U.S. at 130–33.
52. Doe v. McMillan, 412 U.S. at 314–17; Gravel v. United States, 408 U.S. 606, 625–26 (1972).
53. Dombrowski v. Eastland, 387 U.S. 82, 84–85 (1967).
54. Gravel v. United States, 408 U.S. at 616–17. See also Doe v. McMillan, 412 U.S. at 312.
55. Gravel v. United States, 408 U.S. at 626.

Amendment freedom of the press and its right of association. The subcommittee subpoenaed the bank records of an organization active in promoting
dissent toward the Vietnam War. Access to the bank records would have revealed the identities of those who contributed to the organization and thereby
jeopardize its existence. The majority opinion concluded that the actions of
the subcommittee, the individual Senators, and the chief counsel of the subcommittee were protected by the Speech or Debate Clause and therefore immune from judicial interference. The balancing test, even though it tilts easily
in the government's favor, did not even come into play. Whenever the courts
are faced with a situation in which an activity by Congress is within its "legitimate legislative sphere, balancing plays no part."[56] Justice Douglas wrote
a dissenting opinion. Three members of the Court (Marshall, Brennan, and
Stewart) concurred in the judgment but rejected its sweeping interpretation
of the Speech or Debate Clause.

In the second case, spanning more than a decade, Alan and Margaret Mc-
Surely won a damage suit against Senator John McClellan, two of his aides,
and a rural Kentucky prosecutor. The couple, convicted of contempt of Congress in 1970 for refusing to surrender certain documents to a Senate subcommittee, successfully challenged the conviction on the ground that the
subcommittee had violated their Fourth Amendment right to be free of unreasonable searches and seizures. During oral argument in 1978, the government told the Supreme Court that congressional investigators could "probably" break into a private home and take papers from a locked drawer or safe,
and even commit murder with impunity, if they sought information for a legislative purpose.[57] Instead of endorsing this position (which the government
conceded was not "intuitively appealing"), the Court let stand a lower court
ruling that members of Congress and their aides are not immune from liability in a suit for damages involving illegal search and seizure. In 1983 a jury
awarded the McSurelys $1.6 million in damages because of the illegal search
and the violations of their First Amendment right to free speech.[58] The damage suit against the estate of Senator McClellan was overturned on appeal, and
a smaller award of $21,000 was upheld against one of the committee investi-
gators. The appellate court concluded that there was no evidence that Senator
McClellan had ordered or approved the conduct of the investigator.[59]

56. Eastland v. United States Servicemen's Fund, 421 U.S. 491, 501, 510 n.16 (1975).

57. McAdams v. McSurely, oral argument before the Supreme Court, No. 76-1621, March
1, 1978, at 14–15.

58. Washington Post, January 8, 1983, at A1. See McSurely v. McClellan, 521 F.2d 1024
(D.C. Cir. 1975); McSurely v. McClellan, 553 F.2d 1277 (D.C. Cir. 1976), cert. denied, 438
U.S. 189 (1978).

59. McSurely v. McClellan, 753 F.2d 88 (D.C. Cir. 1985), cert. denied, 474 U.S. 1005
(1985); Washington Post, December 3, 1985, at A9. Through a statute enacted in 1988, mem-

Some members of Congress and their aides insist that they have total immunity for their actions under both the Speech or Debate Clause and the common law (inherent) doctrine of official immunity. To narrow that protection to qualified immunity, they argue, would defeat the underlying purpose of legislative independence. The courts are comfortable with absolute immunity only when restricted to a core area of legislative acts. To grant Congress absolute immunity for all acts—legislative and investigative, with or without authorization, within the halls of Congress and outside, by members as well as by aides—would jeopardize the individual rights of free speech, free association, due process, Fourth Amendment freedoms, and other basic liberties protected by the Constitution.

A new challenge to the Speech or Debate Clause occurred on May 23, 2006, when FBI agents turned up at a closed House office building at about 7:15 on a Saturday evening armed with a search warrant. They demanded entry to the office of Representative William J. Jefferson (D-La.) and spent until 1:00 the next afternoon going through his records and taking his computer files as part of a criminal investigation. Throughout that period they refused to have Jefferson's staff or the House General Counsel in the room to supervise the search. Although some members of Congress excused the search on the ground that "no man is above the law," a competing value was at stake: the independence of the legislative branch from executive intimidation. If FBI agents can obtain a search warrant to enter a lawmaker's office, they can enter any room on Capitol Hill, including the office of the House General Counsel or the Senate Legal Counsel, and gain access to both legislative and nonlegislative documents. The damage done to Congress as a coequal branch would be severe. There need to be clear protocols to ensure that congressional leaders are notified in advance of any attempt to search a legislative office and to devise procedures that will safeguard institutional interests.[60]

Presidential Immunity

The Constitution does not contain an express immunity for the President, but a doctrine of official immunity for executive officials and the President

bers of Congress now have immunity from suit when they act within the scope of their "office or employment." 102 Stat. 4564, sec. 3 (1988); 28 U.S.C. 2679 (2000); Williams v. United States, 71 F.3d 502 (5th Cir. 1995).

60. Dan Eggen and Shailagh Murray, "FBI Raid on Lawmaker's Office Is Questioned," Washington Post, May 23, 2006, at A1; Dan Eggen and Allan Lengel, "Officials Defend Raid on Lawmaker's Office," Washington Post, May 24, 2006, at A4; Carl Hulse, "F.B.I. Raid Divides G.O.P. Lawmakers and White House," New York Times, May 24, 2006, at A1; Allan Lengel, "FBI Threatened to Pick Lock, Filing Says," Washington Post, June 8, 2006, at A6.

has been developed by the courts. In 1959 the Supreme Court weighed two conflicting values: the right of a citizen to be protected from oppressive or malicious actions on the part of federal officials, and the interest of the general public in shielding federal officials from harassment by vindictive or ill-founded damage suits. The Court decided this particular case (a libel action) by the narrow vote of 5 to 4 in favor of official immunity. The Court believed that the threat of damage suits might inhibit the "fearless, vigorous, and effective administration of policies of government." Officials enjoy immunity whenever they perform "discretionary acts at those levels of government where the concept of duty encompasses the sound exercise of discretionary authority." The acts are privileged whenever taken "within the outer perimeter" of an official's line of duty.[61] Subsequent decisions elaborated on and refined the doctrine of official immunity.[62]

Presidential immunity was singled out for special protection in 1982 when the Supreme Court held that the President is entitled to absolute immunity in civil suits regarding all his official acts. This immunity is "rooted in the constitutional tradition of the separation of powers." Personal vulnerability to suits for civil damages, said the Court, "could distract a President from his public duties."[63]

On the same day that the Court recognized an absolute immunity for the President, it conferred only a qualified immunity on presidential aides. This middle-level test supposedly allows aides to defeat "insubstantial claims without resort to trial."[64] Three years later the Court held that Cabinet members and other high government officials do not have absolute immunity from lawsuits for illegal conduct even when they claim that their actions were necessary to protect the national security.[65]

The next question raised at the presidential level was whether someone currently serving as President is entitled to immunity from civil liability for unofficial acts—acts committed in a personal capacity rather than in the capacity as President. The particular circumstances of this case—brought by Paula Corbin Jones against Bill Clinton—concerned actions that occurred before Clinton became President. Are actions prior to becoming President immune from civil liability?

61. Barr v. Matteo, 360 U.S. 564, 571, 575 (1959). This decision relied heavily on Judge Learned Hand's opinion in Gregoire v. Biddle, 177 F.2d 579 (2d Cir. 1949).
62. E.g., Bivens v. Six Unknown Named Agents of Fed. Bur. of Narc., 456 F.2d 1339 (2d Cir. 1972); Bivens v. Six Unknown Fed. Narcotics Agents, 403 U.S. 388 (1970); Imbler v. Pachtman, 424 U.S. 409 (1976); Butz v. Economou, 438 U.S. 478 (1978).
63. Nixon v. Fitzgerald, 457 U.S. 731, 749, 753 (1982).
64. Harlow v. Fitzgerald, 457 U.S. 800, 813 (1982).
65. Mitchell v. Forsyth, 472 U.S. 511 (1985).

Jones, a former employee of the Arkansas state government, claimed that in 1991 Clinton, then the governor of Arkansas, had sexually harassed and assaulted her during a conference at a hotel in Little Rock. Clinton moved to dismiss the case on the ground of presidential immunity, though he recognized that Jones would have the right to reinstate the lawsuit after he left the presidency. In 1996 a federal appellate court held that a President enjoys absolute immunity only for official, not unofficial, acts. That decision allowed the Jones suit against Clinton to proceed to discovery and trial. Starting with the "truism" that the Constitution "did not create a monarchy," the court said that the President "is cloaked with none of the attributes of sovereign immunity."[66] A concurring judge noted prior examples of sitting Presidents acting either as defendants in civil actions or as witnesses in other judicial proceedings.[67]

In 1997 a unanimous Supreme Court decided that the Constitution did not afford Clinton temporary immunity in this case. The Court was not persuaded that its ruling would generate a large volume of politically motivated, harassing, and frivolous litigation or that national security concerns might prevent Clinton from explaining the need for a delay in the trial. If Congress believed that the President needed stronger protection from civil lawsuits, the Court invited it to provide the necessary legislation.[68]

The Court's prediction that the case could proceed without substantially burdening Clinton has been much maligned. However, the resulting burden had less to do with the Jones lawsuit than with new allegations about Clinton's relationship with White House intern Monica Lewinsky and his decision to lie, suborn witnesses, and obstruct justice. As explained in the next section, those actions led to his impeachment. The Jones lawsuit was dismissed in 1998 when a district court judge held that there were "no genuine issues for

66. Jones v. Clinton, 72 F.3d 1354, 1358 (8th Cir. 1996). The district court held that Jones's trial could occur only after Clinton left the presidency, but the appellate court reversed that ruling. Jones v. Clinton, 858 F.Supp. 902 (E.D. Ark. 1994); Jones v. Clinton, 869 F.Supp. 690 (E.D. Ark. 1994).

67. President Nixon was ordered by the Supreme Court to produce tapes subpoenaed by a special prosecutor. United States v. Nixon, 418 U.S. 683, 713 (1974). In another case he was held to be amenable to legal process, even in his official capacity. National Treasury Employees Union v. Nixon, 492 F.2d 587 (D.C. Cir. 1974). President Carter gave videotaped testimony at a criminal conspiracy trial of two Georgia state officials, gave videotaped testimony for a grand jury investigating charges that Robert Vesco had enlisted White House aid to quash extradition proceedings against him, and was interviewed under oath by Justice Department investigators probing the nature of relations between his brother (Billy Carter) and the Libyan government. President Ford was compelled to testify by videotape deposition in the criminal trial of Lynette (Squeaky) Fromme, who was charged with attempting to assassinate him. Jones v. Clinton, 72 F.3d at 1366.

68. Clinton v. Jones, 520 U.S. 681 (1997).

trial in this case." After Jones appealed, Clinton agreed to settle the case by giving her $850,000.

The scope of presidential immunity was explored in two lawsuits aimed at Vice President Dick Cheney. Both cases involved efforts to obtain documents related to the energy task force he chaired. Members of Congress and private groups wanted to look into the influence of nongovernmental officials on the energy bill drafted by the Bush administration and presented to Congress. The General Accounting Office (GAO) initiated the first suit, which a district court dismissed on the ground that the Comptroller General lacked standing.[69] GAO decided not to appeal.

The second case came from two private groups, Judicial Watch and the Sierra Club. The D.C. Circuit rejected the administration's argument that the President and Vice President have broad immunity that protects them from any litigation to determine how they formulate legislative proposals. It also directed the two groups to narrow their request for documents. The Supreme Court declined to accept the administration's broad doctrine, preferring to return the case to the D.C. Circuit with instructions to seek an accommodation to protect the President from litigation that might distract from the performance of his constitutional duties.[70]

Impeachment

The investigative power, in its most solemn form, is invoked during the impeachment process. The Constitution provides that the President, Vice President, and all civil officers of the United States shall be removed from office upon "Impeachment for, and Conviction of, Treason, Bribery, or other high Crimes and Misdemeanors." The House impeaches by a majority vote; a two-thirds vote of the Senate is needed for conviction.

The grounds for removal remain uncertain. Treason does not present much of a problem, for it is defined in Article III, Section 3, of the Constitution. Bribery, although not defined in the Constitution, is generally understood to mean the giving, offering, or taking of rewards as payment for favors. But what of "other high Crimes and Misdemeanors"? Does impeachment apply only to actions indictable in the courts (statutory offenses), or does it extend to abuses of office and "political crimes" against the government? A separate issue is whether courts may review an impeachment and conviction by Congress. On all such questions the authorities disagree.

69. Walker v. Cheney, 230 F.Supp.2d 51 (D.D.C. 2002). For further details, see Fisher, The Politics of Executive Privilege, at 183–98.

70. Cheney v. United States District Court for D.C., 542 U.S. 367 (2004).

"What, then, is an impeachable offense?" asked Minority Leader Gerald Ford in 1970, during the attempted impeachment of Justice Douglas. The only "honest answer," he said, "is that an impeachable offense is whatever a majority of the House of Representatives considers it to be at a given moment in history; conviction results from whatever offense or offenses two-thirds of the other body considers to be sufficiently serious to require the removal of the accused from office."[71] That kind of open-ended definition parallels the vague grounds that James Madison so quickly and successfully opposed at the Philadelphia convention.

Madison understood that impeachment was indispensable to defend the community against the "incapacity, negligence or perfidy of the chief Magistrate." The President might "pervert his administration into a scheme of peculation of oppression. He might betray his trust to foreign powers." But when George Mason moved to add "maladministration" as a basis for impeachment, because treason and bribery might be insufficient to reach other "great and dangerous offenses," Madison objected. He said that ill-defined and loose terms would be equivalent to having the President serve at the pleasure of Congress. Mason withdrew the language and substituted "other high crimes & misdemeanors," which passed by a vote of 8 to 3.[72]

During impeachment proceedings it is characteristic for counsel of the accused to contend that the phrase "other high crimes and misdemeanors" refers only to an indictable offense.[73] Although the framers rejected vague grounds ("maladministration"), they did not insist on specific statutory offenses. In Federalist 65, Alexander Hamilton called the object of impeachment "those offenses which proceed from the misconduct of public men, or, in other words, from the abuse or violation of some public trust. They are of a nature which may with peculiar propriety be denominated POLITICAL, as they relate chiefly to injuries done immediately to the society itself." Hamilton conceded in the same essay that there is a danger that the decision to impeach will be regulated "more by the comparative strength of parties than by the real demonstrations of innocence or guilt." The framers chose to live with the risk of unwarranted impeachments. The alternative (which they rejected) would be to permit an unfit person to remain in office, to the detriment of the government and the people, because the grounds for removal were too narrowly drawn. Federal judges enjoy life tenure during "good behaviour," again indicating that tenure may be terminated by conduct short of criminal.

71. 116 Cong. Rec. 11913 (1970).
72. 2 Farrand 65–66, 550.
73. For example, see the position of President Nixon's attorneys, "An Analysis of the Constitutional Standards for Presidential Impeachment," 10 Wkly Comp. Pres. Doc. 270–83 (February 28, 1974).

Madison later reinforced the view that impeachment covers abuses of office. In the First Congress he argued that the removal power of the President would make him responsible for the conduct of department heads "and subject him to impeachment himself, if he suffers them to perpetrate with impunity high crimes and misdemeanors against the United States, or neglects to superintend their conduct, so as to check their excesses."[74]

To insist on an indictable offense contradicts this record. Moreover, the emphasis on statutory crimes does not automatically yield the advantage claimed by supporters. Congress, by rewriting the criminal code, could subject Presidents to impeachment for minor infractions. Even if unrevised, the criminal code contains actions of insufficient stature to merit impeachment. Impeachment is a political, not a judicial, act. The purpose is to remove someone from office, not to punish that person for a crime. Impeachable conduct need not be criminal.[75]

Both Irving Brant and Raoul Berger, authors of two leading works on impeachment, relied on British precedents. Although some language in the U.S. Constitution is lifted from English history, care must be taken not to borrow too much. The English Parliament has far greater power to punish than its American counterpart; the American President has more independence and a more coequal status than the British Prime Minister; and the American system of separated branches differs fundamentally from the close executive-legislative linkage that exists in England. After the development of ministerial responsibility to Parliament, impeachment in England became an anachronism. It remains a necessary check in America.

Is there a need for judicial review? The question turns in large part on what constitutes an impeachable offense—statutory offenses or political abuses. If the latter, the court seems an inappropriate forum. Raoul Berger, relying heavily on *Powell v. McCormack* (1969), concluded that the courts may review impeachment and conviction. But *Powell* involved explicit criteria for the qualifications of members of Congress: age, citizenship, and residence in the state from which they are elected. The standards for impeachable activity are not spelled out in the Constitution with the same precision.[76]

---

74. 1 Annals of Congress 372–73 (May 19, 1789).

75. This is also the conclusion reached by the staff of the House Committee on the Judiciary in preparation for the impeachment of President Nixon. "Constitutional Grounds for Presidential Impeachment," Report by the Staff of the Impeachment Inquiry, House Committee on the Judiciary, 93d Cong., 2d Sess. (Comm. Print February 1974). Even Irving Brant, who repudiated Gerald Ford's position and insisted on a narrow definition of the grounds needed for impeachment, did not go so far as to insist on statutory offenses alone. He believed that a President or judge could be impeached for violating the oath of office (such as by gross and willful neglect of duty). Irving Brant, Impeachment 20–23, 67, 73 (1972).

76. Powell v. McCormack, 395 U.S. 486 (1969); Raoul Berger, Impeachment 103–21 (1973).

It is possible to conceive of circumstances in which courts might play a role. There could be blatant procedural irregularities, such as providing inadequate time for the accused to prepare a defense or denying the accused an opportunity to cross-examine. Treason is defined in the Constitution, so Congress cannot apply the term loosely. Some grounds for impeachment, moreover, might be of a frivolous nature. For example, Article X against Andrew Johnson charged that he attempted to disgrace Congress by making and delivering "with a loud voice certain intemperate, inflammatory, and scandalous harangues . . . amid the cries, jeers, and laughter of the multitudes." Such thin-skinned reactions from Congress obviously fall short of an impeachable offense. Also, Article VII charged him with violating the Tenure of Office Act of 1867, which I believe (but a majority of Congress then did not) was itself an unconstitutional limitation on the President's control over his Secretary of War.

If Congress decides that an officeholder has committed "high crimes and misdemeanors," even if unindictable in the courts, and it builds a record to demonstrate that the individual acted in a manner harmful to the political system and must be removed, there is no recourse to the judiciary. Congress acts essentially as a political body when it impeaches and convicts. Courts are likely to rule that they lack jurisdiction and competence to review these decisions entrusted to legislators.[77]

Congress has been unusually active in recent years in removing federal judges through the impeachment process. District Judge Harry Claiborne, who had been found guilty of income tax evasion, was impeached and removed in 1986. District Judge Walter L. Nixon Jr., convicted of lying to a federal grand jury, was impeached and removed in 1989. District Judge Alcee L. Hastings, acquitted in 1983 of criminal activities, was nevertheless impeached by the House in 1988 and removed by the Senate in 1989.[78] To manage the heavy workload that results from these impeachments, the Senate appoints a committee of twelve Senators to view the evidence and take the testimony of witnesses. Judge Nixon challenged that procedure as unconstitutional, contending that the entire Senate must sit as judge and jury, but a district judge and appellate court decided that the claim was not justiciable.[79] In 1993 the Supreme Court held that the Senate had sole discretion to choose the procedures to be used for impeachment.[80]

President Clinton was impeached in 1998 as a result of federal investigations into the death of White House aide Vincent Foster, the Whitewater

77. Ritter v. United States, 84 Ct. Cl. 293 (1936), cert. denied, 300 U.S. 668 (1937).

78. Louis Fisher, American Constitutional Law 131–32 (2005).

79. Nixon v. United States, 744 F.Supp. 9 (D.D.C. 1990); Nixon v. United States, 938 F.2d 239 (D.C. Cir. 1991).

80. Nixon v. United States, 506 U.S. 224 (1993).

investment company, and the White House's misuse of confidential FBI files. On January 16, 1998, the jurisdiction of the investigation was expanded to include allegations that Clinton had committed perjury, obstructed justice, and intimidated witnesses with regard to his affair with White House aide Monica Lewinsky.

On December 19, 1998, the House of Representatives adopted two articles of impeachment against President Clinton, one for perjury and the other for obstruction of justice. Voting on February 12, 1998, the Senate "acquitted" Clinton on both articles. On the perjury article, 45 Senators voted "guilty" and 55 voted "not guilty." The vote on obstruction of justice was 50 to 50, far short of the two-thirds required for removal. The meanings of the phrases "acquitted," "guilty," and "not guilty" require explanation, however, because the voting process used by the Senate was distorted. From 1789 to 1936, the Senate voted twice—first on the question of guilt, and then on the question of removal—allowing the Senators to find someone guilty of the charges but then to decide that the person should not be removed from office. After 1936 the two questions were collapsed into a single vote.

Many Senators who voted "not guilty" explained that they thought Clinton was indeed guilty of the charges. For example, Senator Robert C. Byrd (D-W.Va.) voted "not guilty" on both articles even though he thought that Clinton's behavior constituted "an impeachable offense, a political high crime or misdemeanor against the state." But because he did not want to remove Clinton from office, Byrd had only one choice: to vote "not guilty." Other Senators, including Susan Collins (R-Me.), Olympia Snowe (R-Me.), James Jeffords (R-Vt.), Fred Thompson (R-Tenn.), Ted Stevens (R-Alaska), and Slade Gorton (R-Wash.) also concluded that Clinton was guilty on one or both articles but voted "not guilty" because they thought removal was unwarranted. John Breaux, a Democrat from Louisiana, voted against the articles but cautioned that his vote "is not a vote on the innocence of this President. He is not innocent." Bob Kerrey, a Democrat from Nebraska, added: "While there is plenty of blame to go around in this case, the person responsible for it going this far is the President of the United States."[81]

On January 19, 2001, his last day in office, Clinton admitted that he had provided—under oath—false responses to questions about his relationship with Lewinsky. In a statement made to Independent Counsel Robert W. Ray to avoid further prosecution after he left office, Clinton acknowledged that in his deposition in the Jones case he had "knowingly violated Judge Wright's

81. For details on the Clinton impeachment and the Senate votes, see Louis Fisher, "The Independent Counsel Statute," in Mark J. Rozell and Clyde Wilcox, eds., The Clinton Scandal and the Future of American Government 66–79 (2000).

discovery orders" and that some of his responses to questions about Lewinsky "were false." In addition, he agreed to pay a fine of $25,000 to the Arkansas Bar Association, promised not to seek reimbursement of any legal fees from a federal court, and accepted a five-year suspension of his Arkansas law licence.[82]

Executive Privilege

The claim of executive privilege invites a confrontation between the power of Congress to investigate and the power of a President to withhold information. Although these prerogatives are often cast in unqualified and unconditional terms, generally there are opportunities to negotiate a settlement satisfactory to both branches. If the two branches cannot agree, the matter may find its way into the courts. Based on political and legal controversies over the past two centuries, it is possible to identify some general areas where control is exclusive and others where it is shared.

Access by Congress

The House of Representatives has the "sole Power of Impeachment." It cannot discharge that constitutional responsibility unless it has full access to materials needed for an investigation. When President Washington refused to share with the House certain papers regarding the Jay Treaty, he did so on the ground that the House is constitutionally excluded from the treaty-making process. Had the House sought the papers as part of an impeachment, Washington suggested, the information would have been made available.[83] The power of impeachment, said President Polk, gives to the House of Representatives

> the right to investigate the conduct of all public officers under the Government. This is cheerfully admitted. In such a case the safety of the Republic would be the supreme law, and the power of the House in the pursuit of this object would penetrate into the most secret recesses of the Executive Departments. It could command the attendance of any and every agent of the Government, and compel them to produce all papers, public or private, official or unofficial, and to testify on oath to all facts within their knowledge.[84]

82. "Exiting Job, Clinton Accepts Immunity Deal: Admits Testimony Was False—Long Legal Fight Ends," New York Times, January 20, 2001, at A1.
83. 1 Richardson 187 (March 30, 1796).
84. 5 Richardson 2284 (April 20, 1846).

Even short of impeachment, executive privilege is inappropriate when there are charges of administrative malfeasance. President Jackson, a jealous defender of executive prerogatives, told Congress that if it could "point to any case where there is the slightest reason to suspect corruption or abuse of trust, no obstacle which I can remove shall be interposed to prevent the fullest scrutiny by all legal means. The offices of all the departments will be opened to you, and every proper facility furnished for this purpose."[85] The Supreme Court has noted that the power of Congress to conduct investigations "comprehends probes into departments of the Federal Government to expose corruption, inefficiency or waste."[86]

Attorney General William French Smith, although upholding a very broad theory of executive privilege in 1982, admitted that he would not try "to shield documents [from Congress] which contain evidence of criminal or unethical conduct by agency officials from proper review."[87] During a news conference in 1983, President Reagan said: "We will never invoke executive privilege to cover up wrongdoing."[88] After the Iran-Contra story broke in November 1986, President Reagan permitted his two former national security advisers (Robert McFarlane and John Poindexter) to testify before Congress, allowed his Cabinet officials (including Secretary of State George Shultz and Secretary of Defense Caspar Weinberger) to discuss with Congress conversations they had had with the President, and made available to Congress thousands of sensitive, classified documents.

In 1995 President Clinton initially refused to hand over to Congress a document relating to Whitewater, but as explained earlier in this chapter, the administration relented and released the material. A year later, he invoked executive privilege to deny Congress access to a secret internal report on his 1994 decision to tacitly approve Iranian weapons shipments to Bosnian Muslims. The report was withheld even from the House and Senate Intelligence Committees. In 1996 President Clinton again asserted executive privilege to withhold from Congress documents relating to Travelgate, but after the House moved to cite the White House Counsel for contempt, Congress was given access to the materials.

Several barriers stand in the way of full disclosure to Congress. The Supreme Court noted in 1959 that Congress "cannot inquire into matters which are within the exclusive province of one of the other branches of the Govern-

85. Cong. Debates, 24th Cong., 2d Sess., vol. 13, part 2, Appendix, at 202, but see entire discussion at 188–225.

86. Watkins v. United States, 354 U.S. at 187.

87. Letter of November 30, 1982, to Congressman John Dingell, reprinted in H. Rept. No. 968, 97th Cong., 2d Sess. 41 (1982).

88. Public Papers of the Presidents, 1983 (I), at 239.

ment."[89] Were Congress to seek information concerning a pardon, for example, the President could decline on the ground that the matter is solely executive in nature and of no concern to Congress (unless the pardon required appropriations for an amnesty program). Likewise, the President need not disclose to anyone in Congress the details of a treaty being negotiated. He may do so to enlist the support of legislators, but it is purely voluntary. It is done for political, not constitutional, reasons.

Similarly, until the President submits to the Senate the name of a nominee, Congress has no grounds for gaining access to the applicant's file. Requests for personnel and medical files might be regarded by the President as an unwarranted intrusion into personal privacy. The removal power over top executive officials is strongly attached to the President's office. Grover Cleveland once withheld from the Senate various papers and documents that pertained to a suspended official. The power to remove, he said, was solely an executive prerogative and could not be shared or compromised with the Senate.[90]

The politics of the nomination process can force the release of documents that are normally protected. President Reagan invoked executive privilege in 1986 to deny to the Senate certain internal memos that Chief Justice–designate William H. Rehnquist had written while serving in the Justice Department from 1969 to 1971. The purpose was to protect the confidentiality and candor of the legal advice submitted to Presidents and their assistants. When it appeared that the dispute might delay Rehnquist's confirmation indefinitely, Reagan agreed to give the Senate access to many of the documents.[91] Two years later, other internal documents from the Justice Department were turned over to the Senate to secure the confirmation of Stephen S. Trott to the Ninth Circuit.[92]

Investigatory files in the executive branch may enjoy a protected status. Whereas the judicial process calls for strict rules of evidence and procedural safeguards to protect the accused, looser standards prevail during congressional investigations. The President may therefore feel an obligation to protect an individual against the disclosure of allegations and hearsay. It is possible to extend this argument to the protection of security files for federal employees (except for confirmation purposes). In 1950 President Truman wrote to Senator

89. Barenblatt v. United States, 360 U.S. at 112.

90. Louis Fisher, "Grover Cleveland Against the Senate," 7 Cong. Stud. 11 (1979); Grover Cleveland, The Independence of the Executive 48–82 (1913). President Jackson, also operating on the theory that the removal power lay exclusively with the President, refused to give the Senate information concerning a dismissed official; 3 Richardson 1352.

91. Washington Post, August 1, 1986, at A1; August 6, 1986, at A1; August 8, 1986, at A3; Fisher, The Politics of Executive Privilege, at 76–81.

92. Washington Post, March 25, 1988, at A23.

Millard E. Tydings that he was denying his request for investigative files relating to federal employees charged with disloyalty. Release of the investigative files, he said, might prejudice the effectiveness of FBI investigations, embarrass and endanger confidential informants, and injure innocent individuals accused by malicious or misinformed people.[93]

Formulation of a policy requires trust and confidentiality among presidential aides. Therefore, no one in Congress was entitled to the preparatory materials that led to the Camp David accords under President Carter, to the Reagan administration's early drafts proposing the sale of military aircraft (AWACS) to Saudi Arabia, or to the Clinton administration's version of a Bosnia plan that was later ratified by the parties in Dayton, Ohio. When a witness before a congressional committee in 1971 commented that the President's first draft of a message was none of Congress's business, Senator William Fulbright replied: "Sure. What did he say to Mr. Kissinger this morning before breakfast? I think that is out."[94] Congressional committees recognize that advisers to the President need not disclose discussions of a confidential nature.[95] However, grave scandals, such as the Iran-Contra affair, may convince the President to waive executive privilege in its entirety, including confidential talks with the President.

Congressional investigations into matters pending in the courts have unique hurdles to overcome. The Senate Watergate Committee failed in its attempt to obtain certain documents and tapes directly from President Nixon. Stymied in this effort, the committee appealed to the judiciary, only to be told by a district court that it lacked jurisdiction. Congress passed a special statute to confer jurisdiction, but this time the lower courts held that the release of material to the committee created the undue risk of pretrial publicity in the pending Watergate prosecutions.[96] The courts also concluded that the Senate had failed to demonstrate an immediate need for the tapes, partly because the House Judiciary Committee already possessed copies of the tapes acquired during its impeachment investigation.[97]

The existence of an impeachment effort underscores the extraordinary circumstances surrounding the Watergate case. On other occasions the spirit

93. Public Papers of the Presidents, 1950, at 229–32, 240–41. See also 40 Op. Att'y Gen. 45 (1941), and Archibald Cox, "Executive Privilege," 122 U. Pa. L. Rev. 1383, 1427 (1974).
94. "Transmittal of Executive Agreements to Congress," hearings before the Senate Committee on Foreign Relations, 92d Cong., 1st Sess. 31, 33 (1971).
95. Donald G. Morgan, Congress and the Constitution 16–21 (1966).
96. Senate Select Com. on Pres. Campaign Activities v. Nixon, 366 F.Supp. 51 (D.D.C. 1973); 87 Stat. 736 (1973).
97. Senate Select Com. on Pres. Campaign Activities v. Nixon, 370 F.Supp. 521 (D.D.C. 1974), aff'd, Senate Select Com. on Pres. Campaign Activities v. Nixon, 498 F.2d 725, 732, 734 (D.C. Cir. 1974).

between the branches has been more cooperative. In order not to interfere with the government's prosecution of a criminal case, congressional committees may decide to defer their investigation until completion of the criminal trial. For example, after Senator Harrison A. Williams Jr. was indicted on several criminal counts, the Senate suspended its own investigation until he was found guilty in 1981. Facing an almost certain expulsion vote later that year, he resigned.[98]

Kilbourn and other early decisions suggested that a congressional investigation could not interfere with matters pending before a court. Under that doctrine, however, legislative inquiries could be frustrated for years while awaiting the outcome of a lawsuit. Congress is free to investigate a matter even if it results in publicity prejudicial to a defendant. In such situations a court may find it necessary to postpone a trial until the prejudice has been removed.[99] When Congress seeks a document that it could have had in the absence of a lawsuit, the mere existence of a suit or a grand jury action is inadequate reason to withhold information from Congress.[100]

Investigations by the independent counsel often compete with congressional efforts to probe the same dispute. Congress may decide to accommodate the independent counsel by delaying a legislative investigation, but Independent Counsel Lawrence E. Walsh recognized that his investigation into the Iran-Contra affair did not automatically trump Congress's decision to hold hearings and conduct its own inquiry. In order to publicize and facilitate its investigation, Congress can grant immunity to witnesses, and "there is no way that it can be avoided. They have the last word and that is a proper distribution of power."[101]

Executive officials sometimes claim that they cannot share information with Congress without it being leaked to the public. For example, Congressman John E. Moss sought information about a company's reserve estimates for all its natural gas leases and contracts. This information is protected by Exemption 4 of the Freedom of Information Act (FOIA), which exempts "trade secrets and commercial or financial information obtained from a person and privileged or confidential." However, Moss requested the information not as a member of the public but in his capacity as subcommittee chairman, and the FOIA expressly states that the exemption "is not authority to withhold

98. S. Rept. No. 187, 97th Cong., 1st Sess. 2 (1981).

99. Delaney v. United States, 199 F.2d 107, 114–15 (1st Cir. 1952). See also Hutcheson v. United States, 369 U.S. 599, 612–13, 623–25 (1962), and Sinclair v. United States, 279 U.S. 263, 295 (1929).

100. In re Hearings before the Committee on Banking and Currency of the United States Senate, 19 F.R.D. 410, 412 (N.D. Ill. 1956).

101. Lawrence E. Walsh, "The Independent Counsel and the Separation of Powers," 25 Houston L. Rev. 1, 9 (1988).

information from Congress."[102] Another argument used to deny the information to Moss relied on language in the Federal Trade Commission Act, which empowers the commission to release information "except trade secrets and the names of customers." The company maintained that the restriction also applied to Congress, implying that what was shared with Congress would soon find its way to the public domain. Two courts refused to conclude that the transfer of information from the Federal Trade Commission to the subcommittee would lead "inexorably to either public dissemination" or disclosure to the company's competitors. Judges presume that congressional committees will exercise their powers responsibly.[103]

When executive officials refuse to comply with a congressional request for information, one of the instruments of coercion is the contempt power. A 1975 tug-of-war between the branches, with Congress the eventual victor, concerned Arab boycott reports compiled by the Department of Commerce. Secretary Rogers Morton initially refused to comply with a committee subpoena. After facing contempt proceedings, however, he bowed to the will of Congress and released the material. In 1980 President Carter threatened to withhold documents concerning his oil import fee. Secretary Charles W. Duncan Jr., with a contempt citation hanging over his head, yielded the documents to a House subcommittee. A year later Secretary of Energy James B. Edwards narrowly escaped a contempt citation by agreeing to provide information on the synthetic fuels program to a House committee.[104]

This pattern of conflict continued with two members of the Reagan Cabinet: Interior Secretary James Watt and Environmental Protection Agency (EPA) Administrator Anne (Gorsuch) Burford. Watt withheld documents from a House subcommittee in 1981, provoking a committee subpoena for the documents and a recommendation by the Committee on Energy and Commerce that he be cited for contempt. Several weeks later Watt made the documents available to the subcommittee. The documents were to be delivered to a secure room on Capitol Hill and reviewed only by subcommittee members; subcommittee staff would not be allowed to provide technical

102. 5 U.S.C. 552(d) (2000).
103. Ashland Oil, Inc. v. FTC, 409 F.Supp. 297, 308 (D.D.C. 1976), aff'd, 548 F.2d 977 (D.C. Cir. 1976). See also Exxon Corp. v. FTC, 589 F.2d 582, 589–91 (D.C. Cir. 1978), cert. denied, 441 U.S. 943 (1979).
104. "Contempt Proceedings Against Secretary of Commerce, Rogers C. B. Morton," hearings before the House Committee on Interstate and Foreign Commerce, 94th Cong., 1st Sess. (1975), and 121 Cong. Rec. 40768–69 (1975); Duncan: Cong. Q. Wkly Rept., May 17, 1980, at 1352; Edwards: Washington Post, July 30, 1981, at A2. For further details on the power of Congress to issue subpoenas and hold executive officials in contempt, see Fisher, The Politics of Executive Privilege, at 91–134.

assistance. Moreover, the members could not photocopy the documents, but they could take notes. Some subcommittee members objected to the exclusion of staff, who function as a necessary extension and "alter ego" of members of Congress.[105]

In an early phase of the Watt confrontation, Attorney General William French Smith advised President Reagan to invoke executive privilege in response to the subcommittee subpoena. Smith's opinion displayed an extraordinary misconception about the legislative branch. First, he said that "the interest of Congress in obtaining information for oversight purposes is, I believe, considerably weaker than its interest when specific legislative proposals are in question."[106] But the courts have consistently held that the investigative power is available not merely to legislate or when a "potential" for legislation exists but also for pursuits down blind alleys. Even if there were some basis for Smith's argument (and there was not), Congress could have easily neutralized it by introducing a bill whenever it had oversight in mind.

Smith also claimed that "all of the documents in issue are either necessary and fundamental to the deliberative process presently ongoing in the Executive Branch or relate to sensitive foreign policy considerations."[107] The dispute with Watt concerned the impact of Canadian investment and energy policies on American commerce, an issue clearly covered by Congress's enumerated constitutional power to "regulate Commerce with foreign Nations" and its authority to oversee the particular statute that established the nation's policy on foreign investments. Moreover, the record demonstrates that the documents were not of "fundamental" importance to the deliberative process. They could have been, and eventually were, shared with the committee.[108]

The accommodation over the Watt documents should have formed a foundation for better executive-legislative relationships. Indeed, when the oversight subcommittee of the House Public Works Committee sought documents on the EPA's enforcement of the "Superfund" program, it was advised by the agency that there would be no objection "so long as the confidentiality of the information in those files was maintained."[109] The subcommittee had

105. "Contempt of Congress," hearings before the House Committee on Energy and Commerce, 97th Cong., 2d Sess. 385–94 (1982).
106. "Executive Privilege: Legal Opinions Regarding Claim of President Ronald Reagan in Response to a Subpoena Issued to James G. Watt, Secretary of the Interior," prepared for the House Committee on Energy and Commerce, 97th Cong., 1st Sess. 3 (Comm. Print November 1981).
107. Id. at 2.
108. "Contempt of Congress," hearings before the House Committee on Energy and Commerce, 97th Cong., 2d Sess. 385–94 (1982); H. Rept. No. 898, 97th Cong., 2d Sess. (1982).
109. H. Rept. No. 968, 97th Cong., 2d Sess. 11 (1982).

been investigating the $1.6 billion program established by Congress to clean up hazardous waste sites and to prosecute companies responsible for illegal dumping.

Shortly thereafter the Reagan administration decided that Congress could not see documents in active litigation files. The administration's reversal appeared to be triggered by requests from other committees. Another oversight panel from the House Energy and Commerce Committee wanted access to the same type of information. The administration expressed concern that executive branch control would be undermined by these multiple requests.[110] Both oversight subcommittees had reason to suspect that the major chemical companies were not paying their full share of the costs, requiring the taxpayers to pick up the balance.

EPA Administrator Gorsuch, acting under instructions from President Reagan, refused to turn over "sensitive documents found in open law enforcement files." Reagan's memorandum to her, dated November 30, 1982, claimed that those documents represented "internal deliberative materials containing enforcement strategy and statements of the Government's position on various legal issues which may be raised in enforcement actions relative to the various hazardous waste sites" by the EPA or the Department of Justice.[111] The administration's initial position in the Watt dispute had not changed; it assumed that since documents shared with Congress might find their way into the public realm, they should not be shared at all. Following this logic, congressional oversight would have to be put on hold for years until the government completed its enforcement actions.

The Public Works Committee held Gorsuch in contempt and the House of Representatives voted 259 to 105 to support the contempt citation. Although partisan overtones were present, 55 Republicans joined 204 Democrats to build the top-heavy majority.[112] Pursuant to the statutory procedure for contempt citations, the Speaker certified the facts and referred them to the U.S. Attorney for presentation to a grand jury. Instead, the administration asked a district court to declare the House action an unconstitutional intrusion into the President's authority to withhold information from Congress. In 1983 the court dismissed the government's suit on the ground that judicial intervention in executive-legislative disputes "should be delayed until all possibilities for settlement have been exhausted."[113] The court urged both parties to devote their energies to compromise and cooperation, not confrontation. The Reagan administration agreed to release "enforcement sensitive" documents to

110. Id. at 15, 21.
111. H. Rept. No. 968, 97th Cong., 2d Sess. 76 (1982); id. at 42.
112. 128 Cong. Rec. 31746–76 (1982).
113. United States v. House of Representatives, 556 F.Supp. 150, 152 (D.D.C. 1983).

Congress, but only in a series of steps, beginning with briefings and edited versions and eventually ending with the unedited documents.[114]

One of the casualties of this confrontation was former EPA official Rita M. Lavelle, who was sentenced in 1984 to six months in prison, five years' probation, and a fine of $10,000 for lying to Congress about her management of the Super-fund program. She was the only EPA official indicted in the scandal. However, more than 20 top officials, including Anne Burford, left the EPA amid allegations of perjury, conflict of interest, and political manipulation of the agency.[115]

In 1993 House Republicans tried to investigate the firing of seven Travel Office employees from the Clinton White House. The House Judiciary Committee, controlled by Democrats, blocked the effort. After the Republicans gained control of Congress in the 1994 elections, the House Committee on Government Reform and Oversight began a detailed probe of the firings, but the release of documents by the White House was slow and episodic. In 1996, to expedite the inquiry, the House passed a resolution conferring special authorities on the committee. The resolution authorized the committee chairman, after consulting with the ranking Democrat on the committee, to direct a member or staff of the committee to take affidavits and depositions pursuant to notice or subpoena and under oath. This procedure allowed the staff to depose more than 50 potential witnesses. From that effort the chairman could select a handful of witnesses to appear before the full committee during public hearings. This kind of authority is granted only on rare occasions, such as the congressional investigations into Koreagate, Abscam, and Iran-Contra.[116]

Access by the Courts

Efforts to withhold information may have to give ground in cases of criminal prosecution. When government prosecutors attempt to withhold from the judiciary sensitive materials needed for a trial (statements by witnesses for the government, an informer's identity, and the like), the courts offer prosecutors a choice: either produce the information or drop the charges.[117] Congress passed legislation to empower federal judges to inspect sensitive materials *in camera* (in the privacy of their chambers). If the government decides not to comply with this procedure, the courts may strike from the record the testimony of the government's witness or declare a mistrial.[118]

114. H. Rept. No. 323, 98th Cong., 1st Sess. 18–40 (1983).
115. Washington Post, January 10, 1984, at A2.
116. 142 Cong. Rec. 4094–4100 (1996).
117. Roviaro v. United States, 353 U.S. 53 (1957), and Jencks v. United States, 353 U.S. 657 (1957).
118. 71 Stat. 595 (1957). See also Alderman v. United States, 394 U.S. 165, 181 (1969), and Giordano v. United States, 394 U.S. 310 (1969).

Defendants sometimes used the tactic of "graymail," or threatening to disclose classified information. They hoped that this would force the government to dismiss criminal charges to avoid the release of sensitive material. Congress passed legislation in 1980—the Classified Information Procedures Act (CIPA)—to allow a judge to screen classified information to determine whether it could be used during a trial.[119]

A brief written for President Nixon during his impeachment process acknowledged that executive privilege "cannot be claimed to shield executive officers from prosecution for crime." But Nixon believed that the President, not the courts, should determine whether information fell within the scope of the privilege. The brief concluded that the "public interest in a conviction, important though it is, must yield to the public interest in preserving the confidentiality of the President's office."[120] In a subsequent brief, Nixon maintained that the only constitutional recourse against a President in matters of executive privilege "is by impeachment and through the electoral process."[121]

In a unanimous decision, the Supreme Court required Nixon to produce certain Watergate tape recordings and documents relating to his conversations with aides. A federal grand jury had returned an indictment charging seven men—employed either by the White House or by the Committee for the Re-Election of the President—with a number of offenses, including conspiracy to defraud the United States and to obstruct justice. To permit an absolute, unqualified executive privilege would have prevented the judiciary from carrying out its duties under the Constitution. The adversary nature of the American judicial system requires access to information in order to establish guilt or innocence. "The ends of criminal justice," said the Court, "would be defeated if judgments were to be founded on a partial or speculative presentation of the facts." The integrity of the judicial system depends on the compulsory production of evidence needed by the prosecution or the defense.[122]

A prosecutor had to persuade the trial court that the materials sought were relevant, admissible as evidence, and specific. Once this was done, the trial judge could inspect the requested materials *in camera,* determining which portions were required for the trial. Of central importance was the conclusion that the courts, not the President, decide the scope of executive privilege.

119. 94 Stat. 2025 (1980).

120. 9 Wkly Comp. Pres. Doc. 968–69 (August 7, 1973). The brief also stated that "executive privilege does not vanish because the grand jury is looking into charges of criminal conduct." Id. at 967.

121. 10 Wkly Comp. Pres. Doc. 662 (June 21, 1974).

122. United States v. Nixon, 418 U.S. 683, 709 (1974). President Nixon also lost two lower court tests: In re Subpoena to Nixon, 360 F.Supp. 1 (D.D.C. 1973), and Nixon v. Sirica, 487 F.2d 700 (D.C. Cir. 1973).

Also significant was the first recognition by the Supreme Court that executive privilege has its source in the Constitution. The President's privilege regarding communications with aides is "fundamental to the operation of government and inextricably rooted in the separation of powers under the Constitution." The question of what would happen when evidence was needed for *civil* litigation was left for another day.[123]

National Security and Foreign Affairs

Even more privileged than executive confidentiality in communications, according to the Court in *Nixon* (1974), is the President's "need to protect military, diplomatic or sensitive national security secrets."[124] Nothing in the *Nixon* case involved such secrets, and it is unfortunate that the Court indulged in such careless dicta. The ruling mechanically echoed previous decisions that deferred to presidential responsibilities in military and diplomatic matters. In 1948 the Supreme Court said that it would be "intolerable that courts, without the relevant information, should review and perhaps nullify actions of the Executive taken on information properly held secret. Nor can courts sit *in camera* in order to be taken into executive confidences. But even if courts could require full disclosure, the very nature of executive decisions as to foreign policy is political, not judicial."[125]

What happens when "secret" information is needed for a trial? In *United States v. Reynolds* (1953), three women tried to recover damages as widows of civilians killed in the crash of a military aircraft. To support their claim they requested certain documents from the Air Force. A district court and the Third Circuit ruled that the government's claim of privilege did not justify withholding evidence required for a pending lawsuit. At a minimum, the government needed to show the documents to the district judge so that they could be examined in his chambers. After failing to release the documents, the government lost in both district court and the Third Circuit.[126]

The Supreme Court reversed those judgments by a 6-to-3 vote. Although the Court noted that judicial control over the evidence of a case cannot be "abdicated to the caprice of executive officers," it also held that the judiciary "should not jeopardize the security which the privilege is meant to protect by insisting upon an examination of the evidence, even by the judge alone, in

---

123. United States v. Nixon, 418 U.S., at 708, 712 n.19.
124. Id. at 706.
125. C. & S. Air Lines v. Waterman Corp., 333 U.S. 103, 111 (1948).
126. Brauner v. United States, 10 F.R.D. 468 (E.D. Pa. 1950); Reynolds v. United States, 192 F.2d 987 (3d Cir. 1951). For background and analysis, see Louis Fisher, In the Name of National Security: Unchecked Presidential Power and the *Reynolds* Case 29–91 (2006).

chambers." To add weight to its judgment, the Court noted (in the climate of the Korean War) that "this is a time of vigorous preparation for national defense."[127] In essence, then, the Court did indeed abdicate its role to executive officers because it refused to examine the documents requested by the widows. If courts are unwilling to examine national security evidence *in camera*, they cannot know whether administration officials are acting capriciously.

In 2000 the daughter of one of the civilian engineers killed in the military crash found the declassified documents through an Internet search. There were no "state secrets" in the documents. The three families once again returned to the courts for justice, this time charging fraud against the judiciary because the government had misled the courts, but their effort was unsuccessful.[128]

Since the early 1950s the courts have been drawn into several disputes involving secret information. The concept of "national security," used on occasion as an umbrella term to justify any number of executive actions, brings into play many competing sections of the Constitution. The Nixon administration, for example, attempted to have the courts enjoin two newspapers from publishing the Pentagon Papers, a secret study on the origins and conduct of the Vietnam War. The Supreme Court held against the administration. The word "security," said Justice Black, "is a broad, vague generality whose contours should not be invoked to abrogate the fundamental law embodied in the First Amendment. The guarding of military and diplomatic secrets at the expense of informed representative government provides no real security for our Republic."[129] This decision had limited application to executive privilege. Because the Pentagon Papers had been leaked to the press, the question was one of prior restraint on the press—a First Amendment test that an administration would find it difficult to meet.

Access to executive documents is regulated in part by the Freedom of Information Act. First written in 1966, the FOIA directs agencies to make information available to the public, subject to nine exemptions. The first consists

127. United States v. Reynolds, 345 U.S. 1, 9–10 (1953).

128. Herring v. United States, 424 F.3d 384 (3d Cir. 2005), cert. denied, 126 S.Ct. 1909 (2006). For details on this litigation from 2003 to 2006, see Fisher, In the Name of National Security, at 165–211.

129. New York Times Co. v. United States, 403 U.S. 713, 719 (1971). United States v. Marchetti, 466 F.2d 1309 (4th Cir. 1972), cert. denied, 409 U.S. 1063 (1972), required an author to submit to the CIA—prior to publication—any writing relating to the agency. The CIA could excise from the manuscript any passage that contained undisclosed classified information. The decision was based in part on the President's constitutional responsibility in foreign affairs and national security to prevent the disclosure of classified materials (executive privilege), but the court also cited statutory grounds for agency censorship (delegated power). Snepp v. United States, 444 U.S. 507 (1980), also upheld the CIA's prepublication review but appeared to be based on statutory authority (see n. 3 at 509 and 512).

of matters "specifically authorized under criteria established by an Executive order to be kept secret in the interest of the national defense or foreign policy." The exemptions were supposed to limit access to information by the *public,* not Congress. The act explicitly states that the exemptions do not constitute authority "to withhold information from Congress."[130]

Nevertheless, the FOIA has been used to withhold information from individual members of Congress. In 1971, 33 members of the House of Representatives attempted to obtain documents prepared for President Nixon concerning an underground nuclear test scheduled for Amchitka Island, Alaska. The Supreme Court in *Mink* (1973) decided that it had no authority to examine the documents *in camera* to sift out "non-secret components" for their release.[131] Executive privilege was not at issue, since the information had been withheld on statutory grounds (Exemption 1 of the FOIA). The Court's interpretation prompted Congress to rewrite the act in 1974, requiring that material withheld under Exemption 1 be "properly classified" pursuant to an executive order. This provision, coupled with a clarification of court review, overrode the holding in *Mink.* Federal courts are now clearly authorized to examine executive records in judges' chambers as part of a determination of the nine categories of exemptions under the FOIA.[132] This authority brings the courts a long way in terms of attitude, procedures, and capability to pass judgment on national security withholdings. The new doctrine contrasts sharply with the rulings in *C. & S. Air Lines* (1948) and *Reynolds* (1953).

Although it may be proper for the courts to sometimes defer to the President on national security grounds, the same attitude should not be taken by Congress. Unlike the courts, Congress has explicit responsibilities under the Constitution to declare war, provide for the common defense, raise and support armies, and provide and maintain a navy. Legislative expertise exists in the Armed Services Committees, the defense appropriations subcommittees, the Budget Committees, and a number of other congressional panels. By 1977 both houses had established select committees on intelligence to receive classified information from the CIA and other elements of the U.S. intelligence community.

Deference by the courts, therefore, need not mean deference by Congress. In *C. & S. Air Lines,* the Supreme Court declined to settle an issue on the

130. Originally enacted in 1966 (80 Stat. 250), the FOIA was codified the following year with some changes (81 Stat. 54) and amended in 1974 (88 Stat. 1561) and 1976 (90 Stat. 1241). It is codified at 5 U.S.C. 552 (2000).

131. EPA v. Mink, 410 U.S. 73 (1973).

132. 88 Stat. 1562, sec. 4(B). See H. Rept. No. 1380, 93d Cong., 2d Sess. 8–9, 11–12 (1974). For legislative steps in strengthening the role of federal courts in national security issues, see Fisher, In the Name of National Security, at 124–64.

ground that foreign policy decisions "are wholly confided by our Constitution to the political departments of the government, Executive *and Legislative*."[133] In 1986 the Court discussed its role in a case involving "this Nation's foreign relations" and recognized "the premier role which both Congress and the Executive play in this field."[134]

This joint responsibility is illustrated by a confrontation in the 1970s. Congressman John Moss, acting through his subcommittee, issued a subpoena to obtain from the American Telephone and Telegraph Company information on "national security" wiretaps by the administration. A district court, after balancing the investigative power of Congress against the President's executive privilege in foreign affairs, announced in 1976 that "if a final determination as to the need to maintain the secrecy of this material, or as to what constitutes an acceptable risk of disclosure, must be made, it should be made by the constituent branch of government to which the primary role in these areas is entrusted. In the areas of national security and foreign policy, that role is given to the Executive." An appellate court remanded this decision five months later. The election of Jimmy Carter had created new possibilities for resolving the matter out of court. The appellate court returned the case to the lower court with the recommendation that Congress and the executive branch attempt to negotiate a settlement: "A compromise worked out between the branches is most likely to meet their essential needs and the country's constitutional balance."[135]

Additional guidance was needed from the appellate court to break the deadlock between the two branches. Judge Harold Leventhal put pressure on both parties to clarify their major concerns and reach an accommodation. The case was dismissed on December 21, 1978, after the Justice Department and the subcommittee amicably resolved their differences.[136]

In discussing executive privilege, there is a temptation to cede to the President broad scope in military, diplomatic, or national security affairs. This is too great a concession. Generalizations of this order should be avoided. As illustrated by the James Watt dispute, what appears to be "foreign policy" to the President may seem with equal clarity to be "foreign commerce" to Congress. Although the judiciary may decide at times to yield to presidential initiatives

133. C. & S. Air Lines v. Waterman Corp., 333 U.S. 103, 111 (1948). Emphasis added.
134. Japan Whaling Assn. v. American Cetacean Society, 478 U.S. 221, 230 (1986).
135. United States v. AT&T, 551 F.2d 384, 394 (D.C. Cir. 1976). For the district court decision, see United States v. AT&T, 419 F.Supp. 454, 461 (D.D.C. 1976).
136. United States v. AT&T, 567 F.2d 121 (D.C. Cir. 1977). For the settlement, see "Court Proceedings and Actions of Vital Interest to the Congress, Current to December 31, 1978," prepared by the House Select Committee on Congressional Operations, 95th Cong., 2d Sess. 50 (1978).

in military, diplomatic, and national security affairs, no such acquiescence should be expected of Congress.[137]

The scope of executive privilege remains in a state of tension because of three competing demands: the integrity of the judicial process requires evidence; the executive branch needs a measure of confidentiality in its deliberations; and Congress depends on information to carry out its responsibilities. Because the three branches of government are coequal in status and have a right to preserve their independence and influence, it would be contrary to the Constitution for one branch to subordinate its interests to another. Accommodations by all parties are essential. The Supreme Court may claim to be the final arbiter in disputes involving executive privilege, but it can exercise that role only selectively and discreetly. Most of the collisions between Congress and the President over documents and witnesses will be resolved politically, not through litigation.

137. Congress has full constitutional authority to weigh and override national security claims asserted by the executive branch. See Fisher, The Politics of Executive Privilege, at 229–56.

7

THE POWER OF THE PURSE

Based primarily on its power to appropriate funds and its unique status as a representative body, Congress is justly regarded as the "First Branch of Government." The power of the purse, James Madison noted in Federalist 58, represents the "most complete and effectual weapon with which any constitution can arm the immediate representatives of the people, for obtaining a redress of every grievance, and for carrying into effect every just and salutary measure." Article I, Section 9, of the Constitution places this weapon squarely in the hands of Congress: "No Money shall be drawn from the Treasury, but in Consequence of Appropriations made by Law." Using pithier language in Federalist 48, Madison said that "the legislative department alone has access to the pockets of the people."

Constitutional Limitations

The appropriations power, though broad, is restricted by other provisions in the Constitution. Congress cannot lawfully use its funding power to establish a religion,[1] diminish the compensation of members of the federal judiciary,[2] or take other actions specifically proscribed by the Constitution. Congress may not impose unconstitutional conditions on recipients of federal funds.[3] When statutory directives conflict with constitutional rights, the courts are available to police the boundaries. The flow of federal money is not "the final arbiter of constitutionally protected rights."[4]

1. Flast v. Cohen, 392 U.S. 83, 104–5 (1968). However, the courts may deny plaintiffs standing to challenge federal assistance to religious institutions; Valley Forge College v. Americans United, 454 U.S. 464 (1982). In this 5-to-4 decision, the dissenters disagreed sharply with the Court's paper-thin distinction between the Spending Clause (*Flast*) and the Property Clause (*Valley Forge*).

2. United States v. Will, 449 U.S. 200 (1980); Booth v. United States, 291 U.S. 339 (1934); O'Donoghue v. United States, 289 U.S. 516 (1933).

3. Comments, "The Federal Conditional Spending Power: A Search for Limits," 70 Nw. U. L. Rev. 293 (1975). See also Smith v. Ehrlich, 430 F. Supp. 818 (D.D.C. 1976), although in this instance the condition was upheld.

4. Clark v. Board of Education of Little Rock Sch. Dist., 374 F.2d 569, 571 (8th Cir. 1967). See also Califano v. Westcott, 443 U.S. 76, 92–93 (1979).

A celebrated example of judicial supervision concerned a rider to an appropriations bill in 1943 that prohibited the payment of federal salaries to three named "subversives." The courts struck down the section because it represented a bill of attainder (legislative punishment without judicial trial) proscribed by Article III, Section 3, of the Constitution.[5] In addition, when a proviso in an appropriations act collides with the President's power to pardon and attempts to prescribe to the judiciary the effect of the pardon, the proviso cannot stand.[6]

In recent years the courts have reviewed the constitutionality of provisions in appropriations bills that deny public funds to indigent women seeking abortions. In 1976 a district court struck down the following language in an appropriations act: "None of the funds contained in this Act shall be used to perform abortions except where the life of the mother would be endangered if the fetus were carried to term."[7] In 1980 the same court held unconstitutional a congressional restriction (the Hyde Amendment) on the use of federal funds for abortions.[8] In response, 238 members of Congress signed an amicus brief instructing the Supreme Court that the district court had violated the appropriations power of Congress. Claiming that the "appropriation and expenditure of tax funds is inherently a political question," the brief argued that the Supreme Court "has never taken the position that the judiciary may oversee the appropriations process or set itself up as the ultimate arbiter of federal fiscal policy."[9] The brief was overstated, to be sure, but later that year the Court upheld the Hyde Amendment. It refused to extend the constitutional freedom of choice to have an abortion to include a right of federal financial support. The latter was "a question for Congress to answer, not a matter of constitutional entitlement."[10]

The Constitution prohibits the appropriation of funds to raise and support armies for a term of more than two years. Yet Congress, supported by opinions of the Attorneys General, has been able to provide funds to the Defense Department for longer periods—even providing "no-year" funds for defense procurement and research and development (making funds available until expended). This practice came to an end in 1970 when Congress decided that appropriations would be made on a two-year basis for research and development,

5. United States v. Lovett, 328 U.S. 303 (1946). See also Blitz v. Donovan, 538 F.Supp. 1119 (D.D.C. 1982).
6. United States v. Klein, 13 Wall. 128 (1872); Hart v. United States, 118 U.S. 62 (1886).
7. McRae v. Mathews, 421 F.Supp. 533 (E.D. N.Y. 1976).
8. McRae v. Califano, 491 F.Supp. 630, 728–31 (E.D. N.Y. 1980).
9. 126 Cong. Rec. 5949 (1980).
10. Harris v. McRae, 448 U.S. 297, 318 (1980).

three years for procurement, and five years for shipbuilding. Congress made the changes for policy, not constitutional, reasons.[11]

The legal justification for appropriating funds to the Defense Department for more than a two-year term relies on the following distinction: "raising and supporting" (subject to the two-year limit) and "equipping" (which is not). The drafts of the Constitution offer some support for this interpretation. The verb "equip" was initially applied to the Navy, as in "raise armies, (& equip Fleets)"; "raising a military Land Force—and of equiping a Navy—"; or "Raise Armies; to build and equip Fleets." When the draft was completed, the Constitution used "raise and support" for the Army and "provide and maintain" for the Navy. The two-year limit applied to armies, not navies. The framers, primarily concerned about a standing army, were less concerned that funds might remain available over a period of years for the construction of vessels. Taking this reasoning a step further, it can be argued that the two-year limit does not apply to a construction item that takes years to produce, even if for the Army, Air Force, or Marine Corps.[12]

These topics have been of recurrent interest throughout America's constitutional history, flaring up at times to cause major controversies. Of more permanent concern, and forming the heart of this chapter, are three issues: (1) the establishment of budget priorities by Congress and the President, (2) reliance on confidential and secret funds, and (3) efforts to combine the purse with the sword (the Iran-Contra affair).

The Budget and Accounting Act of 1921 attempted to pull together the scattered parts of a process that had become fragmented and uncoordinated over the years. Neither branch, prior to the act, could be said to exercise financial control. The legislation remained faithful to constitutional principles by making the President responsible for budget estimates and giving Congress final control over appropriated levels. The two branches were supposed to work in tandem, each carrying out distinct and specific duties.

Presidential Responsibility for Estimates

The President formulates budget estimates and submits them to Congress in accordance with the Budget and Accounting Act of 1921. Although this is the statutory source, the authority for submitting such estimates can also be derived from the Constitution. Under Article II, Section 3, the President "shall from time to time give to the Congress Information of the State of the Union,

11. Louis Fisher, Presidential Spending Power 127–30 (1975).
12. 2 Farrand 143, 158, 168, 182. See 25 Op. Att'y Gen. 105 (1904), and 40 Op. Att'y Gen. 55 (1948).

and recommend to their Consideration such Measures as he shall judge necessary and expedient." Therefore, the President did not have to await statutory authority to submit a budget. Indeed, President Taft submitted a budget in 1912 despite opposition from Congress.

The dispute about Taft's budget originated in 1910 when Congress appropriated $100,000 to finance a study into more efficient and economical ways of conducting the public business. Taft used the money to set up a five-member Commission on Economy and Efficiency. In June 1912 he released the commission's report, which called for a national budget initiated by the President and for which he would be held responsible. In that same month Taft ordered department heads to prepare two sets of estimates: one for the customary "Book of Estimates" (a loosely organized report consisting of unrelated bureau estimates) and one for the national budget recommended by the commission. Congress tried to stop Taft by passing legislation that directed executive officials to prepare estimates only in the customary manner.[13]

Treating the statute as unconstitutional, Taft directed department heads to prepare two sets of estimates. In a forceful statement, he argued that the Constitution empowered him to recommend measures to Congress and "to advise it as [to] the existing conditions and their betterment." In his opinion, it was "*entirely competent for the President to submit a budget,* and Congress can not forbid or prevent it."[14] Taft proceeded with his plan to prepare and submit a model budget. Congress ignored it.

The Budget and Accounting Act

The financial implications of World War I—especially the huge national debt that had to be managed by the Treasury Department—provided the main stimulus for the Budget and Accounting Act of 1921.[15] A central purpose of the act was to place responsibility on the President. The House Select Committee on the Budget condemned the existing process on a number of grounds. Budget estimates submitted to Congress represented "only the desires" of the individual departments, establishments, and bureaus. Their requests were not subjected to a "superior revision with a view to bringing them into harmony with each other, to eliminating duplication of organization or activities, or of making them, as a whole, conform to the needs of the Nation as represented by the condition of the Treasury and prospective

13. 37 Stat. 415 (1912).

14. Frederick A. Cleveland, "The Federal Budget," 3 Proceedings of the Academy of Political Science 167–68 (1912–13). Emphasis in original.

15. Taft's model budget appears at 49 Cong. Rec. 3985 (1913). For the evolution of the executive budget from 1789 to 1921, see Fisher, Presidential Spending Power, at 9–35.

revenues." No one was responsible. Budget estimates were "a patchwork and not a structure." A great deal of the time of congressional committees was taken up "in exploding the visionary schemes of bureau chiefs for which no administration would be willing to stand responsible." The committee concluded that definite responsibility had to be placed on the President to subject agency estimates to scrutiny, revision, and correlation.[16]

The 1921 act contained two exceptions to this principle of presidential responsibility. First, he was to set forth in his budget all estimates necessary "in his judgment" except those of the legislative branch and the Supreme Court. In a spirit of comity and mutual respect among coequal branches, those estimates are included in the budget without revision. Second, the act prohibited agency officials from submitting appropriations requests directly to Congress or submitting recommendations on how revenue needs should be met, "unless at the request of either House of Congress." For the most part, then, Congress authorized a newly created Budget Bureau to "assemble, correlate, revise, reduce, or increase the estimates of the several departments or establishments."[17] In 1970 the Budget Bureau was renamed the Office of Management and Budget (OMB).

This structure of presidential responsibility has slowly eroded over time. Budgets not subject to presidential review at the present time include those of the legislative branch and the judiciary, the Milk Market Orders Assessment Fund, the International Trade Commission, the Federal Reserve System Board of Governors, and a number of privately owned, government-sponsored enterprises.[18]

The Trade Act of 1974 provided that the estimated expenditures and proposed appropriations for the International Trade Commission (formerly the Tariff Commission) would be included in the President's budget "without revision." Budget watchers on Capitol Hill (including the author) learned of the provision months after enactment. President Ford had made no mention of the provision when he signed the bill.[19]

Some of the congressional intrusions were rebuffed. In 1978 President Carter vetoed a bill that would have required three Cabinet officers to report to Congress whenever the President's budget requests for certain activities were less than the amounts authorized by Congress and to explain why the higher amounts were not requested. Carter regarded the requirement as an "unacceptable intrusion" on his obligations and ability to make budget recommendations.[20] In 1981 President Reagan interpreted narrowly a veterans bill

16. H. Rept. No. 14, 67th Cong., 1st Sess. 4–5 (1921).
17. 42 Stat. 20, secs. 210(a), 206, and 207.
18. OMB Circular No. A-11, §11.2 (June 1995).
19. 88 Stat. 2011, sec. 175(a)(1) (1975); 19 U.S.C. 2232 (2000).
20. Public Papers of the Presidents, 1978 (II), at 1250.

that might have required him to request specific amounts. He dismissed the latter possibility "for it is the President's constitutional duty to make recommendations to Congress of such measures as he judges necessary and expedient."[21]

Congressional Revision of Estimates

The Budget and Accounting Act provided for an "executive budget" only in the sense that the President initiated the budget and took responsibility for it. The act allowed members of Congress full freedom, either in committee or on the floor, to decrease or increase the President's estimates.

The Prerogative to Add

When John J. Fitzgerald, chairman of the House Appropriations Committee, met with the New York constitutional convention in 1915, he supported a procedure that would make it as difficult as possible for legislators to increase the amounts proposed by the President. He believed that Congress should be prohibited from appropriating any money "unless it had been requested by the head of the department, unless by a two-thirds vote, or unless it was to pay a claim against the government or for its own expenses."[22]

Charles Wallace Collins, whose studies on budget reform contributed to the 1921 act, was of similar mind. In 1916 he published an article that argued for a form of parliamentary government. "Our institutions," he said, "being more nearly akin to those of England, it is to the English budget system that we more naturally look for the purpose of illustration." He noted that Parliament had long ago yielded the initiative in financial legislation to the Cabinet. The budget in England was ordinarily ratified as introduced. A prime feature of the national budget system in America, according to Collins, would be "the relinquishing of the initiative in financial legislation to the executive by the Congress. . . . The President would possess the functions of a Prime Minister in relation to public finance. He would take the responsibility for the preparation of the budget. Complementary to this the Congress would yield its power of amendment by way of increasing any item in the budget, and also its power to introduce any bill making a charge upon the Treasury, without the consent of the executive."[23]

21. Public Papers of the Presidents, 1981, at 1011.
22. "Budget Systems," Municipal Research, No. 62 (June 1915), at 312, 322, 327, 340. See also William Franklin Willoughby, The Problem of a National Budget 146–49 (1918).
23. Charles Wallace Collins, "Constitutional Aspects of a National Budget System," 25 Yale L. J. 376 (1916).

Other changes were necessary to complete Collins's scenario. He would have granted members of the Cabinet a seat in the House and a voice (but not a vote) in all legislative proceedings involving the budget. The committee system of making appropriations "would cease." Since the budget bill represented an administrative measure, Congress "should relinquish its power to add any new item, to increase any item, or to consider any measure which would impose a burden upon the Treasury unless such a measure had the sanction of the executive."[24]

In 1918 Representative Medill McCormick (strongly influenced by Collins) introduced a number of bills and resolutions calling for budget reform. He proposed a House budget committee to replace the Committees on Ways and Means and Appropriations; it would have the power to reduce presidential estimates but not to add to them, unless requested by the Secretary of the Treasury upon the authority of the President or unless the committee could muster a two-thirds majority. Members of the House would not be allowed to add to the budget bill when it reached the floor, except to restore what the President had originally requested.[25]

William McAdoo, Wilson's first Secretary of the Treasury, supported a system to prohibit Congress from increasing the President's requests: "Let us be honest with ourselves and honest with the American people. A budget which does not cover the initiation or increase of appropriations by Congress will be a semblance of the real thing."[26] When Secretary of the Treasury Carter Glass submitted budget estimates in 1919, he said that the budget "as thus prepared for the President and on his responsibility should not, as such, be increased by the Congress."[27] David Houston, the next Secretary of the Treasury, asked Congress in 1920 not to add to the President's budget unless recommended by the Secretary of the Treasury or approved by a two-thirds vote.[28]

This version of an executive budget was explicitly rejected by the Budget and Accounting Act. The budget was executive only in the sense that the President was responsible for the estimates submitted. It was legislative in the sense that Congress had full power to increase or reduce his estimates. Increases could be made in committee or on the floor, and in either place by a simple majority vote. The act did not contemplate in any fashion the surrender of congressional power. It did not make Congress subordinate to the

24. Id. at 382–83.
25. H. Doc. No. 1006, 65th Cong., 2d Sess. (1918).
26. Annual Report of the Secretary of the Treasury, 1918–19, at 121 (from his testimony of October 4, 1919, to the House Select Committee on the Budget).
27. Id. at 117.
28. David Houston, Eight Years with Wilson's Cabinet 88 (1926).

President's plan. In reporting the bill, the House Select Committee on the Budget explained in straightforward language:

> It will doubtless be claimed by some that this is an Executive budget and that the duty of making appropriations is a legislative rather than Executive prerogative. The plan outlined does provide for an Executive initiation of the budget, but the President's responsibility ends when he has prepared the budget and transmitted it to Congress. To that extent, and to that extent alone, does the plan provide for an Executive budget, but the proposed law does not change in the slightest degree the duty of Congress to make the minutest examination of the budget and to adopt the budget only to the extent that it is found to be economical. If the estimates contained in the President's budget are too large, it will be the duty of Congress to reduce them. If in the opinion of Congress the estimates of expenditures are not sufficient, it will be within the power of Congress to increase them. The bill does not in the slightest degree give the Executive any greater power than he now has over the consideration of appropriations by Congress.[29]

Although Congress formally retained the power to increase budget estimates, the President gained an important advantage by shaping the agenda for legislative action. Because Congress works off his budget, a majority is needed to delete funds recommended by the President. This power of initiative has far-reaching implications. In 1982 Congressman Joseph Addabbo, chairman of the House's defense appropriations subcommittee, failed on a tie vote (26 to 26) to delete MX missile production funds. If proponents of the missile system had had to *add* the funds to a congressional budget, a tie vote would have gone against the President. Congress can change this practice at any time, working off a newly prepared draft bill rather than the President's budget.

Impoundment

After Congress completes the appropriations process, reductions can occur when Presidents impound funds. Harry Truman, Dwight Eisenhower, and John Kennedy refused to spend funds that Congress had added to their defense budgets. Impoundment also affects funds that Congress adds to domestic programs. In signing an agriculture appropriations bill in 1966, President Johnson objected to $312.5 million that Congress had added to his budget request. Rather than veto the bill, he simply reduced expenditures for certain

29. H. Rept. No. 14, 67th Cong., 1st Sess. 6–7 (1921).

items "in an attempt to avert expending more in the coming year than provided in the budget."[30]

On an entirely different order were the impoundments carried out by the Nixon administration. They set a precedent in terms of magnitude, severity, and belligerence. The message from the White House came across without equivocation: congressional add-ons to the President's budget were irresponsible and wholly lacking in merit. Programs were either cut back to the President's request or, in some cases, terminated and dismantled.[31]

The administration justified some of the impoundments on the ground that the President's budget contained requests to rescind (cancel) certain funds. Since the President wanted to rescind the funds, it was reasoned that he should not spend the money until Congress had an opportunity to consider his request. In three rescission cases, the federal courts found the administration's rationale totally inadequate. A President's budget was merely a recommendation, the courts noted. The budget had no special standing. What deserved implementation was not a President's budget but a public law.[32] This principle, which the Nixon administration had ignored in its eagerness to alter federal programs, was reiterated many times by federal courts.

In a decision involving the Office of Economic Opportunity (OEO), a district court ruled that it was not permissible for the Nixon administration to begin dismembering the OEO simply because the President decided to omit funds for the agency in his budget. The President's budget was "nothing more than a proposal to the Congress for the Congress to act upon as it may please."[33] In another decision, affecting mental health funds, a federal judge noted that the President "does not have complete discretion to pick and choose between programs when some are made mandatory by conscious, deliberate congressional action."[34] The courts denied that the administration could withhold funds as a means of combating inflation.[35]

---

30. Public Papers of the Presidents, 1966 (II), at 981. For defense impoundments, see Fisher, Presidential Spending Power, at 161–65.

31. Fisher, Presidential Spending Power, at 175–201.

32. National Association of Collegiate Veterans v. Ottina, Civ. Action No. 349–73 (D.D.C. 1973); Minnesota Chippewa Tribe v. Carlucci, Civ. Action No. 628–73 (D.D.C. 1973); National Association of State Universities and Land Grant Colleges v. Weinberger, Civ. Action No. 1014–73 (D.D.C. 1973).

33. Local 2677, the American Federation of Government Employees v. Phillips, 358 F.Supp. 60, 73 (D.D.C. 1973).

34. National Council of Community Mental Health Centers v. Weinberger, 361 F.Supp. 897, 902 (D.D.C. 1973).

35. State of Iowa ex rel. State Highway Com'n v. Brinegar, 512 F.2d 722 (8th Cir. 1975); State of Minnesota v. Coleman, 391 F.Supp. 330 (D. Minn. 1975); State Highway Commission of Missouri v. Volpe, 479 F.2d 1099 (8th Cir. 1973).

Only one of these cases reached the Supreme Court. In 1975 the Court decided that the Clean Water Act, despite ambiguities in its language and legislative history, did not permit the President to withhold from allotment and obligation the funds provided by Congress. The basic thrust of the act convinced the Court that Congress had made a firm commitment of substantial sums to build waste treatment plants.[36] The decision turned essentially on questions of statutory interpretation, but important constitutional principles were underscored: the authority of Congress to mandate spending, the President's obligation to carry out the laws, and the legitimacy of court orders to compel presidential action.

In response to the massive impoundments by the Nixon administration, Congress passed legislation in 1974 to limit the President's power. The Impoundment Control Act requires special messages from the President whenever he proposes to rescind (terminate) or defer (delay) appropriations. To rescind funds, both houses must complete action on a bill or a joint resolution within 45 days of continuous session. Deferrals would remain in effect unless one house passed a resolution of disapproval. The Supreme Court's decision in *INS v. Chadha* (1983), striking down the legislative veto, invalidated the one-house veto for deferrals. The federal courts later determined that the one-house legislative veto was tied inextricably to the deferral authority. Because they were inseverable, the authority vanished with the legislative veto. Congress promptly converted the judicial decision into statutory law.[37]

Some members of Congress objected to the rescission procedure because it put the burden on the President to convince both houses of Congress within 45 days to support the termination of funds. If Congress ignored the President's proposal, as sometimes happened, the money would have to be released and spent. Out of this dissatisfaction came two proposals. One was called "expedited rescission," which would force at least one house to vote on the President's rescission proposals. If one house disapproved, the other house would not have to act, since both houses had to support rescission. The House of Representatives passed expedited rescission in 1992, 1993, and 1994.[38] These bills were not acted on by the Senate.

In 1995, after the Republicans gained control of Congress, the House of Representatives passed a stronger version called "enhanced rescission." The purpose was to shift the burden from the President to Congress. Under this

36. Train v. City of New York, 420 U.S. 35 (1975). See also Fisher, Presidential Spending Power, at 184–92.
37. City of New Haven, Conn. v. United States, 809 F.2d 900 (D.C. Cir. 1987); 101 Stat. 785, sec. 206 (1987).
38. 138 Cong. Rec. 30600–11, 31015–16 (1992); 139 Cong. Rec. 8502–13, 8519–40, 8617–43 (1993); 140 Cong. Rec. 16551–82 (1994).

procedure the President's rescission proposals would become law unless Congress passed a resolution of disapproval within a fixed number of days. If Congress failed to act during that period, the proposals would take effect. If Congress did disapprove, its resolution could be vetoed by the President, and it would take a two-thirds majority in each house to override the veto and restore the funds. The House adopted that version in 1995,[39] the Senate passed a different measure, and in 1996 both houses agreed to a modified form of enhanced rescission called the Line Item Veto Act (P.L. 104-130).[40]

The Supreme Court decided in 1998 that the statute violated the legislative procedures required by the Constitution. In 2006 Congress considered—but did not enact—legislation to grant the President an "item veto" not by enhanced rescission but by expedited rescission (discussed in chapter 5).

The Budget Act of 1974

The model of an executive budget looked appealing to Congress when it considered reform legislation in the early 1970s. The 1921 act had assumed that presidential control and responsibility would be improved by centralizing the budget process in the executive branch. But advantages for the President need not flow to Congress, given its unique institutional qualities.

The Budget Act of 1974 anticipated a contest between two budgets: presidential and congressional. The analogy is weak because the President heads an executive branch, fortified by a central budget office. This hierarchical system restricts the size of budget requests as they move upward from bureaus and departments to the OMB and the President. But there is no head in Congress and no possibility of a central budget office comparable to the OMB. Congress is inherently decentralized, and no amount of procedural innovation can disguise that reality.

The Budget Act of 1974 contained a number of provisions designed to strengthen congressional control. It created Budget Committees in the House and the Senate, established a Congressional Budget Office (CBO) to supply technical support, and required the adoption of budget resolutions to set overall limits on budget aggregates (such as total outlays and revenues) and to permit debate on spending priorities. Because of bicameralism, decentralization, and committee autonomy within Congress, the CBO can never have the institutional strengths of an OMB.

39. 141 Cong. Rec. 3443–509, 3546–70, 3759–800 (1995).
40. For further details on Senate action and the Line Item Veto Act, see Louis Fisher, Congressional Abdication on War and Spending 146–53 (2000).

The gap between promise and performance has been stunning, even if technical and procedural complexities help obscure the results of the Budget Act. Members of Congress praised the new process for exerting a restraining influence on federal spending. Many of the compliments, however, depended on illusion. Instead of keeping within the President's aggregates, members voted on generous ceilings in budget resolutions and announced to their constituents that they had "stayed within the budget." *Which* budget was never made clear.

Budget resolutions are highly touted as vehicles for centralized, systematic, and coherent legislative action. The Budget Act assumed that members of Congress would behave more responsibly by having to vote explicitly on budget aggregates, facing up to totals rather than deciding in "piecemeal" fashion the spending actions in separate appropriations and legislative bills. In 1974, as now, it was difficult to defend fragmentation, splintering, and decentralization when reformers pressed eagerly for "coordination" and a "unified budget process." But the risks are high when Congress, possessing very different institutional qualities, tries to emulate the President. Increasing the size of a legislative vehicle—from an appropriations bill to a budget resolution—magnifies the scope of legislative conflict and encourages additional concessions to members. It costs more to build a majority. And when conflict exceeds a certain point in Congress, the result is escapist budgeting. Members become less, not more, responsible.

Presidential responsibility for the budget was undermined by the Budget Act of 1974 because the nation now had not one budget but two: a presidential budget and a congressional budget. Furthermore, the congressional budget is not one but many: the first budget resolution, the second budget resolution (later repealed), and various House and Senate versions. Under these conditions, the phrases "below budget" and "above budget" no longer have meaning. The country lost a visible benchmark (the President's budget) that provided a fixed reference point to measure executive leadership and congressional action.

As a result, the public and the press now have more difficulty keeping the two branches accountable. In 1983, when members of Congress wondered whether a pending bill was below budget or above budget, House Majority Leader Jim Wright gave this response: "This bill is not over the budget; the amounts proposed in this amendment are well within the budgeted figures. The amounts that we have agreed to and have discussed are not in excess of the congressional budget resolution. That, of course, is the budget." Wright conceded that the amounts might be in excess of what the President requested in his budget, but "that, of course, is not the budget. Congress makes the budget; the President does not."[41]

41. 129 Cong. Rec. 25417 (1983).

Instead of staying within the President's aggregates, members of Congress could raise the ceilings in a budget resolution and tell their constituents that they had "stayed within the budget." Even Presidents found the convention attractive. In 1985 President Reagan announced that he "would accept appropriations bills, even if above my budget, that were within the limits set by Congress' own budget resolution."[42]

Although the 1974 act has generally weakened the President's budget, under special conditions it can strengthen executive power. Those conditions materialized in 1981. President Reagan was able to gain control over the budget resolution in both houses and thereby use it as a blueprint to enforce his priorities: a tax cut, defense buildup, and retrenchment of domestic programs. Having seized control of the budget resolution, action on the tax bill, appropriations bills, and the reconciliation bill became the inevitable and necessary steps to carry out White House policy. When the President's theory of supply-side economics failed to generate predicted revenues, the nation faced budget deficits of $150 billion to $200 billion a year.

Would the actions and miscalculations in 1981 have happened without a budget resolution? Possibly, but President Reagan would have faced almost insurmountable hurdles in trying to enact his radical, supply-side economics with the pre-1974 budgetary process. Most likely his program would have been chopped to bits by successive committee and subcommittee actions. The budget resolution gave him the centralizing vehicle he needed. The incrementalism of the budget process before 1974 would have functioned as an effective brake on radical proposals.[43]

The growth of budget deficits after 1981, combined with President Reagan's refusal to offer constructive solutions, paved the way for the Gramm-Rudman-Hollings (GRH) Act of 1985. The statute symbolized many things: an admission that the congressional budget process created in 1974 was useless in dealing with such large deficits, a conclusion that the political stalemate between Reagan and Congress required a new statutory framework to force action, and an unwillingness by Congress to delegate any additional authorities or powers to the executive branch.

GRH attempted to direct both branches to meet specified targets for the federal deficit, gradually lowering it to zero by fiscal year 1991. The decision by Congress to dictate certain numbers (an anticipated deficit) in the President's budget served to undermine the President's budget even more. An

42. Public Papers of the Presidents, 1985 (II), at 1401.

43. Rudolph G. Penner, "An Appraisal of the Congressional Budget Process," in Allen Schick, ed., Crisis in the Budget Process 69 (1985); Allen Schick, "How the Budget Was Won and Lost," in Norman J. Ornstein, ed., President and Congress: Assessing Reagan's First Year 25 (1982).

executive budget, by its very nature, must reflect the numbers chosen by the President. The executive budget is a proposal, and Congress cannot tell the President what numbers to propose. Nevertheless, the White House evidently found it convenient to accept the statutory mandate as a way of evading political responsibility.

Not trusting the President or the OMB, Congress decided to shift the duty of administering GRH to the Comptroller General. If the two branches failed to adhere to the deficit targets set forth in the statute, the Comptroller General would prepare a "sequestration" report to withhold whatever funds were necessary to keep deficit numbers on target. This transfer of power to the Comptroller General raised constitutional questions. Although appointed by the President and confirmed by the Senate, the Comptroller General is subject to a joint resolution of removal passed by Congress. The President can veto the joint resolution, but the procedure at least gives Congress the opportunity to initiate a removal. The Supreme Court in 1986 decided that Congress cannot delegate executive functions to an officer removable by Congress.[44]

During GRH's existence, President Reagan submitted budgets that supposedly complied with the statutory targets, but only by making wildly optimistic assumptions about economic growth, inflation, and interest rates. Congress accepted the phony figures because the use of honest figures (which were available) would have increased the size of the projected deficit and made it appear that Congress was the "big spender." Once the President ducked responsibility by submitting a dishonest budget, Congress was politically bound to embrace the same mistaken assumptions.

After the President and Congress failed to meet the deficit targets in GRH, Congress enacted a new version in 1987, delaying to fiscal 1993 the goal of a balanced budget. When it became obvious that President Bush I and Congress could not comply with GRH II, a Budget Enforcement Act was passed in 1990 promising a $500 billion reduction in the federal deficit over a five-year period. The fixed deficit targets of GRH were abandoned. Once again the two branches chose to hide behind a supposedly statutory mandate.

President Clinton adopted the same approach in 1993 by signing an extension of the Budget Enforcement Act. Presidents Reagan, Bush I, and Clinton all promised action against budget deficits, and Congress took credit for passing legislation that dealt with the problem. But the deficits unleashed by the 1981 budget changes were remarkably uniform from one administration to the next. Almost like clockwork, a trillion dollars of debt was added every four years. It took almost two centuries—from 1789 to 1981—to create a national debt of $1 trillion. By the time Reagan left office in 1989 that figure

44. Bowsher v. Synar, 478 U.S. 714 (1986).

had jumped to $3 trillion, and the national debt continued to climb to $5 trillion by 1996.

The inability of either branch to control these deficits led to two dramatic shutdowns of the federal government in 1995 and 1996. The Republicans in Congress were intent on a plan that would balance the budget in seven years. Their particular mix of spending cuts was resisted by President Clinton, who vetoed a number of appropriations bills and also a continuing resolution (a short-term, stopgap funding vehicle to keep government afloat) because he claimed that it would raise Medicare premiums on senior citizens and cut education and environmental protection too deeply. The result was a six-day government shutdown.

Clinton signed two continuing resolutions in 1995 that promised a balanced budget no later than fiscal year 2002. Those measures were hailed as a major breakthrough in budget negotiations, but Congress and Clinton quickly locked horns on the precise means of reaching a balanced budget. What would be the size of the tax cut? How would the cost growth of Medicare and Medicaid be curtailed? Those disagreements, and others, persisted. In December 1995 the government began a record-setting shutdown of 21 days. During those confrontations, the Republicans managed to impose significant spending restraints on a number of federal programs, but their insistence on a tax cut (Clinton agreed on a tax cut, but a smaller one) made it difficult to make much progress in eliminating deficits.[45]

Clinton's initiative in 1993 promised to break the pattern of federal deficits. The Omnibus Budget-Reconciliation Act of 1993, which relied on tax increases to reduce the deficit, narrowly passed the House and required Vice President Al Gore to break a tie vote in the Senate. The White House estimated that the bill would reduce the deficit by $500 billion over five years. It did more than that. The legislation not only reduced the deficit but also produced surpluses for fiscal years 1998 through 2001. However, sharp tax cuts by President George W. Bush in 2001 once again threw the country into the red, with fiscal years 2003 to 2006 averaging almost $400 billion a year in deficits. By fiscal year 2006 the gross federal debt topped $8 trillion.

Secret Spending

The framers placed in Article I, Section 9, of the Constitution an explicit safeguard for financial accountability: "A regular Statement and Account of

---

45. Louis Fisher, "Government by Continuing Resolution: Smaller Is Inevitable," Los Angeles Times, January 28, 1996, at M2.

the Receipts and Expenditures of all public Money shall be published from time to time." It is remarkable that this provision, so essential to democratic budgeting, did not appear in the draft of the Constitution until the final few days. The manner in which it was added clouds its meaning. Aided by this ambiguity, billions of dollars are appropriated each year for covert spending without a statement or accounting.

The Statement and Account Clause

On September 14, 1787, George Mason proposed that "an Account of the public expenditures should be annually published." Gouverneur Morris objected that publication would be "impossible in many cases."[46] Morris, a supporter of executive authority, probably believed in some element of secrecy and confidentiality. During his service with the Continental Congress he chided those who assumed that legislative committees could manage the people's business. The burden fell on the committee chairman, who at that time performed the role of executive. As Morris recalled: "Necessity, preserving the democratical forms, assumed the monarchical substance of business"—that is, the chairman did the work of the committee. At the Philadelphia convention, Morris favored executive power, regarding the President as the "guardian of the people, even of the lower classes, agst. Legislative tyranny." He warned that Congress would "continually seek to aggrandize & perpetuate themselves."[47] This kind of attitude does not make for open government.

Rufus King faulted Mason's proposal: "The term expenditures went to every minute shilling. This would be impracticable. Congs. might indeed make a monthly publication, but it would be in such general Statements as would afford no satisfactory information." Unlike Morris, King appeared to be concerned about detail and frequency of publication rather than the need for secrecy.

James Madison proposed to delete "annually" from the motion and insert "from time to time." The purpose was to give Congress discretion over the timing of the publication instead of imposing an arbitrary schedule that might be ignored altogether. Several statements at this point suggest the need for secrecy. James Wilson, supporting Madison, said, "Many operations of finance cannot be properly published at certain times"; Thomas FitzSimons insisted that it was "absolutely impossible to publish expenditures in the full extent of the term." The convention accepted Madison's amendment without

46. 2 Farrand 618.
47. Id. at 52–54. See also 1 Diary and Letters of Gouverneur Morris 12 (Anne Cary Morris ed., 1888).

a dissenting vote. Mason's proposal, as rewritten, included an accounting for receipts as well as expenditures and applied the requirement for publication to "all public Money."[48]

This clause was discussed at the Virginia ratifying convention in 1788. Mason said that the phrase "from time to time" had been added because "there might be some matters which might require secrecy." His explanation indicates that Congress could delay the publication of sensitive material: "In matters relative to military operations, and foreign negotiations, secrecy was necessary sometimes. But he did not conceive that the receipts and expenditures of the public money ought ever to be concealed. The people, he affirmed, had a right to know the expenditures of their money."[49] This position makes sense only if Mason believed that the cost of secret operations, after some period of time, would be made public.

The Growth of Secret Funding

With such a fragmentary and cryptic record, it would be hasty to conclude that the framers insisted on the publication of every expenditure of the federal government. The men who assembled at Philadelphia had just been through a decade of secret operations in the war against Great Britain. In Federalist 64, drawing on his own experiences, John Jay justified secrecy in the diplomatic area: "It seldom happens in the negotiation of treaties, of whichever nature, but that perfect *secrecy* and immediate *dispatch* are sometimes requisite. There are cases where the most useful intelligence may be obtained, if the persons possessing it can be relieved from apprehension of discovery." Expenditures made public, then, could not reveal the parties involved.

This special need for diplomacy was soon recognized by statute. In 1790 Congress provided the President with a $40,000 account to be used for foreign intercourse. It was left to his judgment to decide the extent to which the expenditures should be made public. Three years later Congress specified that the President could make a certificate of the amount of expenditures in foreign intercourse "he may think it advisable not to specify." A certificate (a statement that funds have been spent, but providing no details) was regarded as a sufficient voucher for the sums expended.[50] Over the years, Congress would authorize other unvouchered funds.

---

48. 2 Farrand 619.
49. 3 Farrand 326.
50. 1 Stat. 129 (1790), 1 Stat. 300 (1793), codified at 31 U.S.C. 3526(e) (2000). For an unsuccessful effort by a newspaper to examine these expenditures, see Washington Post Co. v. U.S. Dept. of State, 501 F.Supp. 1152 (D.D.C. 1980).

Confidential funds in diplomatic affairs led to a dispute between President Polk and Congress. In an effort to embarrass Senator Daniel Webster, the House of Representatives passed a resolution in 1848 requiring the President to deliver certain State Department records covering the period from March 4, 1841, to May 9, 1843. That interval dovetailed with Webster's tenure as Secretary of State. Part of the information requested dealt with confidential funds in foreign intercourse. Polk refused to give the House the information on funding, pointing out that Congress, by statute, had given the President total discretion over the degree to which such funds should be made public. Although it was his practice to settle all expenditures for contingent expenses of foreign intercourse by regular vouchers, he declined to surrender the certificates made by his predecessor.[51]

On another occasion, in 1811, Congress passed a secret statute that gave President Madison $100,000 to take temporary possession of territory south of Georgia. The law was not published until 1818.[52] The only annual exception to the Statement and Account Clause throughout the nineteenth century was the President's contingency account in foreign intercourse. By 1899 the yearly amount had reached $63,000.

The next exception occurred in 1916, just before the United States entered World War I. Congress authorized the Secretary of the Navy to make a certificate of expenses for "obtaining information from abroad and at home." Congress added a third unvouchered account in 1935 by giving the FBI a confidential fund of $20,000 (later raised to $70,000).[53] This is a revealing record. From 1789 to 1935— a period of 146 years—Congress departed from the Statement and Account Clause only on rare occasions and for relatively small amounts of money.

The record changed dramatically with the onset of World War II, which had a profound and lasting effect on democratic budgeting. Millions of dollars were given to the President on a confidential basis to expedite war production. The atomic bomb, costing billions of dollars, was developed and produced with secret funds. Congress authorized a confidential fund for the newly created Atomic Energy Commission. In quick succession Congress established

51. 5 Richardson 2281–86. Secret spending by President Lincoln for the purpose of paying a spy during the Civil War was upheld by the Supreme Court in Totten, Administrator v. United States, 92 U.S. (2 Otto.) 105 (1875). In 1974 a district court stated that *Totten* "is inapplicable to criminal actions and has been modified by a century of legal experience, which teaches that the courts have broad authority to inquire into national security matters so long as proper safeguards are applied to avoid unwarranted disclosures"; United States v. Ehrlichman, 376 F.Supp. 29, 32 n.1 (D.D.C. 1974).

52. 3 Stat. 471–72. See David Hunter Miller, Secret Statutes of the United States (1918).

53. 39 Stat. 557 (1916), 10 U.S.C. 7231 (2000); 49 Stat. 78 (1935), 28 U.S.C. 537 (2000).

unvouchered funds for the White House, the Defense Department, the District of Columbia, the Attorney General, the Bureau of Narcotics and Dangerous Drugs, the Secret Service, the Coast Guard, the Bureau of Customs, the Immigration and Naturalization Service, and other agencies.

In 1973 and 1974, prompted by revelations about the Watergate scandal, several of the confidential funds were deleted because they lacked authorizing language. Congress responded by enacting most of the necessary authorizations. It also consolidated some of the smaller confidential funds into larger accounts to provide for better administrative control.[54]

The General Accounting Office Act of 1980 permitted the GAO to carry out a limited audit of unvouchered expenditures, although the statute did not cover the CIA, and it allowed the President to exempt certain sensitive foreign intelligence and law enforcement activities. The basic purpose of the statute was to allow the GAO to determine whether an unvouchered expenditure was, in fact, actually made and whether the expenditure was authorized by law.[55]

Despite these reforms, it is still difficult to even identify the confidential funds authorized by Congress. A researcher must be aware of language (sometimes clear, sometimes opaque) that appears in authorization bills, appropriations bills, and the United States Code. It is often uncertain whether an account is confidential (unvouchered) or merely discretionary (subject to full GAO audit). These problems could be alleviated by adopting standard language for confidential funds. Appropriations bills should state the amount of the fund, stipulate in explicit language that the account is unvouchered, and provide references to the authorizing law. Appropriation accounts could use this language: "Not to exceed [dollar amount] can be used for emergencies and extraordinary expenses, as authorized by [U.S. Code citation], to be expended on the approval or authority of the Secretary, and payments may be made on his certificate of necessity for confidential purposes."

The justifications for unvouchered funds deserve scrutiny. Law enforcement seems a legitimate reason when confidentiality is used to protect the identity of informers. However, identities can be protected through the regular voucher system. Other justifications seem weak: the use of unvouchered funds for entertaining foreign dignitaries (for example, tickets to theaters and sports events, sightseeing tours), gifts, and travel by White House aides. These reasons appear related less to national security than to agency convenience and the desire to minimize agency embarrassment.

54. Louis Fisher, "Confidential Spending and Governmental Accountability," 47 G. W. L. Rev. 347 (1979).
55. 94 Stat. 311, sec. 101 (1980); 31 U.S.C. 3524 (2000).

The Intelligence Community

Overshadowing other confidential funds, both in dollar amount and in the character of operation, are those spent on the U.S. intelligence community. The Central Intelligence Act of 1949 provided several extraordinary features of financial independence. The Director of the Central Intelligence Agency may spend funds on a confidential basis, using certificates rather than vouchers. More important, the CIA does not receive a direct appropriation from Congress. Funds are included in a number of departmental budgets. After the appropriations bills are signed, the OMB transfers the appropriate amount to the CIA. The 1949 act authorized the CIA to transfer to and receive from other governmental agencies "such sums as may be approved" by the OMB for the performance of any "functions or activities" authorized by the National Security Act of 1947.[56]

Precisely what Congress anticipated by "functions or activities" has long been at issue. Covert operations in Laos and Chile, secret funding of Radio Free Europe and Radio Liberty, and subsidies to religious organizations, student groups, and labor unions have all sparked intense controversies about the proper scope of CIA activities. But of direct interest in this chapter is the tension between the Statement and Account Clause and the method used to fund the CIA.

William B. Richardson, a resident of Greensburg, Pennsylvania, asked the federal courts to declare the Central Intelligence Act a violation of the Statement and Account Clause. A series of rulings from 1969 to 1974 ended with the Supreme Court's decision that Richardson lacked standing to maintain his suit.[57] But he picked up some significant support along the way. An appellate court in 1972 emphasized the importance of the clause in these terms:

A responsible and intelligent taxpayer and citizen, of course, wants to know how his tax money is being spent. Without this information he cannot intelligently follow the actions of the Congress or of the Executive. Nor can he properly fulfill his obligation as a member of the electorate. The Framers of the Constitution deemed fiscal information essential

56. For CIA statutory authority for funding, see 50 U.S.C. 403f, 403j (2000). The relationship among Congress, the CIA, and the OMB is discussed in a letter from OMB Director Roy Ash to Senator William Proxmire, April 29, 1974, reprinted at 120 Cong. Rec. 17487–89 (1974). Further discussion of CIA funding appears in Fisher, Presidential Spending Power, at 214–23, and Stansfield Turner, Secrecy and Democracy 257–59 (1985).

57. United States v. Richardson, 418 U.S. 166 (1974). Challenges from any citizen, whether as a taxpayer under *Richardson* or as a plaintiff under the Freedom of Information Act, fail because of lack of standing and the political question doctrine; Halperin v. CIA, 629 F.2d 144 (D.C. Cir. 1980).

if the electorate was to exercise any control over its representatives and meet their new responsibilities as citizens of the Republic.[58]

Justice Douglas, one of four members dissenting, rejected the proposition that Congress, by statute, is at liberty to suspend a constitutional provision. The claim that Congress had the power to read the Statement and Account Clause out of the Constitution was to him "astounding."[59]

Pressure gradually mounted in Congress to publish an aggregate figure for the entire intelligence community budget. Past CIA Directors William E. Colby and James R. Schlesinger, as well as Director Stansfield Turner (appointed in 1977), agreed that publication of the aggregate figure would not jeopardize national security. What made them uneasy was the possible political demand for further details and the risk that trends and "bumps" in the budget totals from year to year might communicate useful information to America's enemies. But as Colby noted on one occasion, the American constitutional system probably requires publication of more information on the CIA budget than might be convenient from the agency's point of view.[60]

In 1976 the House Select Committee on Intelligence (the Pike Committee), at the end of its tumultuous existence, recommended "that there be disclosure of the total single sum budgeted for each agency involved in intelligence, or if such an item is a part or portion of the budget of another agency or department that it can be separately identified as a single item."[61] Less ambitious was the conclusion of the Senate study committee on intelligence activities (the Church Committee) to publish the aggregate figure for the intelligence community budget. In voting 8 to 3 for this recommendation, the committee highlighted one of the major objections to secret budgeting: "Most Members of Congress and the public are deceived about the appropriations and expenditures of other government agencies whose budgets are inflated to conceal funds for the intelligence community."[62] Sums were not only concealed; they also distorted the totals of other appropriations accounts.

58. Richardson v. United States, 465 F.2d 844, 853 (3d Cir. 1972), footnote omitted.

59. United States v. Richardson, 418 U.S. at 200–201. In 1977 an appellate court decided that Congressman Michael J. Harrington lacked standing to bring suit against the use of public funds for illegal CIA activities; Harrington v. Bush, 553 F.2d 190 (D.C. Cir. 1977). In 1976 a federal court held that the Freedom of Information Act exempted disclosure of the CIA budget; Halperin v. Colby, Civ. Action No. 75–676 (D.D.C. June 4, 1976).

60. "Nomination of William E. Colby," hearings before the Senate Committee on Armed Services, 93d Cong., 1st Sess. 17, 181 (1973); "Nomination of James R. Schlesinger, to Be Secretary of Defense," hearings before the Senate Committee on Armed Services, 93d Cong., 1st Sess. 67–68 (1973); "Nomination of Admiral Stansfield Turner," hearings before the Senate Select Committee on Intelligence, 95th Cong., 1st Sess. 83–84 (1977).

61. H. Rept. No. 833, 94th Cong., 2d Sess. 3 (1976).

62. S. Rept. No. 755, 94th Cong., 2d Sess. 384 (1976).

President Ford intervened in 1976 to urge the Senate committee to reconsider its decision. He believed that the "net effect of such a disclosure could adversely affect our foreign intelligence efforts and therefore would not be in the public interest." CIA Director George Bush wrote to the Senate Appropriations Committee, agreeing with the President's position.[63] Also during that time, the Senate was in the process of creating a new committee (the Senate Select Committee on Intelligence) that would have jurisdiction over the authorization of intelligence activities. A specific responsibility placed on this new committee was to study whether the disclosure of budgetary figures would be in the public interest. The Senate deferred action while awaiting the committee's recommendation.

In 1977 the Senate Select Committee voted 9 to 8 in favor of disclosing the aggregate amount of funds appropriated for national foreign intelligence activities for fiscal year 1978. CIA Director Turner had testified that neither he nor President Carter objected to the publication of this figure.[64] Since that time, Congress has often included nonbinding language in intelligence authorization bills, recommending publication of the aggregate budget number. For example, a statute in 1991 provided: "It is the sense of Congress that, beginning in 1993, and in each year thereafter, the aggregate amount requested and authorized for, and spent on, intelligence and intelligence-related activities should be disclosed to the public in an appropriate manner."[65] In 1994 the chairman of the House intelligence committee supported disclosure of the aggregate figure, but his amendment lost 194 to 221.[66] In 1996 a presidential commission recommended the disclosure of the aggregate intelligence budget, inadvertently revealing the individual budgets of the National Reconnaissance Office ($6.2 billion), the National Security Agency ($3.7 billion), the Central Intelligence Agency ($3.1 billion), and the Defense Intelligence Agency ($2 billion).[67] This constitutional issue awaits action by the political branches, not the courts.

Steven Aftergood has filed a succession of Freedom of Information Act requests and lawsuits to uncover the aggregate budgets of the intelligence community. His efforts paid off in 1997 when the CIA voluntarily released an

63. "Whether Disclosure of Funds Authorized for Intelligence Activities Is in the Public Interest," hearings before the Senate Select Committee on Intelligence, 95th Cong., 1st Sess. 391–94 (1977).

64. S. Rept. No. 274, 95th Cong., 1st Sess. 6, 8 (1977).

65. 105 Stat. 1270, sec. 701 (1991).

66. 140 Cong. Rec. 17047–52 (1994). See "Public Disclosure of the Aggregate Intelligence Budget Figure," hearings before the House Permanent Select Committee on Intelligence, 103d Cong., 2d Sess. (1994).

67. "Making Connections with Dots to Decipher U.S. Spy Spending," Washington Post, March 12, 1996, at A11.

aggregate figure of $26.6 billion (with the CIA budget accounting for about $3 billion of the total) and a figure of $26.7 billion the following year. But the agency has blocked access since that time. Aftergood's lawsuits have been repeatedly dismissed by district courts.[68] The CIA appeared willing to release its budget for fiscal year 1948 but told Aftergood that the records could not be found.[69] He advised the judiciary that he had independently obtained and released CIA budget information for fiscal years 1953 to 1955.[70] Also, the CIA conceded in court that it had inadvertently released the aggregate intelligence budget for 1963.[71] Aftergood claimed that the CIA had officially disclosed the aggregate intelligence budget for fiscal years 1963 to 1966, but the agency submitted evidence that the figures for 1964 to 1966 were not accurate.[72]

Aftergood found in the papers of former Senator Styles Bridges the CIA budget for fiscal year 1955.[73] Other scholars looking at archival papers have also discovered budget figures for the intelligence community. David Barrett, while looking at the private papers of George Mahon, who served on the relevant House appropriations subcommittee, found specific budget figures for the CIA.[74] In 2005 a top U.S. intelligence official inadvertently revealed at a public meeting what she thought to be the annual intelligence budget: $44 billion.[75]

Combining Purse and Sword: The Iran-Contra Affair

Of the revelations emanating from the Iran-Contra affair, the most startling constitutional claim was the assertion that whenever Congress uses its power of the purse to restrict the President in foreign affairs, the President may pursue his goals by soliciting funds from private citizens and foreign countries. Beginning in 1982, Congress enacted a number of statutory restraints on the Reagan administration's assistance to the Contras in Nicaragua. When those

68. Aftergood v. C.I.A., 355 F.Supp.2d 557 (D.D.C. 2005); Aftergood v. C.I.A., 2004 WL 3262743 (D.D.C. 2004); Aftergood v. C.I.A., 225 F.Supp.2d 27 (D.D.C. 2002); Aftergood v. C.I.A., Civ. No. 8-2107 (TFH) (D.D.C. 1999).

69. Letter from CIA to Aftergood, "Reference: Freedom of Information Act request for FY 1947–48 aggregate intelligence budget figures (F-2002-01910/F-2002-00144)."

70. Aftergood v. C.I.A., 355 F.Supp.2d at 563.

71. Id.

72. Id.

73. Id. at 565.

74. David M. Barrett, The CIA and Congress: The Untold Story from Truman to Kennedy 102 (2005).

75. Scott Shane, "Official Reveals Budget for U.S. Intelligence," New York Times, November 11, 2005, at A24.

curbs proved insufficient, Congress in 1984 adopted strict language in the Boland Amendment to prohibit all executive assistance of any kind to support the Contras. The statutory language, in effect from October 1984 to October 1986, was sweeping: "During fiscal year 1985, no funds available to the Central Intelligence Agency, the Department of Defense, or any other agency or entity of the United States involved in intelligence activities may be obligated or expended for the purpose or which would have the effect of supporting, directly or indirectly, military or paramilitary operations in Nicaragua by any nation, group, organization, movement, or individual."[76]

Despite the all-embracing nature of this restriction, some members of Congress suspected that the Reagan administration might find ways to assist the Contras. During hearings in March 1985, Senator Christopher Dodd asked an administration witness whether there might be efforts to evade the Boland Amendment by seeking funds from private parties or other nations. The witness assured the Senator that there would be no attempt to circumvent the Boland Amendment. The administration's spokesman provided similar assurances a month later before a House committee.[77]

When President Reagan signed the statute that contained the Boland Amendment, he did not issue a statement claiming that Congress had overstepped its powers and that the administration would pursue its course of action in Nicaragua. The Attorney General did not question the constitutionality of the Boland Amendment. The Office of Legal Counsel in the Justice Department did not conclude in any internal memorandum or report that the amendment was invalid or nonbinding.

Nevertheless, at the very moment that the administration witness was providing assurances to two congressional committees, executive officials in the Reagan administration were actively soliciting funds to assist the Contras. Private citizens contributed money for the purchase of military weapons and supplies, and administration officials tried repeatedly to obtain aid from foreign governments, including Saudi Arabia.

Because members of the Reagan administration destroyed official documents and refused to tell the truth about what had happened, the full story of the Iran-Contra affair may never be known. However, if there had been evidence that President Reagan had used the National Security Council as a substitute for the CIA as a means of circumventing the Boland Amendment, and that he intended to use private and foreign funds as a substitute for public

76. 98 Stat. 1935, sec. 8066(a) (1984).
77. "Security and Development Assistance," hearings before the Senate Committee on Foreign Relations, 99th Cong., 1st Sess. 908–10 (1985); "Department of Defense Appropriations for 1986" (part 2), hearings before the House Committee on Appropriations, 99th Cong., 1st Sess. 1092 (1985).

funds, he would have committed an impeachable offense by trying to combine the power of the sword (Commander in Chief) with the power of the purse.

The framers were familiar with the experience of English kings who had been denied funds by Parliament. Monarchs turned to revenue from other sources—private citizens as well as foreign governments. These attempts to circumvent Parliament finally erupted in civil war and resulted in Charles I's loss of both his office and his head.[78] The growth of democratic government is intimately tied to legislative control over revenues and appropriations.

The U.S. Constitution is designed to avoid the civil wars, bloodshed, and regicide of British history by placing the power of the purse squarely in Congress. The framers deliberately divided government by making the President the Commander in Chief and reserving to Congress the unquestioned power to finance military expeditions. Under their design, a single branch could not both make and fund war. In Federalist 69, Hamilton argued that the American President was far less threatening than the King of England because the power of the latter "extends to the *declaring* of war and to the *raising* and *regulating* of fleets and armies." In contrast, all those powers were expressly granted to Congress. Madison warned against placing the power of Commander in Chief in the same hands as the power to go to war: "Those who are to *conduct a war* cannot in the nature of things, be proper or safe judges, whether *a war ought* to be *commenced, continued, or concluded.* They are barred from the latter functions by a great principle in free government, analogous to that which separates the sword from the purse, or the power of executing from the power of enacting laws."[79] George Mason advised his colleagues at the Philadelphia convention that the "purse & the sword ought never to get into the same hands <whether Legislative or Executive>."[80]

Congress can place conditions and prohibitions on presidential activities in foreign affairs, just as it limits presidential actions in domestic matters. Congress used the power of the purse to halt military operations in Southeast Asia in 1973.[81] Three years later, with the Clark Amendment, Congress prohibited all assistance for conducting military or paramilitary operations in Angola.[82] In 1986 Congress inserted language in an appropriations bill to prohibit U.S. forces from operating within 20 miles of the Nicaraguan border while providing assistance to the Contras.[83] In 1993 Congress set a deadline for American troops to leave Somalia. No funds could be used for military

78. Paul Einzig, The Control of the Purse 57–62, 100–106 (1959).
79. 5 The Writings of James Madison 148 (Hunt ed.) Emphasis in original.
80. 1 Farrand 139–40.
81. 87 Stat. 129; 87 Stat. 134; Fisher, Presidential Spending Power, at 110–18.
82. 90 Stat. 757, sec. 404 (1976).
83. 100 Stat. 3341–307, sec. 216 (1986).

action after March 1, 1994, unless the President requested an extension from Congress and received explicit legislative authority.[84]

It is possible to conduct federal operations with private and foreign funds, but only when specifically authorized by Congress. Statutes have created trust funds to receive gifts from the private sector and from foreign governments.[85] Gift funds must be placed in the Treasury Department and spent only for objects defined by Congress.[86] The purpose is to "ensure that the executive branch remains dependent upon the congressional appropriations process."[87] The 1991 Gulf War against Iraq was financed largely with funds contributed by other nations, but those funds went directly to the Treasury Department and first had to be appropriated by Congress.

Beginning with the Neutrality Act of 1794, Congress has forbidden private citizens from organizing military expeditions against a foreign government.[88] U.S. foreign policy must be conducted through political institutions, not private parties. A Department of Justice analysis in 1979 concluded that the legislative history of the Neutrality Act "clearly shows that the evil it proscribed was precisely and exclusively one which threatens the ability of the Government to carry on a coherent foreign policy."[89]

Despite these long-standing principles and precedents, Colonel Oliver North testified during the Iran-Contra hearings that the President could authorize and conduct covert operations with nonappropriated funds.[90] He was asked at the hearings: "If Congress told the President he could not ask foreign countries or private individuals for financial or other official assistance for the Contras, there would be serious doubt whether Congress had exceeded its constitutional power, correct?" North replied: "If the Congress had passed such a measure, it would clearly, in my opinion, be unconstitutional."[91]

This argument suffers from weaknesses both political and constitutional. If President Reagan had defied the Boland Amendment by seeking financial or other assistance from foreign countries or private individuals, at a minimum this would have subjected the United States to ridicule and humiliation. Having been rebuffed by Congress, the President would go, hat in hand, around

84. 107 Stat. 1476, sec. 8151(b)(2)(B) (1993).

85. 31 U.S.C. 1321 (2000); 5 U.S.C. 7342 (2000).

86. 31 U.S.C. 3302 (2000).

87. General Accounting Office, Principles of Federal Appropriations Law 5-65 (1982); see also 5-82 to 5-89.

88. 1 Stat. 369 (1794); 18 U.S.C. 960–62 (2000).

89. Office of Legal Counsel, U.S. Department of Justice, "Applicability of the Neutrality Act to Activities of the Central Intelligence Agency," memorandum from Larry L. Sims to Philip B. Heymann, Assistant Attorney General, Criminal Division, at 5 (October 10, 1979).

90. Iran-Contra hearings, vol. 100-7 (part 2), at 37.

91. Id., vol. 100-7 (part 1), at 207.

the globe seeking assistance to implement his foreign policy. Such conduct would risk a major confrontation with Congress, with the President acting in defiance of a congressional policy enacted into law. In such circumstances, a President would invite, and deserve, impeachment proceedings. He would have failed in his constitutional duty to see that the laws are faithfully executed, and he would have precipitated a constitutional crisis by merging the power of the sword with the power of the purse.

Moreover, soliciting funds from foreign governments to promote U.S. foreign policy opens the door to widespread compromise and corruption. Admiral John Poindexter testified that the administration could withhold information from Congress because the Contras were being assisted with non-appropriated funds: "We weren't using appropriated funds. They were private, third-country funds."[92] That is a statement of phenomenal ignorance. Accepting funds from foreign governments to sustain the Contras not only violated national policy but also created an implicit quid pro quo, requiring the United States to reciprocate by giving donor countries special consideration in such tangible forms as foreign assistance, military assistance, arms sales, and trade concessions.[93]

Legislation already existed to outlaw quid pro quos. The Pell Amendment in 1985 prohibited the use of any U.S. funds to provide "assistance of any kind, either directly or indirectly, to any person or group engaging in an insurgency or other act of rebellion against the Government of Nicaragua." The purpose was to prevent recipients of U.S. funds and materials from giving assistance to the Contras as a condition, or quid pro quo, for obtaining aid.[94] In 1989 President Bush vetoed a bill that contained criminal sanctions to punish quid pro quos.[95] In that same year he vetoed another bill establishing restrictions on quid pro quos, even though this measure omitted criminal sanctions.[96] In each of his veto messages Bush said that he was "sensitive to the concerns" that prompted Congress to add such language.[97] The principle that Congress was asserting merited presidential support. It was a matter of finding the right language.

Bush signed a revised bill aimed at quid pro quos. The new law stated that appropriated funds for foreign assistance may not be provided to "any foreign government (including any instrumentality or agency thereof), foreign

92. Id., vol. 100-8, at 158.
93. Id., vol. 100-1, at 25, 201, 279–80. See Alex Whiting, "Controlling Tin Cup Diplomacy," 99 Yale L. J. 2043 (1990).
94. 99 Stat. 254, sec. 722(d) (1985).
95. Public Papers of the Presidents, 1989 (II), at 1567–69.
96. Id. at 1546.
97. Id. at 1546, 1569.

person, or United States person in exchange for that foreign government or person undertaking any action which is, if carried out by the United States Government, a United States official or employee, expressly prohibited by a provision of United States law."[98] In signing the legislation, Bush agreed that the section prohibited quid pro quo transactions "in which U.S. funds are provided to a foreign nation on the express condition that the foreign nation provide specific assistance to a third country, which assistance U.S. officials are expressly prohibited from providing by U.S. law."[99]

For reasons both constitutional and practical, U.S. foreign policy must be conducted only with funds appropriated by Congress. Allowing the President to carry out foreign policy with private or foreign contributions would create what the framers feared most: the union of the purse and the sword.

98. 103 Stat. 1251, sec. 582 (1989).
99. Public Papers of the Presidents, 1989 (II), at 1573.

8

TREATIES AND EXECUTIVE AGREEMENTS

American public interest in international agreements has been spare and spasmodic. Geographic isolation, an abundance of natural resources, and a native distrust of "entangling alliances" have been some of the inhibiting factors. Occasionally an emotional issue such as the Jay Treaty, the Versailles Treaty, or the North American Free Trade Agreement (NAFTA) commands public attention, but for more prosaic disputes it has been difficult to sustain interest.

This general record is undergoing some change. The United States now depends heavily on foreign trade, finds itself vulnerable to oil embargoes and other interruptions of essential supplies, experiences world price effects, and sees its currency fluctuating widely because of international pressures. Cooperation on many matters can be resolved only by regional and worldwide compacts. As executive agreements are relied on more frequently as a substitute for the treaty process, creating demands on the Treasury, both houses of Congress scrutinize them with greater care. These pressures force the House of Representatives to participate on a more equal basis with the Senate.

Treaties

It is commonplace today to assign to the President a leading role in foreign policy and international affairs. But quite late in the deliberations at the Philadelphia convention, the delegates entrusted the predominant voice to the Senate. As late as August 6, 1787, the constitutional draft gave the Senate exclusive power to make treaties and appoint ambassadors. Opposition developed, however, and by early September the convention decided that the President should make treaties "by and with the advice and consent of the Senate" and should nominate "and by and with the Advice and Consent of the Senate, . . . appoint Ambassadors."[1]

Article II, Section 2, of the Constitution requires that treaties receive the support of "two thirds of the Senators present." A roll-call vote is not necessary (as it is for veto overrides), nor is there even a requirement that a quorum be present. In 1952, with two Senators on the floor, the Senate gave its

---

1. 2 Farrand 155, 169, 183, 297–98, 392–94, 495.

220

advice and consent to the ratification of three treaties. One of the Senators did not even vote. The other, the presiding officer, cast an "aye" vote and stated that "two-thirds of the Senators present concurring therein, the resolution of ratification is agreed to, and the convention is ratified." A year later Senate Majority Leader William Knowland announced that future treaties would be preceded by a quorum call and subjected to "a yea-and-nay vote, at least on the first of a series of treaties." That remains the general practice.[2]

The use of the word "treaty" in a statute does not necessarily mean an international agreement requiring the advice and consent of the Senate. Unless Congress specifically defines the word in that sense, courts may interpret treaties to mean an international agreement concluded between sovereigns without Senate participation.[3]

Negotiation

Does Senate "advice" on treaties apply only to the final product, as fashioned by the President and his assistants, or to the earlier stages of negotiation as well? Contemporary judgment often excludes the Senate from any participation in treaty negotiation. The process of drafting and negotiating a treaty is widely regarded as a "presidential monopoly."[4] And yet this conclusion is contradicted by the Philadelphia debates, the precedents established by the Washington administration, and the practices and understandings developed thereafter.

The Constitution does not divide treaty-making into two distinct and sequential stages: negotiation by the President and approval by the Senate. The President "makes" treaties by and with the advice and consent of the Senate. The constitutional language in Article II, Section 2, for treaties differs significantly from that used for appointments, a process that does depend on exclusive and sequential steps. The President "shall nominate, and by and with the Advice and Consent of the Senate, shall appoint Ambassadors." Here the President's authority to nominate is set apart as an executive responsibility. For treaties, the President "shall have Power, by and with the Advice and Consent of the Senate, to make Treaties." Treaty-making from this language appears to be done jointly by the two branches.

---

2. 99 Cong. Rec. 9231 (1953). See 98 Cong. Rec. 7217–23 (1952), and Carl Marcy, "A Note on Treaty Ratification," 47 Am. Pol. Sci. Rev. 1130 (1953). For contemporary practice, see "Treaties and Other International Agreements: The Role of the United States Senate," prepared for the Senate Committee on Foreign Relations, 106th Cong., 2d Sess. 97–111 (January 2001).

3. Weinberger v. Rossi, 456 U.S. 25 (1982).

4. The Constitution of the United States of America: Analysis and Interpretation, S. Doc. No. 108-17, at 492 (2004); Edward S. Corwin, The President 211–12 (1957); United States v. Curtiss-Wright Corp., 299 U.S. 304, 319 (1936).

When President George Washington first communicated with the Senate regarding the appropriate procedure for treaties, he did not assume that the process of negotiating treaties was a "presidential monopoly." Instead, he stated that oral communications with the Senate "seem indispensably necessary; because in these a variety of matters are contained, all of which not only require consideration, but some of them may undergo much discussion; to do which by written communications would be tedious without being satisfactory."[5] This policy suggests an active role for the Senate, not a mere yea or nay to what a President submits.

A subsequent letter from Washington underscores the partnership status of the Senate on treaty-making: "In the appointment to offices, the agency of the Senate is purely executive, and they may be summoned to the President. In treaties, the agency is perhaps as much of a legislative nature and the business may possibly be referred to their deliberations in their legislative chamber." Repeatedly he expressed his intention to send "propositions" to the Senate, again implying that the Senate would be invited to make changes and offer recommendations to treaty drafts.[6] Hamilton, in Federalist 75, did not see an exclusive executive role in treaties. He said that the power of making treaties "will be found to partake more of the legislative than of the executive character, though it does not seem strictly to fall within the definition of either of them."

Washington sent a message to the Senate on August 21, 1789, stating his intention to meet with Senators in the Senate Chamber "to advise with them on the terms of the treaty *to be negotiated* with the Southern Indians."[7] He was coming to them before, not after, negotiating a treaty. He met with Senators the following day and put to them a series of questions, requesting advice on the instructions to be given to the commissioners selected to negotiate the treaty.[8]

The disappointments experienced by both sides have often been recounted. The Senators did not want to rely solely on the information supplied by the Secretary of War, who had accompanied Washington. The noise from the carriages traveling past made it difficult to follow the discussion. When the Senators announced that they would not commit themselves to any positions that day, Washington felt inconvenienced by the trip. He returned two days later and obtained the Senate's answers to his questions and its consent to the treaty, but he never again met personally with the Senators to obtain their advice on a treaty draft.[9]

5. 30 The Writings of Washington 373 (Fitzpatrick ed.).
6. Id. at 378.
7. 1 Annals of Congress 67 (1789). Emphasis added.
8. Id. at 69–71.
9. William Maclay, Sketches of Debate in the First Senate of the United States 122–26 (1880).

It is a misreading of this unhappy incident to conclude that henceforth the Senate was excluded from any role in the negotiation process. Washington continued to seek its advice, but he did so through written communications rather than personal appearances.[10] Senators were asked to approve the appointment of treaty negotiators and even to advise on their negotiating instructions.[11] Far from being a "presidential monopoly," the negotiation of treaties has often been shared with the Senate in order to secure legislative understanding and support.[12]

President Andrew Jackson understood the value of seeking the advice of Senators on how best to pursue treaty negotiations. Inviting the Senate to participate in the negotiation process for an Indian treaty seemed good sense to him. Obtaining the Senate's views "on this important and delicate branch of our future negotiations would enable the President to act much more effectively in the exercise of his particular functions. There is also the best reason to believe that measures in this respect emanating from the *united counsel* of the treaty-making power would be more satisfactory to the American people and to the Indians."[13]

President James K. Polk adopted a similar attitude, asking the Senate to give its advice on the negotiation of a treaty because it was prudent for a President to consult Senators in advance of "important measures of foreign policy which may ultimately come before them for their consideration." Through such consultation the President "secures harmony of action between that body and himself."[14] Presidents William McKinley, Warren Harding, and Herbert Hoover included Senators as members of U.S. delegations that negotiated treaties.[15]

Woodrow Wilson held a different view. As a scholar he urged the President not to consult with the Senate and treat it as an equal partner. Instead, he recommended that negotiations be pursued independently. After these unilateral executive actions, legislative compliance would be compelled by getting the country "into such scrapes, so pledged in the view of the world to certain courses of action, that the Senate hesitates to bring about the appearance of dishonor which would follow its refusal to ratify the rash promises or to support the indiscreet threats of the Department of State."[16] This mousetrap

10. 1 Richardson 64–65, 68–69, 71–72, 81–84, 110–13, 115.

11. Thomas M. Franck and Edward Weisband, Foreign Policy by Congress 136 (1979).

12. Many examples are cited in 2 George H. Haynes, The Senate of the United States 576–602 (1938).

13. 4 J. Sen. Exec. Proc. 99 (1887). Emphasis added.

14. 5 Richardson 2299.

15. Treaties and Other International Agreements: The Role of the United States Senate, S. Prt. 106-71, 106th Cong., 2d Sess. 109 (2001).

16. Woodrow Wilson, Congressional Government 233–34 (1885). Similar views appear in his Constitutional Government in the United States 77–78 (1908). His constitutional analysis

theory of the treaty power had disastrous consequences for Wilson's record in office as well as for international events after World War I. One of his gravest miscalculations was his decision to exclude prominent Senators from the negotiation of the Versailles Treaty. When administrations decide to present the Senate with a fait accompli, the Senate may retaliate by tacking on amendments, shelving treaties, or rejecting them outright.[17]

A healthier model of Senate-presidential cooperation appears in the legislative history of the United Nations Charter. The details of this Charter were hammered out at a conference in San Francisco in 1945. Half of the eight members of the U.S. delegation came from Congress: Senators Tom Connally (D-Tex.) and Arthur H. Vandenberg (R-Mich.) and Representatives Sol Bloom (D-N.Y.) and Charles A. Eaton (R-N.J.). John Foster Dulles, later to be Secretary of State under President Eisenhower, told the Senate Foreign Relations Committee in 1945 that in the past he had had "some doubts as to the wisdom of Senators participating in the negotiation of treaties." However, because of his experience at the San Francisco conference, those doubts "were dispelled."[18] He failed to note that the legislative participants included not only two Senators but two members of the House as well.

Another example of Senate-presidential cooperation is the North Atlantic Treaty. It was foreshadowed by Senate Resolution 239, passed in 1948, calling for "regional and other collective arrangements for individual and collective self-defense." The Senate developed the resolution in close collaboration with the State Department. Between the time of its passage and ratification of the treaty, ranking members of the Senate Foreign Relations Committee consulted with the State Department. The committee as a whole helped formulate the terms of the treaty. Dean Acheson, who entertained inflated notions of executive prerogatives during his tenure as Secretary of State, testified in 1971 that the treaty process was formally divided into negotiation and ratification stages, but "anybody with any sense would consult with certainly some of the members of the ratifying body before he got himself out on the very end of a limb from which he could be sawed off." He recalled that during the negotiations of the North Atlantic Treaty, Senators Thomas Connally and

is effectively refuted by William Whitwell Dewhurst, "Does the Constitution Make the President Sole Negotiator of Treaties?" 30 Yale L. J. 478 (1921); Forrest R. Black, "The United States Senate and the Treaty Power," 4 Rocky Mt. L. Rev. 1 (1931); and Richard E. Webb, "Treaty-Making and the President's Obligation to Seek the Advice and Consent of the Senate with Special Reference to the Vietnam Peace Negotiations," 31 Ohio State L. J. 490 (1970).

17. Franck and Weisband, Foreign Policy by Congress, at 136–37.
18. "The Charter of the United Nations," hearings before the Senate Committee on Foreign Relations, 79th Cong., 1st Sess. 644 (1945).

Arthur Vandenburg "were with me all the time," and Senator Walter George actually wrote one of the provisions of the treaty.[19]

The substantial overlap between domestic and foreign matters creates the need to include congressional leaders in the negotiation of international agreements and to establish machinery to permit more effective integration of congressional interests.[20] The volatile politics of the Panama Canal Treaty prompted Senate Majority Leader Robert Byrd, Minority Leader Howard Baker, and several other key Senators to visit Panama and negotiate changes in the treaty with General Omar Torrijos and Panamanian officials. These rescue missions might have been averted had President Carter reached out earlier for Senate advice.[21] The Carter administration consulted with at least 70 Senators during the final negotiations of the Panama Canal Treaty.[22]

Members of both houses of Congress are formal participants in the broad network of international boards and commissions. They attend international conferences and serve as delegates to the North Atlantic Assembly, the Interparliamentary Union, and other interparliamentary groups. They serve as U.S. Representatives to the UN General Assembly. Through such participation and experience, members of Congress become deeply involved in negotiation. During 1977 and 1978, 26 Senators went to Geneva as official advisers to the Strategic Arms Limitation Talks (SALT II) negotiating team.[23] Since 1962 it has been the practice of Congress to require that a specific number of Representatives and Senators be accredited as official advisers to the U.S. delegations that negotiate trade agreements.[24] Foreign leaders customarily contacted only the President (except for ceremonial addresses before Congress). Beginning in the 1970s, however, foreign leaders appealed directly to the leaders and committees of Congress, lobbying them for arms sales, enriched nuclear fuel, and other benefits.

19. "Executive Privilege: The Withholding of Information by the Executive," hearing before the Senate Committee on the Judiciary, 92d Cong., 1st Sess. 262–64 (1971). See also Richard H. Heindel et al., "The North Atlantic Treaty in the United States Senate," 43 Am. J. Int'l L. 633 (1949).

20. See Bayless Manning, "The Congress, the Executive, and Intermestic Affairs: Three Proposals," 55 Foreign Affairs 306 (1977).

21. Cecil V. Crabb Jr. and Pat M. Holt, Invitation to Struggle: Congress, the President, and Foreign Policy 77–79 (1980); John Spanier and Joseph Nogee, eds., Congress, the Presidency, and American Foreign Policy 92–93 (1981).

22. I. M. Destler, "Treaty Troubles: Versailles in Reverse," 35 Foreign Policy 45, 50 (Winter 1978–1979).

23. I. M. Destler, "Executive-Congressional Conflict in Foreign Policy: Explaining It, Coping with It," in Lawrence C. Dodd and Bruce I. Oppenheimer, eds., Congress Reconsidered 310 (1981).

24. Robert C. Cassidy Jr., "Negotiating About Negotiations: The Geneva Multilateral Trade Talks," in Thomas M. Franck, ed., The Tethered Presidency 267–68 (1981).

Private groups are also more active in the negotiation of international agreements. Advisory committees, consisting of representatives from the private sector, serve on dozens of panels in the foreign affairs field. Their functions include assisting in the preparation of international negotiations and advising the State Department on positions to take at conferences.[25] State governments, in their search for export trade and foreign investment, maintain direct contact with both private and government officials of foreign countries. This activity is encouraged by the Commerce Department and American embassies and consulates.[26]

The notion that the President is the exclusive negotiator of treaties and international agreements has been undermined even more by recent trade legislation, which gives Congress a direct role in the negotiation process. It is now the practice of Congress to offer the President a "fast-track" legislative procedure for implementing trade agreements with other nations. Under the fast-track system, the President's implementing bill is automatically introduced in Congress, committees must act within a specified number of days, Congress must complete floor action within a limited time, and amendments to the bill are prohibited either in committee or on the floor. Through this procedure, leaders of foreign governments (often with parliamentary systems that vest strong powers in the executive) are assured that the trade pact will be given expedited consideration by Congress.

In obtaining these procedural benefits, Presidents recognize that members of Congress must be closely involved in the negotiations that produce the implementing bill. In 1991, after President Bush asked Congress to extend the fast-track procedure to a trade pact with Mexico, U.S. Trade Representative Carla A. Hills told the Senate Finance Committee that the fast track "is a genuine partnership between the two branches." Because Congress retained the power to defeat the implementing bill, Hills emphasized that Congress "has a full role throughout the entire process in formulating the negotiating objectives in close consultation as the negotiations proceed."[27] President Bush gave Congress his "personal commitment to close bipartisan cooperation in the negotiations and beyond."[28] This initiative in the Bush administration led to NAFTA, which became law in 1993. President Clinton continued to involve members of Congress closely in the negotiations and last-minute changes in the draft implementing bill.

25. "The Role of Advisory Committees in U.S. Foreign Policy," prepared for the Senate Committee on Foreign Relations, 94th Cong., 1st Sess. 4 (Comm. Print April 1975).

26. Harold G. Maier, "Cooperative Federalism in International Trade: Its Constitutional Parameters," 27 Mercer L. Rev. 391 (1976).

27. "Extension of Fast Track Legislative Procedures," hearings before the Senate Committee on Finance, 102d Cong., 1st Sess. 9 (1991).

28. Public Papers of the Presidents, 1991 (I), at 450.

The Logan Act

Efforts to protect the President's responsibility for negotiating with foreign nations go back to the Logan Act of 1799. The previous year, after American negotiations with France had foundered, a Philadelphia physician by the name of George Logan set sail for Europe to try his hand at diplomacy. His trip provoked a resolution in Congress directed against private citizens who "usurp the Executive authority of this government, by commencing or carrying on any correspondence with the Governments of any foreign Prince or State." The same Congress that passed the Alien and Sedition Acts gave birth to the Logan Act, which provided for fines and imprisonment to punish American citizens who carry on unauthorized correspondence or intercourse with foreign governments for the purpose of influencing American policy.[29]

Hundreds of individuals have defied this act, but only one has been indicted, and he was found not guilty. During the Vietnam War, pacifist leaders and American office seekers maintained frequent contact with North Vietnam and the peace delegations at Paris. The State Department has taken the position that members of Congress may engage in discussions with foreign officials in pursuance of their legislative duties under the Constitution, provided they advise the officials that they have no authority to negotiate on behalf of the United States.[30]

In 1976 former President Nixon traveled to China around the time of the New Hampshire primary. Senator Barry Goldwater said that Nixon had violated the Logan Act and would do the United States a favor by remaining in China.[31] The State Department regarded Nixon's visit as one undertaken entirely as a private citizen and was "unaware of any basis for believing that Mr. Nixon acted with the intent prohibited by the Logan Act."[32]

After more than 50 Americans were held hostage in Iran beginning in November 1979, American legislators, professors, clergymen, and parents of the hostages traveled to that country to try to negotiate a release. President Carter appeared to support such ventures. In 1979, after American citizens had traveled to the Middle East to talk to Arab and Israeli leaders, he said: "I don't have any authority, nor do I want to have any authority, to interrupt or to interfere with the right of American citizens to travel where they choose

---

29. 1 Stat. 613 (1799); 18 U.S.C. 953 (2000). The resolution is cited in Annals of Congress, 5th Cong., 3d Sess. 2489 (1798). See also Charles Warren, History of Laws Prohibiting Correspondence with a Foreign Government and Acceptance of a Commission, S. Doc. No. 696, 64th Cong., 2d Sess. (1917).

30. Digest of United States Practice in International Law, 1975, at 749–50.

31. 122 Cong. Rec. 4216, 4919 (1976); Washington Post, February 26, 1976, at A7:1.

32. Digest of United States Practice in International Law, 1976, at 75–76.

and to meet with whom they choose. I would not want that authority; I think it would be a violation of the basic constitutional rights that are precious to our Nation."[33]

Carter's patience snapped during the summer of 1980 when former Attorney General Ramsey Clark attended a conference in Iran despite a presidential ban. Several members of Congress were outraged by the visit, labeling Clark the "Benedict Arnold of the 20th century" and urging the Justice Department to prosecute him for violating the Logan Act and the International Emergency Economic Powers Act.[34] Carter said that he was inclined to prosecute Clark and several others who had violated his directive on the travel ban.[35] This statement was attributable to presidential pique, however, and the incident was soon forgotten. Attorney General Benjamin R. Civiletti later announced that it would be "inappropriate" to prosecute Clark in a criminal suit, and no action was ever taken in a civil suit.[36]

Jesse Jackson was an active traveler to foreign countries during the Reagan years, visiting with government leaders in Syria, Cuba, Central America, and other regions, often negotiating for the release of U.S. citizens. Jackson's visit to Cuba in 1984 and his talks with Fidel Castro prompted President Reagan to remind reporters that "there is a law, the Logan Act, with regard to unauthorized personnel, civilians, simply going to . . . other countries and, in effect, negotiating with foreign governments. Now, that is the law of the land." But he said that he had no plans to take legal action.[37] A trip by Louis Farrakhan in 1996 to African and Middle Eastern countries, including Libya, Nigeria, Iraq, and Iran, prompted some legislators to charge that he had violated the Logan Act.[38]

Because the Logan Act is vague in meaning and restricts First Amendment freedoms, it is of doubtful constitutionality.[39] The historical record certainly suggests that the sanctions are too harsh to be applied. As part of an effort to revise and unify the federal criminal code, Congress has considered repealing the Logan Act.

    33. Public Papers of the Presidents, 1979, at 1861.
    34. 126 Cong. Rec. 13005–8, 13581–82, 13727–31, 13842–43 (1980).
    35. Public Papers of the Presidents, 1980–1981 (II), at 1087.
    36. Washington Post, January 8, 1981, at A6:1.
    37. Public Papers of the Presidents, 1984 (II), at 990.
    38. 142 Cong. Rec. 3667 (1996).
    39. Detlev F. Vagts, "The Logan Act: Paper Tiger or Sleeping Giant?" 60 Am. J. Int'l L. 268 (1966), analyzed the act and concluded that it is probably unconstitutional. The same conclusion was reached by Kevin M. Kearney, "Private Citizens in Foreign Affairs: A Constitutional Analysis," 36 Emory L. J. 285 (1987). Other constitutional doubts are raised in Waldron v. British Petroleum Co., 231 F.Supp. 72, 88–89 (S.D. N.Y. 1964).

The Role of the House

In 1976 President Ford vetoed a bill that Congress had passed to implement U.S. obligations under a treaty. The bill contained a one-house veto that, he said, "would allow the House of Representatives to block adoption of what is essentially an amendment to a treaty, a responsibility which is reserved by the Constitution to the Senate."[40] Ford's assumption that the House is excluded from treaty matters has been contested in the past and is challenged even more vigorously today.

Several delegates at the Philadelphia convention favored a check on treaties by both houses rather than by the Senate alone. They reasoned that treaties, accorded the status of law under the Constitution, should be approved by Congress as a whole. At one point it was suggested that "no Treaty shall be binding on the U.S. which is not ratified by a law." Madison wondered whether a distinction might not be made between different types of treaties, allowing the President and the Senate to make "Treaties eventual and of Alliance for limited terms—and requiring the concurrence of the whole Legislature in other Treaties." A later proposal, joining the House with the Senate in advising and consenting to treaties, was decisively beaten back with only one state in favor and ten opposed.[41] The Constitution adopted in September reserved the treaty-making power to the President and to the Senate.

Some of the framers raised specific objections to any role for the House in treaty affairs. In Federalist 75, Hamilton said that the "fluctuating and . . . multitudinous composition" of the House necessarily excluded it from a position of trust: "Accurate and comprehensive knowledge of foreign politics; a steady and systematic adherence to the same views; a nice and uniform sensibility to national character; decision, *secrecy*, and dispatch, are incompatible with the genius of a body so variable and so numerous." In Federalist 64, Jay claimed that decisions on treaties should be placed in the hands of the Senate, whose members would be chosen by the "select assemblies" of state legislatures and presumably would possess greater expertise than members of the House. Those arguments became less compelling after the Seventeenth Amendment subjected Senators to popular election and the Senate grew until it exceeded the original House membership of 65.

Before those two developments, however, the power to make laws and to appropriate funds propelled the House into an active role in international

---

40. Public Papers of the Presidents, 1976–1977 (III), at 2481. Substantially the same bill (substituting a two-house for a one-house veto) became law the following year; 91 Stat. 308 (1977). See H. Rept. No. 447, 95th Cong., 1st Sess. (1977).
41. 2 Farrand 392–94, 538.

affairs. President Washington recognized political reality in 1793 when he included both the House and the Senate in treaty-making with Algiers because of the need for funds.[42] A major dispute erupted in 1796 when President Washington notified the House of Representatives that the Jay Treaty had been ratified. Congressman Edward Livingston offered a resolution requesting the President to transmit to the House a copy of the instructions that had been given to the U.S. minister who negotiated the treaty, together with correspondence and other documents relating to the treaty. Five days later he modified the resolution to permit the President to withhold any papers that it might be improper to disclose in view of existing negotiations. Livingston maintained that the House possessed "a discretionary power of carrying the Treaty into effect, or refusing it their sanction."[43] Congressman Albert Gallatin of Pennsylvania was even more explicit. He said that certain powers delegated to Congress by the Constitution, such as the authority to regulate trade, might clash with the treaty-making powers. The House did not have to acquiesce in decisions agreed to by the President and the Senate. The legislative powers specifically delegated to Congress served as limitations on the treaty process; the general power of granting funds constituted yet another restraining force.[44]

After weeks of debate the House supported Livingston's resolution by a margin of 62 to 37. Washington denied the request for papers and documents and cited a number of reasons, including the need for caution and secrecy in foreign negotiations as well as the Senate's exclusive participation as a member of the legislative branch. Shortly thereafter Congressman Thomas Blount introduced a resolution (adopted 57 to 35), stating that the House of Representatives did not claim any agency in making treaties,

> but that when a Treaty stipulates regulations of any of the subjects submitted by the Constitution to the power of Congress, it must depend, for its execution, as to such stipulations, on a law or laws to be passed by Congress. And it is the Constitutional right and duty of the House of Representatives, in all such cases, to deliberate on the expediency or inexpediency of carrying such Treaty into effect, and to determine and act thereon, as, in their judgment, may be most conducive to the public good.[45]

42. Louis Fisher, The Politics of Executive Privilege 30–33 (2004).
43. Annals of Congress, 4th Cong., 1st Sess. 426–28.
44. Id. at 437, 466–74.
45. Id. at 771–82. This language has been adopted on other occasions, such as on April 20, 1871; 2 Hinds' Precedents §1523. See also Ivan M. Stone, "The House of Representatives and the Treaty-Making Power," 17 Ky. L. J. 217 (1929).

Some of the issues of the Jay Treaty resurfaced during the debate on the Louisiana Purchase. On the basis of a provisional appropriation of $2 million to be applied toward the purchase of New Orleans and the Floridas, the Jefferson administration entered into an agreement with France to buy the whole of Louisiana. Congressional support required not only the advice and consent of the Senate to the treaty but also funds supplied by both houses. Accordingly, Jefferson sent copies of the ratified treaty to the House of Representatives and to the Senate, explaining: "You will observe that some important conditions can not be carried into execution but with the aid of the Legislature, and that time presses a decision on them without delay."[46] The House debated at length a resolution requesting that Jefferson provide certain papers and documents relating to the treaty. Some portions of the resolution were adopted, others rejected. The resolution as a whole went down to defeat, 59 to 57. The House subsequently joined the Senate in passing legislation to enable Jefferson to take possession of the Louisiana Territory.[47]

On other occasions the House has opposed treaties that required appropriations, two examples being the Gadsden purchase treaty with Mexico in 1853 and the Alaskan purchase treaty with Russia in 1867. The need to have support from both houses for certain treaties was recognized in a reciprocity treaty with the Hawaiian Islands in 1876. A proviso made the treaty dependent on legislative consent by both houses.[48]

Article I, Section 8, of the Constitution empowers Congress to "regulate Commerce with foreign Nations, and among the several States, and with the Indian Tribes." For nearly a century Congress treated the tribes as independent nations, subject to the treaty-making power of the President and the Senate. The Civil War changed the government's policy toward assimilation and citizenship. During this time the Office of Indian Affairs came under heavy fire for corruption and maladministration. In response to those developments the House of Representatives began to voice strong opposition to its exclusion from Indian affairs. When the Senate inserted funds in a bill to fulfill treaties it had ratified with the Indians, the House withheld its support. The session expired in 1869 without an appropriation for the Office of Indian Affairs. Congress fashioned a compromise the following session, but the dispute between the two houses persisted. Finally, an act approved in 1871 contained the following clause: "*Provided,* That hereafter no Indian nation or tribe within the territory of the United States shall be acknowledged or

46. 1 Richardson 350–51 (October 21, 1803).
47. Annals of Congress, 8th Cong., 1st Sess. 385–419; 2 Stat. 245, 247 (1803).
48. Chalfant Robinson, "The Treaty-Making Power of the House of Representatives," 12 Yale Rev. 191 (1903).

recognized as an independent nation, tribe, or power with whom the United States may contract by treaty."[49]

In 1880 the House declared that the negotiation of a commercial treaty, fixing the rates of duty to be imposed on foreign imports, would be "an infraction of the Constitution and an invasion of one of the highest prerogatives of the House of Representatives."[50] The commerce power was again at issue a few years later. A commercial treaty with Mexico in 1883 contained a clause making its validity dependent on action by both houses of Congress. The House Ways and Means Committee interpreted the language to mean that the House had a right to a voice in treaties affecting revenue. Although additional conventions were entered into to extend the time available for congressional approval, the House did not support the treaty, and it did not take effect.[51] The prerogatives of the House in matters of foreign commerce, tariffs, and revenues have been protected by the use of statutes that authorize reciprocal trade agreements.[52]

Legislation sometimes serves as a direct substitute for treaties. When the Senate failed to ratify a treaty for the annexation of Texas, President John Tyler advised the House of Representatives: "The power of Congress is, however, fully competent in some other form of proceeding to accomplish everything that a formal ratification of the treaty could have accomplished."[53] He laid before the House the rejected treaty, together with all the correspondence and documents that had previously been made available to the Senate. Instead of having to obtain a two-thirds vote from the Senate, the annexation of Texas was consummated by simple majority votes from both houses.[54] Hawaii was annexed in 1898 by the same method after Senate opposition prevented action on a treaty. The St. Lawrence Seaway plan, rejected by the Senate in 1934 in treaty form, passed Congress in 1954 as a regular bill.[55] The Carter administration created a stir when it considered submitting SALT agreements as a joint resolution rather than as a treaty.[56]

49. 16 Stat. 566 (1871). See also U.S. Department of the Interior, Federal Indian Law 138–214 (1958).

50. 2 Hinds' Precedents §1524.

51. 24 Stat. 975 (1883), 25 Stat. 1370 (1885), 24 Stat. 1018 (1886), and 2 Hinds' Precedents §§1526–28.

52. For the development of reciprocal trade legislation, see Louis Fisher, President and Congress 133–55 (1972).

53. 5 Richardson 2176 (June 10, 1844).

54. 5 Stat. 797 (1845).

55. For an opinion by Acting Attorney General James McGranery in 1946 upholding the legality of an executive agreement made pursuant to a joint resolution (instead of a treaty), see 40 Op. Att'y Gen. 469 (1946).

56. Armen R. Vartian, "Approval of SALT Agreements by Joint Resolution of Congress," 21 Harv. Int'l L. J. 421 (1980); "Treaty Ratification Process and Separation of Powers," hearing before the Senate Committee on the Judiciary, 97th Cong., 2d Sess. (1982).

During World War II, proposals were put forth to give the House equal treaty-making powers with the Senate. In part this development reflected criticism of the Senate's performance over the previous half century.[57] Members of the House also challenged the traditional arguments offered in support of the Senate's treaty prerogative. In Federalist 64, Jay had claimed that treaties should be in the hands of Senators because they are chosen by the "select assemblies" of state legislatures and would therefore possess greater expertise than members of the House. The force of that reasoning evaporated after the Seventeenth Amendment subjected Senators to popular election. Jay had also argued that the small size of the Senate permitted greater secrecy and dispatch than could be expected of the House, but by 1944, the Senate had grown from 26 members to 96, or larger than the original House membership of 65. On the basis of these changes in the political system, the House in 1945 adopted, by a vote of 288 to 88, a resolution to amend the Constitution to provide for treaty ratification by a majority of both houses. Not surprisingly, the Senate took no action on the measure.[58]

But the issue persists. A dispute over the Spanish Bases Treaty of 1976 began as an executive-legislative conflict. The Senate successfully argued that an agreement with Spain over military bases should be accomplished not by executive agreement, as in the past, but by treaty. Having conceded that point to Congress, the administration ran into other difficulties. Members of both houses objected to language in the treaty that appeared to make mandatory the appropriation of funds over a five-year period. The administration also maintained that the treaty constituted an *authorization* to have funds appropriated, thus threatening to bypass the jurisdiction of the Senate Committee on Foreign Relations and the House Committee on Foreign Affairs.

Responding to both issues, the Senate Resolution of Advice and Consent contained a declaration that the sums referred to in the Spanish treaty "shall be made available for obligation through the normal procedures of the Congress, including the process of prior authorization and annual appropriations." Although the administration had wanted the treaty itself to serve as the authorization, the Senate resolution guaranteed congressional involvement for the authorizing and appropriating committees of *both* houses. Congress enacted legislation in 1976 to authorize the appropriation of funds needed to implement the treaty.[59]

The Spanish Bases Treaty was replaced by an executive agreement in 1982. The agreement stipulates that the supply of defense articles and services is

57. H. Rept. No. 2061, 78th Cong., 2d Sess. 4–5 (1944).
58. 91 Cong. Rec. 4326–68 (1945).
59. 90 Stat. 765, sec. 507; 90 Stat. 2498.

subject to "the annual authorizations and appropriations contained in United States security assistance legislation." Although the agreement promises support "in the highest amounts, the most favorable terms, and the widest variety of forms," it also conditions such support on what "may be lawful and feasible."[60] In short, negotiators may negotiate whatever they want; what is actually supplied depends on congressional action.

The lesson of the Spanish assistance agreement can be applied broadly. When the Ford administration signed an executive agreement with Turkey in 1976, it earmarked in Article XIX specific sums for defense assistance. President Ford sent Congress draft legislation to implement the agreement, but the measure was never even reported from committee.[61] Draft legislation the next year was again ignored.[62] Instead, Congress continued the existing arms embargo on Turkey until 1978. After the embargo was lifted, the Carter administration entered into an executive agreement with Turkey in 1980 without making a specific pledge of economic or military assistance. The United States promised to make its "best efforts" to provide mutually agreed assistance. The level of that assistance depended on annual authorization and appropriation by Congress.

The history of the Panama Canal is one of Senate participation in the treaty process followed by House involvement. Ever since Theodore Roosevelt "took" Panama in 1903, the United States has been under pressure to compensate other nations for the venture. In 1922 the Thompson-Urrutia Treaty gave Colombia (the previous owner of Panama) special canal rights and a cash grant of $25 million as penance for Roosevelt's use of force.[63] The American presence in the Canal Zone remained a problem. A riot in 1964 precipitated talks for a new treaty.

The House of Representatives watched these negotiations with growing apprehension. The prospect of surrendering control of the canal raised questions of military needs and national security. But the constitutional interest of the House was twofold: the power to appropriate and the power to cede U.S. property. Article IV, Section 3, Clause 2, of the Constitution states: "The Congress shall have Power to dispose of and make all needful Rules and Regulations respecting the Territory or other Property belonging to the United States." In 1975, on a floor vote of 246 to 164, the House adopted an amendment to prohibit the use of any funds "for the purpose of negotiating the

60. "Agreement on Friendship, Defense, and Cooperation Between the United States of America and the Kingdom of Spain," Complementary Agreement Three, Article 2 (signed July 2, 1982).

61. H. Doc. No. 531, 94th Cong., 2d Sess. (1976). Introduced as S.J. Res. 204.

62. H. Doc. No. 57, 95th Cong., 1st Sess. (1977).

63. Robert K. Murray, The Harding Era 340–41 (1969).

surrender or relinquishment of any U.S. rights in the Panama Canal Zone." Here was an effort not only to control a treaty but to influence negotiations as well. In fact, opponents of the amendment contended that it would make further negotiation impossible. As softened by the conference committee and enacted into law, the language was nonbinding and general: "It is the sense of the Congress that any new Panama Canal treaty or agreement must protect the vital interests of the United States in the Canal Zone and in the operation, maintenance, property and defense of the Panama Canal."[64]

Advocates of House prerogatives continued to insist that a treaty with Panama, providing for the transfer of American property or the payment of money to Panama, could not be accomplished by the treaty process alone. Congressman Mickey Edwards and 59 other members of the House filed suit, asking the courts to declare illegal President Carter's submission of the Panama Canal Treaties to the Senate. They argued that he had violated their constitutional right to vote on the disposition of U.S. property.

A district court in 1978 held that the members lacked standing to challenge the President's action, particularly when legislative solutions were still available to them (both before and after Senate ratification).[65] The D.C. Circuit affirmed this ruling and held that the Property Clause of the Constitution is not the exclusive method for disposing of federal property. The use of treaties for that purpose is constitutionally authorized.[66]

Even after these setbacks in the courts and the Senate's ratification of the Panama Canal Treaties, opponents had one last opportunity: They could defeat the implementing legislation. Congress had to set up a Panama Canal Commission and enact other implementing mechanisms, but the chief focus fell on the overall cost to the federal government (and therefore to taxpayers). Despite a concerted effort by opponents in the House of Representatives, Congress passed the implementing legislation in 1979.

The role of the House in international agreements was debated again in 1994 when President Clinton submitted the Uruguay Round Agreements to Congress as a bill rather than as a treaty. The purpose of the bill was to implement the worldwide General Agreement on Tariffs and Trade (GATT). Professor Laurence H. Tribe testified that certain features of the bill would so alter the dynamics of state-federal relations that ratification of a treaty by two-thirds of the Senate was necessary, given the Senate's special role in representing the states as political units.[67] However, there are no clear guidelines

---

64. 89 Stat. 617, sec. 104 (1975). See the debate at 121 Cong. Rec. 20945–56 (1975).
65. Edwards v. Carter, 445 F.Supp. 1279 (D.D.C. 1978).
66. Edwards v. Carter, 580 F.2d 1055 (D.C. Cir. 1978), cert. denied, 436 U.S. 907 (1978).
67. "S. 2467, GATT Implementing Legislation," hearings before the Senate Committee on Commerce, Science, and Transportation, 103d Cong., 2d Sess. 302–12 (1994).

on the types of national policy that must be included only in a treaty and not in a statute. The subject matter of NAFTA and GATT—international trade—was certainly within the jurisdiction of Congress as a whole to "regulate Commerce with foreign nations" and therefore merited action by both houses through the regular statutory process.[68]

Treaty Termination

Although the Constitution requires joint action by the President and the Senate for the making of treaties, it does not address the question of treaty termination. The issue was not discussed at the Constitutional Convention. Article VI, however, vests treaties with the same domestic status as federal statutes. Treaties may therefore be terminated by subsequent acts of Congress through the regular legislative process. Indeed, some of the early treaties were terminated or abrogated by statute. To the extent that a statute conflicts with an existing treaty, it operates to abrogate those portions of the treaty.[69] Other treaties were terminated by presidential action without prior congressional authorization, by Senate resolutions, and by new treaties.[70]

After President Nixon's overtures to the People's Republic of China (PRC), some members of Congress became concerned that the Carter administration might unilaterally terminate U.S. treaties with the Republic of China (Taiwan), especially the Mutual Defense Treaty of 1954. The treaty of 1954 allowed "either party" to end the pact after giving the other country a year's notice. The treaty did not specify the process by which "a party" would reach that decision. In a bill enacted in 1978, Congress included this nonbinding language: "It is the sense of the Congress that there should be prior consultation between the Congress and the executive branch" on any changes affecting the U.S.-Taiwan treaty.[71] Nevertheless, two months later, while Congress was out of session, Carter announced his decision to recognize the PRC and terminate the defense treaty with Taiwan.

Senator Harry F. Byrd Jr. submitted a Senate resolution stating that it was the sense of the Senate that "approval of the United States Senate is required

68. Bruce Ackerman and David Golove, "Is NAFTA Constitutional?" 108 Harv. L Rev. 799 (1995). See also Laurence H. Tribe, "Taking Text and Structure Seriously: Reflections on Free-Form Method in Constitutional Interpretation," 108 Harv. L. Rev. 1223 (1995).
69. The Chinese Exclusion Case, 130 U.S. 581, 600–602 (1889). See also Whitney v. Robertson, 124 U.S. 190, 193–94 (1888); the Head Money Cases, 112 U.S. 580, 597–99 (1884).
70. Digest of United States Practice in International Law, 1978, at 734–65.
71. 92 Stat. 746, sec. 26 (1978).

to terminate any Mutual Defense Treaty between the United States and another nation." On June 6, 1979, the Senate called up for consideration Byrd's resolution. As rewritten by the Senate Foreign Relations Committee, it became the sense of the Senate that U.S. treaties or treaty provisions should not be terminated or suspended by the President without the concurrence of *Congress* (not just the Senate, as Byrd had provided). The committee also added a number of exceptions to take into account various circumstances.[72]

Byrd offered an amendment to restore the original language of his resolution. The Senate adopted his amendment, 59 to 35. A colloquy between Byrd and Senator Frank Church established that the resolution would apply only to future actions, not to past terminations. Senator Barry Goldwater pointed out that the Taiwan treaty would not be terminated, under the one-year notice requirement, until January 1, 1980. The Byrd Amendment, even if modified or clarified by Church, would therefore still apply to the Taiwan treaty.[73]

While the Senate debated Church's amendment to make Byrd's resolution clearly prospective, Goldwater placed in the *Congressional Record* a decision by District Judge Oliver Gasch handed down earlier that day. Gasch concluded that the power to terminate treaties "is a power shared by the political branches of this government, namely, the President and the Congress." But he also noted that Congress had yet to indicate an intention to assert its prerogatives. Three resolutions were pending in the Senate. Gasch said that only after the Senate or Congress had taken action to withdraw support from the President's termination of a treaty would the controversy be ripe for judicial determination.[74]

Senator Church, realizing that his amendment to make the resolution prospective would still apply to the treaty with Taiwan, withdrew his amendment. He sharpened the language and resubmitted an amendment stating that the Byrd resolution "shall not apply with respect to any treaty the notice of termination of which was transmitted prior to the date of adoption of this Resolution."[75] The Senate recessed without voting on this amendment or taking final action on the Byrd resolution. Majority Leader Robert Byrd asked Senator Goldwater to draft an alternative amendment, which he did, but Senators Church and Jacob Javits found the language unacceptable. Church said that he had "no quarrel with the fact that the Senate, by a substantial majority, wishes to make it plain to the President that, in the future, it does not wish the President to attempt to terminate a mutual defense treaty without the concurrence of the Senate."[76]

72. 125 Cong. Rec. 475, 13672 (1979).
73. Id. at 13705, 13712–13.
74. Id. at 13707–9.
75. Id. at 13716. See also 13714 for the amendment's withdrawal.
76. Id. at 15210. See also 15209–11.

The inability or unwillingness of the Senate to reach a final vote proved fatal in the effort to protect congressional interests. Judge Gasch's subsequent decision in October 1979 concluded that the historical precedents, taken as a whole, supported the position that the power to terminate treaties is shared by the President and Congress. Gasch reasoned that if the President lacked the lesser power to amend a treaty without first receiving the Senate's advice and consent, he could not possess the greater power to annul a treaty. Some form of congressional concurrence was required—either the approval of a majority of both houses or the consent of two-thirds of the Senate.[77]

However, his decision was rejected by both the appellate court and the Supreme Court. The D.C. Circuit ruled that the President, in the precise circumstances before the court, was empowered to terminate the Taiwan treaty. The judiciary, it said, was incapable of distinguishing between treaties that could be terminated by the President alone and those that required joint executive-legislative action. It also pointed out that Congress was aware that it possessed strong powers to state its disapproval and "simply did not take those measures." Even if the Senate had acted on the Byrd resolution, it was merely a sense-of-the-Senate measure and would not have been legally binding on the President. The court highlighted the crucial issue: "Congress as a body has chosen not to confront the President directly on the treaty termination."[78]

Acting without oral argument and within days of the scheduled treaty termination, the Supreme Court dismissed Goldwater's complaint. The Justices split along so many lines that their opinions shed little light on how treaty terminations should be handled in the future.[79] Justice Powell would have dismissed the complaint as not ripe for judicial review. He said that the judiciary should not decide executive-legislative conflicts until the two branches reach an impasse. A congressional challenge would have required the Court to resolve the issue. Rehnquist, joined by Burger, Stewart, and Stevens, viewed the matter as a nonjusticiable political question that should never be considered by the courts. Blackmun, joined by White, believed that the Court should have heard oral argument and given the case plenary consideration. Brennan disagreed that the matter was a political question. He would have given the President the authority to terminate treaties as an incident of his power to recognize foreign governments. Marshall, without writing a separate opinion, concurred in dismissing the complaint.

The question of treaty termination was pushed to the side only temporarily, ready to resume its prominence when the moment was ripe. Senator

77. Goldwater v. Carter, 481 F.Supp. 949, 963–64 (D.D.C. 1979).
78. Goldwater v. Carter, 617 F.2d 697, 707, 712, 714 (D.C. Cir. 1979).
79. Goldwater v. Carter, 444 U.S. 996 (1979).

Goldwater introduced legislation in 1981 to require a two-thirds affirmative vote in the Senate to terminate defense treaties. Two years later he introduced a concurrent resolution to require congressional action by either a two-thirds vote of the Senate or a majority vote of both houses. In 1985 he proposed that the Senate act by simple resolution to establish the procedures for terminating defense and security treaties. Two members of the House of Representatives introduced legislation in 1987 for treaty termination procedures. None of these measures has been acted on by Congress.[80]

On December 13, 2001, President George W. Bush announced the withdrawal of the United States from the Antiballistic Missile (ABM) Treaty that had been signed with the Soviet Union in 1972. He concluded that the treaty hindered the ability of the United States "to develop ways to protect our people from future terrorist or rogue state missile attacks."[81] Thirty-two members of the House of Representatives filed suit, contending that because the Supremacy Clause classifies treaties, like statutes, as the "supreme law of the land," the President may not terminate a treaty without congressional consent. A federal district judge held that the lawmakers lacked standing to bring the action, which raised a nonjusticiable political question.[82] The House members did not appeal the decision.[83]

Treaty Reinterpretation

Once a treaty takes effect, the President and executive officials are largely responsible for interpreting the treaty. Federal courts are also called on to interpret a treaty, sometimes in ways that may contradict executive interpretations.[84] A substantially different issue arises when the President "reinterprets" a treaty to arrive at a meaning contrary to what the Senate understood at the time it granted approval.

The reinterpretation issue developed in 1983 after President Reagan advocated a sophisticated antimissile defense shield consisting of satellites armed with laser weapons. The concept became known as "Star Wars" in the press and the Strategic Defense Initiative (SDI) in administration announcements.

80. S.J. Res. 31 (1981); 127 Cong. Rec. 2286–87 (1981); 129 Cong. Rec. 3414–15 (1983); 131 Cong. Rec. 678–80 (1985); 133 Cong. Rec. 36646, 36666–67 (1987).

81. Public Papers of the Presidents, 2001 (II), at 1510.

82. Kucinich v. Bush, 236 F.Supp.2d 1 (D.D.C. 2002).

83. See David Gray Adler, "Termination of the ABM Treaty and the Political Question Doctrine: Judicial Succor for Presidential Power," 34 Pres. Stud. Q. 156 (2004).

84. Rainbow Nav., Inc. v. Department of Navy, 699 F.Supp. 339 (D.D.C. 1988); Rainbow Nav., Inc. v. Department of Navy, 686 F.Supp. 354 (D.D.C. 1988).

Members of Congress were concerned that deployment or even testing of SDI would violate the ABM Treaty with the Soviet Union. In what was called the traditional or restrictive interpretation of the treaty, funds could be spent on SDI only for research and development. Administration officials argued for a broader interpretation to permit development, testing, and deployment of space-based ABMs contingent on future technologies. The conflict heightened when proponents of the broader interpretation relied on the treaty negotiation record, which was classified and not shared with the Senate.[85]

Although the administration adopted the broad interpretation and believed that the Soviets had never committed themselves to the narrow interpretation, President Reagan limited SDI to research and development and shared with the Senate the administration's study of the negotiation record.[86] What disturbed many Senators, however, was the administration's position that the Senate gives advice and consent to a treaty, not to the explanations of the treaty offered by executive officials.[87] Under that analysis, executive officials could provide explanations to the Senate about the meaning of a treaty but not be bound by those explanations. During hearings in 1987, Senator Arlen Specter asked: "Can we function in a system where the Senate cannot rely on representations made by executive officers?"[88]

Congress had the power to enforce the restrictive interpretation by withholding appropriations. In 1987, for example, legislation stated that the Secretary of Defense "may not deploy any anti-ballistic missile system unless such deployment is specifically authorized by law after the date of the enactment of this Act."[89] The Senate also attempted to hold the administration accountable for its representations of the meaning of a treaty. Secretary of State George Shultz stated in a letter that the testimony of all executive branch witnesses and any submissions for the hearing record by the executive branch could be regarded by the Senate as authoritative. He told the Senate that it could accept executive representations as authoritative without incorporating executive testimony and material into the Senate resolution of ratification through understandings, reservations, amendments, or other materials.[90] White House Counsel Arthur B. Culverhouse Jr. prepared a letter to the Senate in which he

85. Abram Chayes and Antonia Handler Chayes, "Testing and Development of 'Exotic' Systems under the ABM Treaty: The Great Reinterpretation Caper," 99 Harv. L. Rev. 1956 (1986); Abraham D. Sofaer, "The ABM Treaty and the Strategic Defense Initiative," 99 Harv. L. Rev. 1972 (1986).

86. "The ABM Treaty and the Constitution," joint hearings before the Senate Committees on Foreign Relations and the Judiciary, 100th Cong., 1st Sess. 122–23 (1987).

87. Id. at 130.

88. Id. at 143.

89. 101 Stat. 1057, sec. 226 (1987).

90. S. Exec. Rept. No. 100-15, 100th Cong., 2d Sess. 442 (1988).

agreed that the President, as a matter of domestic law, is required "to adhere to the interpretation of a treaty authoritatively shared with, and clearly intended, generally understood and relied upon by the Senate at the time of its advice and consent to ratification."[91]

These general formulations were subject to various interpretations, some of which favored presidential power and prerogatives. In 1988 the Senate added an amendment to the Intermediate-Range Nuclear Forces (INF) Treaty stating that treaties shall be interpreted "in accordance with the common understanding of the Treaty shared by the President and the Senate at the time the Senate gave its advice and consent to ratification." The term "common understanding" was defined to include the text of the treaty, the provisions of the resolution of ratification, and the authoritative representations provided by the President and his representatives to the Senate. Any interpretation different from the common understanding would require action through another treaty or through the enactment of a statute. The amendment was adopted by a vote of 72 to 27.[92]

Following the Senate's approval of the INF Treaty, President Reagan sent a letter to the Senate expressing some concern about this amendment. He acknowledged that in accordance with U.S. law, the President "must respect the mutual understandings reached with the Senate during the advice and consent process" but added that executive statements "should be given binding weight only when they were authoritatively communicated to the Senate by the Executive and were part of the basis on which the Senate granted its advice and consent to ratification." However, Reagan also stated that the administration "does not take the position that the Executive branch can disregard authoritative Executive statements to the Senate."[93]

A President is primarily responsible for interpreting a treaty, but he may not interpret to the point where he amends the treaty or makes a new one. If that is the President's desire, he must submit such a proposal to the Senate to obtain its advice and consent through the regular constitutional process. The Senate cannot single-handedly change the meaning of a treaty through its interpretation, but neither can the President. The meaning of treaties can shift to some extent over time, especially to reflect the practices and implementation of the countries involved, but not to the extent of reaching a result that contradicts the original meaning and understanding.[94]

91. Id. at 443.
92. 134 Cong. Rec. 12593, 12655 (1988).
93. Public Papers of the Presidents, 1988 (I), at 760–61.
94. The treaty reinterpretation issue is debated in detail at 137 U. Pa. L. Rev. 1351–1557 (1989). See also Gary Michael Buechler, "Constitutional Limits on the President's Power to Interpret Treaties: The Sofaer Doctrine, the Biden Condition, and the Doctrine of Binding Authoritative Representations," 78 Geo. L. J. 1983 (1990).

Executive Agreements

The precise boundary between treaties and executive agreements has never been defined to anyone's satisfaction. Of course, treaties require the advice and consent of the Senate, and executive agreements do not. In addition, treaties (unlike executive agreements) may supersede prior conflicting statutes.[95] Otherwise, there is considerable discretion on the part of administration officials to make international compacts either by treaty or by executive agreement. Among the more controversial executive agreements are the destroyers and bases deal made with Great Britain in 1940, the Yalta and Potsdam agreements of 1945, the Vietnam peace agreement of 1973, the Sinai agreements of 1975, and recent agreements pertaining to military bases entered into with Spain, Diego Garcia, and Bahrain. Executive agreements are subject to legislative and judicial constraints.

Sources of Authority

During the early years of the Republic, executive agreements were carried out under statutory authority. For example, legislation in 1792 authorized the Postmaster General to make arrangements with foreign postmasters for the receipt and delivery of letters and packets.[96] Executive officials entered into reciprocal trade agreements on the basis of statutory authority. Although such agreements lacked what the Supreme Court in 1912 called the "dignity" of a treaty, since they did not require Senate approval, they were nonetheless valid international compacts.[97] Treaties are sometimes a source of authority for executive agreements.

The executive branch claims four sources of constitutional authority under which the President may enter into executive agreements: (1) the President's duty as chief executive to represent the nation in foreign affairs; (2) the President's authority to receive ambassadors and other public ministers, and to recognize foreign governments; (3) the President's authority as Commander in Chief; and (4) the President's authority to "take care that the laws be faithfully

---

95. United States v. Schooner Peggy, 5 U.S. (1 Cr.) 103 (1801); memorandum by Monroe Leigh, Legal Adviser to the State Department, October 8, 1975, reprinted at 121 Cong. Rec. 36718–21 (1975).

96. 1 Stat. 239 (1792).

97. Altman & Co. v. United States, 224 U.S. 583, 600–601 (1912). In United States v. Pink, 315 U.S. 203, 230 (1942), Justice Douglas regarded executive agreements as having a "similar dignity" with treaties. For an opinion by Acting Attorney General McGranery in 1946 upholding the legality of an executive agreement made pursuant to a joint resolution, see 40 Op. Att'y Gen. 469.

executed."[98] These powers are so open-ended that Congress may find its own sphere of action constricted because of ambitious executive interpretations. Particularly nebulous are the first, second, and fourth sources. On the one hand, the commander-in-chief authority is a reasonable argument to permit the President to enter into an armistice or cease-fire agreement with a foreign power (subject to Senate action on a peace treaty at a later date). The President as Commander in Chief may also have to enter into agreements to protect troops, control occupied areas, and carry out military training. On the other hand, Presidents should not have the authority as Commander in Chief to commit the nation to military engagement, yet that is precisely what President Clinton did in 1995 by sending U.S. ground troops to Bosnia without obtaining congressional support or authority.[99]

The President has constitutional authority to recognize foreign governments, but the exercise of that power can encroach on the prerogatives of Congress. For example, President Jackson declined to recognize the independence of Texas after it broke from Mexico in 1836. Both houses of Congress passed resolutions stating that the independence of Texas ought to be acknowledged, but Jackson refused to buckle to the pressure. He believed that recognizing the independence of Texas could provoke war with Mexico and therefore invade the prerogatives of Congress.[100]

Also, recognition of other countries may involve the settlement of claims that affect other provisions of the Constitution. Recognition of Soviet Russia by President Roosevelt led to the "Litvinov Assignment" in 1933 and subsequent property claims in the courts. In 1937 the Supreme Court unanimously upheld the assignment as a valid international compact.[101] Five years later, in another case involving Roosevelt's recognition of the Soviet Union, Justice Douglas declared that the powers of the President in the conduct of foreign affairs "included the power, without consent of the Senate, to determine the public policy of the United States with respect to the Russian nationalization decrees." To Douglas, the President had authority to do more than simply determine which government to recognize. Presidential authority included the power to determine the policy to go with recognition. Objections to the policy or the recognition were to be "addressed to the political department and not to the courts." And yet the judiciary could not sidestep the subject so easily. Suppose that an executive agreement, affecting private claims,

98. 11 FAM [Foreign Affairs Manual] 723.2-2(C) (September 25, 2006), accessed at http://foia.state.gov/masterdocs/11fam/11fam0720.pdf.

99. Louis Fisher, "The Bosnia Commitment," Legal Times, March 11, 1996, at 22.

100. 4 Richardson 1486.

101. United States v. Belmont, 301 U.S. 324 (1937).

interfered with such constitutional privileges as the Due Process and Just Compensation Clauses of the Fifth Amendment?[102]

Inevitably the courts were drawn back into the dispute. The Litvinov Assignment represented the exercise of an implied presidential power: recognition of foreign governments. It also involved a federal question: the balancing of interests between the national government and legislation adopted by a state government. These circumstances were unique and narrowly drawn. But the President is not free to enter into executive agreements that violate constitutional provisions. As the State Department concedes, an agreement cannot be "inconsistent with legislation enacted by the Congress in the exercise of its constitutional authority."[103] This principle was given substance by the *Capps* decision of 1953, which struck down an executive agreement because it contravened an existing commercial statute with Canada. Imports from a foreign country represented foreign commerce "subject to regulation, so far as this country is concerned, by Congress alone."[104]

The timing of these decisions on executive agreements should be noted. *Capps*, as a restriction on executive authority, was handed down less than a year after *Youngstown* declared invalid President Truman's seizure of the steel mills. *Belmont*, a ringing affirmation of executive agreements, was decided just five months after Justice Sutherland, in his *Curtiss-Wright* dicta, lent enthusiastic support to presidential prerogatives in external affairs.

Other court decisions have limited the reach of executive agreements. *Seery v. United States* (1955) involved an executive agreement under which the United States agreed to pay Austria a flat sum to settle all obligations incurred by U.S. armed forces. A naturalized American citizen brought suit to recover damages to her home in Austria, which had been used by American troops as an officers' club. The Court of Claims held that the woman was entitled to compensation under the Fifth Amendment: "We think that there can be no doubt that an executive agreement, not being a transaction which is even mentioned in the Constitution, cannot impair Constitutional rights."[105] And in *Reid v. Covert* (1957), the Supreme Court declared invalid an executive agreement that permitted American military courts in Great Britain to rely on trial by court-martial for offenses committed by American military personnel or their dependents. The plaintiff fought successfully for the constitutional right to a trial by jury. The Court declared that an executive agreement with a

---

102. United States v. Pink, 315 U.S. 203, 229 (1942). See Note, "United States v. Pink—A Reappraisal," 48 Colum. L. Rev. 890 (1948).

103. 11 FAM 723.2-2(C).

104. United States v. Guy W. Capps, Inc., 204 F.2d 655, 660 (4th Cir. 1953), aff'd on other grounds, 348 U.S. 296 (1955).

105. Seery v. United States, 127 F.Supp. 601, 606 (Ct. Cl. 1955).

foreign nation could not confer power "on the Congress, or on any other branch of Government, which is free from the restraints of the Constitution."[106]

The opportunity for presidential action widens when specific legislation on foreign commerce does not exist. The Nixon administration entered into so-called voluntary restraint arrangements with European and Japanese steel companies as a means of protecting domestic suppliers. Consumers Union took the issue to court, contending that the import quotas encroached on Congress's authority over foreign trade and violated the Sherman Antitrust Act. In 1973 a district court declined to issue an injunction, as requested by Consumers Union, but urged the administration and the foreign steel companies to reexamine their actions as a possible violation of the Sherman Antitrust Act.[107] The following year an appellate court held that although the President could not impose mandatory import quotas without legislative authority, nothing in the Constitution or existing legislation foreclosed voluntary arrangements. The issue of the Sherman Antitrust Act was vacated after the plaintiffs requested that it be dismissed. A lengthy dissent by Judge Harold Leventhal viewed the President's action as a transgression on congressional authority over foreign commerce. Far from being "voluntary," the arrangements on steel were negotiated bilateral understandings that could be enforced by sanctions imposed by the President.[108]

The Iranian hostage crisis of 1979 set the stage for a series of extraordinary actions by President Carter, including the freezing of Iran's assets in the United States and the suspension of claims pending in American courts. Although the Supreme Court concluded that the first action had statutory support, it found no specific statutory authority for the second. Legal justification was discovered somewhere in the combination of past presidential practices to settle claims by executive agreement, the history of "implicit" congressional approval, and Congress's failure to contest the Iranian agreement. The Court strained to uphold an agreement that it could not possibly overturn, given the foreign policy implications. It limited the damage of its opinion by confining it to the specific circumstances before the Court.[109] Whether Carter's action

106. Reid v. Covert, 354 U.S. 1, 16 (1957). The treaty power is also subject to the restraints found in the Constitution: "It would not be contended that it extends so far as to authorize what the Constitution forbids, or a change in the character of the government or in that of one of the States, or a cession of any portion of the territory of the latter, without its consent"; Geofroy v. Riggs, 133 U.S. 258, 267 (1890).

107. Consumers Union of U.S., Inc. v. Rogers, 352 F.Supp. 1319 (D.D.C. 1973).

108. Consumers Union of U.S., Inc. v. Kissinger, 506 F.2d 136 (D.C. Cir. 1974), cert. denied, 421 U.S. 1004 (1975).

109. Dames & Moore v. Regan, 453 U.S. 654 (1981). For congressional "support" through acquiescence, the Court relied on Haig v. Agee, 453 U.S. 280, 290 (1981), which upheld the right of the Secretary of State to revoke passports despite the lack of explicit statutory authority.

becomes a precedent for further expansions of presidential power depends on congressional reactions to future executive initiatives.

Reporting

Prior to 1950, executive agreements were published in the *U.S. Statutes at Large.* Since that time they have been printed in *Treaties and Other International Agreements.*[110] A number of sensitive agreements, however, were never made known to Congress or to the public. During a Senate hearing in 1972, a State Department official was asked: "Now, you do have some executive agreements in force that are not listed in this publication, do you not?" He replied: "A very small percentage, classified."[111]

The extent of secret executive agreements was carefully documented by the Symington Subcommittee (of the Senate Foreign Relations Committee) during its hearings in 1969 and 1970. Field trips by committee staff uncovered a number of significant agreements that U.S. administrations had made covertly with South Korea, Thailand, Laos, Ethiopia, and Spain, among others. The Senate hearings revealed that the United States had offered secret subsidies to a number of nations for their modest assistance to the war in Southeast Asia.[112]

Congress passed legislation in 1972 to keep itself informed about such agreements. The statute (known as the Case Act) requires the Secretary of State to transmit to Congress within 60 days the text of "any international agreement, other than a treaty," to which the United States is a party. If the President decides that publication of an agreement would be prejudicial to national security, he may transmit it to the Senate Committee on Foreign Relations and the House Committee on Foreign Affairs (now International Relations) under an injunction of secrecy removable only by the President.[113]

Over the next few years, several Senators protested that the Nixon and Ford administrations had failed to comply with the Case Act. Senator James Abourezk testified that the "administration has admitted to both Senator Case and myself that there are some agreements they do not submit at all under the Case Act."[114] A GAO study in 1976 disclosed that a number of agreements (delicately called "arrangements" by the executive branch) had never been submitted to Congress or even to the Office of Treaty Affairs in the State

110. 64 Stat. 979 (1950).
111. "Congressional Oversight of Executive Agreements," hearing before the Senate Committee on the Judiciary, 92d Cong., 2d Sess. 284 (1972).
112. Louis Fisher, Presidential War Power 135–37 (2004).
113. 86 Stat. 619 (1972), 1 U.S.C. 112b (2000).
114. "Early Warning System in Sinai," hearing before the Senate Committee on Foreign Relations, 94th Cong., 1st Sess. 6 (1975).

Department.[115] A Senate study in 1977 discovered that 39 percent of the executive agreements entered into in the previous year had been submitted after the 60-day period (171 out of 440). Thirty-five of those had been submitted a *year* late.[116]

To improve administrative compliance with the Case Act, Congress passed legislation in 1977 requiring any department or agency of the U.S. government that enters into any international agreement on behalf of the United States to transmit to the State Department the text of the agreement no later than 20 days after its signing.[117] A year later Congress broadened the definition of executive agreement to include the text of any "oral international agreement, which agreement shall be reduced to writing."[118]

As a way of avoiding congressional action on a treaty or an executive agreement, the Carter administration discovered a third option: parallel policy statements. On September 23, 1977, ten days prior to the expiration date of SALT I, the United States and the Soviet Union issued statements that they would adhere to SALT I ceilings. Since the statements were issued separately and unilaterally, the State Department argued that they did not constitute an "agreement" and therefore required no action by Congress.[119]

Congress resorted to its power of the purse in 1987 to tighten the reporting requirements of executive agreements. If any international agreement required to be transmitted to Congress under the Case Act is not transmitted within the 60-day period, "then no funds authorized to be appropriated by this or any other Act shall be available after the end of that 60-day period to implement that agreement until the text of that agreement has been so transmitted."[120]

Problems remain. In 1994 President Clinton entered into an "agreed framework" with North Korea to assist in the replacement of Korea's graphite-moderated reactors with light-water reactor power plants. The purpose was to prevent North Korea from developing nuclear weapons. Since the administration regarded the framework as a "political agreement" that was nonbinding, it did not submit it to Congress under the Case Act. Nonbinding international agreements are viewed as involving political or moral obligations but not legal obligations.[121] President Clinton's letter to North Korea repeatedly promised that he would use "the full powers of my office" to implement the

115. "U.S. Agreements with the Republic of Korea," ID-76-20 (February 20, 1976).
116. 123 Cong. Rec. 16127 (1977).
117. 91 Stat. 224, sec. 5 (1977).
118. 92 Stat. 993, sec. 708 (1978), 1 U.S.C. 112b (2000).
119. Franck and Weisband, Foreign Policy by Congress, at 152–54.
120. 101 Stat. 1347, sec. 139 (1987).
121. 22 CFR §181 (2006).

framework, with much of that effort "subject to the approval of the U.S. Congress." In that sense the framework made political and moral, not legal, commitments.[122]

Congress has the power to subject specific classes of agreements to congressional approval. Fishery agreements are forwarded to Congress for legislative action through the regular process, including passage by both houses and submission of a bill to the President.[123] Certain executive agreements on nuclear energy are handled the same way.[124] The Trade Act of 1974 requires implementing legislation before specific types of agreements can enter into force.[125] Congressional leverage is further strengthened when executive agreements clearly state that the level of U.S. economic and military assistance to foreign governments depends on annual authorizations and appropriations by Congress. Through these actions Congress can successively, and successfully, narrow the reach of executive agreements.

122. 141 Cong. Rec. S4050–53 (daily ed. March 16, 1995).

123. For example, 106 Stat. 5039 (1992); 102 Stat. 3286 (1988); 102 Stat. 660 (1988); 102 Stat. 591 (1988); 101 Stat. 1458 (1987).

124. Public Papers of the Presidents, 1984 (I), at 94–95.

125. 88 Stat. 1983, sec. 102(e); 88 Stat. 2001, sec. 151 (1974).

9

THE WAR POWER

Members of Congress can point to specific language in the Constitution for their authority to declare war and provide armed forces. More difficult to locate are the legal sources for presidential authority to initiate military operations. Yet over the last half century, Presidents have been able to make war before Congress has had a chance to act. Particularly in the period since World War II, executive war-making power has increased dramatically as Presidents seek "authority" from the United Nations and the North Atlantic Treaty Organization (NATO) rather than from Congress.

For constitutional as well as practical reasons, the two branches are supposed to work in concert. The President commands the troops, but only Congress can provide them. Congress declares or authorizes war but depends on the President to wage it. An associate of President Cleveland was present when a delegation from Congress arrived at the White House with this announcement: "We have about decided to declare war against Spain over the Cuban question. Conditions are intolerable." Cleveland responded in blunt terms: "There will be no war with Spain over Cuba while I am President." A member of Congress protested that the Constitution gave Congress the right to declare war, but Cleveland countered that the Constitution also made him Commander in Chief. "I will not mobilize the army," he told the legislators. "I happen to know that we can buy the Island of Cuba from Spain for $100,000,000, and a war will cost vastly more than that and will entail another long list of pensioners. It would be an outrage to declare war."[1]

Commander in Chief

Article I, Section 2, of the Constitution makes the President "Commander in Chief of the Army and Navy of the United States, and of the Militia of the several States, when called into the actual Service of the United States." Scholars have long disagreed whether this merely confers a title (Commander in Chief) or implies additional powers for the President. Justice Jackson underscored the elusive nature of this power by remarking that the Commander-

1. 2 Robert McElroy, Grover Cleveland 249–50 (1923).

in-Chief Clause implies "something more than an empty title. But just what authority goes with the name has plagued presidential advisers who would not waive or narrow it by nonassertion yet cannot say where it begins or ends."[2] The Justice Department has argued that the President was given the title not because he was expected to be skilled in the art of war but to preserve civilian supremacy over the military.[3]

Some scholars construe the Commander-in-Chief Clause narrowly. Raoul Berger wrote: "How narrowly the function was conceived may be gathered from the fact that in appointing George Washington Commander-in-Chief, the Continental Congress made sure . . . that he was to be 'its creature . . . in every respect.'" Instructions drafted by John Adams, R. H. Lee, and Edward Rutledge told Washington "punctually to observe and follow such orders and directions . . . as you shall receive from this or a future Congress."[4] Citing those precedents is misleading for two reasons. First, they ignore the extensive delegations that the Continental Congress soon found necessary. For example, an order to General Washington in 1775 stated that "whereas all particulars cannot be foreseen, nor positive instructions for such emergencies so before hand given but that many things must be left to your prudent and discreet management, as occurrences may arise upon the place, or from time to time may fall out, you are therefore upon all such accidents or any occasions that may happen, to use your best circumspection."[5] Second, the precedents are from the wrong period. The office of President created in 1787 is a separate and independent branch, not a mere agent of Congress (its status under the Continental Congress).

The need to trust in executive judgment and discretion for *defensive* actions more accurately represents the understanding of the framers. At the Philadelphia convention they recognized an implied power of the President to "repel sudden attacks." When it was proposed that Congress be empowered to "make war," Charles Pinckney objected that legislative proceedings "were too slow" for the safety of the country in an emergency. He anticipated that Congress would meet but once a year. Madison and Elbridge Gerry moved to insert "declare" for "make," thereby "leaving to the Executive the power to repel sudden attacks." Their motion carried.[6] This trust in executive judgment applies to defensive actions at a time of emergency, not to general or offensive military actions.

Alexander Hamilton offered a modest definition of commander-in-chief powers in Federalist 69. He claimed that the office "would amount to nothing

2. Youngstown Co. v. Sawyer, 343 U.S. 579, 641 (1952).
3. 10 Op. Att'y Gen. 74, 79 (1861).
4. Raoul Berger, Executive Privilege 62 (1974).
5. 2 Journals of the Continental Congress 101 (1905).
6. 2 Farrand 318–19.

more than the supreme command and direction of the military and naval forces, as first General and admiral of the Confederacy." But as Washington's military aide during the war, surely Hamilton knew that "command and direction" are more than clerical tasks. They can determine the scope and duration of a war. As the Supreme Court noted in 1850, the President as Commander in Chief "is authorized to direct the movements of the naval and military forces placed by law at his command, and to employ them in the manner he may deem most effectual to harass and conquer and subdue the enemy."[7]

This decision indicates two values operating in tandem: executive discretion and legislative limits. What is the power to move forces "placed *by law* at his command"? How much does the President depend on Congress to provide the authorizations and appropriations necessary for military action? Under the Constitution, it is the responsibility of Congress to raise and support the military forces, to make rules for their regulation, to provide for calling up the militia to suppress insurrections and repel invasions, and to provide for the organization and disciplining of the militia.

Nineteenth-century cases placed the power to "make war" with Congress.[8] In a case that reached the Supreme Court in 1889, England had wanted American naval forces to act in concert with France against China. The Court cautioned: "As this proposition involved a participation in existing hostilities, the request could not be acceded to, and the Secretary of State in his communication to the English government explained that the war-making power of the United States was not vested in the President but in Congress, and that he had no authority, therefore, to order aggressive hostilities to be undertaken."[9]

When Congress delegates to the President its power to call forth the militia to suppress insurrections or repel invasions, the decision to use force belongs solely to the President. In order to respond effectively to emergencies and avoid divided control, the power to respond is centered in the Commander in Chief.[10]

Congress is empowered to declare war, but only five wars have been declared. Congress can also *authorize* wars, as it did with the "Quasi-War" against France from 1798 to 1800, the war against Iraq in 1991, the war against Afghanistan in 2001, and the second war against Iraq in 2002. From an early date, the Supreme Court has recognized that Congress can either declare or authorize war.[11]

7. Fleming v. Page, 50 U.S. (9 How.) 602, 614 (1850). Also see the dissenting opinion by Chief Justice Chase—joined by Justices Wayne, Swayne, and Miller—in Ex parte Milligan, 4 Wall. 2 (1866).
8. United States v. Smith, 27 Fed. Cas. 1192, 1230 (C.C. D. N.Y. 1806).
9. The Chinese Exclusion Case, 130 U.S. 581, 591 (1889).
10. Martin v. Mott, 25 U.S. (12 Wheat.) 19 (1827).
11. Bas v. Tingy, 4 U.S. (4 Dall.) 36 (1800); Talbot v. Seeman, 5 U.S. (1 Cr.) 1 (1801).

Emergency Powers

Charles McIlwain, tracing the slow and tortuous evolution of constitutionalism, stressed its antagonism to *gubernaculum:* emergency or extraordinary powers available to the executive. Actions taken for "reasons of state" were solely within the king's province. In contrast was the concept of *jurisdictio,* which limited the king's discretion. An early challenge to *gubernaculum* appears in a seventeenth-century speech in Parliament by Sir Benjamin Rudyard: "This by the way I will say of Reason of State, that, in the latitude by which it is used, it hath eaten out almost, not only the laws, but all the religion of Christendom." Another member of Parliament warned that to admit reason of state in a particular situation would "open a gap, through which Magna Charta, and the rest of the statutes, may issue out and vanish."[12]

The idea of *gubernaculum* has survived in the form of the executive prerogative and "inherent" presidential power. John Locke anticipated circumstances in which the executive should be free to act in accordance with his own perception of the public good. In governments in which the legislative and executive powers are in distinct hands, "the good of the society requires that several things should be left to the discretion of him that has the executive power." Legislators could not foresee, and provide by laws, everything needed by the community. Cases arise in which the executive official has to use power "for the good of the society" until legislators can assemble to pass laws. A strict and rigid observance of the laws, Locke reasoned, might do more harm than temporarily vesting in the executive the responsibility to take action for the community's good. The power to act "according to discretion for the public good, without the prescription of the law and sometimes even against it, is that which is called prerogative." Locke subjected the prerogative to a few general restrictions. It had to be used for the good of the people "and not manifestly against it." But when disputes arose as to whether the power had been properly used, "there can be no judge on earth." The people had no other remedy "but to appeal to Heaven."[13]

A more secular safeguard emerged under the American system. In emergency situations Presidents could take the initiative, in the absence of law or even against it, but they had to seek the legislature's sanction at the earliest opportunity. Thomas Jefferson, remembered as a "strict constructionist" and a sharp critic of Hamilton's liberal interpretations of the Constitution, had occasion to act without specific legislative authority. After Congress had recessed in 1807, a British vessel fired on the American ship *Chesapeake.*

12. Charles Howard McIlwain, Constitutionalism: Ancient and Modern 126 (1947).
13. John Locke, Second Treatise on Civil Government, ch. 14.

Jefferson ordered military purchases for the emergency, reporting his actions to Congress after it convened. "To have awaited a previous and special sanction by law," he wrote, "would have lost occasions which might not be retrieved."[14] In 1801 Jefferson took certain defensive actions against the Barbary pirates in the Mediterranean but immediately came to Congress to request further authority, explaining that actions of an offensive nature needed the explicit support of the legislative branch. Thereafter, Congress enacted a number of authorizing statutes to deal with the Barbary pirates.[15] These precedents by Jefferson offer no legal support for Presidents unilaterally taking the country to war.

After leaving the presidency, Jefferson said that observance of the written law is a high duty of a public official, but not the highest. The laws of self-preservation and national security claim a higher priority: "To lose our country by a scrupulous adherence to written law, would be to lose the law itself, with life, liberty, property and all those who are enjoying them with us; thus absurdly sacrificing the end to the means." The executive may act outside the law when necessity demands it, explain his actions, and ask the legislature for acquittance.[16]

Lincoln followed this philosophy in his extraordinary Civil War actions. In April 1861, with Congress in recess, he issued proclamations calling forth state militias, suspending the writ of habeas corpus, and placing a blockade on the rebellious states. When Congress returned he explained that his actions, "whether strictly legal or not, were ventured upon under what appeared to be a popular demand and a public necessity, trusting then, as now, that Congress would readily ratify them."[17] In this way he conceded that he lacked full constitutional authority to do what he did. Congress proceeded to debate the necessity of his actions and then passed an act "approving, legalizing, and making valid all the acts, proclamations, and orders of the President, etc., as if they had been issued and done under the previous express authority and direction of the Congress of the United States."[18]

Under extraordinary circumstances, Lincoln believed that it was more important to preserve than to observe the Constitution.[19] In his message to Congress in 1861, he claimed that the "war power" was his for the purpose of suppressing the rebellion. No choice was left, he said, "but to call out the war power of the Government and so to resist force employed for its destruction by force for its preservation." With "deepest regret" he found the duty of

14. 1 Richardson 416 (October 27, 1807).
15. Louis Fisher, Presidential War Power 32–37 (2d ed., 2004).
16. 5 The Writings of Thomas Jefferson 542–45 (Washington ed.).
17. 7 Richardson 3225.
18. 12 Stat. 326 (1861).
19. Norman J. Small, Some Presidential Interpretations of the Presidency 34 (1932).

employing the "war power in defense of the Government forced upon him."[20] It was under the "war power" (actually a fusion of legislative and executive powers) that Lincoln took his actions to preserve the Union. Congress supported his initiatives, as did a sharply divided Supreme Court in the *Prize Cases*.[21] Justice Grier, however, carefully limited presidential power to internal, defensive actions, noting that the President "has no power to initiate or declare a war against either a foreign nation or a domestic State."[22] Lincoln's counsel in this case acknowledged that his actions during the Civil War had nothing to do with the right "*to initiate a war, as a voluntary act of sovereignty. That is vested only in Congress.*"[23]

Lincoln suspended the writ of habeas corpus, despite opposition from Chief Justice Taney sitting as circuit judge. Taney argued that the President had no power under the Constitution to suspend habeas corpus and that the prisoner, John Merryman, should be set free. Merryman was suspected of being the captain of a secession force and of assisting in the destruction of railroads and bridges to prevent federal troops from reaching Washington, D.C. Acting under Lincoln's orders, prison officials refused to let Taney's marshal carry out his duties.[24] In 1863 Congress authorized Lincoln to suspend habeas corpus during the rebellion, subject to restrictions and procedures placed in the statute.[25] Not until the war was over and Lincoln in his grave did the Court breathe some life into the privilege of the writ of habeas corpus.[26]

Another controversial use of presidential power was undertaken by Franklin Roosevelt during World War II. More than 100,000 Americans of Japanese descent (about two-thirds of them natural-born U.S. citizens) were herded into "relocation centers" after Roosevelt issued an executive order, based in part on "the authority vested in me as President of the United States, and Commander in Chief of the Army and Navy."[27] Bitter opposition came from members of the Supreme Court. Justice Murphy, concurring in *Hirabayashi* (1943), said that the initial curfew action against Japanese-Americans "bears a melancholy resemblance to the treatment accorded to the members of the Jewish race in Germany and in other parts of Europe." In spite of such mis-

20. 7 Richardson 3224–25, 3232 (July 4, 1861).
21. 2 Black 635 (1863). See also 12 Stat. 284, 326 (1861), and Edward S. Corwin, The President 228–34, 448–53 (1957).
22. 2 Black at 668.
23. Id at 660. Emphasis in original.
24. Ex parte Merryman, 17 Fed. Case No. 9487 (1861), at 153. See 10 Op. Att'y Gen. 74, 81 (1861).
25. 12 Stat. 755 (1863); Louis Fisher, Military Tribunals and Presidential Power 42–45 (2005).
26. Ex parte Milligan, 4 Wall. (71 U.S.) 2 (1866).
27. Executive Order 9066, 7 Fed. Reg. 1407 (1942).

givings, a unanimous Court supported the curfew.[28] *Korematsu* (1944), split-
ting the Court 6 to 3, upheld the exclusion of Japanese-Americans and their
relocation to detention camps. Murphy, one of the dissenters, protested that
the exclusion order resulted from an erroneous assumption of "racial guilt"
found in the commanding general's report, which referred to all individuals of
Japanese descent as "subversives" belonging to "an enemy race" whose "racial
strains are undiluted." Jackson, also dissenting, concluded that "here is an attempt to make an otherwise innocent act a crime merely because this prisoner
is the son of parents to whom he had no choice, and belongs to a race from
which there is no way to resign."[29]

A third controversial invocation of commander-in-chief power was by
President Truman. In the wake of a labor-management dispute in 1952, he
seized steel mills as part of his effort to prosecute the Korean War. He did
so on the basis of the authority vested in him as President "by the Constitution and laws of the United States, and as President of the United States and
Commander-in-Chief of the armed forces of the United States." The Supreme Court struck down this use of power in a 6-to-3 decision, but there
were as many views as there were Justices. Each of the six representing the
majority wrote separate opinions. Justice Jackson divided the commander-
in-chief power along an outward-inward axis: "I should indulge the widest
latitude of interpretation to sustain his exclusive function to command the
instruments of national force, at least when turned against the outside world
for the security of our society. But, when it is turned inward, not because of
rebellion but because of a lawful economic struggle between industry and labor, it should have no such indulgence."[30]

Edward S. Corwin, dean of presidential scholars, held conflicting opinions
on the executive prerogative. He maintained that the framers' view of balanced government carried with it "the idea of a *divided initiative in the matter of legislation and a broad range of autonomous executive power or 'prerogative.'*"[31] Yet the scope of that prerogative became the subject of spirited debate
after President Truman sent troops to Korea without congressional approval.
Henry Steele Commager and Arthur M. Schlesinger Jr. defended his decision.
Corwin rebuked the scholars (calling them the "high-flying prerogative men")

28. Hirabayashi v. United States, 320 U.S. 81 (1943).

29. Korematsu v. United States, 323 U.S. 214, 243 (1944). Some of the convictions of
Japanese-Americans were later vacated because the Justice Department deliberately misled the
courts in the 1940s. Korematsu v. United States, 584 F.Supp. 1406 (N.D. Cal. 1984); Hirabayashi v. United States, 828 F.2d 591 (9th Cir. 1987).

30. Youngstown Co. v. Sawyer, 343 U.S. 579, 645 (1952).

31. Edward S. Corwin, The President 14 (1957); emphasis in original. He discusses the
meaning of "executive power" on pp. 3–30.

and denounced the President's action and the justifications that accompanied it.[32] Less than two decades later both Commager and Schlesinger altered their philosophy of executive power, becoming vociferous critics of President Johnson's conduct of the war in Southeast Asia and strong proponents of legislative prerogatives.[33]

The executive prerogative retains a following, even among those who were bitterly opposed to the Vietnam War. In 1969 the Senate Foreign Relations Committee admitted its failure to properly check presidential power. It had hastily approved the Gulf of Tonkin Resolution, giving President Johnson vast authority. In the future, the committee counseled, it would be better to have a President take an emergency action he regards as necessary "without attempting to justify it in advance and leave it to Congress or the courts to evaluate his action in retrospect. A single unconstitutional act, later explained or pronounced unconstitutional, is preferable to an act dressed up in some spurious, precedent-setting claim of legitimacy."[34]

"Defensive War"

Throughout the nineteenth century the concept of defensive war was limited mainly to protective actions along the borders of the United States. Naval wars against the Barbary pirates and France stretched those boundaries, but such actions were infrequent and fully authorized by Congress.

Congressional control was at its strongest when there was no standing army, for in such cases the President would have to ask the legislative branch for authority. That is what President Adams did in 1798 with the Quasi-War against France and what President Madison did in 1812 with the war against England. But when troops and ships are available to move at the President's

32. For a defense of Truman's action, see Schlesinger's letter, New York Times, January 9, 1951, and Commager's article "Presidential Power: The Issue Analyzed," New York Times Magazine, January 14, 1951. Corwin replied to them in "The President's Power," New Republic, January 29, 1951.

33. By 1966 Schlesinger was counseling that "something must be done to assure the Congress a more authoritative and continuing voice in fundamental decisions in foreign policy"; Arthur M. Schlesinger Jr. and Alfred de Grazia, Congress and the Presidency 28 (1967). Commager, meanwhile, had also altered his view, telling the Senate in 1967 that there should be a reconsideration of executive-legislative relationships in the conduct of foreign relations; "Changing American Attitudes Towards Foreign Policy," hearings before the Senate Committee on Foreign Relations, 90th Cong., 1st Sess. 21 (1967). See also Commager's testimony in "War Powers Legislation," hearings before the Senate Committee on Foreign Relations, 92d Cong., 1st Sess. 7–74 (1971). Schlesinger in 1973 stated that the "idea of prerogative was *not* part of presidential power as defined in the Constitution," although it "remained in the back of [the framers'] mind"; The Imperial Presidency 9 (1973); emphasis in original.

34. S. Rept. No. 129, 91st Cong., 1st Sess. 32 (1969).

command, the balance of power can tip to the executive branch. Those conditions coalesced in 1846 when President Polk sent American troops into disputed territory along the Texas-Mexico border. Two years later the House of Representatives censured him for "unnecessarily and unconstitutionally" starting a war.[35] President McKinley defended intervention in Cuba in 1898 by describing the conflict as "right at our door."[36]

These were isolated events, however. Only after World War II did the idea of defensive war take a quantum jump, both conceptually and in practice. American bases were dispersed around the globe. Military commitments became embedded in various defense pacts and treaties, often with little visibility to Congress or the public. No longer did the administration confine the notion of "repelling sudden attacks" to military actions on our continental boundaries. The Legal Adviser to the State Department offered this ambitious scenario in 1966:

> Under the Constitution, the President, in addition to being Chief Executive, is Commander in Chief of the Army and Navy. He holds the prime responsibility for the conduct of United States foreign relations. These duties carry very broad powers, including the power to deploy American forces abroad and commit them to military operations when the President deems such action necessary to maintain the security and defense of the United States. . . .
>
> In 1787 the world was a far larger place, and the framers probably had in mind attacks upon the United States. In the 20th century, the world has grown much smaller. An attack on a country far from our shores can impinge directly on the nation's security.[37]

This idea of a shrinking globe has been part of the conceptual shift behind the enlargement of presidential power. We apply the concept to travel and communication with neutral effect, but constitutionally it shrinks not merely the globe but congressional power as well. In 1962, after the discovery of missile sites in Cuba, President Kennedy announced that the Western Hemisphere ("as far north as Hudson Bay, Canada, and as far south as Lima, Peru") was in danger. The launching of any nuclear missile from Cuba, against any nation in the Western Hemisphere, would be regarded by the administration as "an attack by the Soviet Union on the United States, requiring a full retaliatory response upon the Soviet Union."[38] When President Johnson requested

35. Cong. Globe, 30th Cong., 1st Sess. 95 (1848); Fisher, Presidential War Power, at 39–44.
36. 13 Richardson 6289 (April 11, 1898).
37. 54 Dep't of State Bull. 484 (1966).
38. Public Papers of the Presidents, 1962, at 485.

the Tonkin Gulf Resolution two years later, he argued that a threat in South-east Asia "is a threat to all, and a threat to us."[39]

During the Reagan administration the State Department justified the CIA's mining of several harbors in Nicaragua as a legitimate means of self-defense.[40] In 1986, after reporting that Libya had launched surface-to-air missiles at U.S. naval aircraft and ships in the Gulf of Sidra, President Reagan autho-rized U.S. forces to fire back, sinking three Libyan patrol boats and damaging another. He explained that the air strikes were an act of "self-defense" and a preemptive strike designed to "deter acts of terrorism by Libya."[41]

In December 1989 President George H. W. Bush intervened in Panama to oust General Manuel Noriega. Bush cited a number of justifications, includ-ing the right of self-defense under Article 51 of the UN Charter (protecting American lives in Panama).[42] However, 13,000 American troops were already stationed in the Canal Zone to provide protection to U.S. citizens, and if the United States had a right to invade whenever American citizens were at risk, it would have cause for intervening in dozens of other sovereign countries.[43] In August 1990, after Iraq invaded Kuwait, President Bush dispatched U.S. forces to the Persian Gulf, justifying his action in part as defensive. American forces were taking up "defensive positions" in Saudi Arabia; "their mission is defensive," he said, and the United States was acting under the "inherent right of self-defense."[44]

In 1993, in response to the attempted assassination of Bush during a visit to Kuwait, President Clinton ordered air strikes against Iraq. He called the attempted assassination "an attack against our country and against all Americans" and char-acterized the air strikes as "the exercise of our inherent right of self-defense."[45] Some legal analysts said that calling the bombing of Iraq an act of self-defense for an assassination plot that had been averted two months previously "is quite a stretch."[46] Often these "defensive actions" are intertwined with expla-nations that the President must act to protect American lives and property.

After the terrorist attacks of 9/11, President George W. Bush announced a new defensive doctrine called "preventive war." Under international law, every nation has a right to engage in "preemptive war" when a military threat is im-

39. Public Papers of the Presidents, 1963–1964 (II), at 931.
40. Cong. Q. Wkly Rept., April 14, 1984, at 835.
41. Public Papers of the Presidents, 1986, at 478.
42. Public Papers of the Presidents, 1989 (II), at 1734.
43. John Quigley, "The Legality of the United States Invasion of Panama," 15 Yale J. Int'l L. 276, 281–97 (1990).
44. Public Papers of the Presidents, 1990 (II), at 1107, 1116.
45. Public Papers of the Presidents, 1993 (I), at 938, 940.
46. Michael Ratner and Jules Lobel, "Bombing Baghdad: Illegal Reprisal or Self-Defense?" Legal Times, July 5, 1993, at 24.

minent and direct and there are no diplomatic means to resolve the crisis and no time for deliberation. When acting in self-defense, such as when enemy troops are massed on one's border or an armada has gathered off the coast, the military response must be proportional to the threat. Preventive war, as explained in a position paper released by the Bush administration, allows military action "against such emerging threats before they are fully formed."[47]

Life-and-Property Actions

With neither statutory authority nor a declaration of war, Presidents have used force abroad on many occasions, ostensibly to protect life and property. They have justified their actions on the basis of executive responsibilities inherent in the Constitution. Expeditions of this nature number around 200; however, if actions that represented merely a show of force (such as deploying a battleship off a nation's coast) were included, the total would be even larger.[48]

The constitutionality of this presidential activity came before a circuit court in 1860. An American vessel had been dispatched to Greytown (now San Juan del Norte), Nicaragua, after an affront to an American diplomat and some property losses suffered by an American firm. When the commander of the ship decided that local authorities had failed to make appropriate amends, he bombarded the town and sent troops ashore to wreak further vengeance. A resident sued for damages to his property. The court, in *Durand v. Hollins,* defended the commander's action: "As it respects the interposition of the Executive abroad, for the protection of the lives or property of the citizen, the duty must, of necessity, rest in the discretion of the President. Acts of lawless violence, or of threatened violence to the citizen or his property, cannot be anticipated and provided for; and the protection, to be effectual or of any avail, may, not unfrequently, require the most prompt and decided action."[49]

47. The National Security Strategy of the United States of America, September 2002, p. 2 of introductory statement by President Bush; Fisher, Presidential War Power, at 202–4.

48. J. Terry Emerson, "War Powers Legislation," 74 W. Va. L. Rev. 53 (1972), and his "Constitutional Authority of the President to Use Armed Forces in Defense of American Lives, Liberty, and Property," reprinted at 121 Cong. Rec. 13205–9 (1975). For further details, see James Grafton Rogers, World Policing and the Constitution (1945); Background Information on the Use of United States Armed Forces in Foreign Countries, prepared for the House Committee on Foreign Affairs, 91st Cong., 2d Sess. 50–57 (Comm. Print 1970); R. Ernest Dupuy and William H. Baumer, The Little Wars of the United States (1968); and Barry M. Blechman and Stephen S. Kaplan, Force Without War (1978).

49. Durand v. Hollins, 4 Blatch. 451, 454 (1860). A description of the bombing appears in Milton Offutt, "The Protection of Citizens Abroad by the Armed Forces of the United States," Johns Hopkins Univ. Studies in Hist. and Pol. Sci., series 44, no. 4 (1928), at 32–34.

Bland legalese cannot hide the ferocity of the Greytown bombing. A more measured and deliberate policy was promised by legislation in 1868 (still in effect) directing the President to demand from a foreign government the reason for depriving any American citizen of liberty. If it appears wrongful and in violation of the rights of American citizenship, the President can demand the citizen's release. If the foreign government delays or refuses, the President may use such means "not amounting to acts of war" as he thinks necessary and proper to obtain the release.[50]

This statute did not put an end to heavy-handed American actions abroad. Theodore Roosevelt, William Howard Taft, and other Presidents resorted to force not simply for the purpose of protecting American lives and property but to pursue foreign policy objectives. Woodrow Wilson, taking the Greytown bombardment as an acceptable precedent, ordered American forces to occupy Veracruz, Mexico, in 1914. Although a Mexican commander apologized for arresting several Americans and President Huerta issued an expression of regret, Wilson wanted a formal 21-gun salute to be given to U.S. naval vessels, a gesture that Huerta declined to give. In a message delivered to a joint session of Congress, Wilson stressed the need for immediate action, offering this legal analysis: "No doubt I could do what is necessary in the circumstances to enforce respect for our Government without recourse to the congress, and yet not exceed my constitutional powers as President; but I do not wish to act in a matter possibly of so grave consequence except in close conference and co-operation with both the Senate and the House."[51]

The House acted with alacrity to authorize the use of armed force, but when Senators had the audacity to pause for one day to think about what they were doing, Wilson went ahead and ordered landing operations by the Marines. The following day—two days after his request—Congress passed a joint resolution justifying the President's use of force. This episode, which began with a trivial incident involving U.S. seamen in Tampico, escalated to the bombardment of Veracruz, American occupation for seven months, and the downfall of the Mexican president. The following year Wilson intervened in Haiti to secure a more acceptable government there, while confiding to his Secretary of State that "we have not the legal authority to do what we apparently ought to do."[52] American troops remained in Haiti until 1934.

50. 15 Stat. 223 (1868); 22 U.S.C. 1732 (2000). It is possible to derive the life-and-property prerogative from the Privilege and Immunity Clause. Justice Miller, in enumerating some of the rights protected by this constitutional provision, included the right to be protected abroad; the Slaughter-House Cases, 83 U.S. (16 Wall.) 36, 79 (1872).

51. 16 Richardson 7936.

52. Arthur S. Link, Wilson: The Struggle for Neutrality 536 (1960). For the joint resolution of support for the Veracruz action, see 38 Stat. 770 (1914). A vivid account is given

Recent decades have lengthened the list of life-and-property actions. President Eisenhower sent troops to Lebanon in 1958 "to protect American lives and by their presence there to encourage the Lebanese government in defense of Lebanese sovereignty and integrity."[53] President Johnson intervened in the Dominican Republic in 1965 to prevent what he feared would be a communist takeover, though he later explained that "99 percent of our reason for going in there was to try to provide protection for these American lives and for the lives of other nationals."[54] President Nixon justified his invasion of Cambodia in 1970 on the ground that enemy actions "clearly endanger the lives of Americans who are in Vietnam now and would constitute an unacceptable risk to those who will be there after withdrawal of another 150,000."[55] When the Nixon administration provided support for the South Vietnamese invasion of Laos the following year, the State Department said that the action would "protect American lives."[56] President Ford used troops for evacuations from Southeast Asia and for the rescue of the *Mayaguez* vessel. President Carter sent troops to Iran in 1980 in an abortive effort to free American hostages. President Reagan dispatched Marines to Grenada in 1983, ostensibly to rescue American students and other U.S. citizens, but Russian and Cuban influence in that region was the overriding motivation. President Bush offered a number of justifications in 1989 for ordering U.S. military forces into Panama, including the protection of American citizens in that country.[57] In sending troops to Saudi Arabia in 1990, he claimed that the action was necessary in part to protect the lives of American citizens abroad.[58]

Contemporary use of force cannot be justified on the basis of gunboat diplomacy and forays into Mexico or the Caribbean a half century ago. Ratification of the United Nations Charter imposes restrictions on member states that can be ignored only at some political cost. Article 2, Paragraph 4, states that all members "shall refrain in their international relations from the threat or use of force against the territorial integrity or political independence of any state, or in any other manner inconsistent with the purposes of the United Nations." There are only two exceptions: the right of individual or collective self-defense against an armed attack (Article 51), and collective action taken by the United Nations to deal with serious disturbances of the peace.

by Robert E. Quirk, An Affair of Honor: Woodrow Wilson and the Occupation of Veracruz (1962).
53. Public Papers of the Presidents, 1958, at 549.
54. Public Papers of the Presidents, 1965 (II), at 616.
55. Public Papers of the Presidents, 1970, at 406.
56. New York Times, February 9, 1971, at 17:6. For a discussion of the constitutional limits when force is used to protect troops, see 65 Am. J. Int'l L. 34–35, 79–80 (1971).
57. Public Papers of the Presidents, 1989 (II), at 1734.
58. Public Papers of the Presidents, 1990 (II), at 1108.

Even the Nixon administration, after its intervention in Cambodia in 1970, acknowledged that whatever the practices prior to 1945, adoption of the UN Charter "changed the situation by imposing new and important limitations on the use of armed force."[59] A body of international legal norms has developed since 1945 that supposedly constrains the actions of sovereign nations. The Legal Adviser to the State Department during the Reagan administration testified before Congress in 1986: "Our policy has been that the use of force by the United States is restricted by the United Nations Charter. We are not allowed to use force unless it is either authorized by the Security Council or it falls within the inherent right of self-defense under article 51."[60]

Early drafts of the War Powers Resolution of 1973 recognized the responsibility of the President to protect life and property. A bill introduced by Senator Jacob Javits in 1971 would have allowed the President to use armed force "to protect the lives and property, as may be required, of United States nationals abroad." Javits later deleted the words "and property" for fear that they might be interpreted in a nineteenth-century sense of protecting American business investments abroad.[61] The rest of the language disappeared in the House-Senate compromise that became law.

This lack of legislative authority, together with other statutory restrictions on the use of force in Southeast Asia, created an awkward and confusing situation in 1975. President Ford asked Congress to clarify the statutory restrictions so that he could evacuate American citizens and foreign nationals from South Vietnam and Cambodia. He gave Congress nine days to act.[62] Instead of trying to act while a presidential timer was ticking, party leaders in Congress should have issued a statement saying that the President had sufficient authority for the evacuations, provided he used a minimum of force. Ford had already announced that the War Powers Resolution, as he interpreted it, gave the President "certain limited authority to protect American lives. And to that extent, I will use that law."[63] Why then ask Congress for additional legislative authority? The issue was complicated by the need to rescue foreign nationals as well, but it was politically unreasonable and unrealistic to expect Congress to legislate on such an explosive issue in nine days.

59. Statement by John R. Stevenson, Legal Adviser to the Department of State, May 29, 1970, reprinted at 64 Am. J. Int'l L. 933, 940 (1970).

60. Statement by Abraham D. Sofaer, Legal Adviser to the Department of State, in "War Power, Libya, and State-Sponsored Terrorism," hearings before the House Committee on Foreign Affairs, 99th Cong., 2d Sess. 39 (1986).

61. "War Powers Resolution," hearings before the Senate Committee on Foreign Relations, 92d Cong., 1st Sess. 35–36, 95–96, 128 (1971).

62. Public Papers of the Presidents, 1975 (II), at 464.

63. Id. at 414–15.

Members agonized for weeks, trying to discover the right language that would give Ford the authority he wanted without inviting military reinvolvement in Southeast Asia. Legislators were whipsawed by conflicting feelings. On the one hand, they wanted to relate all military operations to the procedures of the War Powers Resolution. On the other hand, they were apprehensive that any legislation, no matter how meticulously drafted, would become anachronous and ambiguous due to the rapidly changing situation in Southeast Asia.

While Congress anguished over the wording of the legislation, Ford went ahead with the evacuations. In each case he based his action on the President's "executive power" under the Constitution and his authority as Commander in Chief.[64] He took those actions before Congress could deliver the "clarifying authority." Even though the evacuations were over, some members of Congress argued that the legislation should be passed. They reasoned that the President had conducted the evacuations within the limitations of the legislation under consideration (although Ford cited only constitutional sources in his reports); Congress should therefore enact the legislation to establish its authority and somehow legalize the President's action. For such legislators, the integrity of the War Powers Resolution was at stake. Others, however, believed that the bill was moot because of the evacuations. Passage of the legislation would merely lift the restrictions that barred the reintroduction of troops into Southeast Asia. The House, capping three weeks of legislative frenzy, voted down the conference report—an ignominious finale to an ill-conceived legislative exercise.[65]

Following the evacuations and Ford's rescue of the *Mayaguez* crew, Senator Thomas Eagleton introduced legislation explicitly recognizing the President's right to protect lives (but not property). It stipulated various conditions limiting this grant of power: the citizens to be rescued had to be held involuntarily, with the express or tacit consent of the foreign government; there had to be a direct and imminent threat to their lives; the foreign government either could not or would not protect the individuals; and the evacuations had to take place as expeditiously as possible and with a minimum of force.[66] Eagleton's proposal and other amendments to the War Powers Resolution have not been acted on by Congress.

64. H. Doc. Nos. 105 and 124, 94th Cong., 1st Sess. (1975).
65. 121 Cong. Rec. 12752–64 (1975). For a GAO decision that the evacuation of Vietnamese nationals was necessarily incident to the rescue of Americans, see 55 Comp. Gen. 1081 (1976).
66. 121 Cong. Rec. 15579–82 (1975).

Delegated Emergency Powers

Claims of "emergency" are convenient for attracting legislative support, but at such times it is necessary to distinguish between genuine emergencies thrust upon the nation and those that develop because of neglect or contrivance. After President Franklin D. Roosevelt declared 39 emergencies within the space of six years, Congressman Bruce Barton protested: "Any national administration is entitled to one or two emergencies in a term of 6 years. But an emergency every 6 weeks means plain bad management."[67]

Once the nation is engaged in war, the reservoir of presidential power fills rapidly as Congress delegates vast new duties and responsibilities to the executive branch. Characteristically, this legislation offers little in the way of guidelines for administrative action, yet the courts regularly uphold such statutes.[68] Furthermore, these delegations remain in the hands of the President long after hostilities have ended, long after American troops have returned home. Here too the courts defer to the chief executive in determining when a state of war is over.[69]

Other statutes contain latent or dormant authority for the President, ready to spring to life whenever he issues a proclamation declaring the nation to be in a state of emergency. It came as a surprise to many members of Congress in 1971 to learn that the United States had been in a state of declared national emergency since March 9, 1933, when President Roosevelt had proclaimed an emergency during the banking crisis. Also still in effect were national emergencies proclaimed by President Truman on December 16, 1950 (after China's entry into the Korean War) and by President Nixon on March 23, 1970, and August 15, 1971.

These discoveries prompted the Senate to establish a special committee to study the possibility of terminating the states of declared national emergency. A committee report in 1973 disclosed that the four proclamations mentioned above had brought to life 470 provisions of federal law. Each statute extended to the President some facet of control over the lives of American citizens. Among other things, he could seize property, organize and control the means of production, institute martial law, control all transportation and communication, and restrict travel.[70]

67. 84 Cong. Rec. 2854 (1939).
68. For example, United States v. Bethlehem Steel, 315 U.S. 289 (1942); Bowles v. Willingham, 321 U.S. 503 (1944); Yakus v. United States, 321 U.S. 414 (1944); and Lichter v. United States, 344 U.S. 742 (1947).
69. For example, United States v. Anderson, 9 Wall. 56 (1870); The Protector, 12 Wall. 700 (1872); Stewart v. Kahn, 11 Wall. 493 (1870); Hijo v. United States, 194 U.S. 315 (1904); Hamilton v. Kentucky Distilleries, 251 U.S. 146 (1919); Commercial Trust v. Miller, 262 U.S. 51 (1923); Chastleton Corp. v. Sinclair, 264 U.S. 533 (1924); and Woods v. Miller, 333 U.S. 138 (1948).
70. S. Rept. No. 549, 93d Cong., 1st Sess. iii (1973).

In 1976 Congress passed the National Emergencies Act to restrict the use of presidential emergency powers. Its general thrust was to terminate emergency authorities two years from the date the act became law (September 14, 1976). In future national emergencies the President had to publish the declaration in the *Federal Register,* and Congress could terminate the national emergency by passing a concurrent resolution. To prevent emergencies from lingering for decades without congressional attention or action, the 1976 legislation included an action-forcing mechanism. No later than six months after a national emergency was declared by the President, and at least every six months thereafter while the emergency continued, each house of Congress was supposed to meet to consider a vote on a concurrent resolution to determine whether the emergency should be terminated.[71]

The use of a concurrent resolution to control executive action was invalidated by the Supreme Court's decision in *INS v. Chadha* in 1983. Congress passed legislation in 1985 to repeal the concurrent resolution procedure for national emergencies and replace it with action by joint resolution, which satisfies *Chadha*'s requirement for bicameralism and presentment of a bill to the President.[72] The requirement for congressional consideration every six months was rendered a nullity through disuse. Despite the statutory mandate for congressional action, no concurrent resolution was ever introduced, much less acted upon, after President Carter declared a national emergency during the Iranian hostage crisis in 1979. The Senate Foreign Relations Committee and the House Foreign Affairs Committee merely wrote letters to Carter stating that action on a resolution of disapproval was unnecessary.[73] The automatic six-month review has remained a dead letter.

The National Emergencies Act exempted certain provisions of law, including Section 5(b) of the Trading with the Enemy Act, originally enacted in 1917. Over the years this provision had been the basis for controlling domestic as well as international financial transactions. Its reach went far beyond trading with the enemy, providing a source of presidential authority in peacetime as well as wartime. For example, it was under Section 5(b) that President Roosevelt declared a national emergency in 1933 and announced a bank holiday to prevent the hoarding of gold. Presidents Johnson and Nixon also invoked this clause to justify other controversial actions.

Legislation passed by Congress in 1977 limits the use of the Trading with the Enemy Act to time of war *as declared by Congress.* A second set of powers,

71. 90 Stat. 1255 (1976). See also "The National Emergencies Act (Public Law 94-412) Source Book: Legislative History, Texts, and Other Documents," Senate Committee on Government Operations and Senate Special Committee on National Emergencies and Delegated Emergency Powers, 94th Cong., 2d Sess. (Comm. Print November 1976).

72. 99 Stat. 448, sec. 801 (1985); 131 Cong. Rec. 14947–48 (1985).

73. 126 Cong. Rec. 11270–71, 11537 (1980).

more restricted than those available during wartime, would be given to the President upon his declaration of a national emergency in time of peace. The legislation subjects those powers to the procedural restrictions of the National Emergencies Act.[74]

Contemporary War Powers

After decades of debate, Congress passed legislation in 1973 to limit war-making actions by the President. The statute calls for "collective judgment" by Congress and the President before U.S. forces are sent into combat, especially for long-term military engagements. The War Powers Resolution permits the President to act unilaterally for up to 90 days, but congressional approval is required after that. For reasons to be explained, that particular provision has never worked as intended. The statute also provides for reports to Congress and encourages the President to consult with Congress before taking action.

Given the political environment at the time the War Powers Resolution was passed, it is natural to view it solely within the context of the Vietnam War. Indeed, the legislative history is replete with partisan attacks on Richard Nixon and even includes motivations to retaliate against the policies of Lyndon Johnson. However, the War Powers Resolution represents something more than a mix of partisan and personal politics. It reflects almost four decades of bipartisan effort to recapture legislative authority that had drifted to the President.

When the Pendulum Stopped Swinging

Executive-legislative conflicts from the Washington administration to the 1930s were characterized by a cycle—strong Presidents (Jefferson, Jackson, Lincoln, and Wilson, among others) followed by a resurgent Congress. Power did not remain lodged in a single branch for very long. The system of checks and balances functioned in a way to disperse power and block institutional ambition. Even after major military conflicts, such as the Civil War and World War I, Congress was able to restore its place as a coequal branch.

Something different happened in the 1930s. The powers transferred to President Franklin D. Roosevelt during the Great Depression and later during World War II did not return to Congress. What had been a temporary dis-

---

74. 91 Stat. 1625 (1977); H. Rept. No. 459, 95th Cong., 1st Sess. (1977); 123 Cong. Rec. 22473–78 (1977). See also "Trading with the Enemy: Legislative and Executive Documents Concerning Regulation of International Transactions in Time of Declared National Emergency," prepared by the House Committee on International Relations, 94th Cong., 2d Sess. (Comm. Print November 1976).

equilibrium in earlier periods—quickly righted to start a new cycle—became a permanent fixture of executive-legislative relations.

After his election in 1932, President Roosevelt sought and obtained major grants of emergency authority from Congress. In his inaugural address in 1933, Roosevelt drew an analogy between the Great Depression and a time of war, urging the country to move forward "as a trained and loyal army." He hoped that the normal balance of executive and legislative authority would be sufficient to meet the crisis, but "it may be that an unprecedented demand and need for undelayed action may call for temporary departure from that normal balance of public procedure." This temporary departure became a permanent condition, in part through Roosevelt's initiatives, and in part through forces beyond his control.

The pendulum seemed ready to swing back toward Congress after Roosevelt's reelection victory in 1936. He had badly miscalculated in his effort to pack the Supreme Court and seize additional executive authority. Congress was clearly poised to recapture power that had slipped to the President. The normal swings of presidential and congressional dominance were about to resume. At that moment, however, rumblings in Europe and the Far East set the stage for World War II and continued executive dominance.

With the United States in the midst of hostilities, Roosevelt warned Congress in 1942 that he would act with or without statutory authority. He gave Congress a deadline and said that in the event that Congress "should fail to act, and act adequately, I shall accept the responsibility, and I will act." In that same address he claimed that when "the war is won, the powers under which I act automatically revert to the people—to whom they belong."[75]

In fact, after the war was won, presidential powers did not revert either to Congress or to the people. President Harry Truman announced the end of the war in Europe on May 8, 1945, and the surrender of Japan on August 14, 1945, yet he did not proclaim the "termination of hostilities" until December 31, 1946. Furthermore, he retained a number of emergency powers by claiming that "a state of war still exists."[76] On April 28, 1952, he finally signed a statement ending the state of war with Japan and terminating the national emergencies that Roosevelt had proclaimed in 1939 and 1941. Although hostilities had lasted for less than four years, Roosevelt and Truman exercised emergency and war powers for more than twelve years.

Truman's initiative in sending troops to Korea in 1950 dramatized the growth of executive power. The legality of his action has been debated ever since. What is not debatable is that the President, for the first time, committed

75. 11 Public Papers and Addresses of Franklin D. Roosevelt 364–65 (1950).
76. Public Papers of the Presidents, 1946, at 512–13.

U.S. troops abroad into a major conflict on his own authority. He acted without a declaration of war or specific authorization from Congress. Significantly, the President's critics at that time were conservative Republicans; liberal Democrats rushed to his defense.[77]

In 1951 Truman announced his intention to send ground forces to Europe without seeking congressional approval, possibly triggering military conflict with the Soviet Union. His action precipitated a major confrontation with Congress. In an extremely powerful floor statement, the leading conservative of the time, Senator Robert ("Mr. Republican") Taft, delivered a 10,000-word speech urging Congress to defend its prerogatives. Taft insisted that Congress had "a constitutional obligation to reexamine constantly and discuss the foreign policy of the United States." The trend toward secrecy on the part of recent administrations, combined with the failure to consult Congress and seek its advice, deprived members of Congress "of the substance of the powers conferred on them by the Constitution."[78] He concluded: "The policy we adopt must be approved by Congress and the people after full and free discussion. The commitment of a land army to Europe is a program never approved by Congress, into which we should not drift. The policy of secret executive agreements has brought us to danger and disaster. It threatens the liberties of our people."[79]

For three months in 1951 the Senate engaged in the "Great Debate" on the relative prerogatives of Congress and the President in exercising the war power. Taft believed that Congress had the power to prevent the President from sending troops anywhere in the world to involve the United States in war. In what could be read as a precursor to the War Powers Resolution, he urged Congress to assert its power in the form of a joint resolution.[80] Senator John McClellan offered an amendment requiring congressional approval of future plans to send troops abroad. Although the amendment was initially rejected, 44 to 46, it was later accepted.[81] The Senate passed the resolution by a vote of 69 to 21, expressing its approval of Truman's sending four divisions to Europe; however, it stated that "in the interests of sound constitutional processes, and of national unity and understanding, congressional approval should be obtained of any policy requiring the assignment of American troops abroad when such assignment is in implementation of article 3 of the North Atlantic Treaty," and no ground troops in addition to the four divi-

77. Louis Fisher, "The Korean War: On What Legal Basis Did Truman Act?" 89 Am. J. Int'l L. 21 (1995).
78. 97 Cong. Rec. 55 (1951).
79. Id. at 61.
80. Id. at 2987.
81. Id. at 3082–83, 3096.

sions should be sent "without further congressional approval."[82] As a Senate resolution, the measure was not legally binding. It merely expressed the sense of the Senate on constitutional processes, although the debate and the votes were highly significant.

Eisenhower's Philosophy of Joint Action

The destructive collisions between President Truman and Congress convinced President Dwight D. Eisenhower to avoid unilateral executive actions in dispatching troops abroad. Instead, he sought the enactment of area resolutions that would delegate congressional authority to the President. In 1955 he urged Congress to pass the Formosa Resolution, which recognized the security risks in Formosa and the Pescadores and authorized the President to use military force "as he deems necessary." Although Eisenhower believed that he possessed some independent constitutional powers as Commander in Chief, he thought it far more prudent for the two branches to act in concert.[83]

Eisenhower repeated this approach in 1957, asking Congress to pass a joint resolution authorizing him to employ armed forces in the Middle East. Congress debated the proposal carefully and added a section that permitted that body to terminate the authority by passing a concurrent resolution, requiring action by both houses but eliminating the President's opportunity for a veto. Eisenhower was committed to the importance of executive-legislative coordination: "I deem it necessary to seek the cooperation of the Congress. Only with that cooperation can we give the reassurance needed to deter aggression."[84]

In his memoirs, Eisenhower discussed the choice between invoking executive prerogatives and seeking congressional approval. On New Year's Day in 1957 he met with Secretary of State John Foster Dulles and congressional leaders of both parties, requesting their support for the Middle East Resolution. House Majority Leader John McCormack asked Eisenhower whether he, as Commander in Chief, did not already possess the power to dispatch troops without congressional authorization. Eisenhower acknowledged the existence of those powers but explained that "greater effect could be had from a consensus of Executive and Legislative opinion, and I spoke earnestly of the desire of the Middle East countries to have reassurance now that the United States would stand ready to help. . . . Near the end of the meeting I reminded the legislators that the Constitution assumes that our two branches of government should get along together."[85]

82. Id. at 3283 (para. 6).
83. Public Papers of the Presidents, 1955, at 209–10; 69 Stat. 7 (1955).
84. Public Papers of the Presidents, 1957, at 11; 71 Stat. 4 (1957).
85. Dwight D. Eisenhower, Waging Peace 179 (1965).

Eisenhower's position was sound but short-lived. President John F. Kennedy made it clear during the Cuban missile crisis of 1962 that he was prepared to act solely on his own constitutional authority as Commander in Chief.[86] Congress passed another area resolution, the Cuba Resolution, but it did not authorize presidential action. It merely expressed the sentiments of Congress and omitted the procedure for terminating the President's authority by passing a concurrent resolution.[87] When Kennedy later acted to interdict weapons being delivered to Cuba, he acted on what he considered to be his constitutional powers.[88] The next area resolution, the fateful Tonkin Gulf Resolution of 1964, shot through Congress with little debate and no time taken for independent legislative judgment. The Senate Foreign Relations Committee, which reported the resolution favorably, later admitted that it had abdicated its institutional duties by assuming that President Lyndon B. Johnson would not abuse the authority delegated to him.[89]

From 1969 to 1973 Congress retraced the arguments made during the Great Debate of 1951 and concluded that commitments abroad required the concerted action of both branches. The National Commitments Resolution of 1969, which passed the Senate 70 to 16, declared that the commitment of armed forces to a foreign territory or the promise of financial assistance could result "only from affirmative action taken by the executive and legislative branches of the United States by means of a treaty, statute, or concurrent resolution of both Houses of Congress specifically providing for such commitment."[90] The resolution, which was not legally binding because it expressed the sentiments of only one house and was not presented to the President, won the backing of both parties. The Democrats supported it 43 to 3; the Republicans favored it 27 to 13.

The War Powers Resolution

In 1970 the House of Representatives passed a War Powers Resolution by a vote of 289 to 39. It recognized that the President "in certain extraordinary and emergency circumstances has the authority to defend the United States and its citizens without specific prior authorization by the Congress." Instead of trying to define the precise conditions under which Presidents may act, the House relied on procedural safeguards. The President would be required,

86. Public Papers of the Presidents, 1962, at 674, 679.
87. 76 Stat. 697 (1962).
88. Public Papers of the Presidents, 1962, at 810.
89. S. Rept. No. 129, 91st Cong., 1st Sess. 23 (1969).
90. 115 Cong. Rec. 17245 (1969).

"whenever feasible," to consult with Congress before sending American forces into armed conflict. He was also to report the circumstances necessitating the action; the constitutional, legislative, and treaty provisions authorizing the action, together with his reasons for not seeking specific prior congressional authorization; and the estimated scope of activities.[91] The Senate did not act on the measure.

Both houses later passed War Powers Resolutions that went beyond mere reporting requirements. The House of Representatives, following its earlier example, did not try to define or codify presidential war powers. It directed the President "in every possible instance" to consult with Congress before sending forces into hostile situations or those where hostilities might be imminent. If unable to do so, he was to report to Congress within 72 hours, setting forth the circumstances and details of his action. Unless Congress declared war within 120 days or specifically authorized the use of force, the President had to terminate the commitment and remove the troops. Congress could also direct disengagement at any time during the 120-day period by passing a concurrent resolution.[92]

The Senate attempted to spell out the conditions under which Presidents could take unilateral action. Armed force could be used in three situations: (1) to repel an armed attack on the United States, its territories, and possessions; retaliate in the event of such an attack; and forestall the direct and imminent threat of such an attack; (2) to repel an armed attack against U.S. armed forces located outside the United States, its territories, and possessions, and forestall the direct and imminent threat of such an attack; and (3) to rescue endangered American citizens and nationals in foreign countries or at sea. The first situation (except for the final clause) conforms to the understanding developed at the Philadelphia convention. The other situations reflect the changes that have occurred in the concept of defensive war and life-and-property actions.

The Senate bill required the President to cease military action unless Congress, within 30 days, specifically authorized the President to continue. A separate provision allowed him to sustain military operations beyond the 30-day limit if he determined that "unavoidable military necessity respecting the safety" of the armed forces required their continued use for the purpose of "bringing about a prompt disengagement."[93] This effort to codify presidential war powers carried a number of risks. Because of ambiguities in the language, legislation might widen presidential power instead of restricting it. Executive

91. 116 Cong. Rec. 37398–408 (1970). Passed again the next year under suspension of the rules (requiring two-thirds support), 117 Cong. Rec. 28870–78 (1971).
92. 119 Cong. Rec. 24653–708 (1973).
93. Id. at 25051–120.

officials could interpret in broad fashion such terms as "necessary and appro-priate retaliatory actions," "imminent threat," and "endangered citizens."

Nixon's Veto

The two houses of Congress presented a compromise measure to President Nixon. He vetoed the bill primarily because he regarded it as impractical and dangerous to fix in a statute the procedure by which the President and Congress should share the war power. He also believed that the legislation encroached on the President's constitutional responsibilities as Commander in Chief. He reminded Congress that the "only way in which the constitu-tional powers of a branch of the Government can be altered is by amending the Constitution—and any attempt to make such alterations by legislation alone is clearly without force."[94] Both houses mustered a two-thirds majority to override the veto: the House narrowly (284 to 135), and the Senate by a more comfortable margin (75 to 18).[95]

Although the War Powers Resolution of 1973 overcame a veto, it did not survive doubts about its quality and motivation. Some congressional support for the resolution was based on party politics and the resolution's symbolic value rather than its contents. Consider the voting record of 15 members of the House.[96] After voting against the House bill and the conference version, they inconsistently voted to override the veto. If they opposed the legislation because they considered it inadequate or unsound, why vote to make it public law?

This reversal occurred in part because of fear that a vote to sustain Nixon might lend credence to the views advanced in his veto message. Despite seri-ous misgivings about the quality of the bill, some legislators concluded that congressional inaction could be interpreted as a concession to the constitu-tional claims of Nixon (and Johnson). Other legislators used the override to propel the House toward impeaching Nixon. One of those who voted against the House resolution and the conference version but then voted in favor of overriding the veto, Democrat Bella Abzug of New York, advised her colleagues that "this could be a turning point in the struggle to control an administration that has run amuck. It could accelerate the demand for the impeachment of the President."[97]

Another factor was that Democrats were determined to override a Nixon veto. Eight times during the 93d Congress he had vetoed legislation; eight

94. Public Papers of the Presidents, 1973, at 893.
95. 87 Stat. 555 (1973).
96. Representatives Abzug, Drinan, Duncan, Flynt, Harsha, Hechler (W. Va.), Holtzman, Hungate, Landrum, Lott, Maraziti, Milford, Natcher, Stubblefield, and Whitten.
97. 119 Cong. Rec. 36221 (1973).

times Congress had come up short on the override. A number of members looked on the War Powers Resolution as a vehicle to test congressional power.[98] This attitude was especially tempting in the wake of the Watergate scandals. The "Saturday Night Massacre," which sent Special Prosecutor Archibald Cox, Attorney General Elliot Richardson, and Deputy Attorney General William Ruckelshaus out of the government, occurred just four days before Nixon's veto of the War Powers Resolution. Ten days before the Saturday Night Massacre, Spiro Agnew heightened the politicized climate by resigning as Vice President.

Analysis of the Bill

The War Powers Resolution sets forth three main procedures: presidential consultation with Congress, presidential reports to Congress, and congressional termination of military action. The purpose of the resolution, according to Section 2(a), is "to fulfill the intent of the framers of the Constitution of the United States and insure that the collective judgment" of both branches will apply to the introduction of U.S. forces into hostilities. Yet an examination of other sections, together with executive interpretations and congressional behavior, supplies ample evidence that the legislation undermines the intent of the framers, and collective judgment is by no means assured.

The President is to consult with Congress "in every possible instance." This language obviously gives the President considerable discretion as to the form and timing of consultation. The Carter administration noted that the President's responsibilities under the sections involving consultation and reporting "have not been delegated, so that the final decision as to whether consultation is possible and as to the manner in which consultations be undertaken or reports submitted rests with the President."[99]

The authors of the resolution did not expect the President to consult with 535 legislators. But whom should he contact? The leadership? The chairmen and ranking members of designated committees? Selected advisers? Should they merely be briefed, or does consultation encompass a more active role for Congress? The legislative history makes it clear that consultation is more than simply being informed of a decision. Consultation means that "a decision is pending on a problem and that Members of Congress are being asked by the President for their advice and opinions and, in appropriate circumstances, their approval of action contemplated."[100]

98. See Thomas F. Eagleton, War and Presidential Power 213–20 (1974).
99. 123 Cong. Rec. 21898 (1977).
100. H. Rept. No. 287, 93d Cong., 1st Sess. 6–7 (1973).

The War Powers Resolution requires that the President, after introducing forces into hostilities, report to Congress within 48 hours. Precisely what conditions require a report is unclear from the legislation. If the report is delayed for any reason, so are the mechanisms for congressional control. Under the terms of the statute, the President may introduce U.S. forces into hostilities or imminent hostilities for up to 60 days and extend that period by an additional 30 days if he determines that doing so is necessary to protect and remove American troops. Congress provided two means of legislative control: a decision not to support the President during the 60 to 90 days, or passage of a concurrent resolution at any time to direct the President to remove forces engaged in hostilities.

The problem with the "deadlines" is that the clock does not start ticking for the 60- to 90-day limit unless the President reports under a specific section: Section 4(a)(1). For obvious reasons, Presidents do not submit reports under that section. Only twice has the clock begun. President Ford reported under Section 4(a)(1) after the *Mayaguez* was captured, but by the time he did so, the military operation was already completed. Congress started the clock again through the regular legislative process by passing the Lebanon Resolution on October 12, 1983, which declared that Section 4(a)(1) had been activated on August 29, 1983. The resolution, however, authorized President Reagan to keep troops in Lebanon for up to *18 months,* although Reagan removed most of the Marines in February 1984.[101]

Legislative Veto

The second form of legislative control—passage of a concurrent resolution—is also of questionable potency. The Legal Adviser to the State Department told a House committee in 1975 that if the President has the power to put men into combat, "that power could not be taken away by concurrent resolution because the power is constitutional in nature."[102] That position seemed to be reinforced in 1983 when the Supreme Court, in *INS v. Chadha,* struck down the legislative veto as unconstitutional. The Court said that whenever Congress wanted to control the executive branch, it had to act through a bill or joint resolution that was presented to the President.

In response to *Chadha,* Senator Robert Byrd offered an amendment to the State Department authorization bill to conform the provisions of the War Powers Resolution to the Court's decision. In place of the concurrent resolution,

---

101. 97 Stat. 805 (1983).

102. "War Powers: A Test of Compliance," hearings before the House Committee on International Relations, 94th Cong., 1st Sess. 91 (1975).

Congress would have to act by joint resolution or bill. His amendment passed the Senate, but, as altered in conference, it did not amend the War Powers Resolution. Instead, it was enacted as a freestanding, expedited procedure to require the President to withdraw troops.[103]

During hearings in 1988, the Legal Adviser to the State Department testified that the concurrent resolution was "clearly" unconstitutional and should be repealed.[104] In a committee report in 1987, the Senate Foreign Relations Committee stated that the concurrent resolution in the War Powers Resolution "has been effectively nullified" by *Chadha*.[105]

Should the concurrent resolution be replaced by a joint resolution to comply with *Chadha's* requirements for bicameralism and presentment? That would be both unnecessary and undesirable. The term "legislative veto" should be defined strictly to mean a condition placed on delegated power, such as the one-house veto that accompanied the delegation of reorganization authority to the President or the two-house veto attached to rulemaking authority for the Federal Trade Commission. In the case of the War Powers Resolution, no power was delegated. No one argued that the war power belonged exclusively to the legislative branch and was being delegated to the President in the War Powers Resolution on the condition that Congress retain control by passing a concurrent resolution. Section 8(d)(2) expressly states that nothing in the War Powers Resolution "shall be construed as granting any authority to the President with respect to the introduction of United States Armed Forces into hostilities or into situations wherein involvement in hostilities is clearly indicated by the circumstances which authority he would not have had in the absence of this joint resolution."

The constitutional case for the concurrent resolution in the War Powers Resolution thus rests on fundamentally different grounds than the legislative vetoes invalidated in *Chadha*. The disadvantages of replacing the concurrent resolution with a joint resolution are obvious. If Congress passed a joint resolution ordering the President to withdraw troops, the President could veto the measure, and Congress could enforce its policy only by locating a two-thirds majority in each house to override the President. In other words, the President could continue in the face of majority opposition in both houses simply by securing the support of one-third plus one in a single house.

To make this issue concrete, consider the effort by Congress to use its power of the purse to end the war in Vietnam. In 1973 Congress added language to an

103. 129 Cong. Rec. 28406–8, 28673–74, 28683–84, 28686–89, 33385, 33395–96 (1983); 97 Stat. 1062–63, sec. 1013 (1983); 50 U.S.C. 1546a (2000).

104. "The War Power After 200 Years," hearings before the Senate Committee on Foreign Relations, 100th Cong., 2d Sess. 1061 (1988).

105. S. Rept. No. 100–106, 100th Cong., 1st Sess. 6 (1987).

appropriations bill forbidding the use of any funds to support combat activities in Cambodia or Laos. The language covered not only the supplemental funds in the bill but also funds made available by previous appropriations. President Nixon vetoed the bill, and Congress was unable to muster a two-thirds majority in each house for the override. As a result, the bill had to be revised to delay the cutoff of funds from June 30 to August 15, 1973, giving Nixon 45 additional days to bomb Cambodia.

Congresswoman Elizabeth Holtzman filed a suit in New York, asking a federal court to determine that the President could not engage in combat operations in Southeast Asia without congressional authorization. U.S. District Judge Orrin G. Judd held that Congress had not authorized the bombing of Cambodia. Furthermore, the inability of Congress to override Nixon's veto could not be interpreted as an affirmative grant of authority. As Judd observed: "It cannot be the rule that the President needs a vote of only one-third plus one of either House in order to conduct a war, but this would be the consequence of holding that Congress must override a Presidential veto in order to terminate hostilities which it has not authorized."[106] Judd's order was stayed by the Supreme Court because the August 15 compromise agreed to by Congress had broken the impasse between the two branches.[107] Eventually, Judd's decision was reversed by the Second Circuit, which treated the dispute as a political question.[108]

Converting the concurrent resolution to a joint resolution would not entirely solve the constitutional dispute, even though it might satisfy the Court's test in *Chadha*. It has been argued within Congress and the executive branch that Congress cannot order the President to remove troops even by joint resolution. The claim is that the President has plenary power as Commander in Chief to move and remove troops. If Congress cannot act by concurrent or joint resolution, the next step in constraining the President would be to amend the Constitution.[109] That might resolve some legal niceties, but such a proposal is impractical and unwieldy.

The concurrent resolution in the War Powers Resolution remains a useful and appropriate means for expressing congressional policy. If Congress were to pass such a resolution, the President could argue that it had no legally binding effect because of *Chadha*. However, such reasoning would also pub-

---

106. Holtzman v. Schlesinger, 361 F.Supp. 553, 565 (E.D. N.Y. 1973).

107. Holtzman v. Schlesinger, 414 U.S. 1304, 1316, 1321 (1973).

108. Holtzman v. Schlesinger, 484 F.2d 1307 (2d Cir. 1973), cert. denied, 416 U.S. 936 (1974).

109. For example, the position of Senator Barry Goldwater at 129 Cong. Rec. 28686–87 (1983) and testimony by the executive branch in "War Powers: A Test of Compliance," hearings before the House Committee on International Relations, 94th Cong., 1st Sess. 90–91 (1975).

licize the President's determination to keep U.S. forces engaged in hostilities despite the opposition of a majority of both houses of Congress. Politically, if not constitutionally, that is not a tenable position for the President. It is constitutionally repugnant for a President to initiate and continue a war with the backing of only one-third plus one in a single house. Congress should not have to regain control by securing a two-thirds majority in both houses. Under these conditions, and confining *Chadha* as it should be to questions of delegated authority, the concurrent resolution remains an appropriate vehicle.

Military Initiatives from Ford to Clinton

Presidents have submitted a number of reports under the War Powers Resolution, but the manner of the reports and the responses by Congress underscore the fact that the resolution is simply a framework for executive-legislative relations. The actual outcome in every case depends on a spirit of comity, good-faith efforts by the President and members of Congress, and Congress's willingness to assert itself to control unilateral presidential actions.

On three occasions in April 1975, President Ford reported to Congress the use of military forces to evacuate U.S. citizens and refugees from Vietnam and Cambodia. Typical of these reports under the War Powers Resolution, Ford cited his constitutional authority as Chief Executive and Commander in Chief rather than statutory sources of authority. The following month, the War Powers Resolution was put to a more severe test. The U.S. merchant ship *Mayaguez*, traveling from Hong Kong to Sattahip, Thailand, was seized by Cambodians. Two days later the United States recovered the vessel and its crew, but only after President Ford had ordered air strikes against Cambodia and called on Marine ground forces.

As details of the capture trickled in, Ford's action looked less and less appealing. Approximately 41 Americans lost their lives trying to rescue the 39 crewmen. The administration spent little effort probing diplomatic avenues before resorting to force. The quality of military intelligence was not reassuring. The Marines suffered heavy casualties during the assault on Koh Tang Island, under the erroneous impression that the crewmen were being detained there. A punitive spirit seemed to infuse the operations. The United States bombed the Cambodian mainland *after* the crew had been released. A 15,000-pound bomb—the largest conventional bomb in America's arsenal—was dropped on a Cambodian island that measured just a few square miles.[110]

110. "War Powers: A Test of Compliance"; "Seizure of the Mayaguez," hearings before the House Committee on International Relations, 94th Cong., 1st Sess. (1975); and statement by

In 1980 President Carter reported to Congress on the use of military force in his unsuccessful attempt to rescue American hostages in Iran. In reporting "consistent" with the War Powers Resolution, he relied on the President's authority as Chief Executive and Commander in Chief. Although Carter's effort to consult with Congress was no better than Ford's, there was little criticism from legislators. However, Secretary of State Cyrus Vance resigned to protest the rescue operation.[111]

Military initiatives by President Reagan in 1982 and 1983 in Lebanon highlighted another weakness of the War Powers Resolution. Although hostilities in Lebanon were not merely "imminent" but actual, Reagan sent in troops without reporting under Section 4(a)(1) of the War Powers Resolution. By merely reporting in a manner "consistent" with the resolution, he did not set in motion the clock that would have limited military action to 60 to 90 days unless Congress specifically authorized an extension.[112]

Reagan's refusal to trigger the clock meant that Congress had to pass legislation to invoke Section 4(a)(1). In passing this legislation in the fall of 1983, Congress gave the administration authority for 18 months, deliberately allowing military forces to remain in Lebanon throughout the 1984 election year without further legislative action. Members supported this massive delegation by reasoning that Reagan, upon signing the bill, would concede the legitimacy of the process established by the War Powers Resolution. Instead, Reagan made it clear that he might continue military operations beyond the 18-month period without reauthorization by Congress.[113] But by the spring of 1984 he had withdrawn the Marines from Lebanon.

In 1986 President Reagan ordered bomb strikes on facilities and military installations in Libya. There was no meaningful consultation with Congress on this use of force. Reagan advised Congress that he had taken the actions pursuant to his authority as Commander in Chief.[114] He defended the air strikes against Libya as an act of "self-defense" and a preemptive strike designed to "deter acts of terrorism by Libya."[115]

Senator Javits, 121 Cong. Rec. 18312–13 (1975). See also Jordan J. Paust, "The Seizure and Recovery of the Mayaguez," 85 Yale L. J. 774 (1976); Robert Zutz, "The Recapture of the S.S. Mayaguez: Failure of the Consultation Clause of the War Powers Resolution," 8 N.Y.U. J. Int'l L. & Pol. 457 (1976). In 1980 a federal district judge upheld Ford's action in *Mayaguez* as immune from judicial scrutiny under the political question doctrine; Rappenecker v. United States, 509 F.Supp. 1024 (N.D. Cal. 1980).

111. Cong. Q. Wkly Rept., May 3, 1980, at 1200.
112. Public Papers of the Presidents, 1982 (II), at 1238.
113. Public Papers of the Presidents, 1983 (II), at 1367–68, 1444–45.
114. Public Papers of the Presidents, 1986 (I), at 407.
115. Id. at 478.

On four occasions during the 1980s, members of Congress went to court to charge that President Reagan had violated the War Powers Resolution by taking military actions in El Salvador, Grenada, Nicaragua, and the Persian Gulf. In all these cases, federal courts advised Congress that it had to assert its own legislative powers to constrain the President and not look initially for judicial relief.[116]

On December 20, 1989, President George H. W. Bush ordered U.S. military forces into Panama, citing five justifications: to protect the lives of American citizens there, to defend democracy in Panama, to combat drug trafficking, to protect the integrity of the Panama Canal Treaty, and to bring the Panamanian strongman General Manuel Noriega "to justice in the United States."[117] The idea of invading another country, particularly one in Central America, and toppling its government for the reasons Bush cited seemed to be a throwback to nineteenth-century American adventurism. On February 7, 1990, the House of Representatives passed a resolution stating that the U.S. action in Panama "was a response to a unique set of circumstances, and does not undermine the commitment of the government of the United States to the principle of nonintervention in the internal affairs of other countries."[118]

In August 1990 President Bush sent U.S. troops to Saudi Arabia and neighboring countries after Iraq invaded Kuwait. The administration's justifications were numerous: protection of Saudi and Kuwaiti sovereignty, deterrence of Iraqi aggression, maintenance of security and stability in the Persian Gulf, protection of American citizens abroad, and retention of access to Middle East oil. President Bush claimed that he did not need congressional authorization to take offensive action against Iraq, but under the Constitution, the President has limited authority to take unilateral military action for defensive, not offensive, purposes. On January 8, 1991, President Bush asked Congress to pass legislation authorizing military action against Iraq. Congress enacted that legislation four days later after extensive debate.

In two decisions on December 13, 1990, U.S. district courts rejected legal challenges to the sending of troops to Saudi Arabia. In *Ange v. Bush* it was held that the President's deployment order presented nonjusticiable political questions.[119] In *Dellums v. Bush* the court ruled that the issue was not ready

116. Crockett v. Reagan, 558 F.Supp. 893 (D.D.C. 1982), aff'd, Crockett v. Reagan, 720 F.2d 1355 (D.C. Cir. 1983); Conyers v. Reagan, 578 F.Supp. 324 (D.D.C. 1984), dismissed as moot, Conyers v. Reagan, 765 F.2d 1124 (D.C. Cir. 1985); Sanchez-Espinoza v. Reagan, 568 F.Supp. 596 (D.D.C. 1983), aff'd, Sanchez-Espinoza v. Reagan, 770 F.2d 202 (D.C. Cir. 1985); Lowry v. Reagan, 676 F.Supp. 333 (D.D.C. 1987), aff'd, No. 87-5426 (D.C. Cir. 1988).

117. Public Papers of the Presidents, 1989 (II), at 1722–23.

118. 136 Cong. Rec. 1507 (1990).

119. Ange v. Bush, 752 F.Supp. 509 (D.D.C. 1990).

for judicial determination, but it also rejected many of the sweeping claims for presidential war-making prerogatives presented by the Justice Department. The court concluded that if Congress confronted the President and the President refused to accept a statutory restriction, the issue might be ripe for the courts.[120]

The most striking transformation of the war-making power in the last half century has been the extent to which Presidents seek authority not from Congress but from international and regional institutions, particularly the United Nations and the North Atlantic Council. Truman in Korea, Bush I in Iraq, and Clinton in Haiti, Bosnia, and Kosovo—in each case the President circumvented Congress by going to either the UN or NATO. Truman's action was the most damaging because his decision to go to the UN Security Council rather than Congress was flatly contrary to the legislative history of the UN and the plain language of the UN Participation Act of 1945, which anticipated that the President would have to obtain specific statutory authority from Congress before entering into military activities with the UN.[121] Other Presidents have followed Truman's precedent.

In 1994 President Clinton threatened to invade Haiti after the UN Security Council adopted a resolution "inviting" all states, particularly those in the region of Haiti, to use "all necessary means" to remove the military leadership on that island. At a news conference on August 3, Clinton denied that he needed authority from Congress to invade Haiti: "Like my predecessors of both parties, I have not agreed that I was constitutionally mandated" to obtain the support of Congress.[122] In a televised address on September 15, he told the American public that he was prepared to use military force to invade Haiti, referring to the UN resolution and his willingness to lead a multinational force to "carry out the will of the United Nations."[123] Because of negotiations by former President Jimmy Carter, an invasion was not necessary.

In Bosnia, Clinton relied on a combination of Security Council resolutions and NATO decisions to carry out air strikes against Serb positions. These bombings began in February 1994 and continued through August 1995. At that point he contemplated sending in U.S. ground troops to help implement a Bosnian peace accord he had orchestrated. At a news conference on October 19, 1995, Clinton was asked whether he would send the troops if Congress disapproved. His response: "I am not going to lay down any of my constitutional prerogatives here today."[124] By the end of the year he ordered

120. Dellums v. Bush, 752 F.Supp. 1141 (D.D.C. 1990).
121. Fisher, Presidential War Power, at 81–95.
122. Public Papers of the Presidents, 1994 (II), at 1419.
123. Id. at 1559.
124. Public Papers of the Presidents, 1995 (II), at 1630; Fisher, Presidential War Power, at 183–92.

the deployment of 20,000 American ground troops to Bosnia without obtaining authority from Congress.

In 1999 President Clinton was prepared to take military action against Yugoslavia (reduced in size now to just Serbia and Montenegro). Unable to secure the support of the UN Security Council, this time he depended solely on NATO. Remarkably, he stated that he alone would decide whether "the United States would vote to give NATO the authority to carry out military strikes against Serbia."[125] He did not ask for a vote from Congress, even though in other NATO countries such as Germany and Italy the legislative bodies had to explicitly approve military action against Serbia.[126] The U.S. House of Representatives took a series of votes in March 1999 without ever expressly or implicitly offering support for the bombing operation that would begin within two weeks. The Senate voted 58 to 41 to support military air operations, but because the House did not agree, the Senate vote had no legal effect.[127] An effort by a member of the House to have the dispute resolved in court failed.[128]

The history of the War Powers Resolution has been disappointing to its authors and supporters, but the resolution was never more than a set of procedures to encourage greater collective judgment between Congress and the President. The 60- to 90-day window for presidential initiatives is a conspicuous contradiction of the principle of collective judgment. For the most part, military actions taken by Presidents after 1973 were short term: Grenada, Libya, Panama, and the like. Although the 60-day clock was not running legally, executive officials behaved as though it was. The war against Iraq in 1991 seemed to signal that long-term military actions require joint action by both branches. That was the practice after 9/11 when President George W. Bush went to Congress seeking statutory authority for military action against Afghanistan and Iraq.

Terrorist Attacks of 9/11

Presidential power expanded dramatically after the terrorist attacks of September 11, 2001. President Bush first turned to Congress for statutory authority to act militarily against al Qaeda and Taliban forces that had provided

125. Public Papers of the Presidents, 1998 (II), at 1765.
126. Fisher, Presidential War Power, at 199.
127. Id.
128. Campbell v. Clinton, 52 F.Supp.2d 34 (D.D.C. 1999), aff'd, Campbell v. Clinton, 203 F.3d 19 (D.C. Cir. 2000).

training and support for the 9/11 terrorists. The Authorization for Use of Military Force (AUMF) passed both houses of Congress on September 14 and was signed into law four days later. It cleared the Senate 98 to 0 and the House 420 to 1. The statute authorized the President to use "all necessary and appropriate force against those nations, organizations, or persons he determines planned, authorized, committed, or aided" the 9/11 attacks.[129] On October 9, when Bush notified Congress about U.S. combat activities in Afghanistan, he cited only what he regarded as independent constitutional powers for his actions, not the AUMF. He cited the statute for "support," not authority, and also for provisions regarding routine reporting requirements to Congress.[130]

President Bush acted unilaterally on November 13, 2001, to authorize the creation of military tribunals to try noncitizens who provided assistance to terrorists. His order closely tracked language in a proclamation and military order issued by President Roosevelt in 1942 regarding the military trial of eight German saboteurs. Some months after Roosevelt's action, the Supreme Court upheld the jurisdiction of the military tribunal, but the decision has been criticized over the years by Supreme Court Justices and scholarly analyses.[131] The Bush military order allowed the administration to designate both aliens and U.S. citizens as "enemy combatants" and to deny them the right to challenge their detention in court or to seek legal counsel. In two decisions in 2004 the Supreme Court checked and limited Bush's order,[132] forcing additional litigation in the lower courts. Two years later the Court flatly rejected the administration's claim that the President had inherent authority to create tribunals and determine their rules and procedures; instead, the Court held that the President was required to ask Congress for authorizing legislation.[133] In response, Congress passed the Military Commissions Act, signed into law on October 17, 2006. Portions of that statute, including sections that deny aliens designated as enemy combatants access to habeas petitions, were immediately challenged in court.

Having dispatched U.S. troops to Afghanistan in October 2001 to fight and defeat Taliban and al Qaeda forces, Bush next turned his attention to a ground invasion of Iraq to remove President Saddam Hussein from office and

---

129. 115 Stat. 224 (2001).

130. Public Papers of the Presidents, 2001 (II), at 1211–12.

131. Ex parte Quirin, 317 U.S. 1 (1942); Alpheus Thomas Mason, "Inter Arma Silent Leges: Chief Justice Stone's Views," 69 Harv. L. Rev. 806 (1956); Michal R. Belknap, "The Supreme Court Goes to War: The Meaning and Implications of the Nazi Saboteur Case," 89 Mil. L. Rev. 59 (1980); Michal Belknap, "Frankfurter and the Nazi Saboteurs," Yearbook 1982; S. Ct. Hist. Soc. 66; David J. Danelski, "The Saboteurs' Case," 1 J. S. Ct. Hist. 61 (1996); Louis Fisher, Nazi Saboteurs on Trial: A Military Tribunal and American Law (2003).

132. Rasul v. Bush, 542 U.S. 466 (2004); Hamdi v. Rumsfeld, 542 U.S. 507 (2004).

133. Hamdan v. Rumsfeld 126 S.Ct. 2749 (2006).

spread democracy throughout the Middle East. The administration made a number of unsubstantiated claims to justify the use of military force, including an alleged link between Iraq and al Qaeda. The administration also asserted that Iraq had purchased aluminum tubes to make nuclear weapons, possessed chemical and biological weapons, had mobile laboratories to make and disperse biological agents, and had sought uranium ore from a country in Africa. None of those assertions could be corroborated, but the administration was able to pressure Congress into passing the Iraq Resolution in October 2002.

The Democratic Senate had the power to block action on the legislation by arguing that the administration had failed to provide adequate evidence to support its assertions. Also, Senate Democrats could have insisted that a congressional vote be delayed until after the November elections, giving UN inspectors time to travel to Iraq and uncover intelligence about Iraqi weapons of mass destruction. In addition, taking a vote after the November elections would have duplicated the path taken by President Bush I in 1990, prior to the first war in Iraq. Nevertheless, without adequate information, Congress chose to vote on and pass the Iraq Resolution of 2002. Subsequent inspections by both U.S. and UN experts would demonstrate that Iraq possessed no weapons of mass destruction, it had not tried to purchase uranium ore, the mobile laboratories generated only hydrogen for weather balloons, and none of the other assertions had any basis in fact.[134]

Going to war on false information and false claims was reminiscent of the "second attack" that never occurred in the Gulf of Tonkin in 1964.[135] Failure to take the time to think through military intervention in the Middle East led to a poorly planned and incompetently executed war, at great cost to both the United States and Iraq. The result was not democracy in Iraq but political instability throughout the region. Just as Democrats paid a political price for the Vietnam War, so did the Iraq War lead to Republican losses in the 2006 elections and a precipitous drop in public support for the Bush administration. Neither party seemed to understand that overwhelming U.S. military superiority does not guarantee success against determined insurgents and that transferring congressional prerogatives over offensive wars to the President

134. Louis Fisher, "Deciding on War Against Iraq: Institutional Failures," 118 Pol. Sci. Q. 389 (2003); Louis Fisher, "Justifying War Against Iraq," in James A. Thurber, ed., Rivals for Power: Presidential-Congressional Relations (3d ed., 2005).

135. Fisher, Presidential War Power, at 129–33. See also Scott Shane, "Doubts Cast on Vietnam Incident, But Secret Study Stays Classified," New York Times, October 31, 2005, at A1. The NSA study, explaining that confusion over signals traffic led analysts to incorrectly conclude that a second attack had occurred, was declassified and released on November 3, 2005. Robert J. Hanyok, "Skunks, Bogies, Silent Hounds, and the Flying Fish: The Gulf of Tonkin Mystery, 2–4 August 1964," Cryptologic Quarterly.

undermines constitutional government and the system of checks and balances at home.[136]

The Bush administration triggered another constitutional dispute when the *New York Times* reported in December 2005 that executive officials had allowed the National Security Agency (NSA) to listen to telephone calls and intercept e-mails between international callers and individuals in the United States.[137] The NSA program violated the Foreign Intelligence Surveillance Act of 1978, which requires court warrants before monitoring this type of communication. The administration claimed that the President has inherent power to conduct national security eavesdropping and that any statute that attempted to limit or control that power was unconstitutional.[138] Dozens of lawsuits challenged this scope of presidential power.

The Politics of Comity

The post-Vietnam years underscore the need for the President to reach an accommodation with Congress in foreign policy and national defense. Unilateral actions by the President eventually become counterproductive. To sustain a successful policy, the executive branch must secure the support and cooperation of Congress. As Secretary of State Henry Kissinger noted in 1975: "Comity between the executive and legislative branches is the only possible basis for national action. The decade-long struggle in this country over executive dominance in foreign affairs is over. The recognition that the Congress is a co-equal branch of government is the dominant fact of national politics today. The executive accepts that the Congress must have both the sense and the reality of participation: foreign policy must be a shared enterprise."[139] The record in the five years after 9/11 reflected a Congress that was willing to take a backseat.

The President is not the sole voice in foreign affairs. He cannot, and should not, isolate himself from Congress and the general public, dismissing their

136. Thomas E. Ricks, Fiasco: The Military Adventure in Iraq (2006); Michael R. Gordon and Bernard E. Trainor, Cobra II: The Inside Story of the Invasion and Occupation of Iraq (2006); Ron Suskind, The One Percent Doctrine (2006); Bob Woodward, State of Denial: Bush at War, Part III (2006).

137. James Risen and Eric Lichtblau, "Bush Lets U.S. Spy on Callers Without Courts," New York Times, December 16, 2005, at A1.

138. U.S. Department of Justice, Office of Legal Counsel, "Legal Authorities Supporting the Activities of the National Security Agency Described by the President," January 19, 2006; John Cary Sims, "What NSA Is Doing . . . and Why It's Illegal," 33 Hastings Const. L. Q. 105 (2006); Jason McLure, "DOJ Is Steadily Losing Ground in Wiretap Cases," Nat'l L. J., September 11, 2006, at 21.

139. 72 Dept. of State Bull. 562 (1975).

contributions as narrow, local, or parochial. Patsy T. Mink, after dual careers in Congress and the State Department, warned that it "is folly to believe, as many in the top echelons of State and White House staff sincerely do, that good foreign policy necessarily stands above the pressures of domestic politics and constituent interests. Politics is the art of reconciling and educating, not of avoiding, those interests."[140] For that task the President needs members of Congress to develop and support effective international policies.

Secretary of Defense Caspar Weinberger, a strong defender of presidential power, recognized that combat troops should not be sent abroad unless there is congressional and public support. In an important address in 1984, he identified six major tests to be applied in cases of military force. One of the tests adds this caveat: "Before the U.S. commits combat forces abroad, there must be some reasonable assurance we will have the support of the American people and their elected Representatives in Congress. This support cannot be achieved unless we are candid in making clear the threats we face; the support cannot be sustained without continuing and close consultation. We cannot fight a battle with the Congress at home while asking our troops to win a war overseas."[141]

In testimony before the Senate Foreign Relations Committee in 1988, Abraham D. Sofaer, Legal Adviser to the State Department, offered a similar perspective: "This administration recognizes that Congress has a critical role to play in the determination of the circumstances under which the United States should commit its forces to actual or potential hostilities. No Executive policy or activity in this area can have any hope of success in the long term unless Congress and the American people concur in it and are willing to support its execution."[142]

Congress's influence depends on its willingness to act and take responsibility. Failure to act creates a vacuum that Presidents may try to fill. As Justice Jackson noted in the Steel Seizure Case of 1952, presidential authority reaches its highest level when the President acts pursuant to congressional authorization. His power is at its "lowest ebb" when he takes measures incompatible with the will of Congress. But in between those two categories lies a "zone of twilight" in which Congress neither grants nor denies authority. In such circumstances, "congressional inertia, indifference or quiescence may sometimes, at least as

140. Thomas M. Franck, ed., The Tethered Presidency 74 (1981).

141. Statement made by Caspar Weinberger, Secretary of Defense, news release, Office of the Assistant Secretary of Defense (Public Affairs), November 28, 1984.

142. "The War Power After 200 Years," hearings before the Senate Committee on Foreign Affairs, 100th Cong., 2d Sess. 144 (1988).

a practical matter, enable, if not invite, measures on independent presidential responsibility."[143]

It has been argued that the War Powers Resolution and other statutory provisions create uncertainty in the international arena, preventing the President from negotiating effectively with other nations. Foreign leaders supposedly see these legislative constraints as impediments to long-term commitments. But it would be worse for the President to go it alone, acting in isolation without the backing of Congress and the public. Other nations should feel more secure knowing that the President has consulted closely with congressional leaders in hammering out a policy that finds support in both branches.

143. Youngstown Co. v. Sawyer, 343 U.S. 579, 637 (1952).

10

CONCLUSIONS

The general drift of authority and responsibility toward the President over the past two centuries is unmistakable. This trend by itself should not be cause for alarm. More threatening is executive activity cut loose from legislative moorings and constitutional restrictions—presidential action no longer tethered by law. The record of recent decades is disturbing to those who fear unchecked executive power: Watergate during the Nixon administration; revelations of CIA abuses in the 1970s; the Iran-Contra scandal during the Reagan administration; military initiatives by President Clinton in Haiti, Bosnia, and Kosovo; and the assertion of "inherent" executive power by President Bush after 9/11.

The Supreme Court offers limited help in resolving the basic disputes of separation of powers. Over the last three decades it has bounced back and forth, sometimes embracing a functional, pragmatic approach, and at other times adopting a doctrinaire, formalistic model. The functional approach was used in 1974 when the Court rejected President Nixon's claim of an absolute power to determine the limits of executive privilege. Instead, the Court emphasized checks and balances and the need for a "workable" government.[1] Separation of powers entered the Court's equation only in the sense of preserving "the essential functions" of each branch.[2] No effort was made to establish rigid boundaries or to disallow the slightest encroachment.

Three years later, in another case involving Nixon's papers, the Court again viewed separation of powers in practical terms. It rejected the Court's view in 1935 that the three branches of government must remain "entirely free from the control or coercive influence, direct or indirect, of either of the others"[3] and supported the "more pragmatic, flexible approach" of James Madison and Justice Story.[4] The duty of judges was to inquire into the extent to which a statute prevented the executive branch from accomplishing "its constitutionally assigned functions . . . [and] whether that impact is justified by an overriding need to promote objectives within the constitutional authority of Congress."[5]

1. United States v. Nixon, 418 U.S. 683, 707 (1974).
2. Id.
3. Nixon v. Administrator of General Services, 433 U.S. 425, 441–42 (1977), quoting from Humphrey's Executor v. United States, 295 U.S. 602, 629 (1935).
4. Nixon v. Administrator of General Services, 433 U.S. at 442.
5. Id. at 443.

The Court thus permitted some sharing and overlapping of power, as indeed was anticipated by the framers.

However, in a series of rulings from 1982 to 1986, the Court advanced a doctrinaire notion of separated powers. In 1982 it upheld an absolute immunity for the President in civil cases, treating immunity as "a functionally mandated incident of the President's unique office, rooted in the constitutional tradition of the separation of powers and supported by our history."[6] The Court expressed concern about the "dangers of intrusion on the authority and functions of the Executive Branch."[7] The Court relaxed that doctrine in 1997 when it allowed a private party to sue the President, for unofficial acts, while he was still in office.[8]

The concern about intrusion appeared in another decision in 1982 striking down a statute that allowed bankruptcy judges to exercise judicial powers without the protection of life tenure and irreducible salaries guaranteed to Article III judges. The plurality opinion reasoned that Congress's attempt to establish bankruptcy courts under Article I "threatens to supplant completely our system of adjudication in independent Art. III tribunals and replace it with a system of 'specialized' legislative courts."[9] The Court seemed to go out of its way to present a worst-case scenario of one branch invading another. Nothing in the legislative history of the Bankruptcy Act suggested that Congress was positioning itself to take over the federal judiciary.

In *INS v. Chadha* (1983), the Court continued to endorse a highly formalistic model of separated powers. In striking down the legislative veto, the Court dismissed as irrelevant its usefulness for settling executive-legislative disagreements: "Convenience and efficiency are not the primary objectives— or the hall-marks—of democratic government."[10] The Court cited the framers' fear of despotism and the possibility of encroachments by one branch on another.[11] Although the Court denied that the branches are "hermetically" sealed from one another, it insisted that the Constitution divided government into "three defined categories, Legislative, Executive, and Judicial," and that the Court was compelled to resist the "hydraulic pressures inherent within each of the separate Branches to exceed the outer limits of its power."[12]

It was simplistic to believe that the legislative veto was merely a device by which Congress hoped to dominate the executive branch. The history of the legislative veto clearly shows that it originated as a desire by the executive

6. Nixon v. Fitzgerald, 457 U.S. 731, 749 (1982).
7. Id. at 754.
8. Clinton v. Jones, 520 U.S. 681 (1997).
9. Northern Pipeline Co. v. Marathon Pipe Line Co., 458 U.S. 50, 73 (1982).
10. INS v. Chadha, 462 U.S. 919, 944 (1983).
11. Id. at 946–51.
12. Id. at 951.

branch to exercise a much greater degree of legislative power. The framers did not object to a sharing or partial intermixture of powers. They were not doctrinaire advocates of a pure separation between branches. They knew that the "danger of tyranny or injustice lurks in unchecked power, not in blended power."[13] To the extent that the Supreme Court adopts unrealistic and impractical concepts of separated powers, its decisions will be largely ignored or circumvented, as has been the case with the continuation of committee vetoes after *Chadha*.

The Court persisted with a doctrinaire view of separated powers in *Bowsher v. Synar* (1986). In rejecting the assignment of executive duties to the Comptroller General because that officer is subject to removal by a joint resolution of Congress, the Court claimed that the framers provided for "a separate and wholly independent Executive Branch."[14] Wholly independent? What does that do to checks and balances and congressional oversight? The Court argued that except for impeachment proceedings, the President was responsible not to Congress "but to the people."[15] Anyone who follows government knows that the President is very much responsible to Congress. That responsibility results from a number of congressional powers and practical realities that have nothing to do with impeachment.

Nevertheless, the Court pushed ahead with its doctrine by agreeing with language in a 1935 decision that enshrined separation of powers at the cost of checks and balances: "The fundamental necessity of maintaining each of the three general departments of government entirely free from the control or coercive influence, direct or indirect, of either of the others, has often been stressed and is hardly open to serious question."[16] That dictum was fantastic for many reasons, but particularly because Congress obviously was not "entirely free" from the control or coercive influence of the Court when it declared the legislative veto and the Gramm-Rudman-Hollings Act unconstitutional.

As a final gesture to the cause of pure separation, the Court announced that once Congress "makes its choice in enacting legislation, its participation ends. Congress can thereafter control the execution of its enactment only indirectly—by passing new legislation."[17] No one who reads newspapers can believe that. The Court itself has acknowledged the power of Congress to investigate, issue subpoenas, and hold executive officials in contempt. Continued participation by Congress does not require the passage of public laws.

Oddly, on the same day that the Court released this unrealistic opinion, it resorted to pragmatism in upholding the power of the Commodity Futures

---

13. Kenneth Culp Davis, Administrative Law and Government 54 (1960).
14. Bowsher v. Synar, 478 U.S. 714, 722 (1986).
15. Id.
16. Id. at 725, quoting from Humphrey's Executor v. United States, 295 U.S. 602, 629 (1935).
17. Id. at 733–34.

Trading Commission to handle state law counterclaims in reparations proceedings before the agency. Litigants had argued that executive agencies could not adjudicate, but the Court turned aside their demand for sharp boundaries between the branches. In determining the extent to which a congressional decision to authorize adjudication by executive agencies "impermissibly threatens the institutional integrity of the Judicial Branch, the Court has declined to adopt formalistic and unbending rules."[18] The Court weighed a number of factors "with an eye to the practical effect" that congressional actions would have on the judiciary.[19]

A few years later, the Court jettisoned the rigid doctrines of *Chadha* and *Bowsher* and returned to a pragmatic reading of separation of powers. In *Morrison v. Olson* (1988), the Court upheld the power of Congress to authorize federal judges to appoint an independent counsel to prosecute high-ranking officials in the executive branch. Whereas in the bankruptcy court case (*Marathon*) the Court had seemed alarmed at the slightest interference by Congress in the judicial power, in *Morrison* it upheld the decision of Congress to permit the Attorney General to remove the independent counsel only for "good cause." The Court concluded that the good-cause standard did not "unduly trammel" executive authority; the President's need to control the independent counsel was not "so central" to the functioning of the executive branch as to require that the independent counsel serve at the pleasure of the President.[20] Furthermore, the Court stated that "we have never held that the Constitution requires that the three Branches of Government 'operate with absolute independence.'"[21] The experiment with an independent counsel ended in 1999 because of legislative and executive—not judicial—objections.

In 1989 the Court again embraced a pragmatic, functional attitude toward separation of powers, noting that the framers "did not require—and indeed rejected—the notion that the three Branches must be entirely separate and distinct."[22] Madison, the Court noted, recognized that the Constitution imposed on the branches "a degree of overlapping responsibility, a duty of interdependence as well as independence."[23] The Court explicitly adopted a "flexible understanding" of separation of powers.[24]

Given the Court's failure to develop a consistent and coherent theory of separated powers, as well as its record of avoiding many of the disputes between Congress and the President, it is not surprising that the meaning of separation of powers has, for the most part, developed outside the courts. The substance of

18. Commodity Futures Trading Comm'n v. Schor, 478 U.S. 833, 851 (1986).
19. Id.
20. Morrison v. Olson, 487 U.S. 654, 691 (1988).
21. Id. at 693–94, quoting from United States v. Nixon 418 U.S. 693, 707 (1974).
22. Mistretta v. United States, 488 U.S. 361, 380 (1989).
23. Id. at 381.
24. Id.

various clauses and provisions in the Constitution are the result of compromises and accommodations worked out by legislative and executive officials.[25]

In extraordinary situations the President may have to act promptly without clear constitutional or statutory support. Quick action is not a quality or purpose of a legislative assembly. Congress is essentially a deliberative body. Under extreme conditions it is better to let the President invoke emergency powers without claiming the slightest shred of legal support, perhaps even admitting that the action violates the law. That is what Lincoln did at the start of the Civil War. The burden is then on the President to justify the decision and present the case to Congress and the public. Both would be free, after careful examination of the evidence and the circumstances, to render a verdict of exoneration or condemnation.

The precise jurisdictions and fields of operation for Congress and the President will always elude us. Fortunately, the political process has a self-correcting mechanism, although it sometimes comes late and after heavy costs. Ambiguities in the Constitution permit one branch to infringe upon another. Generally this encroachment consists of brief raids in and out of the neutral zone. But at some point, after passing beyond a threshold of common sense and prudence, aggressive actions become counterproductive. They trigger revolts, leading to the recapture of ground taken not only in the most recent assault but in earlier offenses as well. It is not true that "let one occupant of the presidency exercise an additional power, and the advantage thus acquired is never abandoned."[26] Consider what happened with impoundment, the pocket veto, and executive privilege. Power distorted the judgment of the wielder. The moth circled too near the flame.

To call for "comity" and "consultation" is not enough. The record suggests that this is often an illusion. Representative Paul Findley remarked in 1976 that he had been in Congress for 16 years, most of that time serving on the House Committee on Foreign Affairs. The chairman of that committee, Clement Zablocki, had been in Congress for 28 years. Throughout that period—which spanned Democratic as well as Republican administrations—Zablocki had tried to encourage consultation by the executive branch, but Findley was hard put to think of any cases in which consultation actually occurred *in advance* of an executive decision. It was out of this "rather dismal experience," Findley said, that many members of Congress decided to advocate statutory remedies for executive agreements, the war power, and other conflicts with the executive branch.[27]

25. Louis Fisher, "Separation of Powers: Interpretation Outside the Courts," 18 Pepperdine L. Rev. 57 (1990).

26. Norman J. Small, *Some Presidential Interpretations of the Presidency* 198 (1932).

27. "Congressional Review of International Agreements," hearings before the House Committee on International Relations, 94th Cong., 2d Sess. 150 (1976).

If Congress has strong misgivings about an issue, it should resolve the matter by relying on language in a public law, not by informal understandings with executive officials. In 1977 members of the House were worried about being inundated by reorganization plans submitted by President Carter. OMB Director Bert Lance assured the House Committee on Government Operations that the administration appreciated this concern and would adhere to a reasonable timetable. Congress correctly insisted on specific language in the reorganization act to prohibit more than three plans from being before Congress at one time.[28] When in doubt, legislative policy belongs in the law.

This is a policy of prudence, not paranoia. We need to distinguish between objectives and the means used to attain them. Justice Jackson reminded us of our tendency to ignore the fundamentals of government: "The opinions of judges, no less than executives and publicists, often suffer the infirmity of confusing the issue of a power's validity with the cause it is invoked to promote, of confounding the permanent executive office with its temporary occupant. The tendency is strong to emphasize transient results upon policies—such as wages and stabilization—and lose sight of enduring consequences upon the balanced power structure of our Republic."[29] Theodore Sorensen, reflecting on his views of presidential power during and after his service with the Kennedy administration, warned against shortsighted reactions to immediate events and the failure to take into account the longer view: "I understand this error, having committed it myself a decade ago."[30]

The literature on the presidency, after emphasizing for many years such vague qualities as "vigor," "energy," and "persuasion," is now more cautious about the ends to which power may be put and the legal boundaries needed for presidential action. Commentators are taking into account not merely the exercise of power, directed for whatever purpose the President chooses, but also the source of authority, the rights secured under the Constitution, and the larger system of checks and balances.[31] Too often in the past the legal basis for action has been ignored in the eagerness for results and prompt measures.

Constitutional values are important even when they cannot be entirely satisfied. There is no need for dismay because we aim high and fall short. Machiavelli, often portrayed as the father of political expediency, encouraged us to set high standards:

A prudent man will always choose to take paths beaten by great men and to imitate those who have been especially admirable, in order that if

---

28. 91 Stat. 30, sec. 903(b) (1977); "Providing Reorganization Authority to the President," hearings before the House Committee on Government Operations, 95th Cong., 1st Sess. 43–44 (1977).

29. Youngstown Co. v. Sawyer, 343 U.S. 579, 634 (1952).

30. Theodore C. Sorensen, Watchmen in the Night xvi (1975).

31. John Hart, "Presidential Power Revisited," 25 Pol. Stud. 48 (1977).

his ability does not reach theirs, at least it may offer some suggestion of it; and he will act like prudent archers, who, seeing that the mark they plan to hit is too far away and knowing what space can be covered by the power of their bows, take an aim much higher than their mark, not in order to reach with their arrows so great a height, but to be able, with the aid of so high an aim, to attain their purpose.[32]

The framers of the Constitution settled on a single executive in order to foster unity, responsibility, dispatch, expertise, and a national perspective. To an impressive extent, the office of the presidency has alleviated many of the defects experienced by the Continental Congress. Yet the qualities originally anticipated of the executive have undergone profound transformations. Surely it is arbitrary to highlight the unifying quality of the President. Just as easily we can look at the fragmentation of the executive branch and the many groups within it competing for control. Special interests seek representation within the administration just as they do within Congress. In ways similar to a legislature, these groups barter with one another and conduct their own form of logrolling. With heartless accuracy, Alfred de Grazia reminded us some time ago that the President is "a Congress with a skin thrown over him."[33] We need to pierce the skin and comprehend the forces underneath.

The President remains responsible for the operation of the executive branch, but often only in a technical and formal sense. Vast areas are subdelegated to remote sectors of the executive branch (and even to the private sector). Presidents and staff assistants with unusual diligence and energy find themselves overwhelmed by the task. Joseph Califano, who served as an assistant to President Lyndon Johnson in the area of domestic affairs, doubted that he ever met, "much less consulted or helped guide, more than one-third of these noncabinet agency and commission heads. Hyperactive as he was, President Johnson met even fewer of them."[34] Congress is frequently advised to confine its activities to "broad policy" questions and leave "day-to-day" matters to the executive branch. A similar division of labor takes place within the administration. The President is advised to concentrate on broad policy while delegating details to departments and agencies. Political power generally comes with details, not with broad frameworks.

Executive officials are often so absorbed by operations, tactics, and short-run goals that they lose sight of national objectives, other than the raising of campaign contributions and securing the President's reelection. The 1972

32. Allan Gilbert, trans., Machiavelli: The Chief Works and Others, 1, 24–25 (1965), from The Prince, ch. 6.

33. Alfred de Grazia, Republic in Crisis 72 (1965).

34. Joseph A. Califano Jr., A Presidential Nation 23 (1975).

campaign was conspicuous for its bartering of the public interest. The Internal Revenue Service, the Federal Bureau of Investigation, the Central Intelligence Agency, and other agencies were used by the White House to violate the constitutional rights of citizens. Raised to high visibility were the administration's relationships with such special interests as International Telephone and Telegraph, milk producers' cooperatives, and grain exporters.[35]

Congress is not innocent in such matters, but we expect the worst of legislators and at the same time believe in the high virtues of the President and his entourage. Recent decades reveal conspicuous examples of Presidents and executive officials releasing false claims and presenting as fact what is mere assertion on tenuous, suspect grounds. Agency officials, even when they have their facts correct, find it difficult to place them in perspective or part company with long-held assumptions and predilections. White House officials, by necessity generalists, may ignore agency expertise when it fails to dovetail with the political needs of the President.

The strength of Congress is its capacity for diversity and openness (relative to the executive branch)—the opportunity it provides for the expression of different sentiments, opinions, and values. It is a disorderly operation and disappointing to those who want firm direction and quick action. But this free play of ideas, as well as the freedom not to move until the time is right, is essential to democratic government. What is needed from Congress is the daily grind of overseeing administration policies, passing judgment on them, and behaving with confidence as a coequal branch. That takes courage and an understanding of constitutional responsibilities.

Congress may stand against the President or it may stand behind him, but it should not stand aside as it did year after year during the Vietnam War and more recently the second Iraq War, looking the other way and occasionally complaining about executive usurpation. There, the crucial ingredient is will power, not constitutional power. Congressional influence depends on more than access to information, additional staff, or a revamping of procedure and organization. Congress must be willing to participate actively in questions of national policy, challenging Presidents and contesting their actions. Issues need the thorough exploration and ventilation that only Congress can provide. We must learn, especially when the temptation is great, to resist legal shortcuts because "the cause is good" or it is "the right thing to do." The door is then left open for capricious acts we may later deplore.

---

35. "The Final Report of the Select Committee on Presidential Campaign Activities," S. Rept. No. 981, 93d Cong., 2d Sess. (June 1974).

APPENDIX
THE CONSTITUTION OF THE UNITED STATES OF AMERICA
(SELECTIONS)

We the people of the United States, in order to form a more perfect Union, establish Justice, insure domestic Tranquility, provide for the common defence, promote the general Welfare, and secure the Blessings of Liberty to ourselves and our Posterity, do ordain and establish this CONSTITUTION for the United States of America.

Article I

Section 1

All legislative Powers herein granted shall be vested in a Congress of the United States, which shall consist of a Senate and a House of Representatives.

Section 2

. . . .
The House of Representatives . . . shall have the sole Power of Impeachment.

Section 3

. . . .
The Senate shall have the sole Power to try all Impeachments. When sitting for that Purpose, they shall be on Oath or Affirmation. When the President of the United States is tried, the Chief Justice shall preside: And no Person shall be convicted without the Concurrence of two thirds of the Members present.

Judgment in Cases of Impeachment shall not extend further than to removal from Office, and disqualification to hold and enjoy any Office of honor, Trust or Profit under the United States; but the Party convicted shall nevertheless be liable and subject to Indictment, Trial, Judgment and Punishment, according to Law.

. . . .

Section 6

The Senators and Representatives shall receive a Compensation for their Services, to be ascertained by Law [*Ascertainment Clause*], and paid out of the Treasury of the United States. They shall in all Cases, except Treason, Felony, and Breach of the Peace, be privileged from Arrest during their Attendance at the Session of their respective Houses, and in going to and returning from the same; and for any Speech or Debate in either House, they shall not be questioned in any other Place [*Speech or Debate Clause*].

No Senator or Representative shall, during the Time for which he was elected, be appointed to any civil Office under the Authority of the United States, which shall have been created, or the Emoluments whereof shall have been encreased during such time [*Ineligibility Clause*]; and no Person holding any Office under the United States, shall be a Member of either House during his Continuance in Office [*Incompatibility Clause*].

Section 7

All Bills for raising Revenue shall originate in the House of Representatives; but the Senate may propose or concur with Amendments as on other Bills.

Every Bill which shall have passed the House of Representatives and the Senate, shall, before it becomes a Law, be presented to the President of the United States [*Presentment or Presentation Clause*]; if he approves he shall sign it, but if not he shall return it, with his Objections to that House in which it shall have originated, who shall enter the Objections at large on their Journal, and proceed to reconsider it. If after such Reconsideration two thirds of that House shall agree to pass the Bill it shall be sent, together with the Objections, to the other House, by which it shall likewise be reconsidered, and if approved by two thirds of that House, it shall become a Law. But in all such Cases the Votes of both Houses shall be determined by Yeas and Nays, and the Names of the Persons voting for and against the Bill shall be entered on the Journal of each House respectively. If any Bill shall not be returned by the President within ten Days (Sundays excepted) after it shall have been presented to him, the Same shall be a Law, in like Manner as if he had signed it, unless the Congress by their Adjournment prevent its Return, in which Case it shall not be a Law.

Every Order, Resolution, or Vote to which the Concurrence of the Senate and House of Representatives may be necessary (except on a question of Adjournment) shall be presented to the President of the United States [*Presentment or Presentation Clause*]; and before the Same shall take Effect, shall be approved by him, or being disapproved by him, shall be repassed by two thirds of the Senate and House of Representatives, according to the Rules and Limitations prescribed in the Case of a Bill.

Section 8

The Congress shall have Power To lay and collect Taxes, Duties, Imposts and Excises, to pay the Debts and provide for the common Defence and general Welfare of the United States; but all Duties, Imposts and Excises shall be uniform throughout the United States;

To borrow money on the Credit of the United States;

To regulate Commerce with foreign Nations, and among the several States, and with the Indian Tribes;

To establish an uniform Rule of Naturalization, and uniform Laws on the subject of Bankruptcies throughout the United States;

To coin Money, regulate the Value thereof, and of foreign Coin, and fix the Standard of Weights and Measures;

To provide for the Punishment of counterfeiting the Securities and current Coin of the United States;

To establish Post Offices and Post Roads;

To promote the Progress of Science and useful Arts, by securing for limited Times to Authors and Inventors the exclusive Right to their respective Writings and Discoveries;

To constitute Tribunals inferior to the supreme Court;

To define and punish Piracies and Felonies committed on the high Seas, and Offenses against the Law of Nations;

To declare War, grant Letters of Marque and Reprisal, and make Rules concerning Captures on Land and Water;

To raise and support Armies, but no Appropriation of Money to that Use shall be for a longer Term than two Years;

To provide and maintain a Navy;

To make Rules for the Government and Regulation of the land and naval Forces;

To provide for calling forth the Militia to execute the Laws of the Union, suppress Insurrections and repel Invasions;

To provide for organizing, arming, and disciplining the Militia, and for governing such Part of them as may be employed in the Service of the United States, reserving to the States respectively, the Appointment of the Officers, and the Authority of training the Militia according to the discipline prescribed by Congress;

To exercise exclusive Legislation in all Cases whatsoever, over such District (not exceeding ten Miles square) as may, by Cession of particular States, and the acceptance of Congress, become the Seat of the Government of the United States, and to exercise like Authority over all Places purchased by the Consent of the Legislature of the State in which the Same shall be, for the Erection of Forts, Magazines, Arsenals, dock-Yards, and other needful Buildings;—And

To make all Laws which shall be necessary and proper for carrying into Execution the foregoing Powers, and all other Powers vested by this Constitution in the Government of the United States, or in any Department or Officer thereof.

Section 9

. . . .

The privilege of the Writ of Habeas Corpus shall not be suspended, unless when in Cases of Rebellion or Invasion the public Safety may require it.

No Bill of Attainder [*Bill of Attainder Clause*] or ex post facto Law shall be passed.

. . . .

No Money shall be drawn from the Treasury, but in Consequence of Appropriations made by Law; and a regular Statement and Account of the Receipts and Expenditures of all public Money shall be published from time to time [*Statement and Account Clause*].

. . . .

Article II

Section 1

The executive Power shall be vested in a President of the United States of America. He shall hold his Office during the Term of four Years, and, together with the Vice-President, chosen for the same Term, be elected, as follows.

. . . .

The President shall, at stated Times, receive for his Services, a Compensation, which shall neither be encreased nor diminished during the Period for which he shall have been elected, and he shall not receive within that Period any other Emolument from the United States, or any of them.

Before he enters on the Execution of his Office, he shall take the following Oath or Affirmation:—"I do solemnly swear (or affirm) that I will faithfully execute the Office of President of the United States, and will to the best of my Ability, preserve, protect and defend the Constitution of the United States."

Section 2

The President shall be Commander in Chief of the Army and Navy of the United States, and of the Militia of the several States, when called into the actual Service of the United States; he may require the Opinion in writing, of the principal Officer in each of the executive Departments, upon any subject relating to the Duties of their respective Offices, and he shall have Power to grant Reprieves and Pardons of Offenses against the United States, except in Cases of Impeachment.

He shall have Power, by and with the Advice and Consent of the Senate, to make Treaties, provided two thirds of the Senators present concur; and he shall nominate, and by and with the Advice and Consent of the Senate, shall appoint Ambassadors, other public Ministers and Consuls, Judges of the supreme Court, and all other Officers of the United States, whose Appointments are not herein otherwise provided for, and which shall be established by Law: but the Congress may by Law vest the Appointment of such inferior Offices, as they think proper, in the President alone, in the Courts of Law, or in the Heads of Departments.

The President shall have Power to fill up all Vacancies that may happen during the Recess of the Senate, by granting Commissions which shall expire at the End of their next Session.

Section 3

He shall from time to time give to the Congress Information of the State of the Union, and recommend to their Consideration such Measures as he shall judge necessary and expedient; he may, on extraordinary Occasions, convene both Houses, or either of them, and in Cases of Disagreement between them, with Respect to the Time of Adjournment, he may adjourn them to such Time as he shall think proper; he shall receive Ambassadors and other public Ministers; he shall take Care that the Laws be faithfully executed, and shall Commission all the Officers of the United States.

Section 4

The President, Vice-President and all civil Officers of the United States, shall be removed from Office on Impeachment for, and Conviction of, Treason, Bribery, or other high Crimes and Misdemeanors.

Article III

Section 1

The judicial Power of the United States shall be vested in one supreme Court, and in such inferior Courts as the Congress may from time to time ordain and establish. The Judges, both of the supreme and inferior Courts, shall hold their Offices during good Behaviour, and shall, at stated Times, receive for their Services a Compensation which shall not be diminished during their Continuance in Office [*No-Diminution Clause*].

. . . .

Section 3

Treason against the United States, shall consist only in levying War against them, or, in adhering to their Enemies, giving them Aid and Comfort. No Person shall be convicted of Treason unless on the Testimony of two Witnesses to the same overt Act, or on Confession in open Court.

The Congress shall have Power to declare the Punishment of Treason, but no Attainder of Treason shall work Corruption of Blood, or Forfeiture except during the Life of the Person attainted.

. . . .

Article IV

Section 3

. . . .

The Congress shall have Power to dispose of and make all needful Rules and Regulations respecting the Territory or other Property belonging to the United States [*Property Clause*]; and nothing in this Constitution shall be so constructed as to Prejudice any Claims of the United States, or of any particular state.

Section 4

The United States shall guarantee to every State in this Union a Republican Form of Government, and shall protect each of them against Invasion; and on Application of the Legislature, or of the Executive (when the Legislature cannot be convened) against domestic Violence.

. . . .

Article VI

All Debts contracted and Engagements entered into, before the Adoption of this Constitution, shall be as valid against the United States under this Constitution, as under the Confederation.

This Constitution, and the Laws of the United States which shall be made in Pursuance thereof; and all Treaties made, or which shall be made, under the Authority of the United States, shall be the supreme Law of the Land; and the Judges in every State shall be bound thereby, any Thing in the Constitution or Laws of any State to the contrary not withstanding.

The Senators and Representatives before mentioned, and the Members of the several State Legislatures, and all executive and judicial Officers, both of the United States and of the several States, shall be bound by Oath or Affirmation, to support this Constitution; but no religious Test shall ever be required as a Qualification to any Office or public Trust under the United States.

. . . .

Amendments[1]

Amendment I

Congress shall make no law respecting an establishment of religion, or prohibiting the free exercise thereof; or abridging the freedom of speech, or of the press; or the right of the people peaceably to assemble, and to petition the Government for a redress of grievances.

Amendment II

A well regulated Militia, being necessary to the security of a free State, the right of the people to keep and bear Arms, shall not be infringed.

Amendment III

No Soldier shall, in time of peace be quartered in any house, without the consent of the Owner, nor in time of war; but in a manner to be prescribed by law.

Amendment IV

The right of the people to be secure in their persons, houses, papers, and effects, against unreasonable searches and seizures, shall not be violated, and no Warrants shall issue, but upon probable cause, supported by Oath or affirmation, and particularly describing the place to be searched, and the persons or things to be seized.

Amendment V

No person shall be held to answer for a capital, or otherwise infamous crime, unless on a presentment or indictment of a Grand Jury, except in cases arising in the land or naval forces, or in the Militia, when in actual service in time of War or public danger; nor shall any person be subject for the same offense to be twice put in jeopardy of life or limb, nor shall be compelled in any criminal case to be a witness against himself, nor be deprived of life, liberty, or property, without due process of law; nor shall private property be taken for public use, without just compensation.

Amendment VI

In all criminal prosecutions, the accused shall enjoy the right to a speedy and public trial, by an impartial jury of the State and district wherein the crime shall have been committed, which district shall have been previously ascertained by law, and to be informed of the nature and cause of the accusation; to be confronted with the witnesses against him; to have compulsory process for obtaining witnesses in his favor, and to have the Assistance of Counsel for his defence.

Amendment VII

In suits at common law, where the value in controversy shall exceed twenty dollars, the right of trial by jury shall be preserved, and no fact tried by jury, shall be other-

---

1. The first ten Amendments were adopted in 1791.

wise re-examined in any Court of the United States, than according to the rules of the common law.

Amendment VIII

Excessive bail shall not be required, nor excessive fines imposed, nor cruel and unusual punishments inflicted.

Amendment IX

The enumeration in the Constitution, of certain rights, shall not be construed to deny or disparage others retained by the people.

Amendment X

The powers not delegated to the United States by the Constitution, nor prohibited by it to the States, are reserved to the States respectively, or to the people.

. . . .

SUGGESTED READINGS

Chapter 1. Constitutional Struggles

Alfange, Dean Jr. "The Supreme Court and the Separation of Powers: A Welcome Return to Normalcy?" 58 G.W. L. Rev. 668 (1990).

Bessette, Joseph M., and Jeffrey Tulis, eds. The Presidency in the Constitutional Order (1981).

Bondy, William. "The Separation of Governmental Powers in History, in Theory, and in the Constitution," Studies in History, Economics, and Public Law, vol. 5, no. 2 (Columbia University, 1896).

Bruff, Harold H. Balance of Forces: Separation of Powers Law in the Administrative State (2006).

Carpenter, William S. "The Separation of Powers in the Eighteenth Century," 22 Am. Pol. Sci. Rev. 32 (1928).

Fisher, Louis. "The Efficiency Side of Separated Powers," 5 J. Am. Studies 113 (1971).

Glennon, Michael J. "The Use of Custom in Resolving Separation of Powers Disputes," 64 B.U. L. Rev. 109 (1984).

Goldwin, Robert A., and Art Kaufman, eds. Separation of Powers—Does It Still Work? (1986).

Gwyn, W. B. "The Meaning of the Separation of Powers," Tulane Series in Political Science, vol. 9 (1965).

Harriger, Kay J., ed. Separation of Powers: Documents and Commentary (2003).

McDowell, Gary L., ed. Taking the Constitution Seriously: Essays on the Constitution and Constitutional Law (1981).

Pennock, J. Ronald, and John W. Chapman, eds. Constitutionalism (1979).

Radin, Max. "The Doctrine of the Separation of Powers in Seventeenth Century Controversies," 86 U. Pa. L. Rev. & Am. L. Reg. 842 (1938).

Sargentich, Thomas O. "The Limits of the Parliamentary Critique of the Separation of Powers," 34 Wm & Mary L. Rev. 679 (1993).

Sharp, Malcolm P. "The Classical Doctrine of the 'Separation of Powers,'" 2 U. Chi. L. Rev. 385 (1935).

Wormuth, Francis D. The Origins of Modern Constitutionalism (1949).

Wright, Benjamin F. Jr. "The Origins of the Separation of Powers in America," 13 Economica 169 (1933).

Chapter 2. Appointment Powers

Abraham, Henry J. Justices and Presidents: A Political History of Appointments to the Supreme Court (1992).

Carrier, Michael A. "When Is the Senate in Recess for Purposes of the Recess Appointments Clause?" 92 Mich. L. Rev. 2204 (1994).

Carter, Stephen L. The Confirmation Mess: Cleaning Up the Federal Appointments Process (1994).

Chase, Harold W. Federal Judges: The Appointing Process (1972).

Grossman, Joel B. Lawyers and Judges: The ABA and the Politics of Judicial Selection (1965).

Harris, Joseph P. The Advice and Consent of the Senate: A Study of the Confirmation of Appointments by the United States Senate (1953).

James, Louis C. "Senatorial Rejections of Presidential Nominations to the Cabinet: A Study in Constitutional Custom," 3 Ariz. L. Rev. 232 (1961).

Katzenbach, Nicholas DeB. "The Roles of Executive and Legislative Branches in Judicial Appointments," New York L. J. (November 3, 1971).

MacKenzie, G. Calvin. The Politics of Presidential Appointments (1981).

Morganston, Charles E. The Appointing and Removal Power of the President of the United States, reprinted as S. Doc. No. 172, 70th Cong., 2d Sess. (1929).

Reznick, Lois. "Temporary Appointment Power of the President," 41 U. Chi. L. Rev. 146 (1973).

Sollenberger, Mitchel A. "The President 'Shall Nominate': Exclusive or Shared Constitutional Power?" 36 Pres. Stud. Q. 714 (2006).

Tribe, Laurence H. God Save This Honorable Court (1986).

Chapter 3. Theory in a Crucible: The Removal Power

Cirillo, Richard A. "Abolition of Federal Offices as an Infringement on the President's Power to Remove Federal Officers: A Reassessment of Constitutional Doctrines," 42 Ford. L. Rev. 562 (1974).

Corwin, Edward S. The President's Removal Power Under the Constitution (1927).

Donovan, William J., and Ralston R. Irvine. "The President's Power to Remove Members of Administrative Agencies," 21 Corn. L. Q. 215 (1936).

Fisher, Louis. "Congress and the Removal Power," 10 Congress and the Presidency 63 (1983).

Frug, Gerald E. "Does the Constitution Prevent the Discharge of Civil Service Employees?" 124 U. Pa. L. Rev. 942 (1976).

Hart, James. "The Bearing of Myers v. United States upon the Independence of Federal Administrative Tribunals," 23 Am. Pol. Sci. Rev. 657 (1929).

———. The American Presidency in Action 155–248 (1948).

McBain, Howard Lee. "Consequences of the President's Unlimited Power of Removal," 4 Pol. Sci. Q. 596 (1926).

Miller, Charles A. The Supreme Court and the Uses of History 52–70, 205–10 (1969).

Richardson, Ivor L. M. "Problems in the Removal of Federal Civil Servants," 54 Mich. L. Rev. 219 (1955).

Thach, Charles C. Jr. The Creation of the Presidency 140–65 (1969 ed.).

U.S. Congress. "Power of the President to Remove Federal Officers," S. Doc. No. 174, 69th Cong., 2d Sess. (1926).

Chapter 4. Legislative Powers

Barber, Sotirios A. The Constitution and the Delegation of Congressional Power (1975).

Blachly, Frederick F., and Miriam E. Oatman. Administrative Legislation and Adjudication (1934).

Black, Henry Campbell. The Relation of the Executive Power to Legislation (1919).

Bruff, Harold H. "Presidential Power and Administrative Rulemaking," 88 Yale L. J. 451 (1979).

Cash, Robert B. "Presidential Power: Use and Enforcement of Executive Orders," 39 Notre Dame Lawyer 44 (1963).

Chamberlain, Lawrence H. The President, Congress, and Legislation (1946).

Cooper, Phillip J. By Order of the President: The Use and Abuse of Executive Direct Action (2002).

Fairlie, John A. "Administrative Legislation," 18 Mich. L. Rev. 181 (1920).

Fisher, Louis. "Delegating Power to the President," 19 J. Pub. L. 251 (1970).

———. "Laws Congress Never Made [Proclamations and Executive Orders]," 5 Constitution 59 (1993).

Fleishman, Joel L., and Arthur H. Aufses. "Law and Orders: The Problem of Presidential Legislation," 40 L. & Contemp. Prob. 1 (1976).

Foster, Stephen A. "The Delegation of Legislative Power to Administrative Officers," 7 Ill. L. Rev. 397 (1913).

Harlow, Ralph Volney. The History of Legislative Methods in the Period Before 1825 (1917).

Hart, James. "The Ordinance Making Powers of the President of the United States," Johns Hopkins University Studies in Historical and Political Science, series 43, no. 3 (1925).

Hebe, William. "Executive Orders and the Development of Presidential Power," 17 Vill. L. Rev. 688 (1972).

Jaffe, Louis. "Delegation of Legislative Power," ch. 2 of Judicial Control of Administrative Action (1965).

Merrill, Maurice H. "Standards—A Safeguard for the Exercise of Delegated Power," 47 Neb. L. Rev. 469 (1968).

Neighbors, William D. "Presidential Legislation by Executive Order," 37 U. Colo. L. Rev. 105 (1964).

Rosenberg, Douglas H. "Delegation and Regulatory Reform: Letting the President Change the Rules," 89 Yale L. J. 561 (1980).

Schoenbrod, David. Power Without Responsibility: How Congress Abuses the People Through Delegation (1993).

Stewart, Richard B. "The Reformation of American Administrative Law," 88 Harv. L. Rev. 1667 (1975).

Strobel, Mary H. "Delegation and Individual Rights," 56 So. Cal. L. Rev. 1321 (1983).

U.S. Congress. Executive Orders in Times of War and National Emergency, Senate Special Committee on National Emergencies and Delegated Powers, 93d Cong., 2d Sess. (Comm. Print June 1974).

Weeks, O. Douglas. "Legislative Power Versus Delegated Legislative Power," 25 Geo. L. J. 314 (1937).

Chapter 5. Vetoes: Presidential and Legislative

Clineberg, William A. "The President's Veto Power," 18 S.C. L. Rev. 732 (1966).

Condo, Joseph A. "The Veto of S. 3418: More Congressional Power in the President's Pocket?" 22 Cath. U. L. Rev. 385 (1973).

Cooper, Joseph, and Ann Cooper. "The Legislative Veto and the Constitution," 30 G.W. L. Rev. 467 (1962).

Cotter, Cornelius P., and J. Malcolm Smith. "Administrative Accountability to Congress: The Concurrent Resolution," 9 West. Pol. Q. 955 (1956).

Craig, Barbara Hinkson. Chadha: The Story of an Epic Constitutional Struggle (1988).

Derrick, Butler C. Jr. "Stitching the Hole in the President's Pocket: A Legislative Solution to the Pocket Veto Controversy," 31 Harv. J. on Legis. 371 (1994).

Elliott, E. Donald. "INS v. Chadha: The Administrative Constitution, the Constitution, and the Legislative Veto," 1983 Sup. Ct. Rev. 125.

Fisher, Louis. "Judicial Misjudgments about the Lawmaking Process: The Legislative Veto Case," 45 Pub. Adm. Rev. 705 (Special Issue, November 1985).

———. "The Legislative Veto: Invalidated, It Survives," 56 L. & Contemp. Prob. 273 (1993).

Fisher, Louis, and Neal Devins, "How Successfully Can the States' Item Veto Be Transferred to the President?" 75 Geo. L. J. 159 (1986).

Gibson, Martha Liebler. Managing Conflict: The Role of the Legislative Veto in American Foreign Policy (1994).

Gibson, Rankin M. "Congressional Concurrent Resolution: An Aid to Statutory Interpretation?" 37 Am. Bar Ass'n J. 421 (1951).

Ginnane, Robert W. "The Control of the Federal Administration by Congressional Resolutions and Committees," 66 Harv. L. Rev. 569 (1953).

Hoff, Samuel B. "The Presidential Pocket Veto: Its Uses and Legality," 6 J. Am. Hist. 188 (1994).

Kaiser, Frederick M. "Congressional Control of Executive Actions in the Aftermath of the Chadha Decision," 36 Adm. L. Rev. 239 (1984).

Kennedy, Edward M. "Congress, the President, and the Pocket Veto," 63 Va. L. Rev. 355 (1977).

Lee, Jong R. "Presidential Vetoes from Washington to Nixon," 37 J. Pol. 522 (1975).

Note. "The Presidential Veto Power: A Shallow Pocket," 70 Mich. L. Rev. 148 (1971).

———. "The Veto Power and Kennedy v. Sampson: Burning a Hole in the President's Pocket," 69 N.W. U. L. Rev. 587 (1974).

"Pocket Veto Legislation," 29 Record Ass'n Bar of the City of N.Y. 724 (1974).

Spitzer, Robert J. The Presidential Veto (1988).

Strauss, Peter L. "Was There a Baby in the Bathwater? A Comment on the Supreme Court's Legislative Veto Decision," Duke L. J. 789 1983.

Watson, Richard A. Presidential Vetoes and Public Policy (1993).

Chapter 6. Power over Knowledge: Seeking and Withholding Information

Berger, Raoul. Executive Privilege (1974).

Bishop, Joseph W. Jr. "The Executive's Right of Privacy: An Unresolved Constitutional Question," 66 Yale L. J. 477 (1957).

Breckenridge, Adam Carlyle. The Executive Privilege (1974).

Bush, Joel D. "Congressional-Executive Access Disputes: Legal Standards and Political Settlements," 9 J. of L. & Pol. 719 (1993).

Dimock, Marshall Edward. "Congressional Investigating Committees," Johns Hopkins University Studies in Historical and Political Science, series 47, no. 1 (1929).

Eberling, Ernest J. Congressional Investigations (1928).

Fisher, Louis. "Congressional Access to Information: Using Legislative Will and Leverage," 52 Duke L. J. 323 (2002).

————. The Politics of Executive Privilege (2004).

Hamilton, James. The Power to Probe: A Study of Congressional Investigations (1976).

Hamilton, James, and John C. Grabow. "A Legislative Proposal for Resolving Executive Privilege Disputes Precipitated by Congressional Subpoenas," 21 Harv. J. on Legis. 145 (1984).

Henkin, Louis. "The Right to Know and the Duty to Withhold: The Case of the Pentagon Papers," 120 U. Pa. L. Rev. 271 (1971).

Kramer, Robert, and Herman Marcuse. "Executive Privilege—A Study of the Period 1953–1960," 29 G.W. L. Rev. 623, 827 (April and June 1961).

McGeary, M. Nelson. The Developments of Congressional Investigative Power (1940).

————. "Congressional Investigations: Historical Development," 18 U. Chi. L. Rev. 425 (1951).

Murphy, John F. "Knowledge Is Power: Foreign Policy and Information Interchange Among Congress, the Executive Branch, and the Public," 49 Tulane L. Rev. 505 (1975).

Rourke, Francis E. "Administrative Secrecy: A Congressional Dilemma," 54 Am. Pol. Sci. Rev. 884 (1960).

————. Secrecy and Publicity (1966).

Rozell, Mark J. Executive Privilege: Presidential Power, Secrecy, and Accountability (2d ed., 2002).

Schlesinger, Arthur M. Jr., and Roger Bruns, eds. Congress Investigates, 1792–1974 (1975).

U.S. Congress. "Executive Privilege: The Withholding of Information by the Executive," hearing before the Senate Committee on the Judiciary, 92d Cong., 1st Sess. (1971).

Wright, Ronald F. "Congressional Use of Immunity Grants After Iran-Contra," 80 Minn. L. Rev. 407 (1995).

Younger, Irving. "Congressional Investigations and Executive Secrecy: A Study in the Separation of Powers," 20 U. Pitts. L. Rev. 755 (1959).

Chapter 7. The Power of the Purse

Banks, William C., and Peter Raven-Hansen. National Security Law and the Power of the Purse (1994).

Fisher, Louis. Presidential Spending Power (1975).

————. "Confidential Spending and Governmental Accountability," 47 G.W. L. Rev. 347 (1979).

————. "How Tightly Can Congress Draw the Purse Strings?" 83 Am. J. Int'l L. 758 (1989).

Futterman, Stanley N. "Toward Legislative Control of the C.I.A.," 4 N.Y.U. J. Int'l L. & Pol. 431 (1971).

Huzar, Elias. The Purse and the Sword: Control of the Army by Congress Through Military Appropriations, 1933–1950 (1950).

Note. "The CIA's Secret Funding and the Constitution," 83 Yale L. J. 608 (1975).

Powell, Fred Wilbur. Control of Federal Expenditures: A Documentary History, 1775–1894 (1939).

Schick, Allen. Congress and Money (1981).

Schwartzman, Berman. "Fiscal Oversight of the Central Intelligence Agency: Can Accountability and Confidentiality Coexist?" 7 N.Y.U. J. Int'l L. & Pol. 493 (1974).

U.S. Congress. "Whether Disclosure of Funds Authorized for Intelligence Activities Is in the Public Interest," hearings before the Senate Select Committee on Intelligence, 95th Cong., 1st Sess. (1977).

————. "Public Disclosure of the Aggregate Intelligence Budget Figure," hearing before the House Permanent Select Committee on Intelligence, 103d Cong., 2d Sess. (1994).

Walden, Jerrold L. "The C.I.A.: A Study in the Arrogation of Administrative Powers," 39 G.W. L. Rev. 55 (1970).

Wilmerding, Lucius Jr. The Spending Power (1943).

Chapter 8. Treaties and Executive Agreements

Adler, David Gray. "Termination of the ABM Treaty and the Political Question Doctrine: Judicial Succor for Presidential Power," 34 Pres. Stud. Q. 156 (2004).

Bestor, Arthur. "Separation of Powers in the Domain of Foreign Affairs: The Original Intent of the Constitution Historically Examined," 5 Seton Hall L. Rev. 529 (1974).

Cohen, Richard. "Self-Executing Executive Agreements: A Separation of Powers Problem," 24 Buff. L. Rev. 137 (1974).

Fisher, Louis. "Congressional Participation in the Treaty Process," 137 U. Pa. L. Rev. 1511 (1989).

Glennon, Michael J. "The Senate Role in Treaty Ratification," 77 Am. J. Int'l L. 257 (1983).

Johnson, Loch K. The Making of International Agreements (1984).

Mathews, Craig. "The Constitutional Power of the President to Conclude International Agreements," 64 Yale L. J. 345 (1955).

McClure, Wallace. International Executive Agreements (1941).

McDougal, Myres S., and Asher Lans. "Treaties and Congressional-Executive or Presidential Agreements: Interchangeable Instruments of National Policy," 54 Yale L. J. 181, 534 (1945).

Murphy, John F. "Treaties and International Agreements Other Than Treaties: Constitutional Allocation of Power and Responsibility Among the President, the House of Representatives, and the Senate," 23 U. Kans. L. Rev. 221 (1975).

Randall, Kenneth C. "The Treaty Power," 51 Ohio State L. J. 1089 (1990).

Rovine, Arthur W. "Separation of Powers and International Executive Agreements," 52 Ind. L. Rev. 397 (1977).

Slonin, Solomon. "Congressional-Executive Agreements," 14 Colum. J. Transnat'l L. 434 (1975).

Stevens, Charles J. "The Use and Control of Executive Agreements: Recent Congressional Initiatives," 20 Orbis 905 (1977).

Tomain, Joseph P. "Executive Agreements and the Bypassing of Congress," 8 J. Int'l L. & Econ. 129 (1973).

U.S. Congress. "Treaties and Other International Agreements: The Role of the United States Senate," a study prepared for the Senate Committee on Foreign Relations, 106th Cong., 2d Sess. (Comm. Print January 2001).

Chapter 9. The War Power

Adler, David Gray, and Larry N. George, eds. The Constitution and the Conduct of American Foreign Policy (1996).

Draper, Theodore. A Very Thin Line: The Iran-Contra Affairs (1991).

Ely, John Hart. War and Responsibility: Constitutional Lessons of Vietnam and Its Aftermath (1993).

Fisher, Louis. "The Korean War: On What Legal Basis Did Truman Act?" 89 Am. J. Int'l L. 21 (1995).

———. Nazi Saboteurs on Trial (2003).

———. Presidential War Power (2d ed., 2004).

———. Military Tribunals and Presidential Power (2005).

———. In the Name of National Security (2006).

Franck, Thomas M., ed. The Tethered Presidency: Congressional Restraints on Executive Power (1981).

Franck, Thomas M., and Edward Weisband. Foreign Policy by Congress (1979).

Glennon, Michael J. Constitutional Diplomacy (1990).

Henkin, Louis. Foreign Affairs and the United States Constitution (1996).

Javits, Jacob K. Who Makes War: The President Versus Congress (1973).

Jenkins, Gerald. "The War Powers Resolution: Statutory Limitation on the Commander in Chief," 11 Harv. J. Legis. 181 (1974).

Koh, Harold Hongju. The National Security Constitution (1990).

Lofgren, Charles A. "War-Making Under the Constitution: The Original Understanding," 81 Yale L. J. 672 (1972).

May, Ernest R., ed. The Ultimate Decision: The President as Commander in Chief (1951).

Pious, Richard M. The War on Terrorism and the Rule of Law (2006).

Reveley, W. Taylor III. War Powers of the President and Congress (1981).

Rossiter, Clinton. The Supreme Court and the Commander in Chief (1951).

Rostow, Eugene V. "Great Cases Make Bad Law: The War Powers Act," 50 Texas L. Rev. 833 (1972).

Smith, J. Malcolm, and Stephen Jurika. The President and National Security (1972).

Sofaer, Abraham D. War, Foreign Affairs and Constitutional Power: The Origins (1976).

Stern, Gary M., and Morton H. Halperin, eds. The U.S. Constitution and the Power to Go to War (1994).

Turner, Robert F. Repealing the War Powers Resolution: Restoring the Rule of Law in U.S. Foreign Policy (1991).

Whicker, Marcia Lynn, et al., eds. The Presidency and the Persian Gulf War (1993).

Wormuth, Francis D., and Edwin B. Firmage. To Chain the Dog of War: The War Power of Congress in History and Law (1989).

Yoo, John. The Powers of War and Peace (2005).

INDEX OF CASES

Skinner v. Mid-American Pipeline Co., 490
U.S. 212 (1989), 96

Slaughter-House Cases, 83 U.S. (16 Wall.)
36 (1872), 260n50

Smith v. Ehrlich, 430 F.Supp. 818 (D.D.C.
1976), 192

Snepp v. United States, 444 U.S. 507
(1980), 188

Sniadach v. Family Finance Corp., 395 U.S.
337 (1969), 68

Staebler v. Carter, 464 F.Supp. 585 (D.D.C.
1979), 41

State Highway Com'n of Missouri v. Volpe,
479 F.2d 1099 (8th Cir. 1973), 200

State of Iowa ex rel. State Highway Com'n
v. Brinegar, 512 F.2d 722 (8th Cir. 1975),
200

State of Minnesota v. Coleman, 391 F.Supp.
330 (D. Minn. 1975), 200

Steck v. Connally, 199 F.Supp. 104 (D.D.C.
1961), 82

Steelworkers v. Weber, 443 U.S. 193 (1979),
109

Stevens v. Carey, 483 F.2d 188 (7th Cir.
1973), 109

Stewart v. Kahn, 11 Wall. 493 (1870), 264

Stuart v. Laird, 5 U.S. (1 Cr.) 299 (1803),
18

Subpoena, In re, to Nixon, 360 U.S. 1
(D.D.C. 1973), 186

Talbot v. Seeman, 5 U.S. (1 Cr.) 1 (1801),
251

Tavoulareas v. Piro, 527 F.Supp. 676
(D.D.C. 1981), 167

Tenney v. Brandhove, 341 U.S. 367 (1951),
167

Texas v. White, 74 U.S. (7 Wall.) 700
(1869), 92

Totten, Administrator v. United States, 92
U.S. (2 Otto.) 105 (1875), 209

Touby v. United States, 500 U.S. 160
(1991), 96

Train v. City of New York, 420 U.S. 35
(1975), 201

Turner v. Kennedy, 332 F.2d 304 (D.C. Cir.
1964), 82

TVA v. Hill, 437 U.S. 153 (1978), 101

Ullmann v. United States, 350 U.S. 422
(1956), 163

Union Bridge Co. v. United States, 194 U.S.
364 (1907), 87

United Public Workers v. Mitchell, 330 U.S.
75 (1947), 29

United States v. Allocco, 303 F.2d 704 (2d
Cir. 1962), 44

United States v. Anderson, 9 Wall. 56
(1870), 264

United States v. AT&T, 419 F.Supp. 454
(D.D.C. 1976), 190

United States v. AT&T, 551 F.2d 384 (D.C.
Cir. 1976), 190

United States v. AT&T, 567 F.2d 121 (D.C.
Cir. 1977), 190

United States v. Belmont, 301 U.S. 324
(1937), 243

United States v. Bethlehem Steel, 315 U.S.
289 (1942), 264

United States v. Brewster, 408 U.S. 501
(1972), 167

United States v. California, 332 U.S. 19
(1947), 92

United States v. Chemical Foundation, 272
U.S. 1 (1926), 93

United States v. Curtiss-Wright Corp., 299
U.S. 304 (1936), 91–93, 105, 221

United States v. East Texas Motor Fr.
System, 564 F.2d 179 (5th Cir. 1977),
107

United States v. Ehrlichman, 376 F. Supp.
29 (D.D.C. 1974), 209

United States v. Eliason, 41 U.S. (16 Pet.)
291 (1842), 102

United States v. Ferreira, 54 U.S. (13 How.)
39 (1852), 25

United States v. Fort, 443 F.2d 670 (D.C.
Cir. 1970), 160, 162

United States v. Germaine, 99 U.S. (9 Otto.)
508 (1879), 22

United States v. Grimaud, 220 U.S. 506
(1911), 87

United States v. Guthrie, 58 U.S. (17 How.)
284 (1854), 57

United States v. Guy W. Capps, Inc., 204
F.2d 655 (4th Cir. 1953), 244

United States v. Halmo, 386 F. Supp. 593
(E.D. Wis. 1974), 46

United States v. Hartwell, 73 U.S. (6 Wall.)
385 (1868), 22

United States v. Helstoski, 442 U.S. 477
(1979), 11

SUBJECT INDEX